SOCIAL CHANGE:

An Anthology

THE REYNOLDS SERIES IN SOCIOLOGY
Larry T. Reynolds, *Editor*
by **General Hall, Inc.**

SOCIAL CHANGE:

An Anthology

Roxanne Friedenfels
Drew University

GENERAL HALL, INC.
Publishers
5 Talon Way
Dix Hills, New York 11746

SOCIAL CHANGE: An Anthology

GENERAL HALL, INC.
5 Talon Way
Dix Hills, New York 11746

Copyright © 1998 by General Hall, Inc.

All rights reserved. No part of this publication may be
reproduced, stored in a retrieval system or transmitted
in any form or by any means, except for the inclusion of
brief quotations in a review, without the prior permission
of the publisher.

Publisher: Ravi Mehra
Composition: Perfect Setting, Bridgehampton, NY

LIBRARY OF CONGRESS CATALOG CARD NUMBER: **98-71780**

ISBN: 1-882289-60-9 [cloth]
      1-882289-59-5 [paper]

Manufactured in the United States of America

To My Daughters
Robin and Jesse Friebur

Contents

Introduction
1. Some New and Ongoing Themes in Social Change: An Introduction by *Roxanne M. Friedenfels* — 1

Part I: Consciousness, Ideologies, and Change — 15

2. Ideology and the Modern Era by *John B. Thompson* — 16
3. Ideologies in Social Struggles by *Alfred McClung Lee* — 26
4. Multiple Jeopardy, Multiple Consciousness: The Context of a Black Feminist Ideology by *Deborah K. King* — 38
5. The Impact of Ideology on Development in the Third World by *William Tordoff* — 56

Part II: Technology and Divisions of Labor — 70

6. The Role of Technology in Society by *Emmanuel G. Mesthene* — 71
7. The Technology of Production: Making a Job of Gender by *Judy Wajcman* — 91
8. Gender Equality: Toward a Theory of Change by *Janet Saltzman Chafetz* — 108
9. High Technology and the New International Division of Labor by *Manuel Castells* — 125

viii   SOCIAL CHANGE: An Anthology

Part III: Demographic and Social Changes   142

10.   The Role of Mortality Decline in Theories of Social
       and Demographic Transition by *John C. Caldwell*   143

11.   The Mechanisms of Demographic Change in Historical
       Perspective by *John C. Caldwell*   166

12.   Human Migration: A Historical Overview by
       William H. McNeill   189

13.   From Sex Ratios to Sex Roles by *Marcia Guttentag* and
       Paul F. Secord   202

Park IV: Social Movements and Revolutions   223

14.   New Social Movements and Resource Mobilization: The
       European and the American Approach by *Bert Klandermans*   224

15.   Silence, Death, and the Invisible Enemy: AIDS Activism
       and Social Movement "Newness" by *Josh Gamson*   238

16.   Revolutions of the Late Twentieth Century: Comparisons
       by *Ted Robert Gurr* and *Jack Goldstone*   259

17.   Women in Eastern and Central Europe by *Jo Brew*   284

18.   The Future of Eastern Europe: Lessons from the
       Third World by *Ziauddin Sardar* and *Merryl Wyn Davies*   299

Conclusion

19.   Of Rivers and Social Change by *Charles Tilly*   308

References   319
Author Index   357
Subject Index   364

ACKNOWLEDGMENTS

I would like to thank the many people who have helped in some way with this book, though they are too numerous to name individually. I give special thanks, however, to my husband, Jim Burchell, for his steadfast support. James O'Kane, Jonathan Reader, and Carlos De La Torre, fellow members of the sociology department at Drew University, were unstinting in their encouragement. I also thank my typists, Jeannie Kosakowski, Mitzi Pappas, Carolyn Carter, and Carole Stanford, without whom this book could not have been completed.

PERMISSIONS

"From Sex Ratios to Sex Roles" from *Too Many Women?* by Marcia Guttentag and Paul F. Secord, pp. 153–71 (abridged). Copyright 1983 by Sage Publications, Inc. Used by permission.

"The Future of Eastern Europe: Lessons from the Third World" by Ziauddin Sardar and Merryl Wyn Davies, from *Futures: The Journal of Forecasting, Planning, and Policy* 24 (1992): 150–57. Copyright 1992 by Butterworth-Heinemann Ltd. Used by permission.

"Gender Equality: Toward a Theory of Change" by Janet Saltzman Chafetz from *Feminism and Sociological Theory*, Ruth A. Wallace, ed., pp. 135–60 (abridged). Copyright 1989 by Sage Publications, Inc. Used by permission.

"High Technology and the New Industrial Division of Labour" by Manuel Castells, from *Labour and Society* 14 (1989): 16–30 (abridged). Copyright 1989 by the International Institute for Labour Studies. Used by permission.

"Human Migration" by William H. McNeill from *Human Migration: Patterns and Policies*, William H. McNeill and Ruth S. Adams, eds., pp. 3–19 (abridged). Copyright 1978 by Indiana University Press. Used by permission.

"Ideologies in Social Struggles" from *Sociology for People* by Alfred McClung Lee, pp. 60–76 (abridged). Copyright 1986 by Syracuse University Press. Used by permission.

"Ideology and the Modern Era" from *Ideology and Modern Culture* by John B. Thompson, pp. 76–86 (abridged). Copyright 1990 by John B. Thompson. Used by permission.

"The Impact of Ideology on Development in the Third World" by William Tordoff, from the *Journal of International Development* 4 (1992): 41–53. Copyright 1992 by John Wiley & Sons Ltd. Used by permission.

"The Mechanisms of Demographic Change in Historical Perspective" by John C. Caldwell, from *Population Studies* 35 (1981): 5–27 (abridged). Copyright 1981 by John C. Caldwell. Used by permission.

"Multiple Jeopardy, Multiple Consciousness: The Context of Black Feminist Ideology" by Deborah K. King, from *Signs* 14 (1988): 42–72 (abridged). Copyright 1988 by University of Chicago Press. Used by permission.

"New Social Movements and Resource Mobilization: The European and the American Approach" by Bert Klandermans, from *International Journal of Mass Emergencies and Disasters*, pp. 13–37 (abridged). Copyright 1986 by Research Committee on Disasters. Used by permission.

"Revolutions of the Late Twentieth Century: Comparisons" by Ted Robert Gurr and Jack A. Goldstone (authors and eds.), from *Revolutions of the Late Twentieth Century*, pp. 324–44 (updated). Copyright 1991 by Westview Press. Used by permission.

"The Role of Mortality Decline in Theories of Social and Demographic Transition" by John C. Caldwell from *Consequences of Mortality Trends and Differentials*, Population Studies, No. 95 (United Nations publication, Sales No. E.85.Xlll.3), pp. 31–42. Copyright 1986 by the United Nations. Used by permission.

"The Role of Technology in Society" by Emmanuel G. Mesthene, from *Technology and Culture*, pp. 489–536. Copyright 1969 by The University of Chicago Press. Used by permission.

"Silence, Death and the Invisible Enemy: AIDS Activism and Social Movement 'Newness'" by Josh Gamson, from *Social Problems* 36 (1989): 351–67. Copyright 1989 by The Society for the Study of Social Problems. Used by permission.

"The Technology of Production: Making a Job of Gender" from *Feminism Confronts Technology* by Judy Wajcman, pp. 34–53. Copyright 1991 by Judy Wajcman. Used by permission of Penn State Press.

1

SOME NEW AND ONGOING THEMES IN SOCIAL CHANGE: AN INTRODUCTION

Roxanne M. Friedenfels

This book examines a variety of cross-cultural and transhistorical changes, including the move to global capitalism, transformations in gender systems, the demographic transition, and development in the contemporary world. It includes the work of scholars influenced by Marx, Weber, functionalism, feminism, and the movements of people of color. It also examines the impact of demography, an important cause of social change that has been much ignored. While it emphasizes polity and economy, it also examines the role of ideas, culture, and sentiment. Through the articles chosen for inclusion, it asserts that social transformations occur on various levels of social life. While many of the articles focus solely or mostly on macrophenomena, some explore macro/micro links.

    This book is also the result of a long experience of frustration. In one of its recent manifestations, I was participating in Drew University's gender integration project and trying to find a text on social change that incorporated feminist scholarship. I failed. Not only did texts largely ignore feminist theories and research, but there were very few texts on social change, period. So I had to make my own; this book is the result. It is informed by the belief that all social processes, including social change, are gendered. Men or women, or women and men, are the makers of change. Which of these makes change, and the ways each is affected by change, is not accidental or random but needs explaining. Past theorists of change, believing women were not important or interesting subjects of study, "disappeared" them—along with male actors—in highly abstract macroanalysis, or assumed them to be passive. This latter stereotype was the kiss of death in a field focused on violence and resistance. But women have fought in revolutions (Mies 1986), incited and made up the majority of participants in food riots (Tilly and Scott 1978), fomented social movements, and gone on child strike (Brew, this volume). They have been change makers in ways similar to and different from men.

They have also sometimes appeared quiescent while struggling to minimize the impact of surrounding brutalities on themselves and the more helpless beings in their care, the young, the sick, the very old. As Brew says in her article about contemporary women in eastern and central Europe: women are sometimes too busy doing reproductive work to have time to change, or to make change.

But even where women are busy tending to everyday life, and the macro changes are initiated and instituted by men, they are affected by social change. A sociology and history that tell how women have been touched by change, or have reacted to change even when they were not the change makers, will give fuller insight into the past and the present. Scholarship, in short, needs to incorporate gender in studying both the making of change and the effects of change. While not all articles in this book incorporate gender, I have sought to juxtapose articles in such a way that some of the possible connections between the gendered and nongendered articles become apparent. Some of these connections will be brought out here. Others remain for the reader to make.

The chapters in this book cover four broad categories: technology, ideology, demography, and social movements and revolutions. These categories indicate the basic subjects of the articles; each of the four is an important cause of change but is also impacted by change in other parts of society. I discuss not only themes that have been constant in the social change literature but also new frontiers scholars working in this area have begun to traverse. Therefore, I utilize several of the chapter categories in this introduction, but also range beyond them so that I can say more about past and current writings on social change than the chapter categorization allows. Specifically, I cover three "long-standing" themes, and five new themes. The long standing themes are ideology, technology, and struggle/conflict between groups, each as a basis and reflection of change. I focus on one article on each of these long-standing themes, since a number of the articles with these themes also reflect new themes and are covered later. The new themes are exploring gender stratification, consciousness and identity, the emergence of the body, demography and social change, and "bringing the state back in." I discuss specific articles in this book that pertain to each of these themes and show how they fit general trends in the social change literature.

ONGOING THEMES

Ideology as a Basis and Reflection of Change

Social scientists debate whether ideology is a significant cause of social change or largely a result of other changes. Marxists believe that it is not a prime cause of social change but an aspect of the "superstructure" that responds to material changes in technology and the economic base and may or may not have some independent effect. A second group, which includes many scholars utilizing a resource mobilization perspective, sees it as secondary to the goals, structures, and tactics of social movements. Others give it a more central role. They consider it to have some independence from materialist causes, and to be in and of itself an important source of social change, determining whether and which changes will be attempted, as well as the shape and scope of change efforts. The selections in the ideology section of the book suggest that ideology 1) responds to changes in other aspects of society, 2) sometimes has an independent effect on social change, and (3) is itself constantly changing.

Scholars writing about ideology have defined it in many ways. These definitions have been the source of much contention, as can be seen in the articles included in this volume. I do not cover all these definitions, but examine only Thompson's and Tordoff's. (The other ideology articles are covered later in this introduction, as part of the discussion of other themes.)

For Thompson, ideology refers to symbolic forms that establish and sustain relations of domination. In his view, the main disseminator of ideology today is the mass media. I would suggest that in Western societies, and increasingly all over the world, the mass media are the main teller of our stories. Though at first glance, these mass media stories might seem endlessly diverse, some basic stories (pretty girl gets boy, hard work and brains win, the aged are senile and/or silly) get told again and again. Hence, the media tell us ad infinitum the core stories and ideas of our culture. Many core stories obstruct change, sustaining relations of domination, but new stories are also seen. Lesbian and gay characters are increasingly common in films and television; this may well influence many people toward greater acceptance of homosexuals.

Thompson disputes what he calls sociology's "grand narrative of cultural transformation," which suggested that ideology was a symptom of modernization that would disappear as industrial societies reached political and economic maturity. In his view this narrative, which draws from heavily from Marx and Weber, is not a suitable framework with which to analyze the nature and role of ideology in modern societies. Mediazation is of greater significance than either the secularization or rationalization emphasized by the narrative. Thus, technological change has resulted in powerful new ways to communicate ideologies that, in his view, are predominantly conservative.

William Tordoff follows John Plamenatz (1972) in suggesting that ideology is "any system of ideas that acts to support or subvert accepted modes of thought and behavior." He stresses we must look at how these ideas operate in their particular social and political contexts and the programs to which they give rise.

In particular, he examines the relationship of ideology to development, which he defines as a combination of economic growth and movement toward general political participation, protection of civil rights and freedoms, state administrative efficacy, and (at least some) autonomy in foreign affairs. Using Crawford Young's (1982) work on socialist, Marxist, and capitalist states in Africa, he suggests that ideology affects national performance, but often not substantially. Capitalist states had more economic growth, for example, but socialist or Marxist ones may have had less inequality (though in Young's view their edge in egalitarianism was questionable). External restraints, including the greater aid available from Western countries than Eastern, and the support given by the United States and other powers to opposition movements against governments, are themselves frequently ideological and limit the impact of the ideology of state officials. Internal restraints (e.g., natural disasters, the shortage of technical, managerial, and administrative skills) may be less so, but will also limit state efforts toward development. In addition, all regimes must be somewhat pragmatic to operate effectively; hence, there is less difference between socialist, Marxist, and capitalist regimes, at least in Africa, than one might expect.

Struggle as a Basis or Result of Change

The assumption that struggle between groups is a basis of change can be seen in almost all the selections in this volume. While Marxists have long argued that struggle between classes is the primary cause of change in society, most contemporary sociologists believe that struggle between other kinds of groups can also lead to substantial societal change. Struggle between groups occurs because one group dominates another, or desires to do so; the dominator may be a specific group or it may be "society," which develops and maintains norms that favor one group over another (see Gamson, this volume).

Among the things that Lee's article does is to examine group struggle in the context of ideology. He discusses the utilization of ideologies in group conflicts both to maintain the status quo and to foment change. Social groups create ideologies, and modify extant ideologies, to justify unequal power relations or bolster their own societal position. Ideologies are thus central to social competitions, and the ability of a group to wield them skillfully—or its failure to do so—is part of what determines its place in an (unequal) society. States also use ideologies to homogenize their populations, an effort that he suggests is an efficient way to prepare for "eventual chaos," a statement highly salient in light of the revolutions of 1989 but reflective of earlier history as well. Ideologies are thus used to make change and are themselves constantly changing in response to struggles between groups. They may be characterized by the groups with which they are associated, their current social role, and their stage of development.

Ongoing struggles between states can be seen in the article by Sardar and Davies, who argue that east European nations have much in common with the Third World. The Third World is a result of the decolonization of the British, French, and Spanish empires; eastern Europe of the decolonization of the Kremlin. Real liberation and autonomy are not in the offing for either. The Western nations, having lost their empires by the end of World War II, ensured their continued domination through the creation of the World Bank and the International Monetary Fund. These institutions influence and even dictate many of the policies of the Third World and will do the same in eastern Europe. Stability in eastern European nations is also unlikely. Ethnic groups, no longer distracted by colonialism, have returned to old enmities. Internal ethnic conflict and economic poverty will ensure that western European nations do not embrace eastern European states as partners. The latter are unlikely to obtain membership in the European Union (EU), which the western European states created for their own economic and political security. Instead, western and eastern Europe will be separated by a "poverty curtain," and eastern European countries will be a source of cheap labor for their western neighbors. They will develop new elites and a vast majority of "have-nots." Thus, state struggle for domination can be seen as one of many engines for change, resulting in (often nominal) national liberation, changed internal class structures, and new interrelationships between countries. In this case, Sardar and Davies argue that the First World powers-that-be will remain and that dependency more than democracy will be the order of the day in eastern Europe.

Technology as a Basis and Result of Change

Humans have always used technology—indeed, the centrality of technology to our existence, according to some scholars, defines what it is to be human—but the rate of technological change for most of human existence was relatively slow, and technology's importance as a cause of social change less significant than now. The extent, rate, and type of technological change will vary according to societal structure, values, and already existing technological development, as well as (in the current era) global structure and interconnection. Technological change has greatly accelerated since the industrial revolution and continues at an ever faster pace. The most common stance in the social change literature, reflected in the readings in this section, is that new technologies and modes of economic production produce change in social interaction, organization and culture. The salience of the mass media in the dissemination of ideology, seen in Thompson (this volume) is one example. On the other hand, human decision determines technological change, which means that no particular technological change is inevitable. Technology is especially, but not only, important to theories taking a very long view of social change; discussions of short-term change may focus on factors seen as more amenable to manipulation, as can be seen in Chafetz (this volume).

Mesthene defines technology as tools in a general sense, including linguistic, analytical, and mathematical techniques, as well as machines. It creates new physical and social opportunities and new social problems, requiring reexamination of values and transformations of economic and political organization. It leads to physical dispersion, linking ever more technology users and resulting in bigger and more complex systems of social organization. Social issues also become more complex. Experts using sophisticated techniques make increasing numbers of decisions, since the "indirect" nature of the social unit makes it difficult to analyze the resulting problems. Society, in short, becomes increasingly "rationalized." Mesthene suggests that because this runs counter to the elements of Western value systems that suggest direct participation in political processes is desirable, creation of a new democratic ethos and processes could emerge as a pressing challenge.

NEW THEMES

Understanding Gender Stratification

One of the new, but still poorly incorporated, themes in the social change literature might be called "understanding gender stratification." Though a good deal of research now suggests that men have had, and continue to have, more power than women at both the macro and micro levels of many or most societies (Huber 1991), the topic is poorly covered (or covered not at all) in the main texts and anthologies on social change. Marxist theorists of social change have, of course, focused on class, and sociological interest in race predates the 1960s, but gender is a relatively recent arrival on the sociological scene, with research and discussion beginning to have an impact on the discipline only in the 1970s. Gender theory and research are greatly illuminating our understanding of the past as well as informing current gender debates, and their inclusion in social change scholarship, and not just within a separate gender ghetto, is an urgent matter. Increasingly, gender scholarship explores the interconnection of gender with race, class, and (to a lesser extent) age, an important development necessary to an understanding the complexities of people's everyday realities in contemporary societies. As Al Lee argues (this volume), societies are "multivalent," with members of different social groups perceiving, and conceiving, the basic environment in different ways.

Chafetz, looking at the long span of human development, argues that technological change, and the associated increase in economic scale, constitutes the primary mechanism that alters gender divisions of labor and the degree of gender stratification. Demographic changes, such as those caused by war and migration, can also do this, but usually have only short-term effects. These technological or demographic changes may create a demand for labor that men cannot fill, giving women new work responsibilities and opportunities. Thus the essential causes of gender change are material. While women's movements have an important role, they arrive on the scene only after these technological or demographic transformations have altered the roles and status of large numbers of women. They then promote ideological change and define the targets of change. Chafetz suggests that the key target of the current women's movement needs to be the gender division of labor, especially access of women to elite positions. Without this change, other gains can be readily lost.

Looking at industrial societies, Wajcman argues that male workers design machinery and work tasks so as to constitute themselves as capable workers and women as inadequate. While variation exists across age, ethnicity, and class, technological expertise is part of masculine identity. Women operate certain kinds of machines but rarely manipulate their inner workings. While new technologies often disrupt established patterns of sex typing in the workplace and change the sexual division of labor, when women replace men as a result of technological change, they usually do so in jobs that have been "deskilled" and receive less pay than the original job. Hence, gender is commonly exploited in the power struggles between capital and (male) labor.

King examines the "dialectics of three liberation movements to get at the tensions and priorities that influence construction of a black feminist ideology." The three movements—black liberation, movements to end class exploitation, and feminism—have all tended to have "monist" formulations, wherein one oppression was stressed at the expense of others. King suggests the need for a multivalent ideology that would declare the visibility of black women, assert their self-determination, confront multiple jeopardy in society and in liberation movements, and presume black women's image as powerful, independent subjects. She thus asserts that ideology is central to the change needed by black women in the United States and that efforts to understand gender stratification need to incorporate issues of race and class.

Consciousness and Identity

King is also suggesting that consciousness and identity are important to social change, which while certainly not an entirely "new theme" in the social change literature is one that is experiencing a renaissance in sociology. The focus of many researchers in the United States has been on the strategies, goals, and resources of social movements; until recently, there was little emphasis on consciousness and identity, even though slogans such as "black is beautiful" and, in the women's movement, "the personal is political" have long suggested their importance to social change. King argues that the consciousness of a group is determined by their social and historical circumstances and is among the factors determining their ability to make change.

Klandermans compares resource mobilization (RM) theory and new social movements (NSM) theory. RM theory holds that the formation and rise of social movements depends on "changes in resources, group organization, and opportunities for collective action." Grievances are not significant; omnipresent, it is only when there are changes in other facets of society that social movements occur. An additional point not brought out by Klandermans is that identity is assumed, not explained, in RM theory. Groups with particular identities exist; with the availability of resources they may be able to mobilize and make change, but the theory does not consider the conditions under which identity is transformed. NSM theory, in contrast, is concerned with both new grievances and identity change. New grievances are rooted in modernization processes or actions of the welfare state, which according to some versions of this theory lead to loss of identity and traditional ties, opening people to new commitments and utopian ideals. Those who experience these processes are likely to become members of new social movements. (There is more coverage of this theory in the section of this paper entitled "Bringing the State Back In.") While the two theories are very different, they are not, in Klandermans' view, irreconcilable but complementary, covering different aspects of social movements.

According to Josh Gamson, the AIDS activist movement exemplifies the new social movement characteristics of middle-class membership and a mix of instrumental, expressive, and identity-oriented activities. At the same time, strategies in this movement may be quite different from those in other new social movements and analyzing them as like phenomena may be inappropriate. The group he examines, ACT UP, is an AIDS activist group that uses identity-forming strategies that stem from the stigma attached to homosexuality and to AIDS. One general strategy is to take a symbol or phrase used to oppress and invert it. Activists speak of People with AIDS, for example, not AIDS victims, and risk practices, not risk groups. They also use boundary crossing, "reclaiming" spaces that are typically middle-American, as when they put stickers proclaiming "Touched by a Person with AIDS" in phone booths, or unfurl banners proclaiming "Don't balk at safer sex," and "AIDS is not a ballgame" at a Shea Stadium game between the Mets and the Astros. The group has some difficulty in identifying the people its actions are meant to reach due to the nature of the opposition. The state, which controls access to AIDS drugs, and the media and medical establishment, which "denormalize" those who are gay and/or have AIDS, are visible targets. But the bigger enemy is "disembodied and invisible...society itself." Gamson argues that this is a somewhat new phenomenon, since in the eighteenth century the state, not society, would have been the key oppressor. The shift has been very gradual, however, and he argues against NSM theorists who suggest that a fundamental modification of social movements has occurred only since the 1960s. In his view, the transformations giving shape to current movements have been developing for centuries, not decades.

The Emergence of the Body

Gamson's work also shows the "emergence of the body" in the social change literature—a third "trend." Ironically, as "the enemy becomes increasingly disembodied, the body of the dominated becomes more central." In the last two centuries the norm has largely replaced violence as a method of social control. The body has been increasingly subjugated to the rules of society, and at the mercy of societal stigma.

Klandermans also discusses the importance of bodies to new social movements, wherein the private becomes part of political discussion, and the superstructure and the sphere of reproduction take ascendance. Many new social movements fight for freedom of choice in matters relating to the private sphere; they do this in relation to gender roles, to abortion, to death. Bodies are central to each of these issues. Many NSM theorists argue that economic growth and industrialization and/or the increased imposition of the welfare state into private spheres have a negative impact on the satisfaction of important personal needs. New social movements result from these changes.

While Brew makes no major theoretical claims around the body, her article shows the historical and geographical limits of NSM theory, a theory that originated in Europe in relatively stable advanced industrial societies. The discussion below reflects my interpretation of her description of recent developments in eastern and central Europe.

Brew argues that the oppression of women by state, industry, and society is increasing in eastern and central Europe. The picture fits NSM views that the state increasingly oppresses by forcing its way into the private sphere, but whereas Klandermans indicates that many NSM theorists blame the welfare state, we see in eastern and central Europe a dismantling of welfare states and their replacement with states more purely capitalist (and in the case of Poland, theocratic). Most eastern and central European states have taken control of reproduction in ways unheard of since before the socialist revolutions in these countries, increasing abortion restrictions and forcing women back into the home. They have not been able to do this without encountering resistance; women have reacted to their postrevolutionary exclusion from jobs, money, and prestige with nascent feminist organization and with "child strikes," a refusal to reproduce. Brew suggests that the increase of competition that has accompanied capitalism has not benefited most women, who in having responsibility for the reproductive sphere may not have time to gain the new skills necessary to compete. But it is not only that competition has increased and that women lack resources that could make them more competitive, it is also that women are blatantly discriminated against and not allowed to compete. Consequently, in Prague, as well as in other eastern and central European areas not discussed by Brew (Moghadam 1995), prostitution and pornography have increased. Unable to sell their labor power for a fair wage, many sell their bodies instead. Thus, women's bodies bear the brunt of much of the social change in eastern and central Europe.

Brew's article indicates that women in nonwelfare states with laissez-faire market conditions will find their private lives controlled by the market in ways that are at least as pernicious as welfare state intrusion. Welfare states have offered certain advantages to women, such as economic support systems for the old (who are disproportionately women and cared for by women) and publicly funded childcare (which would otherwise be wholly women's "private" work). Brew's article also shows how many women are resisting these changes individually, rather than in collective movement. "Child strikes" are not organized movement actions, but aggregate personal resistance. While it is unclear whether they have any effect, what is obvious is the drastic alteration of women's lives by the 1989 revolutions. And while Brew is hopeful that "one step backward" will end in "two steps forward," it is as likely that many of the new states will not be competitive globally, just as their communist predecessors were not (see Frank 1990; Sardar and Davies, this volume). Where this is the case, life for most of the women—and men—in these countries will be harsh for decades to come.

Demography and Social Change

Less a trend than a recommendation, social change scholars should continue initial explorations of the links between demography and social change.

Generally highly statistical and atheoretical, demography deals with bodies (mortality, fertility, migration, the relative numbers of various groups in a population) via aggregate figures and with little attention to the meaning and emotion of these experiences. It is a subfield of sociology that has been largely separate from the rest of the discipline. At best, one type of demographic change has been used to explain a second type of demographic change. Nonetheless, demographic transformations can and have drastically affected modes of living and the quality of life. I begin with mortality, which is generally considered the *sine qua non* of all subsequent demographic change (Caldwell, "The Role of Mortality Decline," this volume).

Caldwell suggests that scientific revolution and economic modernization caused the mortality decline that began in Europe in the eighteenth century. Thus, social change had a major effect on demographic change. In turn, the lower mortality rates gave people a sense of control over nature, a lessened fatalism that led to yet more mortality decline. Contrary to the current of the literature, Caldwell also argues that mortality decline was not the main cause of fertility decline, since most mortality decline occurred after fertility decline began. It may, however, have accelerated and exacerbated fertility decline. It is possible as well that fertility decline accelerated mortality decline as it would have made it possible to better care for the smaller numbers of children. Unfortunately, these interactions have received relatively little scholarly attention.

Caldwell suggests that mortality decline in the industrializing world today is also due to social changes, albeit different ones than those that drove the process the eighteenth century. New technological developments and the corresponding increased global interconnection make ready export of public health measures and medical technologies possible and accelerate mortality decline in the industrializing world. Increased parental education may also encourage mortality decline. Contemporary theorists of development consider mortality rates to be an important indicator of quality of life.

According to Caldwell's second article ("The Mechanisms of Demographic Change," this volume), fertility decline also signaled a massive change in the human condition. He argues that uncontrolled fertility maintained the relations of production in societies with familial production, but is experienced as uneconomic in contemporary societies: to study demographic transition is to study the change from tradition to modernity. In societies with familial production, children were central to family production, as were women, but both groups consumed little, and wealth flows went to elder males. High fertility provided labor and kept women from competing with men in consumption. In societies based on market production, in contrast, production and consumption are based on the individual. Children are an economic burden, rather than an economic asset, and wealth flows in their direction; fertility is correspondingly low.

Like mortality decline, fertility decline is now a global process. In Caldwell's view, Western values, attitudes and behaviors explain the considerable variation in the pace of fertility decline in industrializing countries. And even though not all societies will be industrialized by the early twenty-first century, most will have experienced a decline in fertility.

The relatively high fertility of industrializing nations continues to feed another demographic process, migration. McNeill explores the links between migration, fertility, and mortality, finding that the historical link with fertility remains. High fertility, combined with low standards of living, creates nomads in search of improved life chances. The long-standing link between migration and mortality, in contrast, has been broken. Population growth, and increased communication between urban and rural areas caused epidemic forms of disease to become endemic by the eighteenth century. As a result, cities, armies, and frontiers no longer acted as "population sumps," attracting masses of people who then died of disease. Migration does remain a major force for social change, however, leading to diffusion of technologies, skills, and ideas, and stimulating cultural exchange. It also remains a significant challenge as the impoverished from Asia, Africa, and Latin America seek better standards of living than their home countries can provide and, concurrently, wealthier nations grapple with conflicts between in-migrants and older populations.

Guttentag and Secord also use demography and venture beyond it to try to explain larger social change. They suggest that sex ratios combine with structural power arrangements to result in particular sex-role arrangements and differing amounts of dyadic power for women and men. They thus pay attention to the meaning and emotion of intimate experiences which result from demographic change. They argue that with sufficient time, an imbalance in sex ratios acts to produce changes in the attitudes and behavior of women and men to each other, associated sex roles, and institutional structures, such as the family.

Bringing the State Back In

The late twentieth century has seen a resurgence in sociologists' interest in the role of the state. Current scholarship considers the ways in which states as organizations and as institutional arrangements affect groups, political conflicts, and demographic trends. It recognizes "states as autonomous actors", with independent goals and explanatory centrality. Theda Skocpol (1985) aptly called this trend "Bringing the State Back In" in Peter Evans's book of the same name, and it constitutes a fifth trend in the social change literature. Among the places where the state has reemerged in contemporary theorizing are social movements and revolution.

Social movement theory up to the 1950s and 1960s stressed relative deprivation and resultant grievances or social strain as the cause of social movements. The movements in the 1960s made clear, however, that membership of movements did not necessarily have to consist of the most deprived; members of the emergent movements were largely people of middle-class origin. The literature then moved in two directions, both of which are relevant to "bringing the state back in." Resource mobilization theory focused on how social movements mobilized while new social movements theory focused on why (Melucci 1984, cited in Klandermans, this volume). While neither Klandermans nor Gamson (this volume) stress the ways in which RM theory has emphasized the state as autonomous actor, such work does exist. Charles Tilly has discussed various state effects on collective action; "repertoires" of collective action, for example, reflect the structure and practice of the states in which they are found (Tilly 1978, 1981).

Klandermans shows that some versions of NSM theory suggest that the intervention of the welfare state in more and more private spheres of life causes these movements. Increased government services along with economic growth have created a sense of entitlement, which nonetheless is often obstructed and "fulfilled" at the same time (Klandermans gives the examples of traffic jams and "little boxes in suburbia"). As a result, people have "new needs," which will remain unsatisfied. Following the general trend outlined by Skocpol in the above-mentioned article, the state in much of NSM theory is an autonomous actor whose policies create grievances; these grievances, in turn, are the impetus for the creation of new social movements.

Early empirical generalizations and theories of political violence, which applied to both social movements and revolutions, did not fully cover the conditions necessary for revolution. Goldstone and Gurr, in contrast, note the centrality of state political crisis. In this state crisis, significant numbers of elites and mass followers believe that the central authorities are acting in ways that are immoral, unjust, or ineffective. Such crisis is the first phase of revolution, followed by a struggle for power of state elites with contending groups, and finally the victors' efforts to reconstruct the state and society. For Goldstone and Gurr, a central issue is the extent to which revolutions can usher in Western democratic institutions and civil and political rights. While they are optimistic that central European leaders intend to do better in this regard than leaders of some other revolutions, Brew's article indicates that the commitment does not extend to the civil and political rights of women. We thus see the continued importance of the state in determining modes of living in general and the shape of women's lives in particular.

New International Division of Labor theory has deemphasized the significance of states to development, arguing that the power of the multinationals is such that individual states and national economies are increasingly inconsequential. According to the NIDL theorists, multinationals operating in the global arena undermine social controls from both organized labor and responsible governments. Castells contends that states remain important, and that some "developmental" Third World governments (in New Industrial Countries such as the Republic of Korea, Singapore, and Taiwan) have successfully spurred national development even as interdependence spreads across national boundaries. He highlights the (present and potential) protectionism of the governments of developed nations, which could hurt a substantial part of the export-oriented Third World. In his view, continued Third World development depends on technological transfer from the industrial nations, supported by a state that fosters the conditions necessary for economic growth, and expansion of both international trade and internal Third World markets.

CONCLUSION

This volume has not attempted to cover all aspects of social change; no articles theorize, for example, the development of capitalism or of bureaucracy, highly important topics to be sure, but covered at length elsewhere. It has necessarily been selective; as Charles Tilly argues in his cogent conclusion to this book, scholars really study many kinds of social changes, not Social Change, and each of these is like a river, with its own currents and eddies. It is impossible in one volume to give even a sampling of all the rivers of change.

The central motivations for this volume, then, have been to make accessible important scholarship that reflects some of the central ongoing themes in social change scholarship, as well as that which explores and develops significant new directions. In doing this, I was interested in work that, even when historical in nature, nonetheless reflected contemporary concerns. The scholarship in this field remains highly salient for a broad and probing understanding of our world. Ideology, technology, demography, and social movements and revolutions all have major impacts on our lives; even so, human imagination and effort also shape these social forces. My hope is that this volume illuminates both the limitations and potentials of this quest.

Part I

CONSCIOUSNESS, IDEOLOGIES, AND CHANGE

2

IDEOLOGY AND THE MODERN ERA

J.B. Thompson

Let me begin by reconstructing a set of assumptions concerning the cultural transformations associated with the rise of modern industrial societies. These assumptions constitute a general theoretical framework, an overarching theoretical narrative, which has shaped many of the problems and debates in social and political analysis, including some of the debates concerned with the nature and role of ideology in modern societies. The original elements of this *grand narrative of cultural transformation* can be discerned in the writings of Marx and Weber, although it was not until the 1950s and 1960s that the story acquired a certain *dénouement*. In examining this theoretical narrative I shall not restrict myself to the work of any particular thinker. For this narrative is not so much a clearly formulated theoretical argument that can be discerned in the writings of one or several authors as a story that has to be gleaned from a variety of texts and that, when reconstructed in this way, offers a vision of the major cultural transformations associated with the development of modern societies. Within this narrative, ideologies have a role to play, as secular belief systems that emerged in the wake of the demise of religion and magic and that served to mobilize political action in a world stripped of tradition. I want to reconstruct this narrative and to examine the twists and turns of its dramatic plot, not only because it offers a vision which has been deeply influential in social and political theory but also because it presents an account of the cultural transformations associated with the development of modern societies, and in particular of the nature and role of ideology in these societies, which is, in my view, misguided in certain fundamental respects.

We can summarize the key elements of the grand narrative in terms of three main points.

1. The rise of industrial capitalism in Europe and elsewhere was accompanied by the decline of religious and magical beliefs and practices,

which were prevalent in preindustrial societies. The development of industrial capitalism at the level of economic activity was accompanied, in the sphere of culture, by the secularization of beliefs and practices and by the progressive rationalization of social life.
2. The decline of religion and magic prepared the ground for the emergence of secular belief systems or "ideologies," which serve to mobilize political action without reference to otherworldly values or beings. The religious and mythical consciousness of preindustrial society was replaced by a practical consciousness rooted in social collectivities and animated by secular systems of belief.
3. These developments gave rise to the "age of ideologies," which culminated in the radical revolutionary movements of the late nineteenth and early twentieth centuries. These movements—according to some theorists writing in the 1950s and 1960s—were the last manifestations of the age of ideologies. Today politics is increasingly a matter of piecemeal reform and the pragmatic accommodation of conflicting interests. Social and political action is less and less animated by secular belief systems that call for radical social change. Hence we are witnessing, according to some proponents of this view, not only the end of the age of ideologies but the end of ideology as such.

Let me elaborate briefly on each of these points.

1. The idea that the rise of industrial capitalism was accompanied by the decline of religious and magical beliefs and practices is an idea shared by many nineteenth- and early twentieth-century thinkers, including Marx and Weber. For Marx, the type of society brought about by the emergence of industrial capitalism is radically different from earlier precapitalist societies. Whereas precapitalist societies were basically conservative in their mode of production, modern capitalist society is constantly expanding, changing, transforming itself; modern capitalist society also dissolves the traditions and cultural forms—including the religious traditions—that were characteristic of precapitalist societies. This emphasis on the progressive, demystifying character of the modern era is particularly striking in the *Manifesto of the Communist Party*. The restless, ceaseless activity of the capitalist mode of production strips social relations of that "train of ancient and venerable prejudices and opinions" that shrouded them in the past, "all that is solid melts into air, all that is holy is profaned" (Marx and Engels 1968, 38). The demystification of social relations is, in Marx's account, an inherent aspect of the development of capitalism. This process of demystification enables human beings, for the

first time in history, to see their social relations for what they are—namely, relations of exploitation. This process places humanity at the threshold of a new era, one that can be and will be ushered in by an enlightened transformation of society, that is, a transformation based on a shared knowledge of demystified social relations. The process of demystification inherent in the development of capitalism is thus an essential precondition for the ultimate elimination of exploitative class relations—even if Marx sometimes acknowledged that symbolic forms transmitted from the past may persist at the heart of the present and deflect the trajectory of revolutionary social change.

Weber was also concerned to highlight the links between the development of industrial capitalism and the transformation of culture and tradition. Like Marx, he saw an association between the rise of industrial capitalism and the dissolution of traditional values and beliefs. But Weber's account differs from that of Marx in several important respects. In the first place, Weber argued that changes in the sphere of culture and tradition were not merely by-products of the autonomous development of capitalism: on the contrary, certain transformations in religious ideas and practices were the cultural preconditions for the emergence of capitalism in the West. Moreover, Weber goes on to argue that, once industrial capitalism had established itself as the predominant form of economic activity in the course of the seventeenth and eighteenth centuries, it acquired a momentum of its own and dispensed with the religious ideas and practices that had been necessary for its emergence. The development of capitalism, together with the associated rise of the bureaucratic state progressively rationalized action and adapted human behavior to criteria of technical efficiency. The purely personal, spontaneous, and emotional elements of traditional action were squeezed out by the demands of purposive-rational calculation and technical efficiency. Whereas the early Puritans had pursued rational economic activity as a calling, for subsequent generations this activity became a necessity, an impersonal power that circumscribed the lives of individuals and constrained them with the inexorability of an iron cage.

> Since asceticism undertook to remodel the world and to work out its ideals in the world, material goods have gained an increasing and finally an inexorable power over the lives of men as at no previous period in history. Today the spirit of religious asceticism—whether finally, who knows?—has escaped from the cage. But victorious capitalism, since it rests on mechanical foundations, needs its

support no longer. The rosy blush of its laughing heir, the Enlightenment, seems also to be irretrievably fading, and the idea of duty in one's calling prowls about in our lives like the ghost of dead religious beliefs. (Weber 1930, 181–82)

While both Marx and Weber discerned a connection between the development of industrial capitalism and the dissolution of traditional religious beliefs, the tone of their accounts is altogether different. Whereas Marx spoke of the *demystification* of social relations and regarded this as the precondition for the ultimate emancipation from exploitative class relations, Weber spoke instead of the *disenchantment* of the modern world, in which some of the traditional and distinctive values of Western civilization were submerged beneath the increasing rationalization and bureaucratization of social life, and he regarded this, with some regret, as the "fate of modern times."
2. The views of Marx and Weber, among others, provide the backcloth against which some thinkers have argued that the formation and diffusion of ideologies is a distinctive characteristic of the modern era. This argument, evident already in the work of Mannheim (1936,5ff), has been developed in recent years by a variety of authors.[1] Here I try to reconstruct the argument in a general way, without adhering too closely to the work of any particular theorist. During the late eighteenth and early nineteenth centuries—so the argument goes—the process of secularization was beginning to take hold in the industrial heartlands of Europe. As more and more people were swept off the land and into the cities to form a labor force for the expanding factories of industrial capitalism, the old traditions, religions and myths began to lose their grip on the collective imagination. The old ties of bondage between lord and serf, ties shrouded in the veil of loyalty and mutual obligation, were increasingly called into question, as individuals were thrust into a new set of social relations based on the private ownership of the means of production and the exchange of commodities and labor power in the market. At the same time as this new set of social relations was being formed, political power was increasingly concentrated in the institutions of a secularized state— that is, a state based on a notion of sovereignty and the formal rule of law and justified by an appeal to universal values, rules, and rights, rather than by an appeal to some religious or mystical value or being that would endow political power with the authority of a divine will. The modern state is distinguished from the political institutions of the *ancien régime* by, among other things, the fact that it is located

entirely *within* the social-historical world, and hence the struggle for and exercise of power becomes a mundane matter embedded in the language of reason and science, interests and rights.

The secularization of social life and of political power created the conditions for the emergence and diffusion of "ideologies." In this context "ideologies" are understood primarily as secular belief systems that have a mobilizing and legitimating function. The late eighteenth and early nineteenth centuries marked the beginning of the "age of ideologies" in this sense, as expressed in the great political revolutions in France and America and in the proliferation of political doctrines or "isms," from socialism and communism to liberalism, conservatism, and nationalism. The diffusion of political doctrines was facilitated, and their efficacy enhanced, by two further developments characteristic of the eighteenth and nineteenth centuries: the expansion of the newspaper industry and the growth of literacy. These developments increasingly enabled individuals to read about the social and political world and to share the experience of others with whom they did not interact in their everyday lives. The horizons of individuals were thereby expanded; they became potential participants of a "public sphere" in which issues were debated and positions were challenged or supported by means of reasons and arguments. It was in the cleared space of the public sphere that the discourse of ideologies appeared, constituting organized systems of beliefs that offered coherent interpretations of social and political phenomena, and that served to mobilize social movements and justify the exercise of power. Ideologies thus provided frames of meaning, as it were, which enabled individuals to orientate themselves in a world characterized by a certain sense of *groundlessness*, a sense produced by the destruction of traditional ways of life and by the demise of religious and mythical worldviews.

3. If the cultural transformations associated with the rise of modern industrial societies created a new space within which ideologies could flourish, this was a space that could, in the view of some theorists, be closed down by the subsequent development of modern societies. The idea that the age of ideologies has come to an end is not a new idea, nor is it an idea shared by all theorists who have argued that ideologies are a distinctive feature of the modern era; it is an idea that could be seen as constituting a particular, but by no means generally shared, twist to the grand narrative of cultural transformation. The "end of ideology" thesis was originally put forward by a range of liberal and conservative thinkers, including Raymond Aron (1957, 1967), Daniel Bell (1960), Seymour Lipset (1959) and Edward Shils

(1958),[2] although an echo of this thesis can be heard today in ongoing theoretical debates. In its original formulation, the end of ideology thesis was an argument about the alleged decline of radical or revolutionary political doctrines in the developed industrial societies of both eastern Europe and the West. In the wake of the Second World War, the defeat of Fascism and Nazism, the Moscow trials, the denunciation of Stalinism, and other political developments and atrocities of recent years, the old ideologies stemming from the late eighteenth and nineteenth centuries had lost, it was argued, much of their persuasive power. These ideologies had taken hold primarily among groups of intellectuals who had become disaffected with existing social and political institutions, and who had expressed their disaffection by calling for radical change. But the political events of the early twentieth century had exposed the naïveté and the danger of such calls. It was becoming increasingly clear to intellectuals and others that the problems confronting developed industrial societies could not be resolved by the kind of radical social change espoused by Marxism and communism, since this kind of change gave rise to similar problems and to new forms of violence and repression. Hence the end of ideology theorists discerned the emergence of a new consensus: the old "ideological politics" were giving way to a new sense of pragmatism in the developed industrial societies. Revolutionary passion was waning and was being replaced by a pragmatic, piecemeal approach to social change within the framework—in the West at least—of a mixed economy and a redistributive welfare state. The end of ideology theorists generally recognized that ideologies would continue to flourish in less developed societies, and they did not altogether rule out the possibility that revolutionary passions might occasionally reappear as isolated and inconsequential outbursts in the developed industrial societies. But they maintained that, as a general situation in which the political arena is animated by radical and revolutionary doctrines that arouse passion and heated conflict, the age of ideologies is over and ideology has ceased to be a significant feature of modern industrial societies.

Of course, the end of ideology theorists were using the term *ideology* in a very special sense. Ideologies, in their view, were not secular belief systems of any kind; rather, they were comprehensive, totalizing doctrines that offer a coherent vision of the social-historical world and that demand a high degree of emotional attachment. For most of these theorists, Marxism was the epitome of ideology in this sense. Marxism offered a systematic, totalizing vision of the social-historical world. It predicted a future that would be radically different from the present, and that could only be realized through the dedicated action of individuals who believed unflinchingly in their cause. These were the characteristics of ideology: totalizing, utopian, impassioned, dogmatic. The end of ideology in this sense was not necessarily the end of political debate and conflict, of contrasting political programs which expressed genuine differences of interest and opinion. But these debates, conflicts, and programs would no longer be animated by totalizing, utopian visions that incited individuals to revolutionary action and blinded them to any considerations that were contrary to their view. With the passing of the age of ideologies, political processes could be increasingly institutionalized within a pluralistic framework in which political parties or groups competed for power and implemented pragmatic policies of social reform. Ideologies were not so much an endemic feature of the modern era as a passing symptom of modernization, a symptom that would gradually disappear as industrial societies reached a state of economic and political maturity.

I have reconstructed this grand narrative of cultural transformation in order to raise a series of issues about the nature and role of ideology in modern societies. It is a narrative with different elements and several subplots and—as I indicated earlier—I do not want to suggest that the whole story can be found in the work of any single author. I have abstracted from detailed variations and elaborations in order to sketch a general line of argument that is deeply embedded in the literature of social and political theory and which continues to structure debates about the nature and role of culture and ideology in modern societies. I now want to turn from reconstruction to critical assessment. In so doing I do not want to suggest that there is nothing of enduring value in the grand narrative: my aim is not to dismiss this narrative in its entirety but to highlight certain respects in which it is, in my view, misleading. I restrict my attention to two main issues. There are many other issues that could be addressed in this context: a line of argument so broad in scope is bound to raise many questions and problems. But my concern is less with detailed difficulties than with general shortcomings; I want to try to show that, for reasons of a fundamental kind, the grand narrative of cultural transformation is not a suitable framework within which to analyze the nature and role of ideology in modern societies.

The first major shortcoming of the grand narrative is that, by characterizing the cultural transformations associated with the rise of modern industrial societies primarily in terms of the processes of secularization and rationalization, this account downplays the significance of what I call the mediazation of modern culture. The problem here is not simply that the processes of secularization and rationalization may have been less sweeping and less uniform than earlier social theorists sometimes suggested—though it is probably the case that these processes were overemphasized and that religious beliefs and practices are more persistent features of modern societies than the early social theorists imagined.[3] More importantly, the problem is that the preoccupation with processes of secularization and rationalization has tended to occlude a development that was of much greater significance for the nature of cultural forms in modern societies—namely, the development of a range of institutions concerned with the mass production and mass distribution of symbolic goods. Insofar as the traditional narrative neglects this development, it offers a seriously misleading account of the cultural transformations associated with the rise of modern societies. The institutions and processes of mass communication have assumed such fundamental significance in modern societies that no account of ideology and modern culture can afford to neglect them.

It is of course true that some of the theorists who could be associated with the grand narrative of cultural transformation have commented on the development of mass communication. For instance, Alvin Gouldner, drawing on Habermas's early work, discusses the ways in which the development of printing and the newspaper industry facilitated the formation of a public sphere in which political issues were debated and ideologies flourished. But Gouldner's account is limited and partial at best, and he hardly considers the implications of more recent forms of mass communication, particularly those involving electronic storage and transmission. Indeed, Gouldner tends to conceive of ideologies as discrete symbolic systems that are realized above all in *writing*, and that serve, as written, rational discourse, to animate public projects of social reconstruction. Hence Gouldner is led to the conclusion that the growth of electronic media, such as radio and television, marks the *decline* of the role of ideology in modern societies. Ideology is increasingly displaced from society as a whole, where consciousness is shaped more and more by the products of the electronic media; ideology is increasingly confined to the restricted sphere of the universities, where intellectuals continue to cultivate the written word (Gouldner 1976, 175–91). This is not exactly a version of the end of ideology thesis, since Gouldner acknowledges a continuing, albeit restricted, role for ideology in contemporary societies. But to argue that ideology bears a privileged relation to writing and hence cannot be implicated in the development of electronic communication is at best a shortsighted view, for it severs the analysis of ideology from the very forms of mass communication that are of greatest significance today. So while the development of mass communication has not been altogether neglected by some authors who could be associated with the grand narrative of cultural transformation, we may doubt whether they have provided a satisfactory account of this development and its implications for the analysis of ideology.

The second major shortcoming of the grand narrative concerns the ways in which the concept of ideology is employed within it. This concept is used in differing ways by different thinkers, and it would be erroneous to suggest that it has a clear, univocal sense within the grand narrative. But if we abstract from the differences of usage, we can see that this concept is generally used to refer to discrete belief systems or symbolic systems that emerged in the wake of secularization and that have served to mobilize political movements and/or legitimate political power in modern societies; the general usage, in other words, is consistent with what I have called a neutral conception of ideology. This general usage is given a specific inflection by particular theorists or groups of theorists. We have seen, for example, that Gouldner tends to use "ideology" to refer to symbolic systems realized primarily in writing, which animate public projects of social reconstruction by means of rational discourse. The end of ideology theorists, by contrast, tend to use the term to refer to that specific subset of discrete political belief systems or doctrines that are comprehensive and totalizing, such as Marxism and communism. This restriction of the term enables them to predict—with a confidence that no doubt contains a good deal of wishful thinking—that the age of ideologies is now over.

The general usage of "ideology" in the grand narrative is questionable in two key respects. In the first place, it obliges us to regard ideology as an essentially *modern* phenomenon, that is, as a phenomenon unique to societies that emerged in the course of capitalist industrialization during the seventeenth, eighteenth and nineteenth centuries. But this, it seems to me, is an overly restrictive view. It is not necessary to define the concept of ideology in terms of a particular body of political doctrines, belief systems, or symbolic systems that are characteristic of certain societies only at a certain stage of their historical development. The concept admits of many other definitions, and it is by no means clear that restricting the concept to modern societies is the most plausible or illuminating way to proceed. Must we accept that it *makes no sense* to speak of ideology in societies that preceded capitalist industrialization in Europe, that it makes no sense to speak of ideology in preindustrial Europe or in nonindustrial societies elsewhere in the world? I think not. It seems to me to be perfectly possible to elaborate a justifiable conception of ideology that is not restricted to a particular body of doctrines that have emerged in the modern era.

The general usage of "ideology" in the grand narrative is also misleading insofar as it directs our attention toward discrete political doctrines, belief systems or symbolic systems, and it therefore turns our attention away from the multiple ways in which symbolic forms are used, in the varied contexts of everyday life, to establish and sustain relations of domination. There is no clear and convincing justification that can be drawn, either from the history of the concept of ideology or from a reflection on the ways in which power is maintained, for restricting the analysis of ideology to the study of discrete political doctrines, belief systems or symbolic systems. To do so would be to take an overly narrow view of the nature and role of ideology in modern societies and to neglect a wide range of symbolic phenomena that support forms of power in the social contexts of everyday life. Once again, it could not be said that all the authors associated with the grand narrative espouse a consistent conception of ideologies as discrete political doctrines, belief systems, or symbolic systems. More often than not, each of these authors uses the term "ideology" in differing ways in different works, or even within the covers of a single work. But it is unquestionably the case that the conception of ideologies as discrete political doctrines features prominently among these uses, and it is primarily as such that the alleged rise and fall of ideologies in the modern era is traced. If we put aside this conception, we can also put aside the view that ideologies first appeared with the dawn of the modern era and have since disappeared from the social and political domain, and we can reoriente the study of ideology toward the multiple and varied ways in which symbolic forms have been used, and continue to be used, in the service of power, whether in modern Western societies or in social contexts situated elsewhere in time and space.

NOTES

1. For recent and differing statements of this argument, see Claude Lefort, "Outline of the Genesis of Ideology in Modern Societies", in *The Political Forms of Modern Society: Bureaucracy, Democracy, Totalitarianism*, John B. Thompson (Cambridge: Polity Press, 1986); and Alvin W. Gouldner, *The Dialectic of Ideology and Technology: The Origins, Grammar and Future of Ideology* (London: Macmillan, 1976).

2. See also Chaim I. Waxman, ed., *The End of Ideology Debate* (New York: Funk & Wagnalls, 1968).

3. Although there has been a decline in regularized participations in Christian churches in many Western industrial societies since the nineteenth century, it remains the case that a large proportion of people declare religious beliefs of some kind. A recent Gallup poll in Britain found that 75 percent of people questioned said they believed in God, and nearly 60 percent said they believed in heaven. See *Gallup Polls 1979* (London: Social Surveys Ltd. 1979), table 3. Comparable figures for the United States are generally higher. See Rodney Stark and William S. Bainbridge, *The Future of Religion: Secularization, Revival and Cult Formation* (Berkeley: University of California Press, 1985). Moreover, Christian churches continue to exercise some influence in the social and political affairs of modern nation-states, although the nature of this influence varies considerably from one national context to another. See David Martin, *A General Theory of Secularization* (Oxford: Basil Blackwell, 1978), and Patrick Michel, *Politics and Religion in Eastern Europe*, trans. Alan Braley (Cambridge: Polity Press, 1991).

3

IDEOLOGIES IN SOCIAL STRUGGLES

Alfred McClung Lee

TO UNDERSTAND CONFLICTING VIEWPOINTS

Aware of the "multiplicity of conflicting viewpoints, the sociologist Karl Mannheim put forward his dramatic relationism as "the only possible way out." Each ideology, "though claiming absolute validity, has been shown to be related to a particular position and to be adequate only in that one." Thus in order for an "investigator to be in a position to arrive at a solution adequate to our present life-situation," the investigator has to have "assimilated all the crucial motivations and viewpoints, whose internal contradictions account for our present social-political tension." Mannheim (1936, 106) called for a "total view" and said that this "implies both the assimilation and transcendence of the limitations of particular points of view." This would have as "its goal . . . the broadest possible extension of our horizon of vision."

In contrast with this vague Mannheim goal, we need to realize as the sociologists P.L. Berger and Thomas Luckman (1966, 118) point out, "Definitions of reality have self-fulfilling potency. Theories can be realized in history, even theories that were highly abstruse when they were first conceived by their inventors." When they gain acceptance and even utility, it is not because a theory has shaped an event or development but because events became hospitable to interpretations of events or aspirations in terms of a given theory.

One can share Mannheim's concern for "the profound disquietude of modern man" in the face of "the multiplicity of conflicting viewpoints" without oversimply interpreting this, as he does, as a crisis to be resolved. He attributes this crisis to the "disruption of the intellectual monopoly of the church." He defines the "greatest exertion of mankind" in current society as "the attempt to counteract the tendency of an individualistic undirected society, which is verging toward anarchy, with a more organic type of social order." This calls, he claims, for the acceptance of dynamic relationism as "the only possible way out" (1936, 13, 32, 98).

The multiplicity exists, as it has for a long time. Like all stimulating situations, it is disquieting, disturbing, even upsetting. It is only claimed to be at a critical point by advocates of one or another integrating ideology who stand to gain from its acceptance. Such advocates are not only academic rationalizers but are especially religious and political propagandists. We are probably no more at a decisive historical moment or turning point in the matter of multiplicity than we have been for centuries.

Ideological multiplicity appears to hold more promise than danger, except for those trying to find the alleged but delusory peace and quiet of a homogeneous society, one more monovalent culturally. Many influences other than the decline of imperial Rome and of ecclesiastical power helped bring forth modern multiplicity. Mannheim might have cited long-time Jewish, Muslim, heretical Christian, primitive magic, commercial, military, and other diversifying influences operative in Europe as sequels to Rome's multiplicity (Gibbon 1782, esp. vol. 1; White 1896).

Talk of a single possible way out, like Mannheim's quest for a transcendent sense of reality, raises such questions as: A way out for whom? For society? For intellectuals only? Why only one way out? Society's multivalence provides and is likely to continue to furnish many perceptions of reality, thus many bases for ideological formulations and interpretations. Certainly each group seems to move in a separate and distinct world of ideas, but one neglects the social realities of cultural conditioning when one says, as does Mannheim, "that these different systems of thought, which are often in conflict with one another, may in the last analysis be reduced to different modes of experiencing the 'same' reality" (1936, 99).

Objective societal symbols, artifacts, and basic environment are presumably present for all to experience, but they differ in their availability and accessibility. They are perceived and conceived differently by members of different social status groups in each society of which we know. Are there not strengths as well as handicaps in ideological multiplicity when it is faced with frankness and tolerance?

Finally, Mannheim's apparent anxiety in the 1920s to replace unplanned individualism with "a more organic type of social order" stresses a type of solution for living in a giant society well illustrated by modern states in a variety of forms. It is a type of solution that has scarcely proven itself in this war-torn century as a way to avoid anarchy more than temporarily. Our vast, centralized, integrated states, with their persistent conformist pressures to homogenize individuals and their values, may merely be more efficient ways to prepare for eventual chaos.

Let us look at an approach or orientation that is more receptive to the implications of cultural multivalence and more appreciative of change and diversity in social life through time and space. Mannheim's position is explored because it resembles that of too many social theorists.

INGREDIENTS OF IDEOLOGIES

The principal ingredients out of which ideologies are constructed are notable for their lack of novelty. They typically include symbols for generalities drawn from a societal culture long embedded in moralistic preachments. The concept (of "reality," of deprivation, need, challenge, and tactics) and referents associated with such symbols, as well as general theories binding them together, derive from the subcultures of the groups to whose concerns the ideologies are chiefly related. Messianism, regal divine right, egalitarian aspirations, puritanical devotion to entrepreneurism, and class conflict are folk theories that long antedated Christianity, absolute monarchy, democracy, the so-called Protestant ethic, and Marxism.

The contributions of the formulator of a given version of an ideology lie chiefly in pattern, relative emphases, topical applications, and rhetorical artistry. The formulator may be an individual writer, a drafting committee, or the impersonal and continuing discussion processes of a group or society that gradually crystallizes a folk aspiration with some clarity and influence. When an ideology is to be mass-communicated in whole or in part, it is often applied to a specific competitive or conflict situation. The same ingredients become those of the related propaganda. In a sense, propaganda is ideology on the march. Much of the continuing impact of a legitimated ideology is through its permeation of a society's formal and informal educational processes.

Bridges of Symbols. Ideologies consist of symbols with which propagandists build bridges from their clients to diverse publics. The symbols represent traditional and habitual values placed in relation to a given leader's or organization's aspirations. Ideologies contain claims to support and thus legitimation from some source of authority—theological, popular, military, economic, historical, scientific—or from a combination of several. "The strength of such legitimations is that they are perceived as independent of the social and political climate in which they are produced. But they can be better understood as reflections of it" (Rose 1986, 732).

An ideology is often used for purposes other than those for which it was presumably developed and given popular acceptance. For example,

> Christianity . . . was harnessed by powerful interests for political purposes with little relationship to its religious contents. . . .

There may be large elements in an ideology that bear no particular relationship to the legitimated interest, but that are vigorously affirmed by the "carrier" group simply because it has committed itself to the ideology. (Berger and Luckman 1966, 114–15)

Thus, Freudianism has been used to combat Marxism. Darwinian theory has been seized upon to give intellectual support to unbridled free-enterprise capitalism.

TO TYPIFY IDEOLOGIES

Rather than by their subject matter alone, it would appear more practical to typify ideologies in terms of their stage of development and vogue (folk, somewhat formulated, crystallized, decadent, modifying), in terms of the groups to which they are related (interest, ethnic, class or stratum, societal), and in terms of their current social role (revolutionary, reformist, legitimated). Interrelations among these three sets of typings could give us sixty possible combinations in a three-dimensional diagram. There are, for example, emerging folk-societal ideologies that are reformist, such as some or those developed by black action groups for the modification of U.S. society. The ideologies most commonly discussed are those that can be characterized as societal, crystallized or modifying, and revolutionary, reformist or legitimated. Some of the ideologies most influential in the subtle coloration of the thoughts and writings of intellectuals in largely unrecognized fashions are those of class, ethnicity (Chapman, 1956, 103–12), occupation, gender, and age. These are often of a folk nature or are only partly (often inaccurately) acknowledged. These ideologies are rationalized and are frequently made to work within the overall legitimated ideological patterning.

In offering such a typology as a way of characterizing ranges of ideological phenomena, it is insisted that actual examples of ideologies are usually typologically "impure." Other dimensions of ideology are also subsumed under the types given—for example, relative absolutism, inclusiveness or exclusiveness, and relative charisma, authority, or pathos. What is principally implied in this suggested typing is that the characteristics of ideologies are relative to their social purposes and roles and to their degree of establishment or nonconformity.

As their social purposes and roles change, ideologies instantly modify, but less in symbolic representation than in associated concepts and referents in interpretation. As the sociologists Severyn T. Bruyn and Paula Rayman conclude: Such interpretations enabled the centralized institutions of the state to perpetuate violence in the "legitimized" battlefields of World War I, the extermination camps of World War II, and the tiger cages of the Indochina War. On a more daily basis, states legitimize the continuation of racism, sexism, and growing worldwide hunger. (1979, 8)

What is also implied by this suggested typing is that rather than announce or even seek an end to ideology or to the influence of ideologies, it would be more useful to study their amazing persistence and adaptability, their many guises and the deep roots of the most useful and the most disastrous ones in family life and in multivalent individual personalities. These roots include the prototypical and successor roles and groups in socialization patterns.[1] As such studies proceed further, social scientists will be able to offer more data about the utility or lack of utility of ideologies to specific types of groups' social actions and to societal welfare broadly considered.

Emotionalism, adroitness, trickery, irrationality, and the use of force recur as one studies ideologies and phenomena related to them. Ideologies are part and parcel of social competitions and conflicts. They demand much more than scholarly wishful thinking or social-scientific technique to brush them aside or deny them.

For all the alleged increase of popular sophistication in political and economic matters through expanded educational facilities, the number of docile voters, soldiers, and customers continues to be abundant and not very questioning. After all, any of the educational facilities are accurately described as impoundment operations devoted to brainwashing and homogenizing.

> The ideology operates not only as a unifying force and a guideline to action in ambiguous situations but also as a language, a set of semantic guides, that makes possible rapid and efficient communications of the wishes of central authorities. (Schein 1966, 608)

As Martin Luther King Jr. (1963, 26), put it, "how often are our lives characterized by a high blood pressure of creeds and an anemia of deeds!"

IDEOLOGIES IN INTERETHNIC RELATIONS

John Stuart Mill (1951, 486) claimed in 1861 that democracy is "next to impossible in a country made up of different nationalities." This view has helped rationalize restrictions of civil liberties and the forceful suppression of ethnic rights movements. After studying interethnic conflicts in many parts of the world, the political scientist Donald L. Horowitz (1985, 684) recognized "recurrent conflict, but the outcomes of conflict are various rather than uniform." His findings did not point to "the futility of democracy or the inevitability of uncontrolled conflict."

Southern white folklore to the contrary, African blacks never did accept slavery or remain in it willingly. Revolts began in the slave-accumulation compounds of West Africa and continued across the Atlantic (Herskovitz 1939, 30). Nonwhite-white struggles have since gone through at least ten significant phases: (1) the 200 slave conspiracies and revolts prior to 1861 (Aptheker 1963, esp. chaps. 6–14); (2) black cooperation with Union armies during the Civil War, the "greatest and most successful slave revolt—a sort of general strike against slavery" (Davie, 1949, 45); (3) white repressive violence featuring the Ku Klux Klan during the so-called Reconstruction at a cost of at least 5,000 black lives (1949, 54); (4) following Reconstruction, white lynchings of 5,000 and killings of uncounted others in terrorist raids on black ghettos (Cutler 1905; Raper 1933; Myrdal et al 1944, chap. 27); (5) from the 1890s, the development of a clearer two-sidedness in interracial clashes (Konvitz 1983);, (6) white rioting against the industrially mobile blacks, especially during the World War I to II period (Sandburg 1969; Rudwick 1964; Lieberson and Silverman 1965, 887–98); (7) nationalism achieving some crystallization in the black Garvey movement of the 1920s and later among Amerindians, black Muslims, and Hispanics (Hill 1983); (8) in the 1950s and later, continuing widespread disorders of blacks and Hispanics against oppression and exploitation (Grimshaw 1969, esp. chap. 12; Lee 1968, vii-xxviii); (9) the emergence of nonviolent confrontations led especially by Martin Luther King Jr. (1929–68) and his followers (Moses 1982; Witherspoon 1985; Garrow 1981); (10) the rise of black political power in the cities and nationally under such leaders as Andrew Young and Jesse Jackson (Cole 1975; Marable 1985).

American whites have yet to give nonwhites adequate aid in their struggles toward equal status and thus toward a more healthful society. Such aid would be a reparation for more than three and one-half centuries of degrading domination and exploitation.

The antiminority positions of the more radical and more conservative white churches are often obscured in interethnic conflicts. Martin Luther King Jr. (1963, 11), recalls that the churches "often served to crystallize, conserve, and even bless the patterns of majority opinion" in this area. He mentions their "erstwhile sanction . . . of slavery, racial segregation, war, and economic exploitation."

The emergence of what is often called "our secular religion" bridges gaps among some ethnic and racial ideologies. It tends to minimize conflicts among the more established or "respectable" segments of the population, to make a degree of "democracy" possible. As King (1963, 8) points out: "success, recognition, and conformity are the bywords of the modern world where everyone seems to crave the anesthetizing security of being identified with the majority." Here is thus another social ambiguity: We need a degree of adherence to an overall "secular religion," but it must be subject constantly to review and criticism in terms of social needs and ideals. As King (1963, 12) appropriately adds: "the hope of a secure and livable world lies with disciplined nonconformists, who are dedicated to justice, peace, and brotherhood."

IDEOLOGIES IN WARS

People with a variety of motives accept ideologies as reasons or excuses for participation in wars as well as in other social conflicts. Propagandist interpretations help obscure unfortunate possible consequences or give a sense of irresistible urgency. As the late clergyman Harry Emerson Fosdick said, "Christianity joined with the state, became sponsor for war, blesser of war, cause of war, and fighter for war. Too often, it tried to carry the cross of Jesus in one hand and a dripping sword in the other (Fosdick, quoted quoted in Ward, 1931:340).[2]

The record of European participation in wars suggests that the United States has carried on its Old World heritage in this respect with little alteration. From the twelfth through the nineteenth centuries, England and France were at war with one another or with some other country from thirty-six to sixty-five of the years in each century (Sorokin 1928, 324).[3] Citing similar figures for these and other European countries ranging from ancient Greece to modern Russia and for the United States, the sociologist Pitirim A. Sorokin noted in 1947 that peaceful periods have been unevenly distributed, have lacked periodicity, and those "as long as a quarter of a century have been exceedingly rare in the history of these countries." Only Holland had a full century of freedom from international military conflict.

Sorokin stresses (1) "that frequency of war is considerably higher than most of us usually think," (2) "that the most primitive peoples—that is, the least literate—are the most peaceful; that with an increase of 'liberalism,' 'humanism,' 'modernism,' and 'relativism' wars have not decreased," (3) "that democracies and republics are not more peaceful than autocracies and monarchies," (4) that more literacy, educational opportunities, scientific knowledge, and mechanical inventions have not diminished the time devoted to war, and (5) that there "is no perpetual historical trend toward either a decrease or increase of war. . . . The theories claiming a progressive pacification of the race constitute merely wishful thinking." The twentieth century's bloodiness, he contends, "is sufficient in itself to refute such utopian theories" (1947, 498–99).[4]

Sorokin's sweeping conclusions are perhaps less surprising today than before the dawn of atomic warfare. In World War II, under various ideological banners, some 16,933,000 soldiers were killed or died of wounds, and 34,325,000 civilians were slaughtered, a total of 51,258,000. The "winning" Allies lost six-sevenths of that total; the "losing" Axis powers lost only one-seventh! When coincident warborne epidemics are also included, the grand total killed was perhaps 60 million in the five-year period, one and one-half times that of World War I (Wright 1965, 1542–43). Our technological efficiency is now such that the same number of people or more could be exterminated in the first few days of a third world war.

Do such unbelievable destructions of human lives accomplish the goals promised in any extant ideology? It is possible that the mobilization and militarization of life among the Allies did at least as much to nurture as to destroy authoritarianisms. Military action did not save the lives of six million Jews, Poles, and others in and on the way to Nazi extermination camps (Morse 1968; Taylor 1969). Effective coping with what became Nazism would have had to start at least as early as the Versailles peace conference, preferably earlier through steps that would have prevented World War I (Barnes, in Waller 1940, 39-99; Millis 1935). As the sociologist Willard Waller cogently pointed out on the eve of the U.S. participation in World War II, "Any valid theory of war . . . must consider the fact that it grows out of the totality of our civilization. . . . War settles nothing because defeated nations will not accept defeat. War is an arbiter whose decisions the contestants refuse to accept as final, for there is always the chance that another trial will turn out differently" (1940, 13, 32).

Ideological rationalizations for a Hitler's existence became complex. In the highly interrelated world of today, the blame—whatever "blame" might be determined to be—for a Hitler is shared so widely by those in power as to be well nigh universal. The trials of Nazi war criminals dealt only with a few obvious instruments. What about the Americans and non-German Europeans who backed Hitler and Hitler's supporters with funds, materials, and silence? Americans too often prefer nationalist (so-called "consensus") historians who carefully select events supportive of pleasant nationalistic myths rather than those who, like Charles A. Beard[5] and Harry Elmer Barnes,[6] insist that unpleasant facts about the American past and present be remembered, pondered, and hopefully used. The latter seek to reverse, at least for a few decision makers, Hegel's futilitarian dictum that "peoples and governments never have learned anything from history, or acted on principles deduced from it" (1858, 6).

How can we explain the depressing frequency of wars, rebellions, riots, and murders throughout the world? No instinct of pugnacity needs to be assumed to account for them. "Peoples have always gone to war with various degrees of relish or repugnance; but such sentiments have been in their traditions and not in any inherited instinct, one way or another" (Sumner and Keller 1927, 1:369),[7] a great many comparative students of society have concluded.

In spite of the efforts of such instinctivists as Robert Ardrey (1966) and Konrad Lorenz (1966), the anthropologist Ralph E. Holloway Jr. (in Fried, Harris, and Murphy 1968, 31) insists that the problem of war "is a political one, not a biological or psychological one." Anthropologist Margaret Mead (in Fried, Harris, and Murphy 1968, 218) argues "that man lacks instinctual controls, and not, as Lorenz and Ardrey do, that warfare is an extension of built-in aggression towards rivals for mates, territory or food." Recourse to interpersonal or intergroup violence varies so greatly in terms of ethnic (including so-called racial) and class differences that it can be traced to social learning and to happenstance rather than to biologically inherited "instinct."

WARS AND SOCIAL INEQUALITY

A large share of the organized violence in and between countries is associated with efforts to facilitate or prevent social changes, especially those that might develop more or less social equality. Only through the use of physical coercion can any dominant group continue for long to maintain a given condition of intergroup inequality.

A relationship of intergroup inequality usually begins with the use of force and is given its justification by myth making later. Masters flatter themselves or accept the flattery of their lackeys about the reasons for their superiority and their consequent high social status. The dominated do not fail to find ways to resist the propagandas that assert and attempt to legitimize their inferiority and their consequent low status. The dominated develop their own counterlegitimacy with which to confer on themselves some degree of dignity and often also some share of social benefits. Intimate views of those living in any deprived area, whether in Calcutta, Tokyo, London, Belfast, Rome, or New York City, provide vivid authentication of this and give pause to any curious-minded person who enjoys power, privilege, and high status in that city.

Our ideological justifications for inequality have become increasingly sophisticated and labored. The more widely held ones are no longer officially based on such disproven crudities as alleged racial superiority and inferiority or the special genetic virtues said to be "bred into" a social-status-group-defined human stock (Kiernan 1969). They are now more commonly couched publicly in terms of IQs, academic grades and degrees, and other types of structures, such as those that do the certifying (Kamin 1974; Sahlins 1976). But the dominated still remain just as "unreasonable" as always about accepting their "inferiority" as a justification for their low status and for their economic and political deprivation. That the criteria are "scientific" or "realistic" or "necessary" for the maintenance of "the system" based upon so-called incentives somehow fails to impress those excluded nationally or internationally from a more proportionate share in what society controls and produces.

Think about what happens to rationalizations for inequality nationally or internationally when we grasp adequately the implications of the statement by the psychologist Kenneth B. Clark (1965, 128): "children who are treated as if they are uneducable invariably become uneducable." That statement has a bearing not only on our expanding prison population but also on the growth of international terrorism and of riots, revolts, and wars. Belief in any child can accomplish educational wonders. On that lesson may hinge significant aspects of society's future, especially whether or not we shall continue to use violence to maintain an unequal society.

THE NEED FOR NONVIOLENT AGGRESSION

As riots, revolts, and wars become more frightful and more destructive, experimentation with alternatives to violence has gained increasing urgency and support. Martin Luther King Jr. (1963, 6) told a congregation: "violence brings only temporary victories; violence, by creating many more social problems than it solves, never brings permanent peace." Nonviolence, he insisted, "combines toughmindedness and tenderheartedness and avoids the complacency and donothingness of the softminded and the violence and bitterness of the hardhearted."

More and more, chiefly the emotionally disturbed, inexperienced, and incompetent among those in positions of leadership try to precipitate armed conflict. Such persons too often achieve great power in social movements and states. When they confront the more competent, the latter get seduced into treacherous spirals of retaliation or of "preventive" violence—fighting to "make the world safe for democracy." Chaotic and overtense social conditions, often carelessly or cynically maintained and stimulated by interests powerful in their own or other states, provide opportunities for the Stalins, Hitlers, Mussolinis, Francos, Japanese warlords, and Third World dictators, not to mention our own members of the list.

Rather than talk about "the violent American" or "the violent human," we need to face these facts and probabilities: A capacity for anger is inherent in human nature. When needs for expression are strongly thwarted, anger may erupt into violence, but violence is not essential to human personality or to human affairs. There are substantial alternatives, for example, to the position of the Algerian activist Frantz Fanon's statement that "decolonization is always a violent phenomenon" (1966, 29). Mohandas K. Gandhi's 1947 achievement in leading India nonviolently to independence from the United Kingdom is one of many examples contrary to Fanon's generalization.

Militarism, as the social analyst Cecelia Kirkman (1986, 3) concludes,

> affects everyone in American society. From children who play with war toys to students who learn the history of warriors but not of peacemakers, from teenagers targeted by military recruitment ads to adults who are constantly bombarded with new rationales for more military spending, we all live in a militarized society.

She adds that women "are directly affected by both the economic violence created, in part, by our militarized national budget and the physical and sexual violence that is part of any militarized culture."

IDEOLOGIES CHANGE: IDEOLOGY PERSISTS

The hopeful increase in popular sophistication in political and economic matters through expanded educational facilities is too often accurately described as increased brainwashing or homogenizing of an excess labor supply. In consequence, the numbers of manipulable voters, soldiers, and customers for mass political parties, armies, and mercantile operations continue to appear to be abundant and too unquestioning.

Thus, one must speak of the persistence rather than the end of ideologies as characteristic of human societies of a massive and literate sort in the world today. Ideologies are the intellectual and emotional patterns in terms of which groups and individuals are provided with ways to organize their cultural symbols for use in communication and action. Ideologies come and go, but the end of ideology is scarcely in sight. In the world's larger countries, men and women with admittedly mixed motives continue to accept ideologies as reasons or excuses for participation in wars, peace efforts, and other social conflicts and competitions; the irrationality or rationality of which propagandas help to obscure and to justify.

When they are functioning as social scientists who care about society, people turn aside from the traditional roles of intellectuals. They refuse to be formulators, curators, disinfectors, interpreters, redefiners, and obfuscators of ideologies for those who employ them and whose social manipulations and exploitations benefit them. They try critically to see such social instruments as ideologies more nearly as they are and to help people generally to have that advantage.

NOTES

1. Conceptions mentioned here are set forth in detail in A. McClung Lee, *Multivalent Man* (New York: George Braziller, 1966), chaps. 11–13.

2. See also Ray Abrams, *Preachers Present Arms* (New York: Round Table Press, 1933); and *The Essays of A.K. Muste*, Nat Hentoff (New York: Simon and Schuster, 1967).

3. See also M.R. Davie, *Evolution of War* (New Haven: Yale University Press, 1929); and Quincy Wright, *A Study of War*, 2nd ed. (Chicago: University of Chicago Press, 1965).

4. See also Sorokin, *Social and Cultural Dynamics*, 4 vols. (New York: Harper Brothers, 1937–41), esp. 3:chaps. 9–11. cf. J.D. Singer et al., *Explaining War* (Beverly Hills: Sage, 1979); and Melvin Small and J.D. Singer, "Patterns in International Warfare, 1816–1965," in *The War System: An Interdisciplinary Approach*, R.A. Falk and S.S. Kim, (Boulder, Colo.): Westview Press, 1980), 551–62.

5. See, for example, C.A. Beard, *An Economic Interpretation of the Constitution of the United States* (New York: Macmillan, 1913); *The Navy: Defense or Portent?* (New York: Harper Brothers, 1932); and *Giddy Minds and Foreign Quarrels* (New York: Macmillan, 1939).

6. See, for example, H.E. Barnes, *The Genesis of the World War*, 2nd ed. (New York: Knopf, 1927); *The Twilight of Christianity* (New York: Vanguard, 1929); *Society in Transition* (New York: Prentice-Hall, 1939); and *An Economic History of the Western World* (New York: Harcourt, Brace, 1938).

7. See also Summner, Keller, and M.R. Davie, *The Science of Society* (New Haven: Yale University Press, 1927), 4:115–52.

4

MULTIPLE JEOPARDY, MULTIPLE CONSCIOUSNESS: THE CONTEXT OF A BLACK FEMINIST IDEOLOGY

Deborah K. King

In the following consideration of the dialectics within each of three liberation movements, I hope to describe the tensions and priorities that influence the construction of a black feminist ideology. To the extent that any politic is monistic, the actual victims of racism, sexism, or classism may be absent from, invisible within, or seen as antagonistic to that politic. Thus, prejudicial attitudes and discriminatory actions may be overt, subtle, or covert; and they may have various manifestations through ideological statements, policies and strategies, and interpersonal relations. That is, black and/or poor women may be marginal to monistic feminism, women's concerns may be excluded from nationalistic activism, and indifference to race and gender may pervade class politics. This invisibility may represent actual exclusion or benign neglect, while marginality is represented in tokenism, minimization, and devalued participation. Antagonism involves two subordinate groups whose actions and beliefs are placed in opposition as mutually detrimental. From this conceptual framework, the following discussion highlights the major aspects of multiple jeopardy within liberation politics.

INTRARACIAL POLITICS

Racial solidarity and race liberation have been and remain a fundamental concern for black Americans. Historically and currently, slavery, segregation, and institutional as well as individual discrimination have been formative experiences in most blacks' socialization and political outlook. The inerasable physical characteristics of race have long determined the status and opportunities of black women in the United States. Since race serves as a significant filter of what blacks perceive and how blacks are perceived, many black women have claimed that their racial identity is more salient than either their gender or class identity.[1] Diane Lewis, an anthropologist, has remarked that when racism is seen as the principal cause of their subordinate status, "their interests as blacks have taken precedence over their interests as women" (Lewis 1977, 343). This political importance of race is evident for other reasons as well. Certainly, the chronological order of the social movements for racial, gender, and class justice in part explains the priority given to racial interests. In both the nineteenth and twentieth centuries, the abolition and civil rights movements predate women's suffrage and the women's movement. Similarly, collective efforts that addressed economic deprivation and exploitation, such as trade unionism beginning in the late 1800s, communist organizing in the 1920s and 1930s, and the anti-imperialist activism of the 1960s were preceded by or simultaneous with race-oriented movements. Considering the order of events, it is reasonable to expect that most black women would have made commitments to and investments in the race movements such that they would not or could not easily abandon those for later movements.

Furthermore, through the necessity of confronting and surviving racial oppression, black women have assumed responsibilities atypical of those assigned to white women under Western patriarchy. Black women often held central and powerful leadership roles within the black community and within its liberation politics. We founded schools, operated social welfare services, sustained churches, organized collective work groups and unions, and even established banks and commercial enterprises. That is, we were the backbone of racial uplift, and we also played critical roles in the struggle for racial justice (Giddings 1983; Harley and Terborg-Penn 1978; Davis 1971: 2–16). Harriet Tubman led slaves to freedom on the underground railroad; Ida Wells Barnett led the crusade against lynching; Fannie Lou Hamer and Ella Baker were guiding political spirits of the southern black efforts that gave birth to SNCC and the Mississippi Freedom Democratic Party; the "simple" act of Rosa Parks catapulted Martin Luther King to national prominence. Black women, therefore, did not experience sexism within the race movement in quite the ways that brought many white women to feminist consciousness within either civil rights or New Left politics (Evans 1980; Carson 1981).

All together, this history constitutes a powerful impetus toward a monistic race approach as the means of liberation for black women. Michelle Wallace concludes that black women simply lack a feminist consciousness as a matter of choice, out of ignorance, misguided beliefs, or an inability to recognize sexual domination both within and without the black community (Wallace 1979).[2] Since the 1800s, however, the writings of such prominent black women as Sojourner Truth, Maria Stewart, Anna Julia Cooper, Josephine St. Pierre Ruffin, Frances Watkins Harper, Pauli Murray, Frances

Beale, Audre Lorde, and Angela Davis have described a broader view of black consciousness.[3] Even among those black women who expressed grave reservations about participating in the women's movement, most recognized sexism as a factor of their subordination in the larger society and acknowledged sexual politics among blacks. They could identify the sexual inequities that resulted in the images of black women as emasculating matriarchs; in the rates of sexual abuse and physical violence; and in black men assuming the visible leadership positions in many black social institutions, such as the church, the intelligentsia, and political organizations.[4] During the civil rights and black nationalist movements of the 1960s and 1970s, men quite effectively used the matriarchy issue to manipulate and coerce black women into maintaining exclusive commitments to racial interests and redefining and narrowing black women's roles and images in ways to fit a more traditional Western view of women. Black feminists Pauli Murray (1975) and Pauline Terrelonge Stone (1975) both agree that the debates over this issue became an ideological ploy to heighten guilt in black women over their supposed collusion with whites in the oppression of black men. Consequently, these intraracial tensions worked against the public articulations of a feminist consciousness by most black women. Nevertheless, a point of concern and contention within the black community was how sexual inequalities might best be addressed, not whether they existed. A few black women responded by choosing monistic feminism, others sought a distinct black feminist activism. While many organized feminist efforts within race-oriented movements, some also adopted a strict nationalist view. Over time, there were also transformations of perspectives. For example, the black women of SNCC created within it a women's liberation group that later became an independent feminists-of-color organization, the Third World Women's Alliance, which is today the only surviving entity of SNCC.

The politics of race liberation have rarely been exclusively race based. Because so many blacks historically have been economically oppressed, race liberation has out of necessity become more pluralistic through its incorporation of economic interests. Whether civil rights or a nationalist activism, the approach to class injustice generally promotes greater economic opportunities and rewards within the existing capitalist order. At the turn of the century, for instance, the collective action known as racial uplift involved the efforts of educated, middle-class blacks to elevate the moral, physical, social, and economic conditions of lower income blacks. The National Association of Wage Earners was established in the 1920s by women like Nannie Burroughs, Maggie Wallace, and Mary McCleod Bethune to assist black female domestic and factory workers (Bennett 1978).

The civil rights movement initially seemed to avoid the value-laden implications of this pattern of middle-class beneficence toward those with fewer economic resources. Both Aldon Morris (1984), a sociologist, and Clayborne Carson (1981), a historian, have written of the genuine grassroots orientation of the black southern strategy in the l950s and early 1960s. The majority of the participants were rural, poorly educated. and economically disadvantaged, but more important, these same individuals set the priorities and the strategies of the movement. The legacy was an affirmation of the strength of seemingly powerless people, and particularly of the black women who were among the principal organizers and supporters (Robinson 1987).

Despite these auspicious beginnings, Cornell West (1984), a black theologian, described the 1960s as a time when the interests of poor blacks were often betrayed. Middle-class blacks were better able to take advantage of the relatively greater opportunities made possible through the race-oriented, legal liberalism of equal opportunity and affirmative action policies and electoral politics. Only such groups as the Nation of Islam and the League of Revolutionary Black Workers, like Marcus Garvey's United Negro Improvement Association earlier in this century, continued to represent the interests of working-class and impoverished blacks. The contemporary controversy over class polarization in the black community is a consequence of the movement's not effectively addressing the economic status of all blacks. Given the particularly precarious economic status of black women, this neglect and marginalization of class is especially problematic for them. The National Welfare Rights Organization, founded in 1967, was one of the few successful, though short-lived, efforts to address the class divisions. Only recently have race-focal groups, including the Urban League and the National Association for the Advancement of Colored People, addressed the plight of impoverished black women.

Racial solidarity has been a fundamental element of black women's resistance to domination. But the intraracial politics of gender and class have made a strictly nationalist approach overly restrictive and incalculably detrimental to our prospects for full liberation. Given a social condition that is also compounded by other oppressions, black women have necessarily been concerned with effecting, at the least, an amelioration of economic and gender discriminations. Consequently, some black women have sought an association with feminism as one alternative to the limitations of monistic race politics.

POLITICS AMONG WOMEN

At one level, black women, other women of color, and white women share many common contemporary concerns about their legal status and rights, encounters with discrimination, and sexual victimization. It is on these shared concerns that feminists have sought to forge a sense of sisterhood and to foster solidarity. This effort is manifest in a variety of ways, but the slogan "Sisterhood is powerful" best exemplifies the importance and the hoped for efficacy of such solidarity in the achievement of women's equality and liberation. For example, all-female restrictions for consciousness-raising sessions, intellectual and artistic programs and publications, organizations, businesses, and communities reflect this singular orientation; and lesbian feminist separatism represents the absolute ideological expression of the monistic tendencies in feminism.

Presumably, black women are included in this sisterhood; nonetheless, invisibility and marginality characterize much of our relationship to the women's movement. The assertion of commonality, indeed of the universality and primacy of female oppression, denies the other structured inequalities of race, class, religion, and nationality, as well as denying the diverse cultural heritages that affect the lives of many women. While contending that feminist consciousness and theory emerged from the personal, everyday reality of being female, the reality of millions of women was ignored. The phrase "The personal is political" not only reflects a phenomenological approach to women's liberation—that is, of women defining and constructing their own reality—but it has also come to describe the politics of imposing and privileging a few women's personal lives over all women's lives by assuming that these few could be prototypical. For black women, the personal is bound up in the problems peculiar to multiple jeopardies of race and class, not the singular one of sexual inequality. This has not necessarily meant that black women rejected feminism, but merely that they were not singlemindedly committed to the organizations and some of the agenda that have come to be called the women's movement, that is, the movement of white, often Protestant, middle-class women.

Feminism has excluded and devalued black women, our experiences, and our interpretations of our own realities at the conceptual and ideological level. Black feminists and black women scholars have identified and critically examined other serious flaws in feminist theorizing. The assumption that the family is by definition patriarchal, the privileging of an individualist worldview, and the advocacy of female separatism are often antithetical positions to many of the values and goals of black women and thus are hindrances to our association with feminism (Lorde 1984, esp. 66–71; hooks 1984; Burnham 1985; Lugones and Spelman 1983). These theoretical blinders obscured the ability of certain feminists first to recognize the multifaceted nature of women's oppressions and then to envision theories that encompass those realities. As a consequence, monistic feminism's ability to foresee remedies that would neither abandon women to other discriminations, including race and class, nor exacerbate those burdens is extremely limited.

Without theories and concepts that represent the experiences of black women, the women's movement has and will be ineffectual in making ideological appeals that might mobilize such women. Often, in fact, this conceptual invisibility has led to the actual strategic neglect and physical exclusion or nonparticipation of black women. Most black women who have participated in any organizations or activities of the women's movement are keenly aware of the racial politics that anger, frustrate, and alienate us.

The case of the struggle for suffrage in the nineteenth century again is an instructive example of the complexity of multiple jeopardy and its politics. Initially, there was an alliance of blacks and women for universal suffrage. As the campaign ensued, however, opponents of universal suffrage, and of any extension of voting privileges, were successful in transforming the debate into one of who should receive the vote, women or black males. Many prominent white suffragists, including Elizabeth Cady Stanton, Susan B. Anthony, and Carrie Chapman Catt, abandoned the alliance and demanded a "women only" enfranchisement. The question of black women's suffrage should have been especially problematical for them. In fact, it was never seriously considered. More damning, however, were their politics of expediency. They cooperated with avowed racists in order to gain the southern vote and liberally used racial slurs and epithets arguing that white women's superior character and intellect made them more deserving of the right to vote than blacks, Native Americans, and eastern European and Asian immigrants.

As Angela Davis observes in her examination of race and class in the early women's rights campaign, even the Seneca Falls Declaration "all but ignored the predicament of white working-class women, as it ignored the condition of black women in the South and North alike (Davis 1981, 53–54). Barbara Andolsen, in one of the most comprehensive studies of racism in the women's suffrage movement observed: "[It] had a bold vision and noble principles . . . but this is a story of a vision betrayed. For the white women who led this movement came to trade upon their privilege as the daughters (sisters, wives, and mothers) of powerful white men in order to gain for themselves some share of the political power those men possessed. They did not adequately identify ways in which that political power would not be accessible to poor women, immigrant women, and black women" (Andolsen 1986, 78). Yet despite the blatant racism and class bias of the women's suffrage movement, black women, discouraged and betrayed, continued to work for their right to vote, both as blacks and as women, through their own suffrage organizations.

This history of racism in the early women's movement has been sustained by contemporary white feminists. Within organizations, most twentieth-century black women encounter myriad experiences that deny their reality. In some instances, it is the absence of materials, information, speeches, readings, or persons representing black women. When present at all, women of color are underrepresented and have marginal and subordinate roles. Recently, Paula Giddings has reported that the National Organization for Women (NOW) remains insensitive to such problematic issues as rape, abortion, sterilization, poverty, and unions. Women of color are rarely elected as officers or appointed to major positions, and NOW has actually encouraged minority women's chapters, rather than the incorporation of their concerns into the "regular" chapters (Giddings 1983, 348). Lawyer and educator Mary Frances Berry, in her analysis of the politics of amending the constitution, has argued that one reason for the defeat of the Equal Rights Amendment was the failure of its proponents to campaign, educate, and mobilize the black community, especially black women (Berry 1986).

Many white feminist activists have often assumed that their antisexist stance abolished all racial prejudice or discriminatory behaviors. At best, this presumption is naive and reflects a serious ignorance of the pervasiveness of racism in this society. Many blacks, women and men alike, see such postures as arrogant, racist, and dangerous to their own interests. Diane Lewis (1977) concluded that the status of black women and our interests within the women's movement and its organizations essentially replicate our structurally subordinate position to white women in the larger society. Different opportunity structures and life options make interracial alliances and feminist solidarity problematic. Conceptually invisible, interpersonally misunderstood and insulted, and strategically marginal, black women have found that much in the movement has denied important aspects of our history and experience. Yet, despite the critical obstacles and limitations, the imperatives of multiple jeopardy necessitate recognizing and resisting sexism.

Beyond race politics in feminism, many black women share concerns of impoverished and working-class women about class politics. What has become mainstream feminism rests on traditional, liberal economic aspirations of equal employment opportunities for women. In practice, however, the emphasis is often on the professional careers of women who are already economically privileged and college educated. It could be argued, for instance, that equal access to all types of vocational training and jobs may not be desirable as a necessary or primary goal. While it is true that men on average earn more than women, all men do not have equally attractive jobs in terms of working conditions, compensation and benefits, prestige, and mobility. Those male jobs may represent, at best, only a minimal improvement over the jobs of many working women. White feminist economic concerns have concentrated on primary-sector employment, but these are not the positions that are most critical and accessible to lower- or no-income women. Referring to the equal opportunity approach, Karen Kollias (1981, esp. 134) points out that "the majority of nonwhite, lower- and working-class women don't have the power to utilize these benefits because their primary objective econonomic conditions haven't changed."

Class stratification becomes an insignificant issue if economic disadvantage is seen as only relevant for feminism to the extent that women are unequal vis-à-vis men. The difference between male and female incomes is dramatically less among blacks than among whites, suggesting that sex alone is not the sole determinant of economic status. From a monist feminist perspective, class exploitation is not understood as an independent system of oppression. Consequently, broad class dynamics are not addressed in liberal and some radical feminisms. Marxist and socialist feminists have sought to correct this biased view of class.[5] While the Marxists attempted to incorporate a concern for gender within traditional Marxist analysis, socialist feminists tried to develop a nonmonist perspective of feminism that saw sexism and classism as coequal oppressions. Ellen Willis concludes that within various feminisms there was limited politics beyond an assertion that class hierarchy was oppressive. A radical feminist, she observes that the consciousness-raising, personal politics approach did not effectively challenge the structural political economy of class oppression. She concludes that as a consequence, "women were implicated in the class system and had real class interests, that women could oppress men on the basis of class, and that class differences among women could not be resolved within a feminist context alone" (Willis 1984, esp. 110–11).

First, the memberships of these class-oriented groups remained mostly middle-class. Economically disadvantaged women have not directly contributed to a feminist theoretical understanding of class dynamics or the development of programs and strategies. Black feminist and literary critic bell hooks notes that "had poor women set the agenda for the feminist movement, they might have decided that class struggle would be a central feminist issue" (hooks 1984, 60–61). She further contends that class oppression has not become central among women liberationists because their "values, behaviors, and lifestyles continue to be shaped by privilege" (hooks 1984, 61). In a similar fashion, feminist and race politics have not informed or established ties between poor and working-class black and white women. Phyllis M. Palmer reasons that from the perspective of a poor black woman, white women individually may suffer wage discrimination because of their sex, but their relations to white males, the top income earners, as daughters and wives, grants them a relatively better quality of material well-being. "Most white women do not in reality live on what they earn; they have access to the resources of white male income earners" (Palmer 1983, 162). Rejecting what she views as the hollow efforts of "slumming" or nonhierarchical organizing, she observes that no serious strategies have been developed for convincing bourgeois women that class liberation is critical for women's liberation or for organizing with poor and working-class women.

This lack of attention to economic issues has significant implications for the participation of black women. Many of the differences of priorities between black and white women are related to class. Issues of welfare, hunger, poor housing, limited health care, and transportation are seldom seen as feminist interests and are rarely the subject of feminist social policies. As Brenda Eichelberger maintains, "the black woman's energy output is more often directed toward such basic survival issues, while the white woman's is more often aimed at fulfillment" (Eichelberger 1977, esp.1). The economic concerns of women from lower-income backgrounds are relatively ignored and distorted in the contemporary women's movement. The feminist interpretation of the "feminization" of poverty is a case in point. While noting that some women, again middle-class, have indeed experienced a recent drastic decline in life circumstances as a consequence of divorce, the feminization analysis has misrepresented many of the causes of female poverty. For example, most impoverished women have been poor throughout their lives as a consequence of their class position or of racial oppression. Linda Burnham writes that race and class are more significant causative factors in black women's impoverishment than is gender. In the thesis of the feminization of poverty, she contends, "the vulnerability of white women to impoverishment is overstated; the impoverishment of Black men is ignored or underestimated; and the fundamental basis in working-class exploitation for the continual regeneration of poverty is abandoned for a focus on gender" (Burnham 1985, 15).

In summary, feminism's neglect of, misunderstanding of, or deemphasis on the politics of race and class have direct implications for the actions of black women in relationship to the movement. Often, our response has been to avoid participation in white female, middle-class dominated organizations and to withhold our support from policies that are not in our race and class interests. Nevertheless, just as the importance of race led many black women to commitments to racially based politics and gender interests compelled our feminist efforts, economic injustices have brought many to consider class politics as a major avenue of liberation.

CLASS POLITICS

Economic exploitation is the third societal jeopardy constraining the lives of black women. Historically, the three major movements to address the deprivations of class in the United States have been trade unionism and the anti-capitalist politics of the 1930s and 1960s, which are colloquially referred to as the Old Left and the New Left. Having their origins in responses to the degradations that accompanied urbanization and industrialization, labor unionists and leftists organized to address the problems of wage labor and economic stratification in a capitalistic society, including the excessive working hours in poor, unsafe conditions, low pay and limited job security, fluctuations in the labor demand, the decline in work satisfaction, the loss of worker autonomy, and poverty. Each movement, although monistic, possessed different objectives. Unionism was reformist in orientation, seeking to ameliorate the worst of the above conditions. In contrast, the socialist and communist ideologies of the left were revolutionary in that they aspired to eradicate capitalism and ostensibly to establish a classless society.

Into the first quarter of this century, organized labor's approach to economic disadvantage held little promise for blacks or women, and thus no promise for black women. Samuel Gompers, the leading force of trade unionism and president of the American Federation of Labor (AFL, founded in 1886), believed that the best means of improving wages for Anglo males was to restrict the labor supply. His strategy was to advocate the return of women to the home and the banning of blacks and Asians from the unions. Although the AFL never formally adopted these restrictions at the national level, many local chapters did so through both formal rules and informal practices.[6] Trade unionists cultivated a cultural image of the worker as a married male who required a family wage to support a wife and children. Labor actively supported protective labor legislation, which effectively excluded women from the jobs that would provide them with sufficient incomes to support themselves and their families. These efforts against women were coupled with the exclusion of black, other racial minorities, and initially southern and eastern European immigrant males from the most economically rewarding labor in the unionized crafts and the closed shops. Blacks, in particular, were specifically denied union membership or else relegated to the unskilled, low-paying jobs. Consequently, the denial of a family wage to black males exacerbated the circumstances of already economically distressed black families and individuals. In occupations where blacks were well represented, unionization often meant their forcible expulsion. Many of the race riots in the early 1900s were related to the tensions between black laborers and white laborers in competition for employment. So, an effective two-prong strategy for improving white men's income required the demand for a family wage and the restriction of labor competition from women and racial minorities.

In response to union discrimination, white women and black women and men organized. The Working Women's Association, founded in 1868, was one of the earlier attempts at synthesizing feminist and white female workers concerns; the Women's Trade Union League, established in 1903, allied white working- and middle-class women, while the International Ladies' Garment

Workers' Union publicized the conditions of white working women, demanded equal pay, demanded female representation in the national labor unions, formed female unions, and organized strikes.[7]

Ironically, most of the women's trade union organizations as well as many socialist feminists, supported protective legislation but with the mistaken belief that involving the state would ensure safer work environments and reasonable labor requirements for both women and men. An unintended consequence of this strategy was that many women's economic situations declined because protective legislation could be used to reinforce occupational segregation and thus limit women's wage-earning opportunities.

As the wives and daughters of men who did not earn a family wage, black women's participation in the labor market was crucial to the survival of themselves and their families. Yet black women benefited little from the unionization efforts among white women. First, they were disproportionately situated in occupations least likely to be unionized, such as domestic and nonhousehold service and agricultural labor. In large industrial workplaces, they were segregated from white female workers, where the organizing took place, and were often pawns in the labor-management contests.[8] Second, white trade unionists failed actively to recruit black females and they often were denied membership because of their race. The protective legislation further hampered their opportunities by closing off numerous employment opportunities simply on the basis of sex. Black women wanted better-paying jobs, but they often had to settle for jobs considered too hazardous, dirty, or immoral for white women, and for which they were not fairly compensated. During the Great Depression, race-gender discrimination was so pervasive that employment in federal work-relief projects often was closed to them. Thus, significant numbers of black women were unemployed and/or underemployed and, therefore, untouched by union activism.

Despite their exclusion from the major unions, black women and men organized caucuses within predominantly white unions and formed their own unions, such as the Urban League's Negro Workers Councils, African Blood Brotherhood, Negro American Labor Council, National Negro Labor Council, and Dodge Revolutionary Union Movement (DRUM). A. Phillip Randolph, founder of the Brotherhood of Sleeping Car Porters, called for a march on Washington in the 1940s to demand the end of wage and job discrimination, the desegregation of schools and public accommodations, protection of immigrant workers, cessation of lynching, and the unionization of black women. During the depression, trade unions and unemployed councils held demonstrations demanding immediate cash relief and unemployment compensation, as well as advocating race solidarity. For blacks in the first half of this century, class and race interests were often inseparable. Black women benefited indirectly from black men's labor activism, and they often supported those efforts by participating on picket lines, providing food and clothing for strikers and their families, and, most important, making financial contributions to the households from their own paid labor. Black women also engaged in labor organizing directly, both through existing predominantly white unions and through their own activism. Black domestics, tobacco workers, garment workers, and others organized strikes and fought for union representation (Janiewski 1987; Lewis 1987).

Not all unions and economic organizations excluded white women and black women and men. The Knights of Labor, established in 1888, the Industrial Workers of the World, created in 1905, and the Congress of Industrial Organizations, formed in 1938, are noted for encouraging the unionization of millions of black men and black and white women workers. But overall, the record of organized labor on issues of import to black women and men and white women has not been outstanding. Until 1971, the major unions opposed the Equal Rights Amendment; and today, many challenge affirmative action and comparable worth policies. The continued need for black and women's labor organizations suggest that the historic barriers remain to their full participation and rewards in unions. But it is also important to recognize that the trade unionist approach has many limitations, and first among these is its focus on the individual worker. As a result, the broad issues of poverty and economic inequality are perceived as beyond the purview of most labor activism. While seeking to ameliorate the worst of industrial society, unionists seldom challenge the economic order of capitalism.

This challenge was left to the socialist and communist activists, but this radical critique of the political economy has never been a part of the political mainstream of the United States as it has in other nations. Nevertheless, a small but significant group of activists and intellectuals have advanced radicalism throughout this century.[9] The political left, in general, supported black women and men and white working women during the Progressive era. In fact, leading intellectuals, including Emma Goldman, Margaret Sanger, Charlotte Perkins Gilman, Elizabeth Curley Flynn, Langston Hughes, Paul Robeson, W.E.B. Du Bois, and C.L.R. James saw socialism as the route for liberation. Two black women, Lucy Parsons and Claudia Jones, were among the early labor activists and socialists of the Old Left. And even Angela Davis (1981), who describes the important role of individual women within the socialist and communist parties during the first half of the twentieth century, does not offer us much insight into the general status of black women, besides noting the Socialist Party's indifference to blacks, both males and females.

But even within these efforts, there still were gaps in recognizing the needs of black women. In 1900, the Socialist Party was founded and immediately began campaigning for women's suffrage and labor rights through its Woman's National Committee. Because it focused on the industrial proletariat, it paid no particular attention to blacks, since they were mostly agricultural laborers. Consequently, the party also paid minimal attention to the black women who were not industrially employed. In contrast, members of the Communist Party were actively involved in organizing industrial workers, sharecroppers, and the unemployed during the depression and in championing racial as well as economic justice for blacks.[10] But the Communist Party remained relatively silent on various feminist concerns. Its vigorous defense of the Scottsboro boys and other victims of racial bigotry linked with its call for black self-determination initially attracted numerous blacks to the party in the 1930s and 1940s. Nevertheless, it became increasingly clear that the international Communist Party was concerned with the liberation of blacks only as long as those efforts advanced its overall objective of aiding the revolutionary leadership of a European working-class. Eventually, the collusion of the American Communist Party with racism and sexism dissuaded many blacks and women of the advantages of Soviet-oriented communist activism.

The second surge of anticapitalism was an integral part of the so-called New Left of the 1960s. Sociologist Stanley Aronowitz (1984) has described the 1960s radicalism as the movements of a generation, which were not oriented around any particular class or race issue. While this might characterize certain aspects of the radical critique of the liberal society, his interpretation does not account for the ideological and activist history that informed both the black and women's liberation efforts of that decade. In an analysis of the contradictions and dilemmas of the New Left, Peter Clecak (1973) described the era as one that lacked a vision of a new society beyond the negation of the present ills of poverty, racism, imperialism, and hegemony. Its apocalyptic perspectives on American society and utopian images of community were founded on a fundamental acceptance of capitalist notions of individualism, personal gain, and personal liberty. By implication, much of the New Left lacked a basic, critical understanding of the dynamics of oppressions as group and systemic processes.

The disillusionment that characterized the New Left movement was compounded by the frustration of its failure to organize the urban poor and racial minorities. The free speech and antiwar activists, Students for a Democratic Society, and the Weather Underground (i.e., the weathermen) mistakenly attempted to organize northern urban communities using SNCC's southern mobilization model. At another level, New Leftists did not understand that most members of oppressed groups desired a piece of the American Dream, not its destruction. The efforts to create coalitions with civil rights and black nationalist groups were strained and defeated because of the conflicting objectives and tactics. The aims of civil rights groups were integrationist through nonviolent means; and while black militants advocated armed defense or even revolution and adopted a Maoist, anticapitalist program, their separatist orientation made black-white alliances almost impossible. Moreover, while the left condemned the role of U.S. imperialism in Southeast Asia, it ignored the advance of Western capitalist interests into the continent of Africa, especially South Africa.

At the same time, women active in the New Left became increasingly frustrated with the theoretical and strategic indifference to the woman question. The sexual politics within the movement subjected women to traditional gender role assignments, sexual manipulation, male leadership and domination, plus a concentration on an essentially male issue, the draft.[11] Once again, invisibility typifies the role of black women in New Left radical politics. Black women responded by incorporating class interest into their race and gender politics. In the founding documents of various black feminist organizations, scathing critiques of the political economy are a cornerstone of the analysis of domination. For example, the Combahee River Collective Statement pointedly declared that "the liberation of all oppressed peoples necessitates the destruction of the political economic systems of capitalism and imperialism, as well as patriarchy . . . We are not convinced, however, that a socialist revolution that is not also a feminist and anti-racism revolution will guarantee our liberation" (Combahee River Collective 1986, 12–13). This excerpt clearly articulated an understanding of multiple jeopardy and its function in the dominant society and within liberation politics. Out of necessity, black women have addressed both narrow labor and broad economic concerns.

Political theorist Manning Marable (1983) has argued that progressive forces must uproot racism and patriarchy in their quest for a socialist democracy through a dedication to equality. Yet a major limitation of both unionism and radical class politics is their monist formulations, wherein economics are exaggerated at the expense of understanding and confronting other oppressions such as racism and sexism. Despite the historical examples of black women and men and white women as union activists and socialists and the examples of the sporadic concern of organized labor and leftists with race and gender politics, class politics have not provided the solution to black women's domination because they continue to privilege class issues within a white male framework. Given the inability of any single agenda to address the intricate complex of racism, sexism, and classism in black women's lives, black women must develop a political ideology capable of interpreting and resisting that multiple jeopardy.

MULTIPLE CONSCIOUSNESS IN BLACK FEMINIST IDEOLOGY

Gloria Joseph and Jill Lewis (1981, 38) have suggested that black women face a dilemma analogous to that of Siamese twins, each of whom have distinct and incompatible interests. Black women cannot, they argue, be wholeheartedly committed and fully active in both the black liberation struggle and the women's liberation movement because of sexual and racial politics within each. The authors recognize the demands of multiple jeopardy politics and the detrimental effect of neglecting these dual commitments. But what they fail to consider are the multiple and creative ways in which black women address their interdependent concerns of racism, sexism, and classism.

Black women have been feminists since the early 1800s, but our exclusion from the white women's movement and its organizations has led many incorrectly to assume that we were not present in the (white) women's movement because we were not interested in resisting sexism both within and without the black community. What appears recently to be a change in black women's position, from studied indifference to disdain and curiosity to cautious affirmation of the women's movement, may be due to structural changes in relationships between blacks and whites that have made black women "more sensitive to the obstacles of sexism and to the relevance of the women's movement" (Lewis 1977, 341). Black women's apparent greater sensitivity to sexism may be merely the bolder, public articulation of black feminist concerns that have existed for well over a century. In other words, black women did not just become feminists in the 1970s. We did, however, grant more salience to those concerns and become more willing to organize primarily on that basis, creating the Combahee River Collective, the National Black Feminist Organization, and Sapphire Sapphos. Some black women chose to participate in predominantly white women's movement activities and organizations, while others elected to develop the scholarship and curriculum that became the foundation of black women's studies, while still others founded black feminist journals, presses, and political organizations.[12]

Several studies have considered the relevance of black women's diverse characteristics in understanding our political attitudes; these reports seem fairly inconsistent, if not contradictory (Cherlin and Waters 1981; Gump 1975; Hershey 1978).[13] The various findings do suggest that the conditions that bring black women to feminist consciousness are specific to our social and historical experiences. For black women, the circumstances of lower socioeconomic life may encourage political, and particularly feminist, consciousness.[14] This is in contrast to feminist as well as traditional political socialization literature that suggests that more liberal, that is, feminist, attitudes are associated with higher education attainment and class standing. Many of the conditions that middle-class white feminists have found oppressive are perceived as privileges by black women, especially those with low incomes. For instance, the option not to work outside the home is a luxury that historically has been denied most black women. The desire to struggle for this option can, in such a context, represent a feminist position, precisely because it constitutes an instance of greater liberty for certain women. It is also important to note, however, that the class differences among black women regarding our feminist consciousness are minimal. Black women's particular history thus is an essential ingredient in shaping our feminist concerns.

Certainly the multifaceted nature of black womanhood would meld diverse ideologies, from race liberation, class liberation, and women's liberation. The basis of our feminist ideology is rooted in our reality. To the extent that the adherents of any one ideology insist on separatist organizational forms, assert the fundamental nature of any one oppression, and demand total cognitive, affective, and behavioral commitment, that ideology and its practitioners exclude black women and the realities of our lives.

A black feminist ideology, first and foremost, thus declares the visibility of black women. It acknowledges the fact that two innate and inerasable traits, being both black and female, constitute our special status in American society. Second, black feminism asserts self-determination as essential. Black women are empowered with the right to interpret our reality and define our objectives. While drawing on a rich tradition of struggle as blacks and as women, we continually establish and reestablish our own priorities. As black women, we decide for ourselves the relative salience of any and all identities and oppressions, and how and the extent to which those features inform our politics. Third, a black feminist ideology fundamentally challenges the interstructure of the oppressions of racism, sexism, and classism both in the dominant society and within movements for liberation. It is in confrontation with multiple jeopardy that black women define and sustain a multiple consciousness essential for our liberation, of which feminist consciousness is an integral part.

Finally, a black feminist ideology presumes an image of black women as powerful, independent subjects. By concentrating on our multiple oppressions, scholarly descriptions have confounded our ability to discover and appreciate the ways in which black women are not victims. Ideological and political choices cannot be assumed to be determined solely by the historical dynamics of racism, sexism, and classism in this society. Although the complexities and ambiguities that merge a consciousness of race, class, and gender oppressions make the emergence and praxis of a multivalent ideology problematical, they also make such a task more necessary if we are to work toward our liberation as blacks, as the economically exploited, and as women.

NOTES

1. See Gloria Joseph and Jill Lewis, *Common Differences: Conflicts in Black and White Feminist Perspectives* (New York: Avon, 1981); Diane K. Lewis, "A Response to Inequality:

Black Women, Racism, and Sexism," *Signs* 3, (1977): 339–61; and bell hooks, *Feminist Theory: From Margin to Center* (Boston: South End Press, 1984), for extended discussions of the dynamics of structural subordination to and social conflict with varying dominant racial and sexual groups.

2. See also Linda C. Powell, "Black Macho and Black Feminism," in *Home Girls: A Black Feminist Anthology*, Barbara Smith 283–92 (New York: Kitchen Table Press, 1983).

3. For statements by Truth, Stewart, Cooper, Ruffin, and Harper, see Bert James Loewenberg and Ruth Bogin, eds., *Black Women in Nineteenth-Century American Life* (University Park: Pennsylvania State University Press, 1976); and Gerda Lerner, ed., *Black Women in White America: A Documentary History* (New York: Vintage, 1973); for Lorde, see Audre Lorde, "Scratching the Surface: Some Notes on Barriers to Women and Loving," *Black Scholar* 13 (1982): 20–24; and *Sister Outsider: Essays and Speeches* (Trumansberg, NY: Crossing Press, 1984); For Davis, see Angela Davis, *Woman, Race and Class* (New York: Random House, 1981); For Beale, see Frances Beale, "Double Jeopardy: To Be Black and Female," Pp. 90–100 in *The Black Woman: An Anthology*, Toni Cade (New York: New American Library, 1979) and "Slave of a Slave No More: Black Women in the Struggle," *Black Scholar* 12 (1981): 16–24; For Murray, see Pauli Murray, "The Liberation of Black Woman," in *Women: A Feminist Perspective*, Jo Freeman, 351–63 (Palo Alto, Calif: Mayfield, 1975).

4. Regarding the church, see Pauline Terrelonge Stone, "Feminist Consciousness and Black Women," in Freeman, ed., 575–88; Joseph and Lewis, *Common Differences*; Jacqueline Grant, "Black Women and the Women Church," in *But Some of Us Are Brave: Black Women's Studies*, Gloria T. Hull et al., 141–52 (Old Westbury, NY: Feminist Press, 1982); and Cheryl Townsend Gilkes, "Together and in Harness; Women's Traditions in the Sanctified Church," *Signs* 10 (1985):678–99. Concerning politics, see Linda LaRue, "The Black Movement and Women's Liberation," in *Female Psychology: The Emerging Self*, ed. Sue Cox (Chicago: Science Research Associates, 1976); Mae C. King, "The Politics of Sexual Stereotypes," *Black Scholar* 4 (1973):12–22; and Manning Marable, *How Capitalism Underdeveloped Black America* (Boston: South End Press, 1983), esp. chap. 3. For a discussion of sexual victimization, see Barbara Smith, "Notes for Yet Another Paper on Black Feminism, or Will the Real Enemy Please Stand Up," *Conditions* 5 (1979):123–27, as well as Joseph and Lewis, *Common Differences*. For a critique of the notion of the matriarch, see Stone, *Feminist Consciousness*; and Robert Staples, "The Myth of the Black Matriarchy," in *The Black Family: Essays and Studies* (Belmont, Calif.: Wadsworth, 1971).

5. See Josephine Donovan, *Feminist Theory: The Intellectual Traditions of American Feminism* (New York: Ungar, 1985); and Lydia Sargent, ed., *Women and Revolution: A Discussion of the Unhappy Marriage of Marxism and Feminism* (Boston: South End Press, 1981); and Zillah R. Eisenstein, ed., *Capitalist Patriarchy and the Case for Socialist Feminism* (New York: Monthly Review Press, 1979), for fuller discussions.

6. For discussion of women, employment, and the labor movement, see Diane Balser, *Sisterhood and Solidarity: Feminism and Labor in Modern Times* (Boston: South End Press, 1987); Carol Groneman and Mary Beth Norton, ed., *"To Toil the Livelong Day": America's Women at Work*, 1780–1980 (Ithaca, New York: Cornell University Press, 1987); Philip S. Foner, *Women and the American Labor Movement: From World War I to the Present* (New York: Free Press, 1980); Bettina Berch, *The Endless Day: The Political Economy of Women and Work* (New York: Harcourt Brace Jovanovich, 1982); and Mary Frank Fox and Sharlene Hesse-Biber, *Women at Work* (Palo Alto, Calif: Mayfield, 1984). For blacks, see Marable, *Capitalism*; Richard Polenberg, *One Nation Divisible: Class, Race, and Ethnicity in the United States since 1938* (New York: Penguin, 1980); Philip S. Foner, *Organized Labor and the Black Worker*, 1619–1973 (New York: International Publishers, 1976); and Dorothy K. Newman et al., *Protest, Politics, and Prosperity: Black Americans and White Institutions, 1940–75* (New York: Pantheon, 1978).

7. See Balser for detailed consideration of the contemporary union activities of women, especially their efforts to organize clerical and other pink-collar workers.

8. See Jacqueline Jones, *Labor of Love, Labor of Sorrow: Black Women, Work and the Family, From Slavery to the Present* (New York: Basic, 1985); Giddings (1983); and Davis (1981), for an examination of black women's work roles and labor activism.

9. See Peter Clecak, *Radical Paradoxes: Dilemnas of the American Left: 1945–1970* (New York: Harper & and Row, 1973), for an illuminating analysis of the Old and New Left.

10. See Vincent Harding, *The Other American Revolution* (Los Angeles and Atlanta: University of California, Los Angeles, Center for Afro-American Studies, and Institute of the Black World, 1980), for discussion of blacks and communist organizing.

11. Heidi Hartmann and Zillah Eisenstein provide theoretical critiques of monist Marxism as an adequate avenue for women's liberation. Both Lydia Sargent and Sara Evans detail the sexual politics on the Left. See Heidi Hartmann, "The Unhappy Marriage of Marxism and Feminism," in Sargent, ed.; Eisenstein, "Reform and/or Revolution: Toward a Unified Women's Movement," 339–62 in Sargent, ed.; Sargent, "New Left Women and Men" in Sargent, ed.; and Sara Evans, *Personal Politics: The Roots of Women's Liberation in the Civil Rights Movement and the New Left* (New York: Vintage, 1980).

12. For information on the development of black feminist scholarship and academic programs, see Patricia Bell Scott, "Selective Bibliography on Black Feminism," in Hull et al., eds; Black Studies/Women's Studies Faculty Development Project, "Black Studies/Women's Studies: An Overdue Partnership," Women's Studies, University of Massachusetts-Amherst, mimeograph, 1983; Nancy Conklin et al., "The Culture of Southern Black Women: Approaches and Materials," University of Alabama Archives of American Minority Cultures and Women's Studies Program, Project on the Culture of Southern Black Women, 1983; the premier issue of *Sage: A Scholarly Journal on Black Women*, Spring 1984, 1; and the establishment of Kitchen Table: A Women of Color Press, New York. The Center for Research on Women at Memphis State University, the Women's Research and Resource Center at Spelman College, and the Minority Women's Program at Wellesley College are among the academic centers.

13. For various opinion polls, see "The 1972 Virginia Slims American Women's Opinion Poll,: conducted by the Roper Organization, Williamstown, Mass: Roper Public Opinion Research Center, 1974. See Barbara Everitt Bryant, "American Women: Today and Tomorrow," National Commission on the Observance of International Women's Year (Washington, D.C.: Government Printing Office, March 1977). Gloria Steinem, "Exclusive Louis Harris Survey: How Women Live, Vote and Think," *Ms. Magazine* 13, (July 1984): 51–54.

14. For analyses of the influence of socioeconomic class and race on feminist attitudes, see Willa Mae Hemmons, "The Women's Liberation Movement: Understanding Black Women's Attitudes," in *The Black Woman*, ed. LaFrances Rodgers-Rose (Beverly Hills, Calif: Sage, 1960), 285–99; and Edward Ransford and Jon Miller, "Race, Sex, and Feminist Outlook," *American Sociological Review* 48 (1983): 46–59.

5

THE IMPACT OF IDEOLOGY ON DEVELOPMENT IN THE THIRD WORLD

William Tordoff

THE FORMULATION OF IDEOLOGIES

Many reasons are given to explain why new state leaders formulate ideologies. According to Clifford Geertz, at independence there is a sort of cultural vacuum, where "institutionalized guides for behavior, thought, or feeling are weak or absent" and "the new states are still groping for usable political concepts, not yet grasping them" (Geertz 1964, 63, 65). Their leaders seek methods of managing social conflict, achieving national integration, and ensuring economic growth, and believe that an ideology may make possible an approach to problems in a systematic and coherent manner. They also want to assert a local identity against the former colonial power. On a more cynical view, they may see ideology as a means of justifying and buttressing their own position. By the same token, the leadership of a group or social class excluded from political power may shape an ideology which attacks the existing institutional and value systems in a bid to assume power itself and shape society in its own image. An ideology may therefore be supportive of the existing power structure and its underlying value system, or subversive of it. In much of the Third World, however, we are concerned with mono-ideological states, where ideologies are not only, in Shils's terms, "the creations of charismatic persons," but also charismatic persons in office (Shils 1968, 69).

To define *ideology* is difficult because, as Geertz put it: "the term "ideology" has itself become thoroughly ideologized" (Geertz 1964, 47). Originally it referred to the study of ideas and systems of ideas. Under the impact of Marxist analysis it became a cloak for interests, while on another view it was seen as a response to deep-rooted social strains. These approaches are not mutually exclusive, and both can be useful. But a difficulty about each of them is that ideology tends to become debased either as a cloak for *vested* interests or as an essentially *irrational* response to social strains (Szeftel 1971; Geertz 1964). Since the bias of the analyst also enters the picture, it is not enough to concentrate solely on the ideas put forward; it is also necessary to examine the impact that the program to which these ideas give rise has on the societies in which they operate.

Brzezinski, in *The Soviet Bloc*, distinguished between the two basic elements in ideology—doctrine and action program. The balance between these elements may vary considerably: some ideologies are high on doctrine and low on explicit action program, while others, notably Marxism, are high on both counts (Brzezinski 1960; Benn 1971). This distinction is worth drawing because the doctrinal element in the ideology of a particular state may be weak (this was predominantly the case with African socialism in the 1960s), yet the ideology may be high on action program. Substantially this applied to Zambian Humanism, which was first elaborated by President Kenneth Kaunda in 1967. Or take Ghana under President Kwame Nkrumah: while we can readily agree with Dennis Austin that Nkrumaism was "a crude ideology," (Austin 1964, 408), we also need to know the relevance of Nkrumaism for, and its impact upon, Ghanaian society. What I am saying, then, is that to label ideas in a pejorative manner will not itself take us very far. We must also consider the way in which the various idea elements operate in their own social context. This is the value of Geertz's work—in directing the investigator toward an assessment of a particular ideology in its own cultural and political context. Similarly in relation to Africa, Clapham has stressed the importance of examining the circumstances under which political ideas are expressed, and the purposes for which they are used (Clapham 1970).

Some definitions of ideology are very exacting; if, for example, we follow Edward Shils, few Third World states can be said to have an ideology at all. For him, ideology is an explicit, systematic, comprehensive, and coherent pattern of beliefs, by means of which an ideological primary group seeks a "total transformation" of society (Shils 1968, 67). However, many Third World "ideologies" are essentially clusters of ideas elaborated by individual national leaders: thus, Nasser gave us Nasserism, Nkrumah Nkrumaism, Sukarno Sukarnoism, and Peron Peronism. Subject to qualification, I prefer therefore the looser definition of John Plamenatz, who takes ideology to be any "system of ideas which acts to support or subvert accepted modes of thought and behavior" (Plamenatz 1972). This is a useful definition, but some emphasis needs to be placed on the word "system": ideology is not just a philosophy but a body of ideas that is shared and organized. Given that there are constraints on policymaking, some actions fall outside the ideology, rendering it irrelevant in certain circumstances. In other cases, as noted below in the section on external constraints on development, the indeterminacy that surrounds the concept of ideology makes difficult precise distinctions between "ideological" and "nonideological" phenomena.

THE MEANING OF "DEVELOPMENT"

It is even more difficult to reach agreement on the meaning of "development" than of ideology. We can say what it is not more easily than what it is: it is not economic growth alone, though economic growth is essential to development. It also embodies social justice: that is, the distribution in a reasonably equitable manner of the benefits of economic growth among the country's regions and people. The difference between growth and distribution is captured in the 1970s story about mutual recriminations between Tanzanians and Kenyans. The former are said to have accused Kenyans of being interested only in material prosperity: by pursuing economic growth alone they were creating "a man-eat-man society." According to the story, the Kenyans responded by saying that the Tanzanians emphasized equality but had nothing to distribute; theirs was therefore "a man-eat-nothing society." Development also has a political component—provision must be made for popular participation in the political process and for the protection of civil rights and essential freedoms; an administrative component, so that the state has the capacity to respond to people's needs; and an international element, enabling the state to exercise some autonomy in the conduct of foreign affairs. Thus development can be said to be multifaceted, with economic, social, political and international dimensions. From this it follows that, as Riggs argued, developing countries should be studied within their entire ecological context (Riggs 1964).

THE RELATIONSHIP BETWEEN IDEOLOGY AND DEVELOPMENT

For each type of regime—whether Marxist, populist socialist or capitalist (to adopt Crawford Young's three-fold classification [Young 1982])—one can say that ideology is helpful if it enables the leadership to instil a sense of direction and purpose in their followers once independence has been achieved. No less obviously, ideology can be a handicap if it is too rigidly applied and makes changes of direction difficult; it can then become an economic straitjacket. This happened in Sekou Toure's Guinea in the early 1960s when the bid to maintain socialist purity had an adverse effect on economic planning and organization (Berg 1964). In Tanzania, a populist socialist state, the experiment in village socialism *(ujamaa vijijini)* initiated by President

Julius Nyerere in 1967 and revolving around communal production, was persisted in for ideological reasons long after it had failed economically. By contrast, Amilcar Cabral, one of Africa's foremost political thinkers who drew substantially upon Marxist theory in his writing, had his feet firmly on the ground. He warned the party cadres in Guinea Bissau against doctrinal rigidity:

> Always remember that people are not fighting for ideas, nor for what is in men's minds. The people fight and accept the sacrifices demanded by the struggle in order to gain material advantages, to live better and in peace, to benefit from progress, and for the better future of their children. National liberation, the struggle against colonialism, the construction of peace, progress and independence are hollow words devoid of any significance unless they can be translated into a real improvement of living conditions. (Cabral, in Chabal 1983, 66)

It may be helpful at this point to summarize the findings of Crawford Young, who, in his book on *Ideology and Development in Africa* (published in 1982), argued that ideology does matter and that it has some bearing on performance. He concluded

1. On *growth*, that to date rapid growth had eluded the Afro-Marxist states and that the capitalist-oriented states, with some exceptions such as Zaire, had a better record; the populist-socialist group of states such as Algeria, Mali and Tanzania were somewhere in between.
2. On *equality*, he found that capitalist states such as the Ivory Coast and Kenya, exhibited high degrees of inequality at the top of the social scale; in other words, there was a wide gap between the very rich and the very poor. This was partly mitigated by effective agricultural policies; in Kenya, for example, fiscal and pricing policy did not hit rural producers as hard as in many other African countries. The socialist states—both Afro-Marxist and populist socialist—had a greater commitment to the egalitarian principle. Although a few states, including Angola in southern Africa and Tanzania in eastern Africa, had good records, their overall performance was not necessarily better. In Young's assessment performance on egalitarianism drew an ambiguous evaluation.
3. On *autonomy*, he found no close correlation between degrees of autonomy and ideology, but noted that all regimes, ranging from Angola to Nigeria, might assert state sovereignty by pursuing policies that ran counter to the interests of their international backers.

4. On *human dignity*, he concluded that "massive and systematic assaults upon human dignity are a function not of ideological strategy but of insecure and paranoid rulers" (p.316).
5. On *popular participation*, he said that participation in the institutions of government was "not a measure that clearly distinguishes the three pathways" (p.320).
6. Finally, Crawford Young assessed *state capacity*, by which is meant the capacity of the institutions of state to fulfill the development goals that the state's leadership, whether civilian or military, set itself. He pointed out that the demands on state capacity were highest for the Afro-Marxist state, with its aspiration for a command economy and comprehensive central planning; given its usually weak legacy of public institutions, that state particularly faced an uphill task in achieving its development goals. But he pointed out that all the development models placed a high premium on the effectiveness and capacity of public institutions, thus lessening the differences between the three regime types in this respect (Young 1982).

From this survey I conclude that while ideology does affect performance in most cases, it often does so only marginally. If one can assume that Young's findings are valid for the Third World generally, it is no less important to point to the internal and external constraints on development faced by all regimes, irrespective of ideological persuasion, than it is to stress the ideological differences between one regime and another. In examining the external constraints, however, it will be seen that some are themselves ideological. This applies, for example, to the interventionist strategies of the IMF, World Bank and the U.S. Agency for International Development (USAID); these strategies are almost explicitly subversive of existing national development strategies, especially those adopted by countries that, like Tanzania, have pursued some variant of socialist planning.

EXTERNAL CONSTRAINTS ON DEVELOPMENT

1. In the preindependence period the colonies in Africa, Asia, and the Caribbean were incorporated into the global capitalist economy dominated by the developed northern states. The price of agricultural and mineral produce was set in hard currencies in European and U.S. markets; similarly, the colonies had no control over the price they paid for the manufactured and other goods they imported. This dependence continued after independence. It was greatly exacerbated for the nonoil states by the sharp increase in oil prices from 1973, a

point vividly illustrated by President Nyerere of Tanzania in his address to the nation on 9 December 1981:

> In 1973 we suddenly began to have to pay more than four times as much for our oil as we had paid before that. Since then the price of oil has gone up many times . . . for the amount of money with which we used to buy thirteen barrels of oil we now only get one.
>
> Other prices of the goods we have to buy from abroad have also increased greatly. We have to give about four times as much cotton to buy a 7-ton lorry as we had to give in 1972, or ten times as much tobacco or three times as much cashew. This means that the amount of tobacco which used to be sufficient for ten lorries is now only enough to buy one lorry. (Nyerere 1981)

In the 1970s, in consequence, most of the non-oil-producing states experienced serious balance-of-payments problems and accumulated substantial foreign debts. In the next decade, once the price of oil had stabilized at about $18 per barrel, these countries were managing to cope with the situation; however, they were again plunged into serious difficulties when the Gulf crisis erupted in August 1990, forcing the price of oil for a time sharply upward.

2. By the end of the 1970s the oil-rich states were experiencing the same problem, though on a much larger scale. This story is familiar enough, so I need only provide a brief outline. A series of events between 1970 and 1974, of which the most important was the Arab-Israeli war of October 1973, enabled the member-states of the Organization of Petroleum Exporting Countries (OPEC), which had been founded in September 1960, to wrest control of oil prices and the determination of production policy from the multinational oil companies. The oil weapon gave certain Third World states a leverage in world politics that they had not previously possessed, and they were able to push up the price of oil from just over $5 per barrel in the early 1970s to over $30. Huge revenues accrued to the oil-producing countries, enabling them to undertake large capital projects. The Middle Eastern states especially had much more money than they could spend at home and therefore deposited billions of petrodollars in Western banks. The latter indulged in "loose lending"—the indiscriminate lending of large sums to Third World countries at what began as low interest rates but which, not being fixed, rose substantially as inflation increased.

But the boom in oil prices did not last. The world recession of the 1970s, of which oil was only one factor, forced Western countries to adopt belt tightening, including energy-saving measures. Oil imports were cut back, and before the end of the 1970s there was excess oil on the market. Oil prices fell sharply, dropping in the early 1980s from a peak of $33 a barrel to $10 at one time. The OPEC member-states, however, which disagreed among themselves over the price and level of production, still seemed a good risk to the commercial banks; they continued to lend heavily in the 1979–82 period to both oil-producing and non-oil-producing states. Mexico, Brazil, and a number of other Latin American countries accumulated massive debts. The crunch came in August 1982 when Mexico, with its economy in a state of acute crisis, declared a moratorium on its debt repayments. Since the banks had obligations well in excess of their capital reserves, the specter of large-scale debt repudiation caused panic in international financial circles. The IMF mounted a rescue operation and put pressure on the banks to reschedule Mexico's debts and grant new loans subject to its accepting stiff conditions; these included heavy devaluation, cuts in public spending, and the removal of urban subsidies. Other Third World countries were treated similarly. Coupled with the crippling burden of debt servicing, which amounted in Mexico's case to over 40 percent of export earning, the conditions imposed adversely affected the development of most Third World states, irrespective of their ideological orientation (Cammack et al. 1988; George 1988, 1989).

3. Increasingly in the 1980s the World Bank, as the primary institution to promote long-term development, made the grant and disbursement of development aid conditional on the applicant country's making specific changes in economic policy, notably towards economic liberalization. More specifically, the World Bank and bodies such as USAID required Third World countries either to overhaul public enterprises that had a poor record of performance and make them efficient or to denationalize them. Some privatization, both in the form of complete divestiture and of ownership change through joint venture and the introduction of private–sector management in a public enterprise, has taken place; it has become a popular strategy in sub-Saharan Africa. As the experience of India, Pakistan and Thailand reveals, however, change has been mostly slow, particularly in respect of divestiture. The reasons are both economic, including the lack of sufficiently developed capital markets, and noneconomic; among the latter are the reluctance, and sometimes opposition, of politicians and bureaucrats to formulate and implement rehabilitative

policies and the negative response of public-sector unions, which fear a loss in employment security (Cook and Minogue 1990; Cook and Kirkpatrick 1988). The example of the Republic of Korea suggests that a combination (rare in Third World states) of efficient bureaucracy and firm political commitment is necessary for privatization to be successfully carried out (Cook and Minogue 1990). By seeking to dictate policy the international institutions concerned infringe the sovereignty of Third World states and expect even socialist states to become increasingly pragmatic in the policies they pursue. In a recent paper on "States and Markets in Africa," Ralph Young has pointed out that while the impact of the divestiture issue has indeed transcended the ideological boundaries separating capitalist and socialist states, some of the latter are less willing than others "to embrace the privatization nettle"; establishing an effective administrative machinery to manage divestiture programs has everywhere proved difficult (Young 1991).

4. This trend is reinforced by the fact that virtually all nonmilitary aid comes from the West. As shown by the experience of Tanzania (a populist socialist state in Crawford Young's classification) in the five-year period up to 1985 a Third World country must accept the IMF's tough conditions if it is to receive what amounts to an IMF certificate of creditworthiness, without which it has no prospect of obtaining aid in any quantity from the World Bank and Western donor countries. While capitalist states gravitate to the West for aid out of choice, socialist states (with the odd exception such as Cuba) increasingly look to the West out of necessity.

5. The lack of management and technical skills makes most Third World states very dependent on multinational corporations (MNCs). Thus, in socialist Chile under President Salvador Allende and state-capitalist Zambia under President Kaunda, when the government in each case assumed ownership of the copper industry in the later 1960s and early 1970s, effective control still lay with the foreign copper companies. The same thing happened in Angola, where the postindependence Marxist government acquired majority shareholding in both the country's oil and diamond industries. The foreign companies concerned—the Gulf Oil Corporation and the Angolan Diamond Company ('Diamang,' a De Beers subsidiary)—retained control, including control of day-to-day operations. The advantage to a MNC of such takeovers is that it is assured of a fee for providing the necessary managerial, technical and marketing inputs, but has no (or reduced) investment commitment in the enterprise. The disadvantage for the Third World state is the substantial loss of that control over its

economy that "nationalization" was designed to achieve. In Bougainville, the fact that Conzinc Rio Tinto, the Australian affiliate of Rio Tinto Zinc, retained majority equity in Bougainville Copper Ltd (BCL) worked to its disadvantage, since the Papua New Guinea government did not stand as a buffer between itself and the landowners and subsequently between itself and the rebels; the activities of the latter closed the Panguna Mine indefinitely in May 1989.

A final point which it may be appropriate to make under the MNC heading is that Namibia's heavy dependence on three South African-dominated mining companies and on South Africa generally, coupled with the enormous political load which its extractive, unbalanced and poorly integrated economy has to bear, have forced South West African People's Organization (SWAPO) leaders to commit themselves to establishing a mixed economy in the post-independence period (Woodsworth 1990). This case affords an excellent example of *realpolitik* prevailing over Marxist-Leninist revolutionary principle—the principle to which SWAPO had committed itself during the long liberation struggle.

6. The last external constraint on development that I propose to mention, and one that is primarily ideological in character, is the support given by certain powers to opposition movements fighting against the established government. Clear cases are/were the support given by South Africa to the Mozambique National Resistance (MNR, or "Renamo") in Mozambique, by South Africa and the United States to the National Union for the Total Independence of Angola (UNITA) in Angola, and by the United States to the *contra* rebels in Nicaragua. This serves to reinforce the conclusion that, while all Third World states suffer from external constraints on their development, states with governments of a socialist orientation are more adversely affected than those that opt for a capitalist approach to development.

INTERNAL CONSTRAINTS ON DEVELOPMENT

These are largely independent of ideological considerations. They include:

1. The existence of communalism or sectionalism, threatening national unity and, in an extreme form as in Lebanon and Sri Lanka, causing serious political instability. When this happens, economic development will be impeded.
2. There is a shortage of administrative, managerial, and technical skills, often caused by inadequate colonial educational and training

programs. In some countries the shortage is severe: Zaire in Central Africa, for example, had only sixteen graduates when Belgium granted independence precipitately in 1960. Countries that achieved independence as a result of a protracted liberation struggle are most likely to be severely handicapped by this constraint; they will probably, though not necessarily, be socialist regimes. Examples are Mozambique, Angola, and Nicaragua. Zimbabwe retains a rhetorical commitment to the creation of a socialist state, but except in the foreign sphere, the impact of ideology on public policy is minimal (Herbst 1990). Namibia has discounted wholesale nationalization and sweeping measures of land redistribution in favour of a mixed economy of public- and private-sector development (Woodsworth 1990); the precise mix remains to be determined—the capitalist ideology permits considerable variation in the extent of a mixed economy.

3. The lack in many Third World states (more in Africa than Asia) of a private entrepreneurial class capable of promoting business activity on a substantial scale has meant that the state itself has become the main agent of development. This, in turn, has led to the creation of a vast parastatal sector, often inefficient and sometimes corrupt. According to the World Bank's *World Development Report* for 1988, in the 1976–78 period public enterprises in Mexico, Brazil, Zambia, and the Philippines accounted for more than half of the outstanding external debt (World Bank 1988). The World Bank's response has been to require Third World governments either to make their public enterprises productive (i.e., responsive to the market) or to privatize them. The ideological debate about the ownership of the means of production—notably whether these enterprises are "socialist" or merely examples of "state capitalism"—has obscured the more important issue of productivity and the need to apply stricter efficiency criteria (Cook and Minogue 1990; Brett 1988).

4. The adoption of policies that subsidize the urban sector at the expense of the rural sector has been one cause of a massive migration to urban centres. Today, Bangkok has a population of some 6 million people. In Africa in 1960 (the year in which most states became independent) no city had a population of 1 million; today there are at least twenty-eight cities. Most urban centers in the Third World are characterized by rising crime rates, unemployment, and acute problems of housing and sanitation that are beyond the capacity of the urban authorities to cope with. The corollary of urban migration may be a fall in agricultural production as able-bodied men drift to the towns. Production may also drop as a result of agricultural neglect when

exports of a particular primary product yield rich returns. When the price of that product drops, the temptation is to try and make up for past neglect by heavy investment in large, state farms that too often have a poor record of production. This has been the experience of both Zambia, with its copper-based economy, and oil-rich Nigeria.
5. Natural disasters due to flooding, as in Bangladesh, and drought, as in Ethiopia and Sudan, have been accentuated by bad land management practices and deforestation. The results have included homelessness and famine.
6. Rulers and elites may be paranoid, self-seeking, and interested in self-enrichment. Susan George recounts that wealthier Mexicans invested half of the $80 billion lent to Mexico between 1980 and 1982 across the U.S. border in California, Florida, and New Mexico. Third World leaders must share with the banks and foreign companies responsibility for such expensive white elephants as the $4 billion invested in a Brazilian steel plant that was never opened, and the Westinghouse, World Bank-financed scheme to site a nuclear plant adjacent to an earthquake zone in the Philippines (George 1989). The strong nationalist undercurrent that underlies most regimes is too often sacrificed to narrow self-interest.

The above internal constraints tend to operate either independently of ideological persuasion or with ideology as a marginal, dependent variable, rather than as a core factor. For example, the parastatals that have mushroomed in capitalist as well as in socialist states have almost everywhere a poor record of performance. Socialist regimes are especially exposed, however, first because of their ambitious development goals, which seek to transform the socioeconomic basis of the state and place heavy demands on state capacity, and second because they receive much less financial underpinning from the East, to which they naturally gravitate, than capitalist-oriented regimes receive from the West. (From the 1970s, the latter consideration became less important since Western donors applied creditworthiness, irrespective of regime type, as their main criterion for granting development aid; socialist regimes benefited accordingly. In June 1990, however, Douglas Hurd, the British foreign secretary, stated, with particular reference to Africa, that the British government would in future apply progress toward "economic and political democracy" as the main criterion. This sort of consideration, events in eastern Europe, and disillusionment with the lack of economic progress made by one-party regimes have given rise to widespread demands for political pluralism in many African states, as well as in certain other parts of the Third World.) In support of Crawford Young's arguments summarized earlier, I would say that in Africa at least the difference between the policies pursued by the two main types of regime—capitalist and socialist—is less wide than we might expect on ideological grounds. This is because internal or external constraints, or a combination of the two, lead most regimes to temper their ideology with pragmatism. This is not, after all, surprising. In an interdependent world even First World states are forced into economic realism. Thus, the governments of Australia, New Zealand and Portugal have pursued Thatcher-style policies despite their supposed espousal of significantly different ideologies.

DEVELOPMENT PROSPECTS

Finally, we must ask: what steps can Third World states take to improve their development prospects? A number of answers might be given. First, they can help establish a new international economic order on the ground that until this is achieved Third World states will remain financially dependent on Western-dominated institutions such as the World Bank, the IMF, and multinational corporations. Unfortunately, Third World states have little leverage in this sphere, and very few of the developed, northern states have a serious interest in creating a new international order. This was borne out by their response to the 1980 Brandt Report, which put forward the concept of mutual interest and argued that a large-scale transfer of resources to the Third World would "simultaneously assist the Third World and alleviate economic difficulties in the industrialized countries" (Brandt Report 1980, 240). The British, U.S. and West German governments regarded the Report as too interventionist and were not convinced that international pump-priming would be a good thing. The British government stressed the role of market forces in contributing to international growth and prosperity and rejected the Report's views of the limitations and imperfections of the world economy. It stated that "the Government believes strongly in the merits of the present world economic system, with its wide reliance on open markets for trade and financial flows" (Kirkpatrick and Nixson n.d.:14).

Second, Third World states can establish regional economic unions, thereby creating bigger markets, improving interstate communications, avoiding the wasteful duplication of projects, and reducing external dependency. Groupings such as the Southern African Development Coordination Conference (SADCC) and the Association of South-East Asian Nations (ASEAN) are important in this respect but it would be rash to expect too much of them. As far as SADCC is concerned, the ideological differences between the ten constituent states have so far been contained, though instances of economic nationalism have occurred, and the grouping remains heavily dependent on Western financial investment, particularly from OECD countries (Anglin 1985; Friedland 1985). To date SADCC has avoided that regional domination by one country (economically Zimbabwe is the obvious present candidate), which has been a marked tendency in other major regions (India in the seven-nation SAARC and Japan, though not even a member, in the six-nation ASEAN group, for example). This domination militates against any substantial restructuring of trading and economic relations in the general regional interest (Bhalla 1988a, 1988b, 1990).

Third, given that Third World countries are predominantly agricultural, steps can be taken to stem the decline of agricultural output where that occurs, as it does in most of Africa. These steps may include currency devaluation on the ground that an overvalued exchange rate tilts the internal terms of trade against rural producers; a substantial increase in the producer prices paid to farmers; the overhaul of parastatal organizations responsible for the purchasing, processing, and selling of major commodities; and the gradual disengagement from those import-substitution industries that are high in cost, low in productivity, and drain foreign exchange (Lofchie 1985, 1986). Most of these policies are prescribed by the IMF, and capitalist-oriented states will have less difficulty in accepting them than socialist states; the latter, understandably, questioning the motives of this Western-dominated institution. Nonetheless, it is the case that many Third World governments have featherbedded the urban sector at the expense of rural producers. Those IMF conditions that seek to redress this imbalance make sense, but they have often been insensitively and too speedily applied and have resulted in popular demonstrations which threaten regime stability. Concerted action by Third World states might succeed in modifying these conditions.

To stress the importance of agriculture is not to deny the key role that industry can play in Third World development. Instead, it is to echo the advice that Arthur Lewis, the West Indian development economist, gave the government of Ghana in 1953; this was that the precondition for industrialization was a strong agricultural base (Lewis 1953). Clearly, this advice is not relevant to Singapore, South Korea, Taiwan, and other newly industrialized countries in Southeast and East Asia. But it remains valid for the great majority of African states, irrespective of their ideological commitment, and I suspect for many other Third World states also.

CONCLUSION

Whereas in Africa there was much evidence, for a decade or so from the mid-1970s, that the second wave of socialist states was releasing new ideological currents in African affairs (Jowitt 1979), with possible divisive effects on the OAU, thereafter, as a result of the sort of development constraints outlined above, there has been a retreat from socialist commitments. The effect of these constraints has been to increase the external dependence of African states and to magnify external leverage on domestic politics. For the time being at least, the 1970s impetus to the ideologization of African politics has all but disappeared, to the extent that many African states seem to have entered an "end of ideology" phase. The current emphasis on implementing IMF/World Bank economic recovery programs is replicated throughout much of the Third World—in Jamaica, Mexico, and Nicaragua, no less than in Algeria, Mozambique, and Tanzania; sometimes, too, it is accompanied by steps to restore a multiparty system of government. There are, of course, a few exceptions to this pattern, Cuba and North Korea being obvious examples; also the pattern is less dramatic in South and Southeast Asia, where for a longer period than in Africa the leadership has inclined toward capitalist strategies of development. Even in Africa the apparent strength of the movement toward deideologization may not prove permanent given the problems that are currently facing many African economies and the likelihood that markets in eastern Europe will prove more attractive to Western investment capital.

Part II

TECHNOLOGY AND DIVISIONS OF LABOR

6

THE ROLE OF TECHNOLOGY IN SOCIETY

Emmanuel G. Mesthene

THREE UNHELPFUL VIEWS ABOUT TECHNOLOGY

While a good deal of research is aimed at discerning the particular effects of technological change on industry, government, or education, systematic inquiry devoted to seeing these effects together and to assessing their implications for contemporary society as a whole is relatively recent and does not enjoy the strong methodology and richness of theory and data that mark more established fields of scholarship. It therefore often has to contend with facile or one-dimensional views about what technology means for society. Three such views, which are prevalent at the present time, may be mildly caricatured somewhat as follows.

The first holds that technology is an unalloyed blessing for humanity and society. Technology is seen as the motor of all progress, as holding the solution to most of our social problems, as helping to liberate the individual from the clutches of a complex and highly organized society, and as the source of permanent prosperity; in short, as the promise of utopia in our time. This view has its modern origins in the social philosophies of such nineteenth-century thinkers as Saint-Simon, Karl Marx, and Auguste Comte. It tends to be held by many scientists and engineers, by many military leaders and aerospace industrialists, by people who believe that we are fully in command of our tools and our destiny, and by many of the devotees of modern techniques of "scientific management."

A second view holds that technology is an unmitigated curse. Technology is said to rob people of their jobs, their privacy, their participation in democratic government, and even, in the end, their dignity as human beings. It is seen as autonomous and uncontrollable, as fostering materialistic values and as destructive of religion, as bringing about a technocratic society and bureaucratic state in which the individual is increasingly submerged, and as threatening, ultimately, to poison nature and blow up the world. This view is akin to historical "back-to-nature" attitudes toward the world and is propounded mainly by artists, literary commentators, popular social critics, and existentialist philosophers. It is becoming increasingly attractive to many of our youth, and it tends to be held, understandably enough, by segments of the population that have suffered dislocation as a result of technological change.

The third view is of a different sort. It argues that technology as such is not worthy of special notice because it has been well recognized as a factor in social change at least since the industrial revolution, because it is unlikely that the social effects of computers will be nearly so traumatic as the introduction of the factory system in eighteenth-century England, because research has shown that technology has done little to accelerate the rate of economic productivity since the 1880s, because there has been no significant change in recent decades in the time period between invention and widespread adoption of new technology, and because improved communications and higher levels of education make people much more adaptable than heretofore to new ideas and new social reforms required by technology.

While this view is supported by a good deal of empirical evidence, it tends to ignore a number of social, cultural, psychological, and political effects of technological change that are less easy to identify with precision. It thus reflects the difficulty of coming to grips with a new or broadened subject matter by means of concepts and intellectual categories designed to deal with older and different subject matters. This view tends to be held by historians, for whom continuity is an indispensable methodological assumption, and by many economists, who find that their instruments measure some things quite well; while those of the other social sciences do not yet measure much of anything.

Stripped of caricature, each of these views contains a measure of truth and reflects a real aspect of the relationship of technology and society. Yet they are oversimplifications that do not contribute much to understanding. One can find empirical evidence to support each of them without gaining much knowledge about the actual mechanism by which technology leads to social change or significant insight into its implications for the future. All three remain too uncritical or too partial to guide inquiry. Research and analysis lead to more differentiated conclusions and reveal more subtle relationships.

SOME COUNTERVAILING CONSIDERATIONS

Two of the projects of the Harvard University Program on Technology and Society serve, respectively, to temper some exaggerated claims made for technology and to replace gloom with balanced judgment. Anthony G. Oettinger's study of information technology in education[1] has shown that, in the schools at least, technology is not likely to bring salvation with it quite so soon as the U.S. Office of Education, leaders of the education industry, and computer enthusiasts and systems analysts might wish. Neither educational technology nor the school establishment seems ready to consummate the revolution in learning that will bring individualized instruction to every child, systematic planning and uniform standards across 25,000 separate school districts, an answer to bad teachers and unmovable bureaucracies, and implementation of a national policy to educate every American to his or her full potential for a useful and satisfying life. Human fallibility and political reality are still here to keep utopia at bay, and neither promises soon to yield to a quick technological fix. . . .

By contrast, Manfred Stanley's study of the value presuppositions that underlie the pessimistic arguments about technology suggests that predictions of inevitable doom are premature and that a number of different social outcomes are potential in the process of technological change. In other words, the range of possibility and of human choice implicit in technology is much greater than most critics assume. The problem—here, as well as in the application of educational technology—is how to organize society to free the possibility of choice.

Finally, whether modern technology and its effects constitute a subject matter deserving of special attention is largely a matter of how technology is defined. The research studies of the Harvard Program on Technology and Society reflect an operating assumption that the meaning of technology includes more than machines. As most serious investigators have found, understanding is not advanced by concentrating singlemindedly on such narrowly drawn yet imprecise questions as "What are the social implications of computers, or lasers, or space technology?" Society and the influences of technology upon it are much too complex for such artificially limited approaches to be meaningful. The opposite error, made by some, is to define technology too broadly by identifying it with rationality in the broadest sense. The term is then operationally meaningless and unable to support fruitful inquiry.

We have found it more useful to define technology as tools in a general sense, including machines, but also including linguistic and intellectual tools and contemporary analytic and mathematical techniques. That is, we define technology as the organization of knowledge for practical purposes. In this broader meaning we can best see the extent and variety of the effects of technology on our institutions and values. Its pervasive influence on our very culture would be unintelligible if technology were understood as no more than hardware.

It is in the pervasive influence of technology that our contemporary situation seems qualitatively different from that of past societies, for three reasons.

1. Our tools are more powerful than any before. The rifle wiped out the buffalo, but nuclear weapons can wipe out humanity. Dust storms lay whole regions waste, but too much radioactivity in the atmosphere could make the planet uninhabitable. The domestication of animals and the invention of the wheel literally lifted the burden from people's backs, but computers could free them from all need to labor.
2. This quality of finality of modern technology has brought our society, more than any before, to explicit awareness of technology as an important determinant of our lives and institutions.
3. As a result, our society is coming to a deliberate decision to understand and control technology to good social purpose and is therefore devoting significant effort to the search for ways to measure the full range of its effects rather than only those bearing principally on the economy. It is this prominence of technology in many dimensions of modern life that seems novel in our time and deserving of explicit attention.

HOW TECHNOLOGICAL CHANGE IMPINGES ON SOCIETY

It is clearly possible to sketch a more adequate hypothesis about the interaction of technology and society than the partial views outlined above. Technological change would appear to induce or "motor" social change in two principal ways. New technology creates new opportunities for people and societies, and it also generates new problems for them. It has both positive and negative effects, and it usually has the two at the same time and in virtue of each other. Thus, industrial technology strengthens the economy, as our measures of growth and productivity show. As Anne P. Carter's study on structural changes in the American economy has helped demonstrate, however, it also induces changes in the relative importance of individual supplying sectors in the economy as new techniques of production alter the amounts and kinds of materials, parts and components, energy, and service inputs used by each industry to produce its output. It thus tends to bring about dislocations of businesses and people as a result of changes in industrial patterns and in the structure of occupations.

The close relationship between technological and social change itself helps explain why any given technological development is likely to have both positive and negative effects. The usual sequence is that (1) technological advance creates a new opportunity to achieve some desired goal; (2) this requires (except in trivial cases) alterations in social organization if advantage is to be taken of the new opportunity; (3) which means that the functions of existing social structures will be interfered with; (4) with the result that other goals served by the older structures are now only inadequately achieved.

As the Meyer-Kain study has shown, for example, improved transportation technology and increased ownership of private automobiles have increased the mobility of businesses and individuals. This has led to altered patterns of industrial and residential location, so that older unified cities are being increasingly transformed into larger metropolitan complexes. The new opportunities for mobility are largely denied to the poor and black populations of the core cities, however, partly for economic reasons, and partly as a result of restrictions on choice of residence by blacks, thus leading to persistent black unemployment despite a generally high level of economic activity. Cities are thus increasingly unable to perform their traditional functions of providing employment opportunities for all segments of their populations and an integrated social environment that can temper ethnic and racial differences. The new urban complexes are neither fully viable economic units nor effective political organizations able to upgrade and integrate their core populations into new economic and social structures. The resulting instability is further aggravated by modern mass communications technology, which heightens the expectations of the poor and the fears of the well-to-do and adds frustration and bitterness to the urban crisis.

An almost classic example of the sequence in which technology impinges on society is provided by Mark Field's study of changes in the system and practice of medical care. Recent advances in biomedical science and technology have created two new opportunities: (1) they have made possible treatment and cures that were never possible before; and (2) they provide a necessary condition for the delivery of adequate medical care to the population at large as a matter of right, rather than privilege. In realization of the first possibility, the medical profession has become increasingly differentiated and specialized and is tending to concentrate its best efforts in a few major, urban centers of medical excellence. This alters the older social organization of medicine that was built around the general practitioner. The second possibility has led to big increases in demand for medical services, partly because a healthy population has important economic advantages in a highly industrialized society. This increased demand accelerates the process of differentiation and multiplies the levels of paramedical personnel between the physician at the top and the patient at the bottom of the hospital pyramid. . . .

The pattern illustrated by the preceding examples tends to be the general one. Our most spectacular technological successes in America in the last quarter of a century have been in national defense and in space exploration. They have brought with them, however, enthusiastic advocates and vested interests who claim that the development of sophisticated technology is an intrinsic good that should be pursued for its own sake. They thus contribute to the self-reinforcing quality of technological advance and raise fears of an autonomous technology uncontrollable by humans. Mass communications technology has also made rapid strides since World War II, with great benefit to education, journalism, commerce, and sheer convenience. It has also been accompanied by an aggravation of social unrest, however, and may help explain the singular rebelliousness of a youth who can find out what the world is like from television before home and school have had the time to instill some ethical sense of what it could or should be like.

In all such cases, technology creates a new opportunity and a new problem at the same time. That is why isolating the opportunity or the problem and construing it as the whole answer is ultimately obstructive of, rather than helpful to, understanding.

HOW SOCIETY REACTS TO TECHNOLOGICAL CHANCE

The heightened prominence of technology in our society makes the interrelated tasks of profiting from its opportunities and containing its dangers a major intellectual and political challenge of our time.

Failure of society to respond to the opportunities created by new technology means that much actual or potential technology lies fallow, that is, is not used at all or is not used to its full capacity. This can mean that potentially solvable problems are left unsolved and potentially achievable goals unachieved, because we waste our technological resources or use them inefficiently. A society has at least as much stake in the efficient utilization of technology as in that of its natural or human resources.

There are often good reasons, of course, for not developing or utilizing a particular technology. The mere fact that it can be developed is not sufficient reason for doing so. The costs of development may be too high in the light of the expected benefits, as in the case of the project to develop a nuclear-powered aircraft. Or, a new technological device may be so dangerous in itself or so inimical to other purposes that it is never developed, as in the cases of Herman Kahn's "Doomsday Machine" and the proposal to "nightlight" Vietnam by reflected sunlight.

But there are also cases where technology lies fallow because existing social structures are inadequate to exploit the opportunities it offers. This is revealed clearly in the examination of institutional failure in the ghetto by Richard S. Rosenbloom and his colleagues. At point after point, their analyses confirm what has been long suspected, that is, that existing institutions and traditional approaches are by and large incapable of coming to grips with the new problems of our cities—many of them caused by technological change, as the Meyer-Kain study has reminded us—and unable to realize the possibilities for resolving them that are also inherent in technology. Vested economic and political interests serve to obstruct adequate provision of low-cost housing. Community institutions wither for want of interest and participation by residents. City agencies are unable to marshal the skills and take the systematic approach needed to deal with new and intensified problems of education, crime control, and public welfare. Business corporations, finally, which are organized around the expectation of private profit, are insufficiently motivated to bring new technology and management know-how to bear on urban projects where the benefits will be largely social. All these factors combine to dilute what may otherwise be a genuine desire to apply our best knowledge and adequate resources to the resolution of urban tensions and the eradication of poverty in the nation.

CONTAINING THE NEGATIVE EFFECTS OF TECHNOLOGY

The kinds and magnitude of the negative effects of technology are no more independent of the institutional structures and cultural attitudes of society than is realization of the new opportunities that technology offers. In our society, there are individuals or individual firms always on the lookout for new technological opportunities, and large corporations hire scientists and engineers to invent such opportunities. In deciding whether to develop a new technology, individual entrepreneurs engage in calculations of expected benefits and expected costs to themselves, and proceed if the former are likely to exceed the latter. Their calculations do not take adequate account of the probable benefits and costs of the new developments to others than themselves or to society generally. These latter are what economists call external benefits and costs.

The external benefits potential in new technology will thus not be realized by the individual developer and will accrue to society as a result of deliberate social action, as has been argued above. Similarly with the external costs. In minimizing only expected costs to himself, the individual decision maker helps to contain only some of the potentially negative effects of the new technology. The external costs and therefore the negative effects on society at large are not his or her principal concern and, in our society, are not expected to be.

Most of the consequences of technology that are causing concern at the present time—pollution of the environment, potential damage to the ecology of the planet, occupational and social dislocations, threats to the privacy and political significance of the individual, social and psychological malaise—are negative externalities of this kind. They are with us in large measure because it has not been anybody's explicit business to foresee and anticipate them. They have fallen between the stools of innumerable individual decisions to develop individual technologies for individual purposes without explicit attention to what all these decisions add up to for society as a whole and for people as human beings. This freedom of individual decision making is a value we have cherished and is built into the institutional fabric of our society. The negative effects of technology that we deplore are a measure of what this traditional freedom is beginning to cost us. They are traceable less to some mystical autonomy presumed to lie in technology and much more to the autonomy that our economic and political institutions grant to individual decision making. . . .

Measures to control and mitigate the negative effects of technology, however, often appear to threaten freedoms that our traditions still take for granted as inalienable rights of individuals and good societies, however much they may have been tempered in practice by the social pressures of modern times: the freedom of the market, the freedom of private enterprise, the freedom of the scientist to follow truth wherever it may lead, and the freedom of the individual to pursue fortune and decide his or her fate. There is thus set up a tension between the need to control technology and our wish to preserve our values, which leads some people to conclude that technology is inherently inimical to human values. The political effect of this tension takes the form of inability to adjust our decision-making structures to the realities of technology so as to take maximum advantage of the opportunities it offers and so that we can act to contain its potential ill effects before they become so pervasive and urgent as to seem uncontrollable.

To understand why such tensions are so prominent a social consequence of technological change, it becomes necessary to look explicitly at the effects of technology on social and individual values.

VALUES

Technology's Challenge to Values

Despite the practical importance of the techniques, institutions, and processes of knowledge in contemporary society, political decision making and the resolution of social problems are clearly not dependent on knowledge alone. Numerous commentators have noted that ours is a "knowledge" society, devoted to rational decision making and an "end of ideology," but none would deny the role that values play in shaping the course of society and the decisions of individuals. On the contrary, questions of values become more pointed and insistent in a society that organizes itself to control technology and that engages in deliberate social planning. Planning demands explicit recognition of value hierarchies and often brings into the open value conflicts that remain hidden in the more impersonal working of the market. . . .

This is another way of pointing to the tension alluded to earlier, between the need for social action based on knowledge on the one hand, and the pull of our traditional values, on the other. The increased questioning and reformulation of values that Robin Williams speaks of (1967, 30), coupled with a growing awareness that our values are in fact changing under the impact of technological change, leads many people to believe that technology is by nature destructive of values. But this belief presupposes a concept of values as eternal and unchanging and therefore tends to confuse the valuable with the stable. The fact that values come into question as our knowledge increases and that some traditional values cease to function adequately when technology leads to changes in social conditions does not mean that values per se are being destroyed by knowledge and technology.

What does happen is that values change through a process of accommodation between the system of existing values and the technological and social changes that impinge on it. The projects of the Harvard Program in the area of technology and values are devoted to discovering the specific ways in which this process of accommodation occurs and to tracing its consequences for value changes in contemporary American society. The balance of this section is devoted to a more extended discussion of the first results of these projects.

Technology as a Cause of Value Change

Technology has a direct impact on values by virtue of its capacity for creating new opportunities. By making possible what was not possible before, it offers individuals and society new options to choose from. For example, space technology makes it possible for the first time to go to the moon or to communicate by satellite and thereby adds those two new options to the spectrum of choices available to society. By adding new options in this way, technology can lead to changes in values in the same way that the appearance of new dishes on the heretofore standard menu of one's favorite restaurant can lead to changes in one's tastes and choices of food. Specifically, technology can lead to value change either (1) by bringing some previously unattainable goal within the realm of choice or (2) by making some values easier to implement than heretofore, that is, by changing the costs associated with realizing them. . . .

One example related to the effect of technological change on values is implicit in our concept of democracy. The ideal we associate with the old New England town meeting is that each citizen should have a direct voice in political decisions. Since this has not been possible, we have elected representatives to serve our interests and vote our opinions. Sophisticated computer technology, however, now makes possible rapid and efficient collection and analysis of voter opinion and could eventually provide for "instant voting" by the whole electorate on any issue presented to it via television a few hours before. It thus raises the possibility of instituting a system of direct democracy and gives rise to tensions between those who would be violently opposed to such a prospect and those who are already advocating some system of participatory democracy.

This new technological possibility challenges us to clarify what we mean by democracy. Do we construe it as the will of an undifferentiated majority, as the result of transient coalitions of different interest groups representing different value commitments, as the considered judgment of the people's elected representatives, or as by and large the kind of government we actually have in the United States, minus the flaws in it that we would like to correct? By bringing us face to face with such questions, technology has the effect of calling society's bluff and thereby preparing the ground for changes in its values.

When technological change alters the relative costs of implementing different values, it impinges on inherent contradictions in our value system. To pursue the same example, modern technology can enhance the values we associate with democracy. But it can also enhance another American value—that of "secular rationality," as sociologists call it—by facilitating the use of scientific and technical expertise in the process of political decision making. This can in turn further reduce citizen participation in the democratic process. Technology thus has the effect of facing us with contradictions in our own value system and of calling for deliberate attention to their resolution.

The Value Implications of Economic Change

In addition to the relatively direct effects of technology on values, as illustrated above, value change often comes about through the intermediation of some more general social change produced by technology, as in the tension imposed on our individualist values by the external benefits and costs of technological development alluded to in the earlier discussion of the negative effects of technology. Nathan Rosenberg is exploring the closely allied relationship between such values and the need for society to provide what economists call public goods and services.

As a number of economists have shown, such public goods differ from private consumer goods and services in that they are provided on an all-or-none basis and consumed in a joint way so that more for one consumer does not mean less for another. The clearing of a swamp or a flood-control project, once completed, benefits everyone in the vicinity. A meteorological forecast, once made, can be transmitted by word of mouth to additional users at no additional cost. Knowledge itself may thus be thought of as the public good par excellence, since the research expenses needed to produce it are incurred only once, unlike consumer goods of which every additional unit adds to the cost of production.

As noted earlier, private profit expectation is an inadequate incentive for the production of such public goods because their benefit is indiscriminate and not fully appropriate to the firm or individual that might incur the cost of producing them. Individuals are therefore motivated to dissimulate by understating their true preferences for such goods in the hope of shifting their cost to others. This creates a "free-loader" problem, which skews the mechanism of the market. The market therefore provides no effective indication of the optimal amount of such public commodities from the point of view of society as a whole. If society got only as much public health care, flood control, or knowledge as individual profit calculations would generate, it would no doubt get less of all of them than it does now or than it expresses a desire for by collective political action.

This gap between collective preference and individual motivation imposes strains on a value system such as ours, which is primarily individualist rather than collective or "societal" in its orientation. That system arose out of a simpler, more rustic, and less affluent time, when both benefits and costs were of a much more private sort than now. It is no longer fully adequate for our society, which industrial technology has made productive enough to allocate significant resources to the purchase of public goods and services, and in which modern transportation and communications as well as the absolute magnitude of technological effects lead to extensive ramifications of individual actions on other people and on the environment.

The response to this changed experience on the part of the public at large generally takes the form of increased government intervention in social and economic affairs to contain or guide these wider ramifications, as noted previously. The result is that the influence of values associated with the free reign of individual enterprise and action tends to be counteracted, thus facilitating a change in values. To be sure, the tradition that ties freedom and liberty to a laissez-faire system of decision making remains very strong, and the changes in social structures and cultural attitudes that can touch it at its foundations are still only on the horizon.

Religion and Values

Much of the unease that our society's emphasis on technology seems to generate among various sectors of society can perhaps be explained in terms of the impact that technology has on religion. The formulations and institutions of religion are not immune to the influences of technological change, for they too tend toward an accommodation to changes in the social milieu in which they function. But one way in which religion functions is as an ultimate belief system that provides legitimation, that is, a "meaning" orientation, to moral and social values. This ultimate meaning orientation, according to Harvey Cox, is even more basic to human existence than the value orientation. When the magnitude or rapidity of social change threatens the credibility of that belief system, therefore, and when the changes are moreover seen as largely the results of technological change, the meanings of human existence that we hold most sacred seem to totter and technology emerges as the villain.

Religious change thus provides another mediating mechanism through which technology affects our values. That conditions are ripe for religious change at the present time has been noted by many observers, who are increasingly questioning whether our established religious syntheses and symbol systems are adequate any longer to the religious needs of a scientific and secular society that is changing so fundamentally as to strain traditional notions of eternity. If they are not, how are they likely to change? Cox is addressing himself to this problem with specific attention to the influence of technology in guiding the direction of change. . . .

Cox notes three major traditions in the Judeo-Christian synthesis and finds them inconsistent in their perceptions of the future: an "apocalyptic" tradition foresees imminent catastrophe and induces a negative evaluation of this world; a "teleological" tradition sees the future as the certain unfolding of a fixed purpose inherent in the universe itself; a "prophetic" tradition, finally, sees the future as an open field of human hope and responsibility and as becoming what humans will make of it (1968, 218–20, 227–31).

Technology, as noted, creates new possibilities for human choice and action but leaves their disposition uncertain. What its effects will be and what ends it will serve are not inherent in the technology, but depend on what people will do with technology. Technology thus makes possible a future of open-ended options that seems to accord well with the presuppositions of the prophetic tradition. It is in that tradition above others, then, that we may seek the beginnings of a religious synthesis that is both adequate to our time and continuous with what is most relevant in our religious history. But this requires an effort at deliberate religious innovation for which Cox finds insufficient theological ground at the present time. Although it is recognized that religions have changed and developed in the past, conscious innovation in religion has been condemned and is not provided for by the relevant theologies. The main task that technological change poses for theology in the next decades, therefore, is that of deliberate religious innovation and symbol reformulation to take specific account of religious needs in a technological age.

What consequences would such changes in religion have for values? Cox approaches this question in the context of the familiar complaint that, since technology is principally a means, it enhances merely instrumental values at the expense of expressive, consummatory, or somehow more "real" values. The appropriate distinction, however, is not between technological instrumental values and nontechnological expressive values, but among the expressive values that attach to different technologies. The horse-and-buggy was a technology too, after all, and it is not prima facie clear that its charms were different in kind or superior to the sense of power and adventure and the spectacular views that go with jet travel.

Further, technological advance in many instances is a condition for the emergence of new creative or consummatory values. Improved sound boxes in the past and structural steel and motion photography in the present have made possible the artistry of Jascha Heifetz, Frank Lloyd Wright, and Charles Chaplin, which have opened up wholly new ranges of expressive possibility without, moreover, in any way inhibiting a concurrent renewal of interest in medieval instruments and primitive art. If religious innovation can provide a meaning orientation broad enough to accommodate the idea that new technology can be creative of new values, a long step will have been taken toward providing a religious belief system adequate to the realities and needs of a technological age.

The Individual in a Technological Age

What do technological change and the social and value changes that it brings with it mean for the life of the individual today? It is not clear that their effects are all one-way. For example, we are often told that today's individual is alienated by the vast proliferation of technical expertise and complex bureaucracies, by a feeling of impotence in the face of "the machine," and by a decline in personal privacy. It is probably true that the social pressures placed on individuals today are more complicated and demanding than they were in earlier times. Increased geographical and occupational mobility and the need to function in large organizations place difficult demands on the individual to conform or "adjust." It is also evident that the privacy of many individuals tends to be encroached upon by sophisticated eavesdropping and surveillance devices, by the accumulation of more and more information about individuals by governmental and many private agencies, and by improvements in information handling technologies such as the proposed institution of centralized statistical databanks. There is little doubt, finally, that the power, authority, influence, and scope of government are greater today than at any time in the history of the United States.

But, as Edward Shils points out in his study on technology and the individual, there is another, equally compelling side of the coin. First, government seems to be more shy and more lacking in confidence today than ever before. Second, while privacy may be declining in the ways indicated above, it also tends to decline in a sense that most individuals are likely to approve. The average Victorian, for example, probably "enjoyed" much more privacy than today. No one much cared what happened to him or her, and he or she was free to remain ignorant, starve, fall ill, and die in complete privacy; that was the "golden age of privacy," as Shils puts it. Compulsory universal education, social security legislation, and public health measures—indeed, the very idea of a welfare state are all antithetical to privacy in this sense, and it is the rare individual today who is loath to see that kind of privacy go.

It is not clear, finally, that technological and social complexity must inevitably lead to reducing the individual to the "mass." Economic productivity and modern means of communication allow the individual to aspire to more than ever before. Better and more easily available education not only provides skills and with it the means to develop individual potentialities, but also improves self-image and one's sense of value as a human being. This is probably the first age in history in which such high proportions of people have felt like individuals; no eighteenth-century English factory worker, so far as we know, had the sense of individual worth that underlies the demands on society of the average resident of the black urban ghetto today. And, as Shils notes, the scope of individual choice and action today are greater than in previous times, all the way from consumer behavior to political or religious allegiance. Even the much-maligned modern organization may in fact "serve as a mediator or buffer between the individual and the full raw impact of technological change," as an earlier study supported by the Harvard Program has concluded.

Recognition that the impact of modern technology on the individual has two faces, both negative and positive, is consistent with the double effect of technological change that was discussed above. It also suggests that appreciation of that impact in detail may not be achieved in terms of old formulas, such as more or less privacy, more or less government, more or less individuality.

ECONOMIC AND POLITICAL ORGANIZATION

The Enlarged Scope of Public Decision Making

When technology brings about social changes (as described in the first section of this chapter) that impinge on our existing system of values (in ways reviewed in the second section), it poses for society a number of problems that are ultimately political in nature. The term "political" is used here in the broadest sense: it encompasses all the decision-making structures and procedures that have to do with the allocation and distribution of wealth and power in society. The political organization of society thus includes not only the formal apparatus of the state but also industrial organizations and other private institutions that play a role in the decision-making process. It is particularly important to attend to the organization of the entire body politic when technological change leads to a blurring of once-clear distinctions between the public and private sectors of society and to changes in the roles of its principal institutions.

It was suggested above that the political requirements of our modern technological society call for a relatively greater public commitment on the part of individuals than in previous times. The reason for this, stated most generally, is that technological change has the effect of enhancing the importance of public decision making in society because technology is continually creating new possibilities for social action, as well as new problems that have to be dealt with.

A society that undertakes to foster technology on a large scale, in fact, commits itself to social complexity and to facing and dealing with new problems as a normal feature of political life. Not much is yet known with any precision about the political imperatives inherent in technological change, but one may nevertheless speculate about the reasons why an increasingly technological society seems to be characterized by enlargement of the scope of public decision making.

For one thing, the development and application of technology seems to require large-scale, and hence increasingly complex, social concentrations, whether these be large cities, large corporations, big universities, or big government. In instances where technological advance appears to facilitate reduction of such first-order concentrations, it tends instead to enlarge the relevant system of social organization, that is, to lead to increased centralization. Thus the physical dispersion made possible by transportation and communications technologies, as Meyer and Kain have shown, enlarges the urban complex that must be governed as a unit.

A second characteristic of advanced technology is that its effects cover large distances, in both the geographical and social senses of the term. Both its positive and negative features are more extensive. Horse-powered transportation technology was limited in its speed and capacity, but its nuisance value was also limited, in most cases to the owner and to the occupant of the next farm. The supersonic transport can carry hundreds across long distances in minutes, but its noise and vibration damage must also be suffered willy-nilly by everyone within the limits of a swath 3,000 miles long and several miles wide.

The concatenation of increased density (or enlarged system) and extended technological "distance" means that technological applications have increasingly wider ramifications and that increasingly large concentrations of people and organizations become dependent on technological systems. A striking illustration of this was provided by the widespread effects of a power blackout in the northeastern part of the United States. The result is not only that more and more decisions must be social decisions taken in public ways, as already noted, but that, once made, decisions are likely to have a shorter useful life than heretofore. That is partly because technology is continually altering the spectrum of choices and problems that society faces, and partly because any decision taken is likely to generate a need to take ten more.

These speculations about the effects of technology on public decision making raise the problem of restructuring our decision-making mechanisms—including the system of market incentives—so that the increasing number and importance of social issues that confront us can be resolved equitably and effectively.

Private Firms and Public Goods

Among these issues, as noted earlier, is that created by the shift in the composition of demand in favor of public goods and services such as education, health, transportation, slum clearance, and recreational facilities that, it is generally agreed, the market has never provided effectively and in the provision of which government has usually played a role of some significance. This shift in demand raises serious questions about the relationship between technological change and existing decision-making structures in general and about the respective roles of government and business in particular. . . .

In Western industrialized countries, new technological developments generally originate in and are applied through joint stock companies whose shares are widely traded on organized capital markets. Corporations thus play a dominant role in the development of new methods of production, of new methods of satisfying consumer wants, and even of new wants. Most economists appear to accept the thesis originally proposed by Schumpeter that corporations play a key role in the actual process of technological innovation in the economy. . . .

There is no similar agreement about the implications of all this for social policy. J.K. Galbraith, for example, argues that the corporation is motivated by the desire for growth subject to a minimum profit constraint and infers (1) a higher rate of new-want development than would be the case if corporations were motivated principally to maximize profit, (2) a bias in favor of economic activities heavy in "technological content" in contrast to activities requiring sophisticated social organization, and (3) a bias in the economy as a whole in favor of development and satisfaction of private needs to the neglect of public needs and at the cost of a relatively slow rate of innovation in the public sector.

But Galbraith's picture is not generally accepted by economists, and his model of the corporation is not regarded as established economic theory. There is, in fact, no generally accepted economic theory of corporate behavior. . . , so that discussions about the future of the system of corporate enterprise usually get bogged down in an exchange of unsubstantiated assertions about how the existing system actually operates. What seems needed at this time, then, is less a new program of empirical research than an attempt to synthesize what we know for the purpose of arriving at a more adequate theory of the firm. . . .

We can hope to do no more than raise the level of discussion of such fundamental and difficult questions, of course, but even that could be a service.

THE PROMISE AND PROBLEMS OF SCIENTIFIC DECISION MAKING

There are two further consequences of the expanding role of public decision making. The first is that the latest information-handling devices and techniques tend to be utilized in the decision-making process. This is so (1) because public policy can be effective only to the degree that it is based on reliable knowledge about the actual state of the society, and thus requires a strong capability to collect, aggregate, and analyze detailed data about economic activities, social patterns, popular attitudes, and political trends; and (2) because it is recognized increasingly that decisions taken in one area impinge on and have consequences for other policy areas often thought of as unrelated, so that it becomes necessary to base decisions on a model of society that sees it as a system and that is capable of signaling as many as possible of the probable consequences of a contemplated action.

As Alan F. Westin points out, reactions to the prospect of more decision making based on computerized databanks and scientific management techniques run the gamut of optimism to pessimism mentioned in the opening of this essay. Negative reactions take the form of rising political demands for greater popular participation in decision making, for more equality among different segments of the population, and for greater regard for the dignity of individuals. The increasing dependence of decision making on scientific and technological devices and techniques is seen as posing a threat to these goals, and pressures are generated in opposition to further "rationalization" of decision-making processes. These pressures have the paradoxical effect, however, not of deflecting the supporters of technological decision making from their course, but of spurring them on to renewed effort to save the society before it explodes under planlessness and inadequate administration.

The paradox goes further and helps explain much of the social discontent that we are witnessing at the present time. The greater complexity and the more extensive ramifications that technology brings about in society tend to make social processes increasingly circuitous and indirect. The effects of actions are widespread and difficult to keep track of, so that experts and sophisticated techniques are increasingly needed to detect and analyze social events and to formulate policies adequate to the complexity of social issues. The "logic" of modern decision making thus appears to require greater and greater dependence on the collection and analysis of data and on the use of technological devices and scientific techniques. Indeed, many observers would agree that there is an "increasing relegation of questions which used to be matters of political debate to professional cadres of technicians and experts which function almost independently of the democratic political process." (Brooks 1965, 71) In recent times, that process has been most noticeable, perhaps, in the areas of economic policy and national security affairs.

This "logic" of modern decision making, however, runs counter to that element of traditional democratic theory that places high value on direct participation in the political processes and generates the kind of discontent referred to above. If it turns out on more careful examination that direct participation is becoming less relevant to a society in which the connections between causes and effects are long and often hidden-which is an increasingly "indirect" society, in other words—elaboration of a new democratic ethos and of new democratic processes more adequate to the realities of modern society will emerge as perhaps the major intellectual and political challenge of our time.

THE NEED FOR INSTITUTIONAL INNOVATION

The challenge is, indeed, already upon us, for the second consequence of the enlarged scope of public decision making is the need to develop new institutional forms and new mechanisms to replace established ones that can no longer deal effectively with the new kinds of problems with which we are increasingly faced. Much of the political ferment of the present time-over the problems of technology assessment, the introduction of statistical databanks, the extension to domestic problems of techniques of analysis developed for the military services, and the modification of the institutions of local government-is evidence of the need for new institutions. It will be recalled that Oettinger's study concludes that innovation is called for in the educational establishment before instructional technology can realize the promise that is potential in it. Our research in the biomedical area has repeatedly confirmed the need for institutional innovation in the medical system, and [Robin] Marris has noted the evolution that seems called for in our industrial institutions. The Rosenbloom research group, finally, has documented the same need in the urban area and is exploring the form and course that the processes of innovation might take.

Direct intervention by business or government to improve ghetto conditions will tend to be ineffective until local organizations come into existence that enable residents to participate in and control their own situation. Such organizations seem to be a necessary condition for any solution of the ghetto problem that is likely to prove acceptable to black communities. Richard S. Rosenbloom, Paul R. Lawrence, and their associates are therefore engaged in the design of two kinds of organization suited to the peculiar problems of the modern ghetto. These are (1) a state- or area-wide urban development corporation in which business and government join to channel funds and provide technical assistance to (2) a number of local development corporations, under community control, which can combine social service with sound business management. . . .

CONCLUSION

As we review what we are learning about the relationship of technological and social change, a number of conclusions begin to emerge. We find, on the one hand, that the creation of new physical possibilities and social options by technology tends toward and appears to require the emergence of new values, new forms of economic activity, and new political organizations. On the other hand, technological change also poses problems of social and psychological displacement.

The two phenomena are not unconnected, nor is the tension between them new: humanity's technical prowess always seems to run ahead of human ability to deal with and profit from it. In America, especially, we are becoming adept at extracting the new techniques, the physical power, and the economic productivity that are inherent in our knowledge and its associated technologies. Yet we have not fully accepted the fact that our progress in the technical realm does not leave our institutions, values, and political processes unaffected.

Individuals will be fully integrated into society only when we can extract from our knowledge not only its technological potential but also its implications for a system of values and a social, economic, and political organization appropriate to a society in which technology is so prevalent. . . .

NOTE

1. Unless otherwise noted, studies such as Oettinger's, which are referred to in this article, are described in the Fourth Annual Report (1967-68) of the Harvard University Program on Technology and Society.

7

THE TECHNOLOGY OF PRODUCTION: MAKING A JOB OF GENDER

Judy Wajcman

New technologies disrupt established patterns of sex typing and thereby open up opportunities for changing the sexual division of labor. As technologies develop and displace each other, there is a disturbance among the technically skilled strata. Some gain and some lose. Many male craft skills have been quite purposively made redundant by new technology that has radically transformed the nature of the work. But technology is not an independent force; the way in which it affects the nature of work is conditioned by existing relationships. There are conflicts and negotiations over technological change and the opportunities for changing the sexual division of labor to women's advantage are often foreclosed by male power. Women lose out in these struggles as powerful groups defend their old skills or monopolize new ones. Craft workers, who have been seen as the defenders of working-class interests in struggles over technical change, in part derive their strength from their past exclusionary practices. Their gains have often been made at the expense of less skilled or less well-organized sections of the workforce, and this has in many cases involved the exclusion of women.

The entry of women into industrial work in Britain, America, and Australia during World War I and, especially, World War II, was followed by an equally deliberate process of their expulsion from that work once the immediate crisis had passed. Thus the gross under-representation of women in engineering and other industrial work, and the lack of confidence often felt by women faced with technology, are evidence of a deeper problem. Official plans to rectify the underrepresentation of women in engineering often proceed as if the problem were simply a lack of self-confidence in women. But male dominance of technology has, in large part, been secured by the active exclusion of women from areas of technological work.

Printing and newspaper publishing in particular is an industry with craft traditions of labor process control. Recent technological developments, particularly in electronic typesetting technologies which have the potential to undermine those traditions, have been resisted by printing workers. Strikes and lockouts throughout the 1970s and early 1980s have characterized attempts to introduce the new technology in the United States, Great Britain, and Australia. The printing industry in Britain provides an illustration of the sexual politics involved in such struggles over technology.

The violent dispute at the new technology newspaper plant at Wapping in London during 1986 was the final phase in a long history of management attempts to wrest control of the labor process from the Fleet Street print unions. Computerized photocomposition systems had been available in the U.S. printing industry from about 1970. This technology enabled journalists and advertising personnel to enter copy directly into a computer. The introduction of this new technology represented an attack on the compositors' control over their work as it meant that their traditional manual skills would become technically redundant.

The restrictive practices of craft labor and the degree of craft control had, not surprisingly, inhibited the introduction of this kind of technological innovation into the newspaper industry in London's Fleet Street. Wages of these craftsmen have been very high in the postwar period. Those of compositors, who prepared the type in hot metal, were the highest of all. In her book on the history of typesetting technology in Britain, Cynthia Cockburn (1983) describes this archetypal group of skilled male workers as they were being radically undermined by cold electronic composition. This is an area of work from which women have been traditionally excluded. Employers saw this technical change as enabling them to replace the men with cheaper women workers. Over the past decade the compositors have fought to defend their position by having sole rights to use the computer typesetting equipment—to retain keyboard work. To varying degrees they managed to maintain their craft control, even though their craft was technologically redundant. But their strategy of resistance has entailed the exclusion of unskilled women from the trade. It should be noted that this exclusionary strategy has also involved racial and religious prejudice. Skilled printing workers have a higher proportion of white Anglo-Saxon Protestants among them than the semi- and unskilled.

Having pointed out the way in which organized male workers have used technology to maintain power over women in the workplace, it needs to be said that this is not a once-and-for-all achievement. Male dominance over machinery is constantly under threat—both by women's direct efforts to undermine it and by actions of employers in seeking to undermine skilled male workers and cheapen their labor costs.

Under some conditions, skilled men do lose out and women enter previously male jobs. The process of feminization is often part of technological change. In such cases, women rarely perform exactly the same tasks, under the same conditions, as the men formerly performed: inherent in this process of technological change is the transformation of jobs. Nevertheless, and this is the crucial point, the introduction of female labor is usually accompanied by a down-grading of the skill content of the work and a consequent fall in pay for the job.

SEX, SKILL, AND TECHNICAL COMPETENCE

It is often said that women are low paid because they are unskilled; certainly women's work tends to fall into the unskilled or semiskilled categories of official classifications. But the crucial question is how definitions of skill are established. To take a simple example, women who assemble digital watches and pocket calculators require considerable manual dexterity ("nimble fingers"), the capacity for sustained attention to detail and excellent hand-eye coordination. Yet these capacities are not defined as "skills." Nurses provide another example of an occupation that requires a great deal of training and ability, as well as technical knowledge. Yet nursing is not thought of as a technical job because it is women's work. Moreover, because such work has been socially constructed as unskilled, it has also been undervalued. Consequently "women's work" is comparatively low paid. The work of women is often deemed inferior simply because it is women who do it.

How has it come about that women have failed to achieve recognition of the skills required by their work? Although it is the case that women workers have generally been refused access to training in traditionally masculine areas of work, the basis for distinctions of skill in women's and men's work is not a simple technical matter. Definitions of skill can have more to do with ideological and social constructions than with technical competencies possessed by men and not by women. It is a question of workers' collective efforts to protect and secure their conditions of employment—by retaining skill designations for their own work and defending that skill to the exclusion of outsiders. These efforts have been predominantly by and on behalf of the male working class. They have been directed against employers who have regularly tried to find ways of substituting cheaper workers for expensive skilled labor.

But men's resistance has also operated against women's interests. Defending skill, preventing "dilution," has almost always meant blocking women's access to an occupation. Moreover employers' own perceptions of the suitability of women for particular types of work must in part be responsible for the craft workers' success in excluding women from skilled work (Liff 1986). Otherwise one would expect the sexual division of labor to be a much more contested area both for management and unions than it is. Skilled status has thus been traditionally identified with masculinity and as work that women do not do, while women's skills have been defined as nontechnical and undervalued.

Thus there are important connections between men's power in the workplace and their dominance over machinery. Likewise, there are important connections between women's relative lack of power and their lack of technological skills. Technology includes not just things themselves but the physical and mental know-how to make use of these things. Know-how is a resource that gives those who possess it a degree of actual or potential power, and we have seen above how this know-how has been central to the class politics of technological work. It is also central to the sexual politics of technological work, as technical competence is a key source of men's power over women—of the capacity, for example, to command higher incomes and scarce jobs.

How can we begin to understand the enduring force of this identification between technical skills and masculinity without making the mistake of treating technology as inherently masculine? We can start, as Cockburn does, by taking seriously the requirement to understand the masculinity of technology as a social product. Men's affinity with technology is then seen as integral to the constitution of male gender identity. "Technology enters into our sexual identity: femininity is incompatible with technological competence; to feel technically competent is to feel manly" (Cockburn 1985, 12).

Once we recognize that gender construction is an ongoing ideological and cultural process with a long history, then the focus shifts to analyzing the social practices involved. The way in which the present technical culture expresses and consolidates relations among men becomes an important factor in explaining the continuing exclusion of women.

This type of analysis stresses the importance of the cultural aspects of gender relations and shows the way that gender is an integral part of people's experience in the workplace. This is illustrated in Cockburn's (1983) study of compositors, where she ascribes the centrality of the craft workers' ease with technology to their masculine identity. The industrial strength of craftsmen derived from their knowledge and competence with machines. The control over this type of industrial technology has traditionally been the province of men, and women workers have been excluded from these technical skills. The technical change from linotype to electronic photocomposition, however, literally makes the compositors feel emasculated. Because the work of composing now resembles typing and involves working with paper instead of metal, that is, a shift from factory work to the office, the compositors no longer consider it to be real work. Traditional craft culture was associated with hot metal, dirt, and physical work, and the elimination of this not only diminishes their control over their work but also represents a threat to their masculinity.

Clearly, however, the appropriation of technical skills plays an important part in the reproduction of inequality among men as well as between men and women. Men do not have power over women in the same sense as capitalists do over workers. In looking at the relations of work one is inevitably looking at class relations. The male culture of craft know-how is the culture of an exploited group. Male employees themselves vary considerably in their capacities to control and benefit from technological innovations. It is important to remember that this source of power is a subordinate one in that technology is also used by some men to dominate others.

The class dimension is also significant in another sense. It is not the case that all women have an identical relationship to machinery and to technical knowledge. There are obviously important differences between the technical skills of, say, women factory workers and those of technically trained professional women. Cockburn found, however, that what they had in common was that they were both to be found operating machinery, but rarely in those occupations that involve knowing what goes on inside the machine. "With few exceptions, the designer and developer of the new systems, the people who market and sell, install, manage and service machinery, are men. Women may push the buttons but they may not meddle with the works" (1985, 11–12). Women may well have considerable knowledge about the machine that they work on, but the key to power is flexible, transferable skills, and these are still the property of men.

To say that technical competence is part of male gender identity is not to presume that there is a coherent single form of masculinity. The masculine culture of technology may take a partially different form for working-class and middle-class men. The cult of masculinity revolving around physical prowess is closely associated with shop-floor culture among manual workers. Working-class men may be more able when it comes to fixing cars and domestic machines, but middle-class men have more power through their possession of abstract and generalizable technical knowledge. Furthermore, it needs to be stressed that ethnic and generational differences, as well as class divisions, produce different versions of masculinity. If we are to avoid essentialist constructions of "men" and "masculinity," we need to pluralize the term and speak of "masculinities".

THE RELOCATION OF WORK

It has been widely noted that the development of microelectronic and telecommunication technology opens up the possibility of radical changes in the location of work. White-collar work, for example, can be decentralized and moved into suburban offices (with lower rents and possibly lower wages), or it can be moved "offshore" altogether. Sending work offshore, while not new, is certainly much easier as a result of greater satellite telecommunications capacity. An international sexual division of labor has emerged based on the breakdown of the production process in computer manufacture, with women performing the labor-intensive assembly of microchips in various Third World countries. More recently, offshore office services have developed where low-wage female labor is used for data entry and data-processing work for firms based in the industrialized countries. It should be noted, however, that just as in manufacturing the development of advanced automation systems has reduced the need for offshore assembly work, so developments in office automation (such as voice recognition and optical character recognition) suggest that the use of offshore office services will be a short-term phenomenon.

The development of computer-based homework, which is also referred to as "telework" or "telecommuting," illustrates further the impact that technology has on the location of work. The combination of computer and telecommunications technology has made it technically feasible for large numbers of workers whose jobs involve information processing to work at terminals in their own homes. The vision of what has become known as the "electronic cottage" features in all scenarios of the future of work. Although the number of people involved in this new form of homework is still small, its potential is quite large. And, according to many writers from a wide variety of political persuasions, it is a paradigmatic case for the future organization of work. According to postindustrial theory, the home as a workplace liberates people from the discipline and alienation of industrial production. Homework offers the freedom of self-regulated work and a reintegration of work and personal life. Moreover, an expansion of homework will allegedly lead to much more sharing of paid and unpaid domestic labor, as men and women spend more time at home together.

Whereas the postindustrial theorists see electronic homework as part of a positive future, for others it evokes the ugly spectre of "sweated" self-exploitative piecework. These writers approach telework with a set of assumptions derived from the study of traditional homeworkers. They expect it to become more widespread because it is a method of production favored by employers seeking to resist competition and protect profits by reducing wage costs. As such it is seen as part of a more general trend toward the casualization of the labor force and the growth of the informal sector. Both perspectives share a largely technologically determinist prophecy of the "collapse of work."

White-collar and service-sector homework, both traditional and modern, have been increasing over the past two decades, even before the new information technology exerted its full influence on work arrangements. From research carried out in Europe, America, and Australia, it is clear that important differences are already emerging between professional and clerical teleworkers.[1] Men predominate among the professionals, such as managerial staff, computer programmers, and systems analysts, while women are the great majority of clerical workers.

Most of these are married women with young children, for whom homework is especially attractive because of their household responsibilities and the lack of affordable quality childcare. In practice, however, balancing childcare with paid work has proved difficult for many women, as they have only limited control over a fluctuating workload. They are often employed precisely for the flexibility that this provides for employers. Like traditional homeworkers, electronic homeworkers are typically paid at piece rates and earn substantially less than comparably skilled employees working in offices, as well as having to meet their own overhead costs. Moreover, as employers do not give homeworkers employee status, they are not entitled to benefits such as sickness pay, and have no security of employment. Electronic homework for clerical women, then, is an extension of traditional homework with all its disadvantages.

The pattern of work of male professionals is quite different from that of clerical workers in that they work from home rather than at home. American research has focused on managerial and professional employees where firms turn to homework in order to retain highly qualified workers such as computer programmers. Our Australian study looked at self-employed programmers who were also able to exploit the skill shortage in their area. Most of these male professionals were earning more working at home, and many pointed to the lower overheads of running a business from home.

In our study we found that what they appreciated was not the opportunity to combine paid work with childcare but their flexible and varied working patterns. In fact, the very long hours they worked militated against any significant change to the balance between work and leisure, or work and family life. When we asked the programmers and word processor operators in our sample how working from home had changed their attitude to work, we found strong evidence of reinforced, rather than transformed, gender differences. Whereas the majority of men had become more work-centered, the women were more likely to have become less work-centered and more family-centered.

Thus even research on new technology homework fails to reveal simple trends. Electronic homework may well mean very different things for professional and clerical workers, and for men and women. For women clerical workers, new technology homework still reflects their labor market vulnerability—vulnerability that stems from the availability of their skill and the domestic division of labor. It is only for male professionals who possess skills that are in short supply that new technology homework presents an unambiguously attractive choice. But this hardly warrants the general enthusiasm for "electronic cottages" that characterizes so much of the literature about the future of work.

Overall, then, new forms of computer-based homework would appear to reinforce sexual divisions in relation to paid work and unpaid domestic work, as well as to the technical division of labor. Once more we see women failing to gain the genuinely technical jobs, in this case producing software for computers. It is a stark example of the reproduction of women's traditional position in the new electronic age.

THE SOCIAL SHAPING OF WORKPLACE TECHNOLOGY

I have been examining the impact of technological change on sexual divisions in the labor market and occupational segregation between women and men. Although new technologies may be important levers of change in the social relations of production, the gendered character of work has inhibited major transformations in the sexual division of labor. In a period of vast technological changes that have profoundly restructured work in every sphere, the resilience of the gendered character of the technical division and hierarchy of labor has been notable.

I now turn the focus around and consider the social factors that cause technological change. The extent to which the invention and diffusion of particular technologies are themselves shaped by social forces are explored. I argue that the sex of the workforce and gender relations in the workplace themselves profoundly affect the direction and pace of technological change. It is only through an analysis of the processes by which technology is itself gendered that its inability to undermine gender divisions can be understood.

New technology typically emerges from modifications to and combinations of existing technology. But this is not the only force shaping technology. Industrial innovation is a product of a historically specific activity carried out in the interests of particular social groups and against the interests of others.

Technological systems are oriented to a goal and that goal is normally to reduce costs and increase revenues. When technologists focus inventive effort on the "inefficient" components of a system, for many practical purposes inefficient means uneconomical. So technological reasoning and economic reasoning are often inseparable.

A vital issue in technical change is the cost of labor, because much innovation is sponsored and justified on the ground that it saves labor costs. In a capitalist society, class relations are a major factor affecting the price of labor.

Placing the class dimension at the center of its analysis, labor process theory is an important and well established approach to the study of technological change. Although limited with respect to gender, it provides a useful starting point for the development of a gender perspective.

INDUSTRIAL CONFLICT AND TECHNICAL INNOVATION

The mechanization of craft work has commonly been presented as the model for understanding major changes in the capitalist labor process. Historically, production was very dependent on the skills and knowledge of craft workers, but over the first quarter of the twentieth century their jobs were subdivided, allowing employers to dispense with skilled labor. Rather than see deskilling as an inexorable tendency, recent studies have emphasized the extent to which worker resistance mediated the deskilling process.[2] Craft skills provided the basis for maintaining control over the utilization of machinery and hence the basis for worker organization. A key part of this strategy was the exclusion of other noncraft workers who offered a threat to their position. As we have already seen, this mechanism of social exclusion was often deployed at the expense of women workers.

Technological innovations have played a major role in these battles for control over production.[3] In the early phases of capitalist development, machinery was used by the owners and managers of capital as an important weapon in the battle for control over production. Marx's classic account of the development of the automatic spinning "mule" (so-called because it was a hybrid of the spinning-jenny and water-frame) in nineteenth-century Britain has, for example, been reexamined from this perspective. In the early production process of spinning the skilled adult male spinner had a central role. The spinner's centrality derived not only from his technical skills but also from his supervisory role through the system of subcontracting labor. The spinners were highly unionized and their frequent strikes were a direct challenge to the power and profits of the cotton-masters. The self-acting mule was the employers' response to this threat.

A major strike in 1824 seems to have galvanized a number of manufacturers into recognizing their common interest in relation to the spinners. They therefore approached Richard Roberts, a well-known mechanical engineer and toolmaker. Roberts told the House of Lords Select Committee in 1851: "The self-acting mule was made in consequence of a turn-out of the spinners at Hyde, which had lasted three months, when a deputation of masters waited upon me, and requested me to turn my attention to spinning, with the view of making the mule self-acting" (Bruland 1982, 103).

The explicit purpose of this invention and its introduction was to break the power of the spinners. By changing the technology of spinning they intended to replace men on the mules with the cheaper labor of women and children. The self-actor was partially successful in its aim of curbing the spinners' militancy. In the period following the innovation, their wages were relatively depressed and strikes declined markedly. This episode exemplifies the way in which particular arenas of industrial conflict may result in the development of particular kinds of technical innovations.

In fact, the diffusion of the self-actor was relatively slow and did not have the anticipated effect of destroying the craft position of the adult male spinners. Despite radical changes in the manual component of mule spinning, these workers retained their position. The spinner-piecer system was merely replaced by an analogous minder-piecer system, which still left minders with responsibility for recruiting assistants and controlling them on the shop floor. This hierarchical division within the workforce persisted because it was the basis of the existing managerial structure in cotton spinning.

William Lazonick (1979) has shown that this reliance of the employers on a very effective form of labor management was more important than the skills or organized strength of the male minders. Thus it was the hierarchical division within the working class that conditioned technical change.

It made it rational for capitalists to work with slightly less automated mules than were technically possible, so that failures of attention by operatives led not to "snarls" that could be hidden in the middle of spun "cops," but to the obvious disaster of "sawney," where the several hundred threads being spun all broke simultaneously, with consequent loss of piecework earnings for the minder (MacKenzie 1984, 497).

The history of the self-acting mule demonstrates that an understanding of technical change as something based on relations of production must include an account of divisions within the working class. It not only shows how workers' resistance depends on their ability to control and restrict entry into their trade but also how employers can exploit these divisions. So the skilled worker typically looks not just in one direction—toward the capitalist who is trying to undermine the worker's position by incorporating the worker's skills into the machine—but also toward the mass of the "unskilled," who can equally be seen as a threat. Typically, this will involve older male white workers looking in the direction of those who have at least one of the characteristics of being young, female, black, or from an ethnic minority.

The development of technology cannot, however, simply be understood in terms of the needs of undifferentiated capital trying to control labor as an undifferentiated mass. Recent labor process work has repeatedly pointed to the weakness of assuming any simple and ubiquitous trend in the social construction of technology for control through deskilling.[4] Further it has highlighted the need to recognize differences of interest and action among capitalists.

The focus has shifted to the interplay between competing managerial strategies and priorities, on the one hand, and various patterns of worker response, on the other. There are now many documented instances where occupational competition was settled in favor of enlarged control by craft workers as well as cases where detailed control and deskilling by technology was the result (Wilkinson 1983). Short-term competitive pressures between capitals or motivational and flexibility concerns clearly lead to compromises over the deskilling potential of technologies.

Studies of how class relations shape technology are overwhelmingly preoccupied with traditional male unionized sections of manufacturing industry. Discussion about the impact of new technologies on the workplace has focused to a remarkable degree on the automation of machine tools. Perhaps this is because many of these male authors, like Braverman, are immersed in the romance of the skilled craftsman tragically becoming obsolete. Skilled machinists, however, have never been typical of workers and certainly women workers do not figure in their number. As there is little empirical analysis of technological development that explicitly challenges technological determinism, it is worth considering this example of a twentieth-century technology to see if lessons can be drawn from it for a gender analysis.

THE AUTOMATION OF MACHINE TOOLS: A CASE STUDY OF CHOICE

The evolution of automatically controlled machine tools is the subject of a detailed study of the design, development, and diffusion of a particular technology, "from the point of conception in the minds of inventors to the point of production on the shop floor" (Noble 1984, xiv). This is a particularly daunting task to undertake for a modern technology when the "heroic inventor" has left the stage to be replaced by major institutions.

The central argument of David Noble's classic study, *Forces of Production*, is that patterns of power and cultural values shape the actual processes of technological development. Noble argues that the concepts of "economic viability" and "technical viability," which are often used to explain technological change, are inherently political. By way of a detailed reconstruction of a lost alternative to numerical control and by examination of variant forms of numerical control that have also vanished, Noble shows that automation did not have to proceed in the way it did. Instead, the form of automation was the result of deliberate selection.

A major goal of machine tool automation was to secure managerial control, by shifting control from the shop floor to the centralized office. There were at least two possible solutions to the problem of automating machine tools. Machining was in fact automated using the technique of numerical control. But there was also a technique of automation called "record-playback" that was as promising as numerical control but enjoyed only a brief existence. Why, asks Noble, was numerical control developed and record-playback dropped? It was the postwar period of labor militancy that provided the social context in which the technology of machine tool automation was developed.

Record-playback was a system that would have extended the machinists' skill. Although the machines were more automated under this system, the machinists still had control of the feeds, speeds, number of cuts, and output of metal; in other words, they controlled the machine and thereby retained shop-floor control over production.

Numerical control, in contrast, offered a means of dispensing with these well-organized skilled machinists. The planning and conceptual functions were now carried out in an office because the machines operated according to computer programs. The machinist became a button pusher. Numerical control was therefore a management system, as well as a technology for cutting metals. It led to organizational changes in the factory that increased managerial control over production because the technology was chosen, in part, for just that purpose.

It would be wrong to assume that managers' goals in preferring numerical control to record-playback were necessarily realized. The introduction of numerical control onto the shop floor did not simply shift control to management. It was met with fierce resistance from the workforce. At the same time, management found that it needed to retain skilled machinists to operate the new machines effectively. Consequently, management was never able to gain complete control over production. In reality, machines do not run themselves and therefore the tendency to deskilling is always contradictory. Indeed, as Noble himself acknowledges, the subsequent development of machine tool technology has made it technically feasible and potentially economical to institute shop-floor programming. As technological advances opened up new areas of application—in smaller firms involved in small batch or specialized production—it also provided opportunities for craft workers to regain control over programming. In fact, the operational requirements of these small firms may be more compatible with shop-floor programming than with a managerial strategy oriented around deskilling.

Noble's study is remarkable for its attempt to encompass many different levels of social determination of the technology. It does not simply rely on treating technology as being determined by management's demand for control over workers. It goes beyond that to include the role and interests of the military in that postwar period, as well as the ideology and interests of engineers. Although it was the social relations of production that tipped the balance in the choice of technology in Noble's example, he demonstrates how the demand for management control coincided with the command and control goals of the military. He also shows how the ideology and interests of engineers who take the view that the most automated is the most advanced and that the human element should be eliminated from production because it is the potential source of "human error" fits in with the idea of management control.

While emphasizing the various class forces that shape the design and application of machine tools, however, Noble fails to consider that there is also a gender dimension to these forces. This could have been observed through the role of the state, capital, and unions, but it is particularly evident in his otherwise excellent account of the ideology and culture of engineers. Engineering culture, with its fascination with computers and the most automated techniques, is archetypically masculine and would have provided an excellent opportunity for an integration of class and gender perspectives on technological change.

THE GENDERED RELATIONS OF TECHNOLOGY

Class divisions have been central to the analysis presented so far, but the relations between women workers and men workers are of fundamental importance for any discussion of the development of technology. One of the ways that gender divisions interact with technological change is through the price of labor, in that women's wage labor generally costs considerably less than men's. This may affect technological change in at least two ways. First, as we have seen, employers may seek forms of technological change that enable them to replace expensive skilled male workers with low-paid, less unionized female workers. Second, because a new machine has to pay for itself in labor costs saved, technological change may be slower in industries where there is an abundant supply of cheap women's labor.

There is some historical evidence that the rate of technical development has depended, at least in part, on the price and skill flexibility of the available labor force. For example, the clothing industry has remained technologically static since the nineteenth century with little change in the sewing process. There are no doubt purely technical obstacles to the mechanization of clothing production, such as the floppy material involved and changing styles and fashions. Leaving aside the technical difficulties, however, there will be less incentive to invest in automation if skilled and cheap labor power is available to do the job.

Thus there is an important link between women's status as unskilled and low-paid workers, and the uneven pace of technological development. Traditionally it is women who sew and they have been available for low wages, either in Third World countries or as migrant labor in Western capitalist countries. The fact that clothing workers are regarded as unskilled reflects in large measure their lack of industrial strength, which is in turn due to the large pool of women whose social situation forces them to compete in this area of work. It is not possible for anybody to sit down at a sewing machine and sew a garment without previous experience. To be a competent machinist demands considerable knowledge and experience with the machine. Although this is one area where women are at ease with machines, this is seen as women's supposed natural aptitude for sewing, and thus this technical skill is devalued and underpaid.[5]

There is a more direct sense, however, in which gender relations leave their imprint on technology. Recent feminist work has emphasized that distinctions of skill between women's and men's work have as much to do with job control and wage levels as they have to do with actual technique. But this formulation understates the tangible basis of skill. Men selectively design tools and machinery to match the technical skills they have cultivated. Machinery is designed by men with men in mind; industrial technology reflects male power as well as capitalist domination.

THE TRANSFORMATION OF TYPESETTING: BUILDING IN SEX-BIAS

The best examples of the gendering of technology come from Cockburn's (1983) history of typesetting, which provides a detailed description of the technological evolution of the computerized photocomposition system. Like Noble, she shows that automation did not have to proceed in the way that it did. Instead, the form of automation was the result of "deliberate" selection. Cockburn suggests that the technical choices made can be understood only by looking closely at the conflictual relations of production, including the central role of gender relations.

Computerized photocomposition technology has what is known as a QWERTY keyboard. Q-W-E-R-T-Y are the characters on the second top row left-hand side of a conventional typewriter. This is now the standard keyboard incorporated into computers. There was nothing inevitable about this. Electronic circuitry is in fact perfectly capable of producing a Linotype lay on the new-style board. The lay of the Linotype keyboard differs greatly from QWERTY. Not only does it have 90 keys in contrast to 44, the relative position of the letters of the alphabet also differs from that of a typewriter and the keys are larger and spread further apart.

So what politics lay behind the design and selection of this keyboard? In choosing to dispense with the Linotype layout, management was choosing a system that would undermine the skill and power basis of the Linotype operators, the highest paid of all the craftsmen. All the operators would be reduced to novices on the new board, as the inputting would now require little more than good typing ability. This would render typists (mainly women) and Linotype operators (men) equal competitors for the new machines; indeed, it would advantage the women typists. The QWERTY technique was designed with an eye to using the relatively cheap and abundant labor of female typists.

The history of mechanized typesetting offers another instance of clear sex bias within the design of equipment. A nineteenth-century rival to the Linotype was the Hattersley typesetter. Compositors hated technical systems such as the Hattersley typesetter that separated the jobs of composing and distribution. It had a separate mechanism for distributing type, designed for use by girls. The separation of the setting (skilled) and distribution (the unskilled job of putting the letters back in their letter box) was devised as a means of reducing overall labor costs. Compositors feared that employers would try to expand this use of cheaper, unskilled labor once it got a foothold into the composing room.

The Linotype machine, in contrast, did not represent the destruction but merely the mechanization of the compositors' setting skills as a whole. The key aspect of this successful machine was that it eliminated distribution as a task—since letters were formed anew each time by the action of brass mold on molten metal. After the type was used it was simply melted down ready to be reused. The compositors actually welcomed the Linotype machine because it did not depend for its success on the employment of child labor. The men's union, the London Society of Compositors, even wrote a letter to the Linotype Company Ltd. in 1893 congratulating them: "The Linotype answers to one of the essential conditions of trade unionism in that it does not depend for its success on the employment of boy or girl labor." On the contrary, by cutting out the task of distribution, it stopped any possible inroads that boys and women might make into the trade. Thus, in deference to the organizational strength of the union, the Linotype manufacturing company adopted a technology that was beneficial to the union men.

Perhaps, finally, there is another level on which the technology of production reflects male power. Feminists have understandably tended to underemphasize the material realities of physical power, given that women's exclusion from numerous occupations has been legitimated in biological terms. It is often still said that men are naturally stronger and therefore more suited to certain types of work. But as Cockburn (1983, 203) correctly stresses, "the construction of men as strong and capable, manually able and technologically endowed, and women as physically and technically incompetent" is a social process. It is the result of different childhood exposure to technology, the prevalence of different role models, different forms of schooling, and the extreme sex segregation of the job market. The effect of this is an implicit bias in the design of machinery and job content toward male strength.

In composing work, the lifting, and carrying of the form is a case in point. The form is heavy and in fact beyond the strength of not only women but also many men, particularly older men and younger apprentices. By defining this task as one that requires muscle, however, women workers cannot threaten to undercut men's labor. The size and weight of the form is in fact arbitrary. Printing presses and the printed sheet could have been smaller too. Tradition alone has decided at what weight the use of hoists and trolleys to transport the form is introduced. There is nothing natural about units of work. Whether it is hay bales or 50-kilo bags of cement or plaster, they are political in their design. Capitalists and workers have a political interest in the design of work processes. Employers prefer workers to use their brawn when it leads to more efficiency and lower production costs. Male workers use their bodily and technical effectivity to design machinery and work tasks so as to constitute themselves as the capable workers and women as inadequate.

It is overwhelmingly males who design technological process and industrial machinery. It is the knowledge and experience of engineers and of the workers who use the machines that filters through into the shape of new technologies. Mechanical equipment is often manufactured and assembled in ways that make it just too big and heavy for the "average" woman to use. This need not be a conscious process or conspiracy. It is, rather, the outcome of a preexisting pattern of power. This is not to imply that men always design technology for their own use and in their own interests. It is more complex than that. Capital's interest cannot be supposed always to coincide with that of men as a sex. As we have seen, some technologies are designed for use by women in order to break the craft control of men. Thus gender divisions are commonly exploited in the power struggles between capital and labor. In this way, the social relations that shape technology include those of gender as well as class.

NOTES

1. See Wajcman and Probert (1988) for a report of our Australian study on new technology homework, which includes a general literature review.

2. See Thompson (1983, chap. 4) for an extensive discussion of the deskilling debate.

3. This argument is developed at greater length in MacKenzie and Wajcman (1985); especially see the extracts by Bruland and Lazonick.

4. See Elger's (1987) review of several recent studies.

5. For a useful discussion of the undervaluing of skills in the clothing industry, see O'Donnell (1984, Chap. 5).

8

GENDER EQUALITY: TOWARD A THEORY OF CHANGE

Janet Saltzman Chafetz

Any complete theory of social change must address at least three analytically distinct issues: (1) What specific social structures and processes are most fundamental, in the sense that their change generates broad-scale systematic change? (2) How does change occur? (3) What are the effects of change on various subpopulations within a society? For activists who are ideologically committed to a specific change goal, such as feminists seeking gender equality in all areas of sociocultural life, the first issue may be seen as a question of targets of change effort (intermediate goals) and the second as an issue of strategies and tactics (means). The third issue refers to the fact that gender system change can be expected to affect different categories of people in diverse ways, thus affecting the degree of both support and opposition to such change. In turn, this issue is directly related to the extent of, and limits to, change.

 An answer to the first question assumes a theory of social stability. The choice of specific social practices or institutions as the key targets, whose change will presumably ramify into broader system change, logically rests on an explanatory system in which the "general problem" is the dependent variable, and the "targets" are critical explanatory variables. In this way, theories about what features of social life are most important to change first in order to result in general systemic change are theories of the maintenance and reproduction of the phenomenon in question, and vice versa. There is no paucity of such theories in the scholarly feminist literature (see Chafetz 1988a, esp. chaps. 3 and 5). Recently, I have attempted to synthesize a variety of theoretical approaches into an eclectic theory of the maintenance and reproduction of systems of gender stratification (Chafetz 1988b). I review this shortly, preparatory to a discussion of change targets.

 The second issue raised above, concerning how change can and does occur, has received surprisingly little attention from feminist social scientists (see Chafetz 1988a, chap. 5). I outline the major components of an eclectic theory of the process of change in systems of gender stratification. Clearly, change in any system of inequality can occur in either of two directions: increase or decrease. As defined here, change is synonymous with a decrease in gender stratification. The third issue, concerning the differential impact of change on subpopulations, is addressed last, in a discussion that focuses on the limits to change in any one historical period.

GENDER SYSTEM STABILITY: A BRIEF REVIEW

My theory of gender system maintenance and reproduction (Chafetz 1988b) asserts that superior male power, which exists by definition in gender-stratified societies, allows men to coerce women into assuming work roles that reinforce their disadvantaged status at both the macro and the micro levels. Moreover, male power also results in the development of social and interpersonal definitions that devalue women and femininity and strengthen and legitimate the gender system. Yet the coercive potential of men is relatively infrequently employed or perceived. This is the result of several processes that together produce gendered personalities and gender normative choices, most importantly for women. In turn, these function to bolster male power while both hiding and further legitimating the entire system. Undergirding both the coercive and the voluntaristic aspects of the process is a gender division of labor that provides unequal power resources to men and women.

THE DIVISION OF LABOR AND MALE POWER

Gender-stratified societies are those in which males have categorically greater access than females, who are otherwise their social peers (e.g., in terms of social class, age, or race/ethnicity), to the scarce values of their society (Chafetz 1984). By definition, any stratification system implies that the superordinate category has superior power (and usually authority) over the subordinate, although the bases and manifestations of such power may vary extensively cross-culturally and across types of stratification systems. When using the concepts "power" and "authority," I am employing the Weberian conception: (1) authority is legitimated power; (2) power exists when a person or group is able to extract compliance from other persons or groups, even in the face of opposition. The exercise of power, in turn, requires control over resources that are needed and desired by subordinates, and not otherwise sufficiently available to them, and/or the ability to inflict harm on subordinates in the absence of a reciprocal ability. Stated otherwise, power wielders have the wherewithal to coerce or bribe compliers.

I begin by assuming superior male power because my theory addresses the issue of how existing systems of gender stratification are perpetuated. I make one further assumption, based on extensive empirical literature in anthropology and sociology: there exists a gender division of labor by which men and women do different work. Moreover, women's work always includes more responsibility for childrearing and family and household maintenance than does men's, regardless of what other kind of work women may do.

Using an exchange perspective, I argue that at least since the development of settled agrarian societies (that is, societies in which workers produce a surplus), and including industrial ones, the gender division of labor has functioned to place a highly disproportionate amount of the economic resources required for survival in male hands (see Sacks 1974; Vogel 1983; Lipman-Blumen 1976; Blumberg 1984). As husbands, men acquire power at the micro level of the household to the extent that women are economically dependent on them. Women grant compliance to their husbands in order to balance exchanges in which men provide more of the important resources (Parker and Parker 1979; Curtis 1986). That power, in turn, can be used by husbands to sustain the gender division of labor and household responsibility that provides relatively less access to economic rewards for women. Male power at the macro level permits elite men, in their roles as economic, educational, political, and other kinds of gatekeepers, to enforce a gender division of labor that advantages their own gender. The result is that women either work entirely within and for the household and are totally dependent on their husbands, or they work in gender-segregated, relatively low-paid jobs and remain chiefly responsible for household tasks (the double workday). In either case, they collectively lack the resources to seriously challenge male macro power (Curtis 1986; Sacks 1974; Hartmann 1984).

DEFINITIONAL POWER

Superior power resources permit men to exercise both macro and micro-level definitional power. At the macro level, social definitions are created and legitimated by elite members, who control dominant social institutions (political, economic, educational, religious, cultural). Their conceptions of the valuable, good, and true become the socially accepted definitions to a substantial degree. Both historically and in the present, elite members have been overwhelmingly male. Therefore, social definitions are fundamentally androcentric, that is, they reflect a masculine perspective of the world, an assertion made by theorists from such diverse perspectives as Marxist-feminist, labeling, and symbolic interaction (Sacks 1974; Vogel 1983; Hartmann 1984; Ferguson 1980; Schur 1984). To the extent that elites create definitions that function to protect and legitimate their own advantaged status, gender-relevant social definitions will devalue women and femininity and support traits and behaviors for both men and women that reinforce the gender division of labor and male power.

Gender ideologies, stereotypes, and norms constitute the relevant types of social definitions. Gender ideologies "explain" in terms of a broader principle (god, nature) why men and women are different and deserve different (and typically unequal) rights, obligations, responsibilities, and rewards. Gender stereotypes describe the ways in which women and men presumably differ, usually in ways that partially devalue presumed feminine traits and serve to justify the gender division of labor. Gender norms specify behaviors expected of men and women, thereby providing the basis for the stigmatization of nonconformists. They specify behaviors congruent with the gender division of labor and superior male power.

At the micro level of interpersonal interaction, superior male power resources also enable them to control the substance of interactions with women and to define the situation of the interaction (Fishman 1982; Ferguson 1980; Bell and Newby 1976). I call this "micro-definitional power." By exercising such power, men reinforce their resource-based power, especially at the micro level of the household, and help to ensure that their wives' perceptions and evaluations of reality support an androcentric view. Again, this helps sustain the gender division of labor that disadvantages women.

Social and micro-definitional phenomena serve as a bridge between the more coerceive aspects of system maintenance available to men because of their resource power advantages, and voluntaristic compliance by women with the requirements of the status quo. To the extent that women choose to comply with gender norms, accept gender ideologies and stereotypes and acquiesce to male definitions of situations, men need not employ their power— micro or macro—to maintain the status quo. In fact, such choices by women serve to reinforce further gender social definitions and to legitimate the gender division of labor and gender stratification.

GENDER DIFFERENTIATION

Why would women make choices that sustain a system that disadvantages them? Because by adulthood they are different from men in personality, priorities, values, competencies, and cognitive skills. I call this "gender differentiation." There exist three explanations for gender differentiation in the literature. The precise contribution of each is as yet an unanswered empirical question. For now, I posit that all three function in the same direction in gender-stratified societies and therefore reinforce one another.

One approach, associated chiefly with learning and cognitive development theorists, stresses the childhood socialization process by which, beginning at birth, people are taught a gender identity that incorporates substantial conformity to gender norms and that is a very central component of their self-identity (Cahill 1983; Lever 1976; Constantinople 1979). From this perspective, as a result of rewards, punishments, and especially modeling, children come gradually to internalize gender social definitions. As adults, everyday life sociologists argue that people actively seek confirmation of their gendered self-identity in interactions with others by behaving in gender normative ways (Goffman 1977; Cahill 1983; West and Zimmerman 1987).

A second perspective is taken by neo-Freudian feminists, who focus on the subtle but far-reaching effects of the fact that primary caretakers in infancy and early childhood are overwhelmingly female (e.g., Chodorow 1978). In turn, the structure of caretaking, which is an integral part of the gender division of labor, produces different relational capacities in males and females. Finally, the engendered personalities produced in this fashion lead to different role choices for men and women, which reproduce the gender division of labor.

The third perspective argues that the specific roles played by adults, including aspects of empowerment, advancement opportunities, and social isolation or integration, create characteristic responses in terms of attitudes, values, behaviors, and priorities. Because they are located in different types of roles, men and women become differentiated (Kanter 1977; Barron and Norris 1976; Schur 1984; Chafetz 1984). In turn, this strongly affects the probability that they will obtain (or even seek) other types of roles in the future.

Despite their differences, what these three perspectives have in common is the idea that, by some point in adulthood, men and women are really different in myriad ways that affect the choices they make concerning the kinds of work they wish to do (both at home and in the economy) and their priorities among varied roles. Women tend to make choices that reproduce the gender division of labor, and with it superior male power and gender stratification. In the process, they perceive their choices as being as unconstrained as those of men. This obviates the need for men to exercise power in order to maintain the status quo, and it functions to legitimate the entire system.

PIVOTAL CHANGE TARGETS

I have argued that systems of gender inequality are sustained, first and foremost, by a gender division of labor that reinforces superior male power at both the macro and the micro levels. It does so because, regardless of the specific tasks assigned to each gender, those assigned to men generate a greater amount of scarce and valued resources than those assigned to women. The same division of labor, and the superior male power it supports, permits elite men to create social definitions that devalue women and legitimate the gender division of labor and the entire gender system. Moreover, they permit most men to impose their definitions of situations on their own wives and other intimate females, thus further reinforcing the entire structure. Finally, the division of labor contributes in fundamental ways to the development of gendered personalities. In turn, this makes male use of power largely unnecessary, as the gender division of labor appears to result from free choice and is thereby legitimated.

The two pivotal mechanisms sustaining the gender system are superior male power and the gender division of labor, which are inextricably intertwined. I suggest that of the two, the gender division of labor is more potentially amenable to manipulation, as superior male power has sources in addition to the division of labor (see Blumberg 1984). Moreover, power advantages can be reduced only when subordinates develop substantial power resources, which women are prevented from doing in great measure precisely because of the gender division of labor.

Two other targets of change have often been stressed both in the scholarly literature and by feminist activists. The first concerns the process by which gendered personalities are constructed in childhood (e.g., Chodorow 1978; Cahill 1983; Lever 1976; Coser 1986). There is both a practical and logical problem with this. If adults have relatively stable engendered personalities that are set in childhood, how are child socializers to be changed in order to change the process of childhood engenderment? If adults are relatively easily changed, the theoretical assumption of the lifelong and fundamental importance of childhood engenderment is wrong. If adults are difficult to change, social change is all but impossible. I suggest that, in lagged fashion, to the extent that important childhood engenderment does occur, its nature will change in response to substantial change in the gender division of labor.

Other theorists and activists have stressed as a change priority those variables (normative, ideological, and stereotypical) that I term social definitional (e.g., Sanday 1981; Ortner 1974; Giele 1978; Kessler and McKenna 1978; Schur 1984). There is little question that definitional phenomena legitimate the status quo and male advantage. In the absence of such legitimation, however, men nonetheless possess superior power resources that can enable them to sustain the status quo by coercion. Again, it appears to me that definitional phenomena will change (and to some extent already have) in response to changes in the gender division of labor, and the resulting distribution of key power resources, more readily than the reverse. This is not to deny the importance of the development of a set of feminist counterdefinitions. Instead, I suggest that definitional phenomena should be viewed not as primary targets of social change but as a central feminist means designed to bring about change.

Change in the division of labor would have to occur both at the household level and within the public sphere to produce greater gender equality. At the macro level, at least two separate subtargets exist. First, income equality must be achieved, which would contribute substantially to the elimination of micro power differences between husbands and wives. Second, equality in incumbency of elite, gatekeeping positions (social, political, cultural, and economic) must be achieved (see Friedl 1975). These are the positions whose incumbents establish social definitions, as well as distribute concrete opportunities and rewards. Although equality in elite incumbency is probably the most difficult of all goals to achieve, in its absence any other forms that might be achieved would be tenuous and rather easily reversed. At the household level, equality in the division of responsibility and work (which virtually presupposes substantial economic equality as a major power resource) should accomplish two things. First, it would affect the process by which new generations become engendered, presumably leading to more androgynous personalities for both genders. Second, it should equalize men's and women's ability to compete outside the household for labor force and other public-sphere roles. This, in turn, should enhance the probability of achieving the two macro subtargets. A central question, then, is how change in the gender division of labor can occur.

TOWARD A THEORY OF GENDER: SYSTEM CHANGE PROCESSES

There are are two analytically distinct but empirically related avenues toward gender system change that reduces gender inequality. On one hand, there are general social processes that produce such change without the willful or conscious intervention of people committed to producing it. On the other hand, in specific times and places, people (mostly women) organize in a conscious attempt to bring about gender system change. The existence of two avenues to gender system change leads to at least four theoretical issues: (1) What are the important variables that produce unintentional gender system change, and how do they do so? (2) What are the important variables that produce intentional change efforts, and how do they do so? (3) To what extent and how are unintentional processes linked to intentional change efforts? (4) What variables explain the outcomes (relative success in goal achievement) of intentional change efforts?

Unintentional Change

If I begin with the premise that the main support of gender inequality is to be found in the gender division of labor, then the logical place to look for the roots of unintentional gender system change is in phenomena that affect the division of labor. A variety of scholars (e.g., Martin and Voorhies 1975; O'Kelly 1980; Nielsen, 1978; Blumberg 1978; Sanday 1974) have noted that the degree of gender stratification varies substantially by type of society, as defined by technological level and subsistence base (e.g., foraging, horticultural, pastoral, agrarian, industrial). In my theory of the causes of variation in the degree of gender stratification (Chafetz 1984), I attempted to distill from discussions of societal types the underlying variables associated with degree of gender inequality. I argued from a broadly Marxian perspective that the key set of variables are those associated with the manner in which societies structure their productive work activities. Of central importance are the extent to which (1) women, relative to men, control the means and products of production; (2) women participate in those work roles socially defined as most highly valued or centrally important; and (3) women workers are easily replaced—by other available women or by a surplus of men—in their productive roles (see also Blumberg 1984).

Although I postulated a large variety of variables that affect (and in several cases are affected by) these work organizational variables, I concluded that technological variation constitutes the primary explanation of variation in the work organization variables and is therefore the primary independent variable for understanding the degree of gender inequality. With only slight modification in conceptualization, the same argument pertains to the issue of how change occurs. The required modification is in terms of how the critical work organization variable is defined. In the theory I am developing in this chapter, I define the gender division of labor as the central variable of interest. This concept subsumes, but is broader than, the work organizational variables enumerated in my earlier work. The question of interest here, then, is what factors produce unintended changes in the division of labor, such that women's work becomes more similar to men's (and vice versa)—within and outside the home—especially in terms of resources generated and incumbency in elite positions. I postulate that technological change, and an associated increase in economic scale, constitute the primary mechanism that alters the gender division of labor. Second, I argue that changes in the demographic profile of a collectivity may affect the gender division of labor, although in most cases this would be temporary.

Technological change can serve to increase equality in the gender division of labor in at least two ways. First, it may function to enlarge the demand for workers in types of work roles previously monopolized by men and/or in newly emerging or expanding jobs so that a new source of labor must be found (Oppenheimer 1970; Berch 1982). For instance, in the decades since World War II, the scale of production of both goods and services has expanded dramatically in the most highly industrialized nations of the world, in fair measure because of ongoing technological innovations, especially in electronics and communication. This has resulted in an enormous increase in the demand for labor (i.e., the total size of the labor force), especially for labor produced by at least moderately well-educated people. The major pool of people available to fill this demand, who were not already members of the labor force, has been married women, including those with preschool children. The gender division of labor has thus changed, to the extent that, unlike the past, a majority of married women are now involved in the formal labor force, from which they receive some power-relevant resources. The division of labor within the labor market has changed relatively little, however. The genders remain largely segregated into different types of occupations and industries; women's jobs pay considerably less than men's; and elite positions are still filled overwhelmingly by men (Fox and Hesse-Biber 1984). The domestic and familial division of labor between the genders has also undergone little change as yet (Huber and Spitze 1983). Among younger cohorts of college-educated people, however, there appears to be somewhat greater gender equality in terms of both pay and the job deployment in the labor force, and possibly more male participation in domestic and family work in dual-earner couples (Hertz 1986).

In the previous paragraph, the focus of discussion centered on the effect of technological change and economic expansion on the demand for female labor. Technological change can also affect the supply of such labor, to the extent that it reduces women's familial and domestic labor. Technological developments that allow women to control their fertility better constitute one example. Research has consistently shown that women are more apt to supply their labor outside the home when they have fewer children (Stewart, Lykes, and LaFrance 1982). In turn, they choose to have smaller families when there are greater opportunities for their labor outside the household (Cramer 1980; Friedl 1975, 137). The development of products that may be used to reduce the time and effort required to maintain home and family can also enhance women's willingness to assume other work roles (e.g., washing machines, vacuum cleaners, refrigerators, no-iron fabrics, microwave ovens, frozen meals and other convenience foods). Whether or not women actually use these technologies to reduce their domestic and familial labor, as opposed to raising the standards of performance within the household, rests heavily on the options available outside that context, that is, on the demand for their labor elsewhere.

In the absence of technological change and economic expansion, an increase in the demand for female workers can also result from a shortage of male adults. There are two primary reasons why this sometimes occurs: war and migration. During wartime, women are often called upon to assume men's jobs. But unless casualty rates are exceptionally high (e.g., the Soviet Union after World War II), the prior status quo follows hard on the heels of the end of hostilities (e.g., the United States after World War II: see Trey 1972). In the absence of technological and economic changes that significantly increase the total demand for labor, the prior status quo will tend to reemerge after a period of time, as the adult sex ratio begins to return to normal.

Migration is often highly gender specific, especially rural-to-urban and cross-national. Where males constitute a disproportionate number of migrants, the demand for female labor may increase in the sending community or society, permitting women access to heretofore male-monopolized roles. This will occur only if there is not a problem of general overpopulation in the sending community. Given overpopulation, the migrants represent a surplus, unemployable male population, which leaves behind enough men to meet demand. This, in fact, is probably the most typical case. That is, selective male migration probably occurs primarily because of the absence of demand for their labor in the sending community or society.

In summary, I am arguing that the gender division of labor sometimes changes in the direction of increasing women's access to resource-generating work roles because technological or demographic changes create a demand for labor that men cannot fill. Technological change may also enhance women's ability and willingness to supply their work in other-than-traditional roles, but, in the absence of demand, this is all but irrelevant.

If the overall demand for women's labor remains high over a long enough period of time, then their increased access to power resources should begin to affect both the division of household labor and their entry into more highly coveted labor force roles, in an equalitarian direction. As the gender division of labor changes, cognitive dissonance theory suggests that social definitions concerning the appropriate duties and attributes of each gender should begin to change as well, to conform to an increasing reality. Given that women take on new work roles well before men's labor in the domestic and familial context increases, social definitions concerning femininity change more quickly and extensively than those concerning masculinity. The United States has experienced precisely this form of attitude change in recent decades. Public opinion became significantly more supportive of married women assuming labor force roles, including mothers of young children; of equal employment and educational opportunity for women; of women as political leaders and elected officials; and of women's reproductive rights. Much less opinion change concerning the roles and obligations of men seems to have occurred, however (see Harris 1987). I predict that, barring economic collapse, in most highly industrialized nations, including the United States, married women will remain firmly entrenched in the labor force, and over time their occupational deployment will become more similar to that of men. The power resources generated by this will result, in time, in change in men's work and in social definitions of masculinity, in a more equalitarian and androgynous direction (which is not to say that I am predicting full gender equality any time soon, but more about that later).

Intentional Change Efforts: The Emergence and Growth of Women's Movements

Relative to men, for several millennia women almost everywhere have been disadvantaged in their access to societal scarce and valued resources. Yet only occasionally and in some societies have they organized and attempted as collectivities to change the gender system of their societies. A. Gary Dworkin and I developed and partially tested a theory that attempts to explain the conditions that give rise to women's movements (Chafetz and Dworkin 1986, 1987b).

We define women's movements as change-oriented, grassroots movements consciously oriented to rectifying socially rooted disadvantages specific to females, which they experience on the basis of their gender. Women's movements are composed of at least one organization that is independent of control by governmental, political party, or other organizational entities, which in turn are controlled by men. We found that they date no further back in time than the mid-nineteenth century, and can be divided into a first (mid-nineteenth to mid-twentieth centuries) and a second wave (those that have arisen since about 1968). While nations around the world have experienced them (we documented thirty-one nations for the first wave, sixteen for the second), they have varied extensively in size.

The theoretical question we raised was this: what accounts for the emergence and growth of women's movements in particular times and places? We found that women's movements arise when macrostructural change results in "role expansion" for women, that is, in the development of new, nontraditional opportunities for a sizable number of especially middle-class women, who constitute the pool from which the vast majority of activists is drawn. Industrialization, urbanization, and the growth of the middle class constituted the critical structural changes in the first wave. They functioned to expand certain public, but not including employment, roles of married middle-class women (e.g., roles in temperance, socialist, nationalist, and other social movements, and social welfare and philanthropic roles). They also served to increase the access of females to formal education, and to expand the employment opportunities of single women. In the second wave, in highly industrialized societies, vastly increased labor force participation by married women was the critical form of role expansion, and it resulted from extensive economic expansion in the 1950s and 1960s. Further increases in educational access again constituted an important form of female role expansion. The greater the magnitude of the structural changes, the larger the women's movement tended to become.

We postulated that role expansion for women often results in "status/role dilemmas" or strains. We defined this as contradictions between socially defined, ascribed gender norms and those associated with newly emerging social roles. Women may find themselves treated according to traditional norms inappropriate to their achieved status/role, or they may be expected to behave in inappropriate or contradictory ways.

Women who experience expanded roles are likely to come into increasing contact with men whose roles, competencies, and credentials are equal—even inferior—to their own, who nonetheless experience superior opportunities and rewards. Using reference-group theory, we argued that this contact prompts at least some of these women to change their comparative reference group from other women—especially those who remain in traditional roles—to men. In turn, change in reference group will prompt feelings of relative deprivation.

Because of their expanded roles, and especially in urban settings, these women are likely to come into increased contact with one another. Their status/role dilemmas and sense of relative deprivation can thereby be shared and refined. As a result, at least some members of this growing pool of women will collectively develop a perception that their problems and disadvantages are not individually caused but are shared on the basis of gender and produced by the social system. They are likely to develop a view that the reward and opportunity systems are unfair and illegitimate. They are, therefore, likely to develop an ideology and set of goals consciously oriented to changing the system that they now perceive as unfairly disadvantaging them. In short, much as Marx argued concerning the development of worker consciousness, we argue for gender consciousness. Moreover, their expanded roles are likely to give women increased access to the tangible and intangible resources that resource mobilization theorists argue are required to mount a social movement, including networks, contacts, organizational and public-speaking skills, and money (Gale 1986; Zald and McCarthy 1979; Jenkins 1983). In this they may be aided by men who benefit from ongoing changes in women's roles and/or suffer by dint of the problems faced by women with whom they have familial or other intimate relationships.

Not all—or even a majority—of women who experience expanded roles become activists. Nevertheless, a larger pool of such women results in a larger-sized movement. The emergence and growth of women's movements, therefore, reflect ongoing changes in the status and roles of women, which in turn result from macrostructural changes.

The Relationship of Unintentional to Intentional Change Efforts: Achieving Goals

Social movements have two basic ways that they can directly influence elite members to enact the changes they wish to see. They can make it costly for elites to fail to make change and/or they can make it rewarding for them to do so. The extent to which a movement is able to raise the cost or reward ante for elites depends in part on the size and resources of the movement itself, but also on factors that are idiosyncratic to each case. In what follows I suggest some means that could or have been employed by women's movements to directly affect the behavior of elites on behalf of their goals.

One way to make the status quo costly is physical violence and property destruction. Black urban riots in the United States during the latter half of the 1960s helped persuade many public policymakers and employers to make at least some token changes on behalf of the black community. With the exception of a minority of militant suffragists in Great Britain, however, women's movements have been overwhelmingly peaceful and nonviolent. Since suffrage, if women are well organized in mass numbers, they have potentially been able to use the ballot to punish political elite members who fail to support their goals. But women's movements have been unable to command sufficient votes to employ this tactic in other than scattered elections, and then usually only on single-issue grounds (e.g., pay equity for state employees, ERA). Nor have women's movements (as distinct from labor unions chiefly composed of women) used the labor strategies of strike and boycott other than around very specific issues of a relatively minor nature (e.g., the dumping of infant formula in Third World nations by Nestlé) or unsuccessfully (e.g., the boycott of states that failed to ratify ERA). The one cost tactic that women's movement groups, at least in the contemporary United States, have used extensively and fairly successfully has been the legal suit against employers who discriminate. This type of action presupposes the existence of antidiscrimination legislation, which already symbolizes extensive elite action on behalf of women. In general, it appears that women's movements have either largely ignored or been unsuccessful in their attempts at tactics that render too costly elite opposition to major demands. This may be because even mass women's movements have lacked sufficient numbers and resources to employ cost tactics, other than violence, effectively, and violence seems to be especially incongruent with a female gender consciousness.

Nonetheless, since the first signs of the emergence of women's movements in the mid-nineteenth century, they appear to have achieved important intermediate goals. In the first wave, women in numerous societies gained expanded access to educational opportunities, some changes in legal and property rights for married women, the vote, and assorted other changes specific to particular cases. In contemporary women's movements, women in a number of nations have achieved better control over their reproduction through access to contraception and abortion, legislation rendering illegal discrimination in the economy and educational institutions, and assorted other legal changes, policies, and programs that are specific to each society. If, by and large, such changes have not resulted from coercion, how have they been won?

In the last section I argued that women's movements emerge and grow to substantial size largely because of a set of factors associated with industrialization, economic expansion, and urbanization. Recall that earlier I argued that unintentional gender system change results primarily from technological development and economic expansion, which serve to open up new role opportunities to women. When we combine these two theoretical arguments, what we see is that the same basic macrostructural factors that spur unintended change contribute in a fundamental way to the emergence and growth of women's movements; the emergence and especially the growth of such movements signifies or indicates that change in the gender system is already under way.

From this vantage point, women's movements do not in fact produce change as much as they manifest and expedite a process already in motion. Women's movements that grow beyond an incipient level and attract substantial grassroots support do so because ongoing changes are producing problems and needed resources for a large pool of women, the pool from which activists are drawn. But that pool is substantially larger than the number who become activists. Moreover, most members of this pool are related to men, many of whom are adversely affected by the problems confronting the women to whom they are attached. In this way, a growing segment of society comes to support at least some of the changes propounded by a women's movement.

The major importance of women's movements is to articulate specific proposed changes and a rhetoric or ideology that legitimates such changes, for the bulk of potential supporters who are not themselves activists, including at least some members of economic, educational, and especially political elites. Women's movements develop a set of social definitions that are counter to the traditional ones that serve to legitimate and perpetuate the status quo. A women's movement ideology falls largely on deaf ears until a sufficiently large pool of women (and the men to whom they are attached) encounter problems that can be made sense of by it. The development and dissemination of such an ideology and programs of specific change targets constitute major mechanisms that allow nonactivists to reformulate into social and political terms their definitions of the origins and solutions to personally experienced problems. In the most recent wave of women's movement activism, this came to be called "consciousness raising." It is important to note that it occurs not only in self-conscious groups of activists but in varying degrees among significant segments of the mass public. It does so primarily through the dissemination of ideas by activists through the media of mass communication.

Often, especially large movements will be characterized by substantial ideological and programmatic diversity, ranging from calls for moderate, relatively minor rule changes to the radical overhaul of the entire system. Not only will the public rarely if ever subscribe to the full ideology and program developed by activists, it will tend to support the more moderate proposals. Moreover, the public will pick and choose among proposals, supporting those that appear most salient to their own personal problems. In this way, elite response, especially governmental response to public pressure, will also be piecemeal. It too will usually support most readily the least radical policies, programs, and laws (see Giele 1978), namely, those that the majority of the public deem most important for their own lives and those of family members.[1] The women's movement per se does not directly reward elites for their support. It expedites public support for change and, therefore, the public rewarding or punishment of elites who support, or fail to support, such change. Activists, even in mass movements, rarely reach sufficient numbers to accomplish this on their own.[2]

In some cases, governments respond to demands made by a women's movement in the absence of such a shift in public opinion. Indeed, they may even respond positively to demands made by a very small women's movement. For instance, four nations enfranchised women before World War I, and in none of these cases had a women's movement grown to mass proportions. Kennedy established a Presidential Commission on the Status of Women and Congress passed the 1963 Equal Pay Act and Title VII of the Civil Rights Act, all before the reemergence of a mass women's movement in this country. These kinds of governmental actions reflect political struggles idiosyncratic to specific times and places. A given political party may have supported (or opposed) female suffrage as part of a calculus of how many additional votes it would net versus its opposition. According to Rupp and Taylor (1987), Kennedy's commission resulted from pressure by those opposed to ERA, including, especially, organized labor, who felt that such a commission could effectively bury the amendment, thereby maintaining protective legislation for women. Title VII of the Civil Rights Act resulted from a failed attempt by southern senators to defeat that act, which was designed to protect blacks. This suggests that women's issues may become enmeshed in other political struggles, and whether women gain or not is less a question of their collective actions than of the political fortunes of contending (male) elite factions. It is possible that women's movements could manipulate political struggles in such a way as to gain some of their objectives in the process. Nevertheless, the historical and cross-national record suggests that when women's movement issues become enmeshed in other political conflicts, women lose more often than they gain in the process (see Chafetz and Dworkin 1986, esp. chap. 1).

In summary of this section, I have argued that when women's movements emerge and gather substantial grassroots support, it is because a change process is already under way that is seriously affecting the roles and status of large numbers of women. Primarily through their development and dissemination of a counterideology and a program of specific targets of change, women's movements affect public opinion. In turn, the pressure of changed public opinion is primarily responsible for new laws, programs, and policies developed by elites. In this way, women's movements expedite rather than directly cause change.

CONCLUSIONS: TARGET AND PROCESS

I have argued that the chief target of change must be the gender division of labor, especially the demand for substantially greater access of women to elite positions. It is possible that in successive "steps" women will gain sufficient power resources, primarily through reductions in the gender division of labor, to be in a position finally to use their resources as consumers, workers, voters, and so on to make their continued exclusion from elite positions too costly for male elites to sustain. Or they may use those resources to up the reward ante for male elites who are in a position to allow them entry.

I do not think that this will happen any time soon for women. The impetus of mass women's movement activism seems to have about played itself out for now, with a substantially incomplete agenda left. Barring economic calamity, the remainder of this century and the early years of the next should witness increasing societal accommodation to the fact that most women spend almost their entire adult life in the labor force in advanced industrial societies.[3] Issues such as childcare, male contribution to household and family work, parental leave, and comparable worth require solutions just to resolve the strains already produced by the wholesale addition of women to the labor force. None of these seriously addresses the issue of the deployment of women within the labor force and especially elite roles. Perhaps when it comes, the next major wave will deal primarily with the unresolved issue of deployment. If it does, it may eventuate in full gender equality.

Acknowledgment: Helen Rose Ebaugh, A. Gary Dworkin, and Ruth Wallace read and commented on earlier drafts of this chapter. I am grateful for their helpful suggestions.

NOTES

1. Nonpolitical elites respond to public opinion just as elected officials may. Economic institutions may alter their hiring practices and advertisements; the media of mass communication may make changes in their programming; universities may institute new courses, programs, and admissions policies; foundations and community agencies may fund new types of projects; religions may change wording and admit women to ritual and organizational roles; police and courts may alter their policies toward rape and family violence victims; and so on.

2. In our research on women's movements, Dworkin and I (1968) found that in the few cases where nations experienced an unambiguously mass movement, only about 3 percent of the public belonged to movement groups or organizations.

3. A more depressing scenario is also quite possible. As advanced industrial societies continue to lose traditionally male manufacturing jobs to both automation and inexpensive Third World labor, men may move into the female service occupations that currently provide jobs for most employed women. If these jobs fail to continue to expand at a rapid rate, it is possible that men will displace women from them, lowering the demand for women's labor outside the home and thereby increasing gender inequality.

9

HIGH TECHNOLOGY AND THE NEW INTERNATIONAL DIVISION OF LABOR

Manuel Castells

Four main processes appear to underlie the conditions for competition and development between countries and between economic units in an economic system characterized by increasing interdependence across national boundaries:

1. Productive decentralization of multinational corporations and their dependent networks, in a worldwide search for comparative advantage in production costs and market penetration
2. Diversification of competitive actors in the world market, with the entry of newly industrialized countries in the international economy
3. The resurgence of protectionism in the core economies, and the countervailing strategies by countries and firms aimed at overcoming or limiting the protectionist threat
4. The growing importance of technology transfer in international economic relations, both as a competitive instrument and as a bargaining chip in strategic alliances

Let us examine sequentially these different processes, with a specific focus on the role played by high technology in each.

DECENTRALIZATION OF MANUFACTURING AND THE SUPERCESSION OF THE NEW INTERNATIONAL DIVISION OF LABOR

A key element in the restructuring of advanced capitalist economies since the late 1960s has been the decentralization of production facilities to lower-cost areas, taking advantage of new technologies in telecommunications, transportation, and manufacturing. This "world assembly line," of which the electronics and automobile industries have been the most characteristic examples, provided the empirical basis for the success of the theory of the "new international division of labor" elaborated in the late 1970s (Frobel, Henricks and Kreye 1980). According to its typical formulation, the theory argued that multinational companies would increasingly shift their manufacturing from the core to the periphery of the capitalist system, to avoid high wages and social controls imposed on them by organized labor and socially responsible governments. Tapping the unlimited reserve of cheap labor in developing countries, as well as the support of Third World governments anxious to attract foreign capital, this process would install a new international division of labor under which advanced services and the upper-level functions of high-technology industries would remain in the core, while unskilled manufacturing would proliferate in a new industrializing, dependent periphery. Manufacturing unemployment at the core and overexploitation and economic disarticulation in the periphery would be the most immediate impacts of the new strategy, a strategy that would reinforce the multinationals' position over each individual national economy.

Indeed, the process of productive decentralization of American electronics companies in Asia (Henderson 1986), of automobile producers in Mexico (Hinojosa and Morales 1986), of American and European manufacturers of consumer durables in Latin America (Touraine 1988), and, later, of Japanese companies in East and Southeast Asia (Ng, Hirono, and Akrasanee 1987) seemed to follow the predicted pattern. High technology played a major role in such developments at two levels: (1) it made materially possible the spatial decentralization of activities in scattered locations, while reintegrating the production and management processes within the same firm (Kaplinsky 1985); (2) because of the sharp division of labor, and of distinct requirements for labor skills resulting from new technologies, both among producers and users of microelectronics, it became possible, and even necessary, to differentiate centers of innovation from skilled manufacturing, and both operations from assembly and testing (Castells 1988a).

But the rapid development of automation technologies has undermined the importance of unskilled labor in overall production costs, thus removing a powerful incentive for decentralizing assembly operations, since these can be easily automated in locations closer to the innovation centers in the core economies (Sanderson 1987). Furthermore, an argument has been made that excessive separation of assembly from both R&D and final markets has affected manufacturing quality, accounting for the loss of competitiveness of American firms (that chose offshoring of production) vis-à-vis Japanese firms (that, until recently, emphasized automation and quality work in Japan) (Stowsky 1987). Finally, the increasing importance of customized production in high technology manufacturing puts a premium on locations that can work in close interaction with the main industrial and advanced services markets, overwhelmingly concentrated in the OECD area (Borrus, n.d.).

On the basis of these different trends, a number of authors, with Juan Rada being most prominent among them, forecast the "relocation back North" of decentralized manufacturing facilities, halting the process of peripheral decentralization and thus reversing the "new international division of labor" (Rada 1982). Yet there is little empirical evidence of such reverses, with the exception of isolated cases, such as the relocation of Fairchild from Hong Kong to Maine in the United States. Indeed, there has been, in fact, a new wave of peripheral industrialization in cheaper areas of the Third World, particularly in Asia (in Thailand, the Philippines, India, Malaysia), as the original locations (e.g., Singapore, the Republic of Korea, Hong Kong and Taiwan, China) upgrade their technological level, thus forming a new echelon in the hierarchy of the decentralized production process (Chen 1987).

Several factors seem to account for the persistence of decentralization under the new technological conditions. And these factors also account for the fact that decentralized manufacturing is being transformed even if the location of the plant does not change.

First, as Dieter Ernst has argued, "Any change in the current pattern of manufacturing and sourcing would involve substantial production costs, both in terms of closing down plants, reshuffling supply and market networks, and in terms of benefits foregone that could be reaped from achieving even higher stages of internationalization. Thus, the mobility of capital invested during previous rounds of internationalization of electronics manufacturing is likely to be much lower than originally expected" (Ernst 1985).

Second, many countries, particularly in Asia, remain attractive not only in terms of labor costs, but in terms of government support, tax incentives, and flexible regulations (Scott and Angel 1986).

Third, existing production sites can upgrade their technological level by improving the quality of their engineering and technical labor force. Thus, Singaporean electrical engineers or Indian software computer scientists have become a major element in determining the comparative advantage of different sites for high-technology manufacturing by raising the labor cost factor to a higher and more significant level: the cost of the engineering labor force (Henderson 1987). Thus, automation is taking place, but very often in the location of existing facilities, provided that the national technological infrastructure is upgraded, in terms of education, training of engineers and technicians, development of higher learning and scientific institutions, and upgrading of the telecommunications and transportation infrastructure (Chen 1987).

Fourth, Japanese companies, stimulated by a rampant yen and increasing land and labor costs in Japan, and aiming at diversifying their locations to overcome protectionism in the United States and Europe, are decentralizing their manufacturing operations, particularly in Southeast Asia, thus contributing to the growth of an advanced industrial complex in the region, in terms of forward and backward linkages both with other multinational companies and with local suppliers (Tan and Kapur 1986).

Fifth, one of the common fundamental assumptions of both the "new international division of labor" theory and of the "relocation back North" thesis is being proven wrong, namely, to equate the use of manual labor in the Third World with the inability to introduce advanced manufacturing technologies. Recently, Shaiken and Herzenberg (1987), in a well-designed study, put this assumption to the test of empirical research. They analyzed three automobile plants of the same company using exactly the same advanced, automated equipment, and manufacturing the same product, in the United States, Canada, and Mexico (confidentiality forbids disclosure of the company's name). The findings are startling. In spite of a young, inexperienced workforce, the Mexican plant achieved, within eighteen months, 80 percent of the machine efficiency of the U.S. plant, and 75 percent of its labor productivity, with quality being intermediate between the Canadian plant (lower) and the U.S. plant (slightly higher). Shaiken and Herzenberg explain the performance by three factors: (1) although inexperienced, the Mexican labor force was highly educated and motivated; (2) work procedures allowed for teamwork and quality-control groups; (3) managers and engineers from around the world were brought into the plant and acted as on-site supervisors, training the workers and forming teams with them, so to avoid a long period of nonsupervised, spontaneous learning. Thus, efficient training of an educated labor force accounted for rapid productivity gains that, combined with major savings in labor costs (one-tenth of equivalent wages in the United States) made the Mexican plant the most profitable of the three, while allowing for the introduction of advanced microelectronics-based equipment.

Thus, against the "relocation back North" thesis, it seems that automation and flexible manufacturing technologies do not reverse the process of decentralization, although multinational companies now have more options, combining automation and location to obtain an optimal mix between production costs, production quality, and market accessibility. There is a slowdown of the process of decentralization of new facilities toward developing countries, but, at the same time, a reinforcement of existing production complexes, with the upgrading of their technological levels and the addition of new companies from Japan and western Europe.

On the other hand, against the "new international division of labor" theory, the new industrialization processes are not limited to routine assembly operations and are not exclusively based on low wages (Deyo 1987). There is a dynamism in the development of the new productive structure organized at the world level. Market penetration becomes more important than labor costs, thus underscoring the importance of locating key facilities in the OECD area (Ohmae 1985). Peripheral industrialization can upgrade its technological level, thus moving up the ladder of the international division of labor. Such dynamism is entirely dependent on the capacity of countries to improve their technological infrastructure, however, particularly in terms of the quality of their technical labor force and in the general level of education, in addition to the introduction of reliable communication facilities. The real cleavage appears to be less between advanced technology and unskilled assembly than between countries integrated into the international structure of production and those excluded from it because they do not offer the minimum conditions required to incorporate up-to-date technologies and so cannot compete in an interdependent world, regardless of labor costs (Ernst 1987). In this fundamental sense, the "new international division of labor" has been made "old" by the strategic importance of advanced manufacturing technologies for the productivity of economies and the profitability of firms (UNCTAD 1984).

Furthermore, the new international division of labor thesis sought to explain the processes of peripheral industrialization by exclusive reference to the patterns of location of multinational corporations from the OECD area. Yet a significant part of the transformation of the international economy originates from competitive strategies by newly industrialized countries, on the basis of government policies and the investment decisions of domestic firms.

THE ROLE OF TECHNOLOGY IN THE COMPETITIVENESS OF NEWLY INDUSTRIALIZING COUNTRIES (NICS)

The high rate of economic growth of a number of developing countries over the past twenty-five years has forced substantial revision of economic development theories (Harris 1986). Starting from a dependent position in the international division of labor, these countries have been able to compete in the world economy on the basis of manufacturing exports, and they have improved their relative position in the world economy (Chen 1985). At the same time, they have substantially raised their standards of living, although often at the price of social equity and political democracy. While the experience of the newly industrializing countries is generally associated with the four "Asian tigers" (the Republic of Korea, Hong Kong, Singapore and Taiwan, China), Brazil has also become a major competitor in the international economy, with a surplus in the manufacturing trade balance for the first time for any Latin American country. In addition, processes of export-oriented industrialization have become very important in the economies of many countries, including Mexico and Chile in Latin America, and Malaysia,

Thailand, the Philippines, and India in Asia. Furthermore, this model of export-oriented growth is making its appeal felt throughout the developing world.

Indeed, at the base of the superior performance of the East Asian NICs, as compared with other developing areas, such as Latin America, there appears to be a combination of an export-oriented economic policy with the ability to compete effectively for and win market shares in the world market for manufactured goods. For instance, in the 1950s South American countries as a whole had a higher level of development and were experiencing higher rates of growth than their East Asian counterparts. Yet the import substitution policies they followed prevented them from benefiting from the dramatic expansion of world trade in the past twenty-five years, so that they fell behind most of East Asia in absolute levels of development, and behind South and Southeast Asia in growth rates, particularly in the 1980s. Fishlow (1986) has analyzed comparatively the composition of the export performance of Asian and Latin American countries. In the export growth of each country, for two periods (1962–72 and 1972–82), he distinguished three components of the change in exports: world trade growth; the internal composition of the export sector of each country; and the competitiveness of each economy in the world market. The main performers in rates of export growth and, ultimately, in rates of GNP growth are those who fare better in competitiveness over the two periods (Republic of Korea, Malaysia, Brazil and Taiwan, China). But among these high competitors in the world economy, some (namely, Malaysia and Brazil) were slowed down because they were unable to change sufficiently the internal composition of their export structure. Thus it is both competitiveness and adaptability to the world economic environment, and particularly to the changes in demand and industrial structure in the OECD countries, that account for sustained export performance, underlying hypergrowth. Although Fishlow does not include Hong Kong and Singapore in his calculations, our educated guess is that the data for these two countries would point in the same direction.

In a different study, Fernando Fanzylber (1986) has compared the performance in the penetration in the world market by exports from the Republic of Korea, Spain, and Yugoslavia, with those from the major Latin American economies, Brazil, Mexico, and Argentina. He uses as an indicator the world market share in capital goods, automobiles, and consumer electronics. The study points to a greatly superior performance of the Republic of Korea both in market shares and competitiveness over time, with Brazil improving its competitiveness during the early 1980s.

The factors that account for the performance of the Asian NICs in world competition, in comparison with the rest of developing countries, are too complex to be discussed in detail in this paper. Nevertheless, for the sake of our analysis, a few remarks could be useful. The four typical NICs are very different in their industrial structure: Singapore is structured around the connection between the state and multinational corporations (Castells 1988b) Hong Kong's manufacturing exports are mainly due to domestic firms, with small and medium business playing a decisive role in both production and exports (Youngson 1982). The Republic of Korea's economy is structured around the tight connection between the state and the large *chaebol* (Lim 1985). And Taiwan, China (Gold 1986) presents a diversified industrial structure made up of large local firms, multinational corporations, and family businesses, all supported financially and technologically by a dirigiste state.

Thus, the NICs do not represent an extension of the "new international division of labor," nor are they an expression of an endogenous process of development based on import substitution and the growth of the domestic market. They combine four common characteristics that seem to be key elements for the performance of developing countries in the new world economy: (1) an outward orientation of the economy that makes international competitiveness the condition for economic growth and redistribution; (2) a developmental state[1] that decisively intervenes in the basic conditions for economic growth, explicitly in the case of Republic of Korea, Singapore, Taiwan, China, and in a more subtle manner in the case of Hong Kong, in spite of the misleading ideology of "positive nonintervention" (Castells, Goh, and Kwok 1988); (3) an educated population, able to adapt to changing conditions of production and trade; (4) a continuous process of technological upgrading, combining government policies and technology transfer from multinational corporations, particularly in electronics. It this latter factor that largely accounts for the ability of the NICs to modify the composition of their output, thus not only enhancing their competitiveness but also benefiting from higher value added in new segments of the world market. Latin America as a whole lags far behind the technological level of the four Asian NICs. The major industrializing country in that region and the only real performer in manufacturing exports, Brazil, is the one that also has the highest level of technological development, particularly in information technologies. Brazil accounts for 75 percent of the computer industry in Latin America and 59 percent of the computer industry in all developing countries. It is in third place in the world, after the United States and Japan, in its ability to supply its own computer needs (Kaplinsky 1986). In more general terms, Dosi and Soete (1983) have shown the statistical relationship between technological level and performance in world trade.

The higher technological level of the Asian NICs and of Brazil, an important element in explaining their competitiveness, seems to derive from a combination of government policies and technology transfer from multinational corporations. The Republic of Korea, Singapore, and Taiwan, China have all had explicit policies of technological upgrading that range from education and training of engineers and scientists abroad, to the formation of science and technology parks and to the financing of technological development programs. Brazil gave full priority to the computer industry, actually closing the microcomputer market to foreign companies to allow a local industry to thrive (Evans 1985). Even the self-declared noninterventionist Hong Kong government reversed its policy and set up a productivity program during the 1980s, as a result of the Report of the Committee on Industrial Diversification (1979) that concluded that there was a gradual loss of competitiveness vis-à-vis other NICs as a result of Hong Kong's lack of adequate technological infrastructure (Castells forthcoming). Multinational corporations accepted some limited technology transfer as a way to locate in a favorable environment and, in the case of Brazil and the Republic of Korea, to penetrate a promising market. The main element in the process of technological development, however, was the ability to diffuse such technology in the industrial structure of the NICs. Such diffusion was possible as a result of a number of key factors: incentives provided by government policies; the existence of a pool of engineering workers; receptivity of firms to technological enhancement as a way to step up their competitiveness vis-à-vis the second-tier NICs, which had started to catch up in terms of production costs but could not compete in quality; and, above all the existence of a well-developed industrial structure that could act as supplier to the multinational firms, learning the new technologies in the process (Carnoy 1987).

It must be emphasized that technological policies always pinpoint information technologies as being strategically decisive and dedicate fewer resources to technologies with less impact on commercial and industrial applications, with the major exception of the Brazilian nuclear program. The strategic choice, made in the early 1970s, of information technologies as tools of manufacturing and management, and as products for expanding world markets, was an important factor in the success of the Asian, and to a lesser extent Latin American, NICs in the midst of the period of crisis and slow growth that have characterized the core economies since the mid-1970s. But this performance triggered the possibility of protectionist policies, which are already reshaping the world economy, even before their implementation.

THE RESTRUCTURING OF THE INTERNATIONAL ECONOMY IN THE SHADOW OF PROTECTIONISM

The competitive challenge of export-oriented peripheral industrialization is met with increasing concern in the core economies. The labor movement in OECD countries leads the charge against unfair competition and accuses multinationals of overexploiting workers in the Third World while destroying jobs in the OECD (Bluestone and Harrison 1982). In fact, the real threat comes from the entry into the international economy of low-production-cost countries that, at the same time, are advancing rapidly along the learning curve of manufacturing quality, while being more flexible in adapting to the world market. To be sure, workers in these countries receive incomparably lower wages and work in much harsher conditions. Compared to the deprivation of rural areas or the petty commodity activities predominant in most Third World cities, however, the new manufacturing industries clearly represent an improvement.

While the prominent Asian and Latin American NICs are generally considered to be the main potential victims of a protectionist era, in fact much of the developing world will be deeply hurt, should such a perspective materialize. In sum, the process of peripheral industrialization has spilled over way beyond the "four tigers" and represents a fundamental element of the development dynamic for most of Asia. This dynamic is currently jeopardized by protectionist policies in the OECD.

Faced with such major threat, firms and governments in the newly industrializing world are adopting several strategies:

1. The first is to invest in the OECD economies. Thus, a good share of the textile industry in the UK, Ireland, Portugal, Greece, and in the southern United States is being revitalized by investments from the Republic of Korea, Hong Kong, and Taiwan, China, among others. Taiwanese surplus in foreign reserves is showing up in Silicon Valley, buying high-technology firms to link them up with firms in Taiwan, China so as to rotate skilled engineers, acquire technology, and retain market access. The Korean automobile industry is following the path of its Japanese teachers, locating complete production plants in the United States and Canada. Thus the new international division of labor theory is being turned upside down, when firms of the poor overexploited countries rush back North to take advantage of the high wages and strong class consciousness of workers in the industrialized countries. But it is obvious that most of the developing world has neither the capital nor the technological capability necessary to reindustrialize America to make up for the offshoring of manufacturing by U.S multinationals. This investment strategy is limited to a few firms of a few countries and cannot counter the protectionist threat for the process of peripheral industrialization as a whole.
2. A second strategy for the upper tier of the NICs consists in establishing subcontracting networks by lower-cost countries so that higher tariffs can be compensated by lower production costs. In

addition, a multilocational pattern allows greater diversification of the import quotas, and builds up a broader base for political lobbying vis-à-vis the OECD countries. This is in particular the case for Hong Kong industrialists, who have proceeded with massive subcontracting to Chinese companies, particularly in the Pearl River Delta region, where it is estimated that about 6,000 firms and 1 million workers produce under such arrangements with Hong Kong parent firms.[2]

3. A third strategy consists in upgrading the technological level of both processes and products, thus becoming competitive in the same terms as advanced industrialized economies, with a bonus for the flexibility of production conditions in the developing countries. Brazil, the Republic of Korea, Hong Kong, and Taiwan, China are clearly engaged in this strategy, as well as Singapore, in a more indirect manner (since the upgrading in the latter case is generally undertaken by foreign multinationals). It seems that, in the medium term, it will become difficult to compete in the world market without a strong technological basis that could make possible better quality, lower cost, and greater flexibility. The problem with this strategy, however, is that it is unlikely to generate as many jobs as did the labor-intensive pattern of the preceding stage of development.

Nevertheless, the bottom line remains that the development process entirely based on an outward-oriented economy, focused on the OECD markets, has reached its limits. While a substantial retrenchment of international trade is unthinkable, barring a major world crisis, it appears that new expansion, still essential for most of the planet, will have to articulate exports with a more dynamic domestic market. Such a strategy implies simultaneous treatment of three major concerns: an increase in purchasing power, through governmental expansionary policies and income redistribution; an improvement in the quality and productivity of domestic industrial production, in order to be able to compete with foreign industries, including those of developed economies in search of new markets; and the transformation of consumption patterns, away from goods and services adapted to the developed economies toward the actual needs of developing societies (e.g., better public transportation, instead of automobiles for export). In all cases, technological development will be a fundamental variable in allowing economic restructuring and in redefining production and consumption patterns.

The threat of protectionism will impose a ceiling on the potential for developing countries to rely entirely on manufacturing exports. It will force them to upgrade their technological level and to expand their domestic markets. But these new markets cannot be generated unless there is a continuing income growth that will still depend, by and large, on competitiveness in the world economy. And the basic condition for the renewal of such competitiveness is the managerial and technological upgrading of the new peripheral industrialization. Thus, under the current conditions of a major technological gap between North and South, one of the keys for access to a new stage of development lies in the effective process of technology transfer.

TECHNOLOGY TRANSFER AS A FOUNDATION FOR DEVELOPMENT IN THE NEW HISTORICAL CONTEXT

As we have seen, technological capability has become a fundamental feature of the development process (Sagafi-Hejad et al. 1981). Yet science and technology are probably the most unevenly distributed goods in the planet, since they depend on the ability of each society to allocate surplus to considerable long-term investments in creating the necessary human and industrial infrastructure (Tovias 1985). Besides, the process of knowledge generation is cumulative and exponential, thus attracting to the key centers of research and development the scientific potential and the skilled labor force of the entire world, in a relentless brain drain.

It follows that the creation of the technological basis for development for most countries implies a major policy emphasis on technology transfer. There are several forms for technology transfer to take (Rosenberg and Frischtak 1985):

1. International aid and cooperation in training programs organized by governments or international institutions.
2. Import of equipment and machinery, together with the necessary instructions and training in its use.
3. Acquisition of licenses to design and produce new technologies.
4. Acquisition of know-how through training scientific and technical personnel by sending them to universities, research institutions, and industrial firms in technologically advanced countries.
5. Location in the country of foreign companies using and producing new technologies so that local personnel learn the technology, while technologically advanced products and processes are available locally.

International aid programs have had a very limited effect on technology transfer, generally focusing on demonstration projects. This is particularly true in the field of information technologies, rarely considered a priority for development until recent years. Furthermore, the military implications of many of the new technologies introduce political factors that make technology transfer dependent on geopolitical strategic alliances.

Licensing is only relevant when a country already possesses a well-developed industrial infrastructure and a highly efficient technical education system. For instance, Japan used licensing as an effective policy to speed up the pace of its technological development in the 1950s, and so did the Republic of Korea in the late 1960s and 1970s. For most countries, however, acquisition of licenses can only be a complement (and an expensive one) to other efforts that constitute the backbone of technological policy.

Among these processes, investment in education and training of scientific and technical personnel seems to be the most relevant and the most effective in the long term. In a new era based on information technologies, human capital investment is more important than ever before. Such investment combines the expansion and quality improvement of the national education system (and not only of its higher education component), the establishment of national R&D centers, and the education abroad of significant numbers of scientists and engineers in the main technological fields. Such a strategy meets many obstacles and tends to be plagued with shortcomings. Access to the best institutions and firms is limited, both in numbers and in terms of the training many foreigners can receive, particularly when military applications are involved (Castells and Skinner, n.d.). Moreover, the risk of this policy is that a high proportion of the researchers, generally the best, never return to the home country, since the dynamics of scientific development and the conditions of living make it almost heroic for them to reintegrate in the difficult conditions of their country. Besides, for those who return there is considerable difficulty in finding a position corresponding to their abilities. Submitted to pressures from jealous colleagues, and unable to adapt to a system that is largely obsolete in relation to the new knowledge they have acquired, the rate of failure of such scientific transplants is very high; in any case, the efficiency of the technological transfer operates at a level much lower than the actual knowledge that has been embodied in the researchers.

These circumstances suggest that training personnel abroad is an indispensable strategy, but one whose effects can only be felt in the long term. Yet a growing technological gap requires short-term and medium-term policies to stop the deterioration of the relative position of a country in a fast-moving, worldwide technoeconomic system. This is why technology transfer must combine a long-term investment in human capital with short-term mechanisms of technological enhancement. There are two main such mechanisms.

The first is importing advanced equipment, both to use it in the production system and to try to imitate it through reverse engineering. This is, in fact, the main policy that developing countries are using to upgrade their technological base in the short term. But there are considerable problems in this approach to technology transfer. Our exploratory study of technology transfer to China, conducted jointly with Bianchi and Carnoy, shows its limits (Bianchi, Carnoy, and Castells 1988). The main obstacle, of course, concerns the scarce resources that most developing countries have, particularly in hard currency, making it impossible to sustain an import effort over a long period of time. In the case of China, after a spending spree in importing machinery in the early 1980s, the Chinese government had to reverse its policy when foreign currency reserves started to be depleted. In addition, low prices for machinery from Japanese exporters were followed by very high prices for spare parts and maintenance, once Chinese industry had become dependent on such supplies. Too often, the equipment was not suited to the actual conditions of its utilization, and the technical instructions and the training programs sometimes lacked sufficient coordination to be effective. Overall, there was considerable waste of resources, leading the Chinese government to emphasize, in 1987, the transfer of know-how over the acquisition of machinery, as the main means of technology transfer. An additional limit to this policy is the political control of technology exports, particularly from the United States, but also through the NATO-related multilateral controls exercised by COCOM, that, for instance, have barred the selling of supercomputers to China (U.S. Congress 1985).

This is why many countries, including China itself, have turned to another method of obtaining technology transfer, namely, attracting multinational corporations. In exchange for favorable location conditions, facilitated by the government, foreign companies are expected to contribute to the technological development of the country, at least at two levels: by producing advanced equipment in the country, thus reducing the need for imports; and by training engineers, scientists, and technicians so that technology transfer takes place through their acquisition of knowledge and skills. It is well known that multinational corporations are not likely to transfer up-to-date technology. If they are sufficiently interested in the conditions offered by the country, however, they can accept to transfer less advanced technology that could still be useful for the learning process of a developing economy. Yet this will happen only if there is a deliberate government policy that specifies clear conditions and processes through which such technology transfer will occur. In the case of China we observed that, given the interest of the multinationals in obtaining an entry into the Chinese market, they were willing to transfer some technology, with Japanese firms being more reluctant. Nevertheless, the lack of adequate industrial supplies in China, and the weak connection of each high-technology producer in China to the rest of the industrial structure, greatly limited the effectiveness of the transfer, since most of the companies were simply assembling components in China or remained isolated in islands of technological modernity.

The main implication of our observations on China, which we believe can be extrapolated to many other countries, is that it is impossible to separate technology transfer from the modernization of the economy and of scientific and educational institutions at large. Multinational corporations can contribute to technological development under conditions well-specified and tightly controlled by national governments. But this can be only one element of a broader process in which the creation of better industrial structure, the flexibilisation of management, and the education of a skilled labor force connect to each other in a self-reinforcing dynamic process in which technological know-how can actually be put to work in production and management.

Technology transfer is a fundamental dimension of the development process in today's world. But it can proceed effectively only when there is an objective interest for the holders of technology in diffusing it into a developing country, and when the economic and institutional structure of the country is organized in such a way that it can receive the technology, modify it, and use it in the perspective of its national development goals.

CONCLUSION: SOME POLICY IMPLICATIONS

Technological progress could be a fundamental tool to tackle the immense problems haunting the Third World. Uses of telecommunications in decentralizing the delivery of public services, of biotechnology in health and agriculture, of microelectronics in industrial production, or of computers in management and education have all been proposed by international experts as a major contribution to the development process (Kaplinsky 1986). But the actual impact of technology depends on the dynamics of the world economic system and on the institutional structure of each country. What we at present observe is a growing differentiation within the Third World, with most countries being threatened with internal dislocation and external disarticulation vis-à-vis the new global technoeconomic structure. Faced with this potential threat, developing countries are emphasizing technological policies as a matter of political priority (Rushing and Brown 1986). But the formulation of policies is not enough if the problems of transfer and appropriate use of the new technologies are not effectively addressed in a conscious strategy.

A handful of countries have succeeded in taking advantage of information technologies to speed up the pace of their development. Yet the economic foundations of newly industrialized countries are threatened by protectionism, and by the need constantly to upgrade their technological level, while expanding their domestic markets to compensate for the potential shrinkage of their international markets.

The largest countries in the Third World could negotiate their integration into the new technoeconomic system on the basis of their gradual opening to the international economy, benefiting, in exchange, from technology transfer that could considerably help their development process. Yet the use of new technologies can be effective only if it goes together with the modernization of the industrial structure, and massive investment in educational and scientific resources (Miljan 1987). Besides, the use of information technologies will have to be adapted to the actual needs of these countries, resulting in a substantial modification of the products and processes of information technologies that we know today.

The majority of Third World countries stand little chance of producing or absorbing new technologies and thus risk being increasingly disarticulated from the dynamic core of the international system, while becoming increasingly dependent on products and processes generated in other societies and for purposes very different from those determined by their own needs (Rada 1985). In fact, for these countries the technological revolution will make development even more difficult, as their balance of trade becomes more unbalanced, and their endogenous potential more obsolete (Cimoli, Dosi, and Soete 1986).

Nevertheless, there is nothing fatal or irreversible in human history. Given the appropriate political and economic conditions, policies can be implemented that would alter the course of events and make it possible for all countries to participate in the creation of the new technoeconomic international order. But such policies must be realistic enough to start from the acknowledgment of the present conditions and an awareness that the technological factor is a key element in the new developmental processes.

Since no Third World country will be able to generate its technological basis on its own, technology transfer should lie at the core of new policies of international aid—and more specifically, transfer of information technology, whose strategic importance determines the effective use of other technologies. Yet, much international aid is concerned with low-level technologies in traditional fields, particularly in agriculture. The ideology that developing countries need simple technologies overlooks the fact that these "simple technologies" will not be able to reverse the process of dependency and underdevelopment because they will not enable countries to engage actively in worldwide economic competition. It is true that computers can do little without a proper organizational structure and a well-developed educational system, but the strategy of development should include as a goal the creation of the conditions for the production and appropriate use of the most advanced technologies.

The technological modernization of the Third World requires such a gigantic effort that it can be achieved only through large-scale regional integration. This integration should include, at least, markets and educational and scientific institutions. For most countries, their potential domestic markets are below the size required for a self-sustaining process of development, and below the level that could be considered attractive enough for foreign firms to engage in technology transfer. Thus, regional trade and production agreements appear to be a necessity in most of the world. In addition, the resources of institutions of higher learning and scientific centers are not sufficient to generate and retain the research and engineering labor force required to support technological development in many areas of the Third World. A major role of international organizations should be the creation of regional universities and research complexes in key areas of the Third World, with the cooperation of governments, private firms, and international institutions. Unless such initiatives are taken, the brain drain toward the OECD countries will continue.

The process of technology transfer will be effective only if two conditions are met. First, countries receiving technology must engage in substantial reform policies concerning their industrial structure, their educational system, and their management of organizations, both public and private. Investment in technology will be wasted if the infrastructural conditions for its use and adaptation do not exist. Second, countries and economic units transferring technology must have an objective interest in this process. Humanitarian feelings toward developing countries are not a sufficient motivation to engage in a process whose outcome will be the reshaping of the world economy and world power. We believe such objective interest exists, in that there is a growing contradiction between the tremendous expansion of productive capacities generated by technological innovation and the relative shrinking of markets sought by a growing number of competitors. The dramatic development of productive forces under the impulse of new information technologies requires a corresponding expansion of markets, and this can only result from the incorporation of the vast areas of the planet that still remain technologically backward. It is in the objective interest of governments and corporations in the OECD countries to contribute to the economic, and thus technological, development of the entire world, expanding markets, and enhancing the dynamism and potential of the whole system. Japan seems to be testing such a strategy in its recent development plan for the Southeast Asian countries. But in most instances, development aid is still proceeding under the old parameters of political clientelism or humanitarian relief. A major technological development plan for each region or country, backed by a consortium of governments, international agencies, and private firms, would be beneficial both for developing countries, which could obtain technology with fewer strings attached, and for the advanced economies, which could achieve, in the medium term, a substantial expansion of their markets and of international trade.

In the absence of such a concerted, self-interested effort, developing countries will have to concentrate their scarce resources on obtaining the indispensable technological tools to compete in the world economy. Most will fail, under the combined pressure of scarce resources and inadequate organizational structures. The few that succeed will do so at a very high human cost. And because their competition in the core markets will be a matter of survival, they will win market share at the expense of the standards of living in countries and regions in the core economies.

The technological imperative of the new international economy leads to a sharply defined policy alternative: international cooperation in ensuring shared technological development in an expanding market or cutthroat competition in a world market shrinking proportionally to the productive potential spurred by high technology. Developing countries must be prepared for both scenarios, since the true new international division of labor will be largely determined by the ability to obtain, produce, use, and adapt the new technological means.

NOTES

1. The concept of the developmental state has been proposed by Chalmers Johnson (1982).
2. Hang Seng Bank, *Monthly Economic Bulletin*, Hong Kong, October 1987.

Part III

DEMOGRAPHIC AND SOCIAL CHANGE

10

THE ROLE OF MORTALITY DECLINE IN THEORIES OF SOCIAL AND DEMOGRAPHIC TRANSITION

John C. Caldwell

A discussion of the role attributed to mortality in demographic transition theories is important for two reasons. First, the onset of mortality decline is often taken to be the major determinant of all subsequent demographic change or at least the *sine qua non* for decisive or persistent change. Second, so much is the primacy of mortality decline taken for granted in a mortality-fertility demographic transition sequence that the assumptions embodied in mortality-transition theory—to the extent that such theory exists at all—are hardly ever subject to the same kind of scrutiny as is frequently the lot of fertility decline assumptions.

Before focusing on demographic transition, however, it is necessary to dispose of the role of mortality in more comprehensive theories of major social change. An earlier examination of major theories of social change or "modernization" showed that most of the grand theories sought neither to explain demographic transition nor to assign demographic movements any major role in causing social change (Caldwell 1982a, 297–332). At the most, they accepted the theories put forward by demographers, in which demographic change largely explained further demographic change, and took it for granted that the desire for a small family and its attainment was a necessary characteristic of "modern man" (Inkeles and Smith 1974). This was true in the heyday of development aid and the publications that paralleled the interest in the conditions of change for traditional societies, as can be seen in the writings during the early 1960s of Lerner (1958), Hagen (1962), Levy (1966), Rostow (1960), and Deutsch (1961, 493–514), although Deutsch does list population growth as one of the seven important aspects of "social mobilization," as it is in the collection of essays edited by Braibanti and Spengler (1961). Nor was the position essentially different by the second half of the 1960s, as is evident from the work of Feldman and Hurn (1966, 378–395) or

Bendix (1964) or Lewis (1955). More surprisingly, mortality decline played no major part in the works of those social and economic theorists of the 1970s who did have strong demographic interests, as can be discovered from the writings of Eisenstadt (1966), Crook (1978, S198–S210) or indeed the Chicago Household Economists (1974). Nevertheless, all these theorists and everyone else who now writes on development regard high mortality as a major characteristic of underdevelopment and its removal as a necessary and prime target in the improvement of the human condition. In the past this was not the viewpoint even of those who advocated urgent change, largely of course because the potential for mortality decline only slowly became clearer. There is implicit (and occasionally explicit) in their demand for greater social and economic egalitarianism the belief that one section of society should not suffer ill health more than any other, but there is no feeling that societies must necessarily be backward and miserable because of the existing overall mortality level. Thomas Paine envisaged a just and happy society in the *Rights of Man*, given that poverty, illiteracy, unemployment, and war were eliminated, even though, at the time of its publication in 1791, the expectation of life at birth in England and France was probably under forty years[1] and that in the United States little above (a level no longer recorded for any nation and probably now past even in the Sahel (*Demographic Indicators of Countries 1980*). Nor did Karl Marx find high average mortality to be a constraining influence on the human race either in *The Communist Manifesto* (Marx and Engels, in Fernback 1973, 67–98). or in *Capital* (Marx 1897), even though when they were published, in 1848 and 1867 respectively, the expectation of life at birth in England had stagnated at around forty years (Wrigley and Schofield 1981), while mortality was undoubtedly higher still in Germany.[2]

Among the social and economic theorists there are exceptions. Alfred Marshall in the *Principles of Economics*, published in 1890, devoted a good deal of attention to mortality decline and consequent population increase (Marshall 1898, vol. 1, esp. 250–71), although even at that date he did not relate these changes to sustained fertility decline, nor apparently did he realize that the latter had begun. Sometimes the decline in mortality is seen as being the necessary determinant of the passing of a fatalistic acceptance of the dictates of nature and man, an occurrence regarded as necessary in producing a modern society. Inkeles regarded decisive social change as being partly dependent on "a general abandonment of passivity and fatalism in the face of life's difficulties," although he evidently regards education as being more important than mortality decline (1969, 208–25).

In contrast, George Foster believed not only that the reduction in the risk of death eroded the fatalistic outlook toward life but that the latter change reinforced the mortality decline in that the population began to search actively for further ways of lessening mortality risk (1962, 66–68). Frank

Notestein expressed the view at its strongest, suggesting that the mortality level determined the nature of much of society:

> When death rates are high, the individual's life is relatively insecure and unimportant. The individual's status in life tends to be that to which he was born. There is, therefore, rather little striving for advancement. Education is brief, and children begin their economic contributions early in life. In such societies, moreover, there is scant opportunity for women to achieve either economic support or personal prestige outside the roles of wife and mother, and women's economic functions are organized in ways that are compatible with continuous childbearing. (1953, 16)

IMPORTANT QUESTIONS AND INFLUENTIAL CONCEPTS WITH REGARD TO MORTALITY TRANSITION

There are many answers in the field of mortality transition, but most are provided without clearly formulated antecedent questions. Some basic questions are the following: Before the recent dramatic and conclusive mortality decline, was there some kind of mortality-fertility equilibrium? If so, what caused it and what determined its level? What caused the subsequent mortality transition? Was the mortality transition a necessary precursor of fertility transition, and did it determine the fertility transition? How, and after what intervening period? If the mortality decline did not determine the fertility decline (and there are a number of explanations of the fertility decline that do not argue that once mortality transition had occurred, fertility transition was inevitable) (Schultz 1974; Caldwell 1982b), how does one explain the relative closeness in time of their occurrence?

Demographers have been deeply influenced when answering these questions by two concepts, that of Malthusian equilibrium, which owes its origin in part to Thomas Malthus, and that of a single demographic transition with mortality and fertility transitions as twin components with the onset of the first preceding that of the second, a model most clearly articulated by Notestein.

Malthus, in *An Essay on the Principle of Population* (1970a) published in 1798, clearly presented the picture of population growth ultimately leading to such pressure on subsistence that mortality rises and population growth ceases, because of a rising proportion of deaths due to starvation or more frequently to other diseases proving fatal because of malnourishment. The underlying mechanism is the propensity of population to outstrip agricultural production, the former, when unrestricted, growing according to geometric progression and the latter by arithmetic progression. Therefore, the picture is one of near-equilibrium, with population increase restricted to the rate of agricultural progress and accordingly with fertility exhibiting only that margin over mortality. Malthus did not claim to be the first to perceive that such an equilibrium situation should exist. Indeed, in the *Second Essay* (1970a, 251, 285, 286) he attributes the question to Captain Cook on his first voyage in 1770 when ruminating on what would now be called the biomass available to the population of New Holland (Australia): "By what means are the inhabitants of this country reduced to such numbers as it can subsist?" The answer was an old one, probably best understood by the human race in palaeolithic times. In 1695 Samuel Dugard had written in *A Discourse Concerning the Having Many Children,* "Where there are many children there is no likelihood that a plentiful provision can be made for them all . . . where there are more brought into a miserable world, larger food is thereby afforded unto Death" (Strangeland 1904, 165).³

The strong modern belief in the pretransitional equilibrium is based also on the observation frequently made that the principle of compound interest (another version of geometric progression) shows that birth and death rates must have been extremely close to each other for all of human history. For instance, it matters hardly at all whether we estimate human numbers 12,000 years ago immediately before the beginning of the neolithic revolution as 1 million or 40 million: with constant growth over those twelve millennia until the beginning of the present century, the former figure implies a crude birthrate one point per thousand above the crude death rate and the latter figure, half a point. In either case there appears to be long-term equilibrium with an insignificant difference between the level of birth and death rates (a conclusion almost equally strong if we confine our attention to growth over the last 2,000 years)—apparent evidence that recent times have been very typical of human history (an argument frequently advanced to show the need for family planning programs).

Demographic transition theory is examined later, but there is one aspect of Notestein's formulation that is of great importance for pretransition demographic theory, and that is the emphasis given to mortality as the prime determinant of demographic change. As early as 1916, Walter Willcox (1916, 1–15) had analyzed European and American population trends and had concluded that mortality decline probably induced fertility decline. Notestein (1945, 41), while noting at various times that mortality and fertility were both affected by the "forces of modernization," nevertheless described a mechanism that would make the fertility level dependent on the mortality level and that would render it almost inevitable that fertility could not change decisively without a prior change in mortality and that mortality decline would be followed, perhaps with a cultural lag, by fertility decline. "Any society having to face the heavy mortality characteristic of the premodern era must have high fertility to survive. All such societies are therefore ingeniously arranged to obtain the required births. Their religious doctrines, moral codes, laws, education, community customs, marriage habits, and family organizations are all focused towards maintaining high fertility" (1945, 39). "These arrangements, which stood the test of experience throughout the centuries of high mortality, are strongly supported by popular beliefs, formalized in religious doctrine, and enforced by community sanctions. They are deeply woven into the social fabric" (Notestein 1945, 16).

Malthusian Equilibrium and Pretransitional Demographic Theory

These formulations raise a series of questions. Is there an equilibrium situation in that pretransitional birth and death rates were usually close together? Was the equilibrium level the same for all societies? If not, was the level for the vital rates determined by the fertility or the mortality level? Is the equilibrium level decided by subsistence, and are population numbers usually pressing against this ceiling?

Stable population theory shows that any number of theoretical equilibrium positions can exist. For premodern societies these could range from crude death and birth rates of 50 per 1,000, with an expectation of life at birth of twenty years and a total fertility rate of 6.6, to vital rates of 30 per 1,000, with an expectation of life at birth of thirty-five years and a total fertility rate of around 4 (Coale and Demeny 1966). Indeed the range can be extended further in either direction but only by postulating mortality or fertility levels that appear to be implausible. But the two extremes of the range cited above probably have characterized historic societies: the first, West Africa before the beginning of the present century[4] (and perhaps much of the rest of Africa) and the second, England in the second half of the seventeenth century (Wrigley and Schofield 1981, 414, 528). It may well be that the English equilibrium was far less stable than the African one.

What determined the equilibrium level? Malthus had little doubt that it was fertility behavior, and indeed his *Essay* is largely a homily on the fearful consequences of not observing a proper restraint on marriage (although he recognized that there were other "preventive checks"). He recognized clearly that there were different levels of demographic balance that were consonant with keeping the population down to the numbers that could subsist but that allowed different lengths of life (and implied a better diet and general standard of living when longevity was greater):

> In a review of the checks to population in the different states of modern Europe, it appears that the positive checks to population

have prevailed less, and the preventive checks more, than in ancient times, and in the more uncultivated parts of the world. (1970, 254)

That Malthusian view is probably emerging again. There is a growing recognition that the insistence in much of tropical Africa on polygyny and widow remarriage compared with much lower levels of encouragement for either in India arises from the nature of society and social goals (Caldwell and Caldwell 1983) and probably allowed the latter to have birth and death rates around five points lower than the former at the beginning of the present century.[5] As examples of rapid fertility decline in the Third World become more common, less emphasis is placed on complex social structures enforcing high fertility and needing substantial periods for dismantling, and more attention is given to the probability that large families were not economically disadvantageous before fertility transition and that persistent high fertility following mortality decline is a sign not of the time taken to remove the cultural props to high fertility but of the continuing economic value of a large family (Schultz 1974; Caldwell 1982b) One cannot attribute no role to either fertility or mortality, at least in the extreme situations. Total fertility rates do not climb above 7 when that can be achieved only by methods traditional societies regard as socially and physically dangerous and counterproductive in terms of the number of surviving children (see Gray 1981, 93–109),[6] and hence it is fertility behavior that sets the upper limit of the equilibrium range. In contrast, health conditions determine the lower level, for, in a premodern society where many diseases were epidemic and incurable, a reduction of fertility below some minimum level (perhaps, the total fertility rate of 4 found in England in the seventeenth century, although this would vary according to the disease level and other factors such as culturally prescribed hygiene practices) would probably find mortality still falling but not sufficiently to reach the low level attained by fertility.

It might be emphasized that Malthus was not necessarily referring to zero population growth but only to one where the margin between birth and death rates was small enough to allow population to grow no faster than the increase in agricultural production or, better still, so small as to reduce the pressure on subsistence.

The evidence is that, in general, birth and death rates do move together, and this does suggest some kind of ceiling or constraint imposed by mortality. Between 1550 and 1750 the series compiled by Wrigley and Schofield for England were roughly parallel with the rates of natural increase exceeding two-thirds of 1 percent for only three of the twenty-eight quinquennia between 1611 and 1751 (Wrigley and Schofield 1981, 528–29). It has become conventional wisdom among demographers to argue that fertility is much less variable than mortality and that the level of the latter is usually much lower than the former, with its average being raised by periodic great crises.[7] The Wrigley-Schofield series provide only limited support for the thesis: certainly the annual fluctuations in the death rate were greater than those in the birth rate—perhaps double the amplitude—but the death rate exceeded the birthrate by any substantial margin only about half a dozen times between 1550 and 1750 (and never thereafter) (Wrigley and Schofield 1981, 496–502 and end paper).

Several qualifications should be made. Malthus was clearly aware of fertility differentials by social class and knew that, although the rich consumed a disproportionate share of subsistence, the limiting pressure exerted upon the population was experienced in the form of higher mortality rates only by the poor (Malthus 1970a, 93ff). He took the differential mortality rate to be proof that subsistence pressure was being exerted with mortal effect, but drew the lesson, not that food should be shared more equally, but that the poor could escape their plight only by following the better-off and limiting their fertility through postponed marriage. Malthus also realized that the size of the subsistence population depended on its foodstuffs and that greater numbers could be supported on a predominantly grain diet than if meat were an important constituent (1970a, 94–95).

The greatest doubts have centered on the nature of the Malthusian ceiling to population growth. Malthus believed that the connection with limiting food supplies was usually visible only if a whole series of other mechanisms failed to keep mortality sufficiently high:

> The positive checks to population include all the causes, which tend in any way prematurely to shorten the duration of human life, such as unwholesome occupations—severe labour and exposure to the seasons; bad and insufficient food and clothing arising from poverty; bad nursing of children; excesses of all kinds; great towns and manufactories, the whole train of common diseases and epidemics; wars; infanticide; plague, and famine. (1970b, 250)

Yet, many of these other causes merely do the work that famine would otherwise have to accomplish, for he then argues that "these checks . . . form the immediate causes which keep the population on a level with the means of subsistence" (1970b, 250).

Clifford Geertz concluded from his work in Java that the equilibrium population itself can reduce the carrying capacity of land under a swidden (shifting cultivation) regime but not under paddy rice cultivation. Referring to the latter, he wrote:

> ... the sociologically most critical feature of wet-rice agriculture [is] its marked tendency (and ability) to respond to a rising population through intensification; that is, through absorbing increased numbers of cultivators on a unit of cultivated land. . . . (Geertz 1963, 32)

> Because even the most intense population pressure does not lead to a breakdown of the system on the physical side (though it may lead to extreme impoverishment on the human side), such pressure can reach a height limited only by the capacity of those who exploit it to subsist on steadily diminishing per capita returns for their labour. Where swidden "overpopulation" results in a deterioration of the habitat, in wet-rice regime it results in the support of an ever increasing number of people within an undamaged habitat. (Geertz 1963, 33)

If Geertz is arguing the ultimate existence of a Malthusian ceiling (and the tenor of much of his discussion suggests this), then the reduced subsistence must mean that rice cultivators had previously either experienced a period of rapid increase in food production, possibly because of the conversion of more sparsely settled land to rice terraces as irrigation was extended, or that the other positive checks, violence and excesses of all kinds as well as disease, especially among infants and small children, had for long allowed the living to feed relatively well. Perhaps in much of Southeast Asia the agricultural revolution of the nineteenth and twentieth centuries as the forests were cleared had meant that the Malthusian ceiling had been banished for generations.

These kinds of considerations have been employed to attack the whole concept of a subsistence ceiling. Marston Bates (1962, 68ff) believed that most people in most societies in history appeared to be sufficiently nourished to make it hardly credible that their numbers were limited primarily either by starvation or by malnourishment sufficiently great to lead to a significant rise in disease. That would be the view of nearly all foreigners visiting West Africa from the end of the fifteenth century onward. They repeatedly reported that the Africans looked well fed and that there was plenty of unused land available for cultivation. Bates was skeptical of a subsistence ceiling not only for human beings but also for wild animals:

> I see few signs of organisms living to this possible limit—some other kind of "limiting factor" seems to come in long before depletion of the food supply starts to operate. (1962, 68)

It seems to me that food supply is the direct limiting factor on population only in rare and catastrophic situations—and that these catastrophic situations, when we examine them, turn out with surprising frequency to involve some direct or indirect form of human activity. (1962, 69)

Bates suggested that the explanation lay, at least in palaeolithic times, in the operation of territoriality, but, within each territory, apart from citing some population limitation through infanticide, he sought an explanation in the limits imposed by the food supply.

The potentially most damaging attack on the Malthusian ceiling, although not fully developed because "our inquiry is concerned with the effects of population changes on agriculture and not with the causes of these population changes," has been made by Ester Boserup (1965, 14). She argued that, when population densities threaten a critical diminution of the food supply, the response is to break the subsistence barrier by altering the mode of agriculture—actually the method and intensity of cultivation—thus allowing not an incremental advance in agricultural production by arithmetic progression but a quantum leap. The new techniques have usually been long known but have been little used because the increase in productivity per unit of land means an increase in the labor needed to produce a unit of food (and hence a drop in the individual's real living standard because of the necessity of working longer hours). She concluded that "the low rates of population growth found (until recently) in pre-industrial communities cannot be explained as the result of insufficient food supplies due to overpopulation, and we must leave more room for other factors in the explanation of demographic trends . . . medical, biological, political etc." (1965, 14).

Boserup's case can be attacked. Mass innovation is difficult, for all kinds of social reasons, even when an invention or a new technique is known, although perhaps not widely, in a society. Critical population densities might result in an epidemic or a disastrous period of warfare on countless occasions before the historical circumstances were exactly right for the innovation to be employed in such a way that its use would become self-sustaining. Even unused land in Africa has been explained in terms of the vast reserves of temporarily fallow land needed in poor lateritic soils to maintain a system of shifting cultivation without declining productivity (Allan, 1965). There is evidence from the West African savannah that this thesis might also be suspect, in that rural densities around some towns can continue to rise steeply (Mortimore 1968, 298–306), although this phenomenon apparently depends on a symbiotic relationship between town and country, where agriculture uses the manure and refuse of the town and may prove possible only as the economic functions of urban populations develop.

Nevertheless, if one abandons the concept of a subsistence ceiling, one must still seek some explanation for the long-term very low growth rate of the human race. The only possible contender seems to be the density of population. It can be shown that epidemic disease is more likely to break out and to spread rapidly in denser populations, and indeed that there are critical minimum densities below which many infections disappear (Fenner 1970, 48–68). We have increasingly abandoned the idea that, given a low expectation of life in ancient Rome, longevity in the earlier period must have been lower still;[8] the mortality levels of contemporary isolated hunters and gatherers appear to be only moderate and it appears likely that the neolithic revolution and the later growth of the first cities in turn raised population densities, the level of infectious diseases, and the consequent death rate (Barnes 1970, 1–18).

We will probably move toward a mortality theory that retains the Malthusian subsistence ceiling, at least for the poorer part of the population, but recognizes that it has been approached in most societies only rarely and then during subsistence rather than population crises. During the greater part of the time the positive checks limiting growth have been disease or violence and some degree of deliberate population control, and most people have not been gaunt with near-starvation. Violence has certainly been a factor and most societies have long held that the sign of a good ruler whose laws were obeyed was that population numbers grew. In recent times we have become aware that population numbers can be raised if food is brought from elsewhere during the great subsistence crises and if individuals are prevented by modern medicine from dying when afflicted even by diseases that struck more easily because of a degree of malnourishment. Sauvy has argued that a downward change in the subsistence level could reduce population growth not only by raising mortality but also by lowering fertility (Sauvy 1969, 3–18). We have evidence now that both factors operate at least briefly during intense famines.[9]

Malthusian theory lies at the core of much of modern economic-demographic theory. Harvey Leibenstein argued:

> On the whole, mortality rates seem to depend on the "standard of life," that is, on the level of consumption. Hence, it is quite reasonable to posit that mortality rates are a monotonically decreasing function of per capita income, given the state of public health measures in existence. (Leibenstein 1957, 159)

> Rapid mortality declines must mean a rapid expansion of the population and an equal, or almost equal, expansion in aggregate output in order to feed and otherwise maintain the expanding

population. That is, even if declines in mortality precede development, some economic expansion in the aggregate sense must occur if these lower mortality rates are to be maintained. (Leibenstein 1957, 240)

Richard Nelson, when analyzing the low-level equilibrium trap, wrote:

> In areas with low per capita incomes short-run changes in the rate of population growth are caused by changes in the death rate, and changes in the death rate are caused by changes in the level of per capita income. Yet once per capita income reaches a level well above subsistence requirements, further increases in per capita income have a negligible effect on the death rate. (Nelson 1956, 898)

It is assumed, of course, that income can be employed to purchase food and other subsistence necessities.

McKeown, writing from a medical viewpoint, strongly supported this stance:

> When death rates are high, as in developing countries today and in all countries in the recent past, mortality is due to a high incidence of infectious diseases. The level of infection is determined mainly by the standard of living, and even modest improvements are reflected rapidly in a lower death rate. (McKeown 1976, 35)

When this widely agreed upon relationship was tested for England by Wrigley and Schofield (1981, 402–453), they discovered no relationship between the movement of real wages and the mortality level. There was a close relationship between the movement of wages and that of marriage and a slightly delayed response from fertility. Thus, population did rise with income, and the positive check apparently did not come into operation because the preventive check was operating massively in English society—and not merely among the upper classes—at least as early as the mid-sixteenth century.

THE CAUSES OF MORTALITY DECLINE

Within modern times the high-level mortality-fertility equilibrium has disappeared, first with the onset of persistent mortality decline in the West. The long Swedish series of vital statistics appears to show that the decline in that country began around 1750 (Hofsten and Lundstrom 1976). The same is also true in the longer series compiled by Wrigley and Schofield for England (1981:528-29) but the latter shows that the century from 1650 to 1750 exhibited particularly high mortality. Indeed, their series indicates that the low mortality of the beginning of the fourth quarter of the sixteenth century was not equaled again until around 1850, and that the unique modern mortality transition was not clearly established as more than a periodic swing until after that date.

Marshall (1898, 266), writing in 1890, attributed mortality decline to "the growth of temperance, of medical knowledge, of sanitation and of general cleanliness." The debate has raged around the balance of these elements ever since, though social scientists, in contrast to social historians, have forgotten the emergence from the era in England, especially in the towns of the eighteenth century, of gin drinking (Trevelyan 1946, 341,343).[10]

The role of medical science has been given even less emphasis, being relegated by Samuel Preston and Etienne van de Walle (1978, 291) to the period after the introduction of diphtheria immunization in the 1890s and by McKeown (1976, 92–109, 153) to the years after 1938 when sulphonamides became available. The role of science in general, if not medical science, may be more complex than this. Bellah (1968, 40), emphasizing the rise of the Protestant outlook in the sixteenth and seventeenth centuries, wrote of "an entirely new conception of the relation of science and society which made the conquest of nature a central social goal and the building of a new civilization a scientific endeavour." Colin Clark (1967, 49) claimed that "the significant decline in mortality . . . clearly began about 1759 [and] was due to medical improvements, due to better knowledge and application of medical science. . . . Attempts by some historians to show that it was the industrialization of England (and other countries) which came first . . . have been unsuccessful and have been abandoned." The emphasis in recent decades has in fact been on sustained economic growth over several centuries, growth that gave birth to the industrial revolution, and, like that revolution, owed much to the new sciences. Yet, the growth of a scientific outlook certainly affected society and individual behavior. It probably contributed as much as did fashion and fastidiousness to the movement toward personal and social cleanliness from the late eighteenth century, which David Razzel (1974, 5–17) regards as being a much underestimated aspect of the early mortality decline. That movement may well have been part of a larger transition to regarding a wide range of behavior affecting health as being an element in human control of nature. In contemporary rural India attitudes to sickness are in the process of being transferred from the religious and mystical realm to the secular one, with a considerable impact on health (Caldwell, Reddy, and Caldwell 1983, 185–205); a similar process has been described as beginning in England as early as the sixteenth century (Thomas 1971). The decline in infant and child mortality with the education of mothers described by John Caldwell (1979, 395–413; Caldwell and McDonald 1981, 79–96) and by Preston (1978, 63–75) and almost certainly a decline later in life in mortality in keeping with an individual's own education, is explained partly by the transmission of secular and scientific attitudes.

Warren Thompson (1953, 77) wrote that, "the great decline in the death rate that has taken place during the last two centuries in the West is due, basically, to the improvement in production and economic conditions. This economic development made better sanitary practices possible and provided the means for research in medicine and for the establishment of good medical education. . . . The importance of the improvement of sanitation in cities can scarcely be overestimated." McKeown (1976, 110–27, 153) dated the impact of sanitation improvements only to the second half of the nineteenth century, agreeing in effect with Winslow that the "Great Sanitary Awakening" began with the publication of Edwin Chadwick's *Enquiry into the Sanitary Conditions of the Labouring Population of Great Britain* in 1842 and the consequent passage of the Public Health Act of 1848 (Winslow 1951, 9). For the earlier period he adopted a strict Malthusian explanation that the death rate fell mainly because of an improvement in nutrition due to greater food supplies (1976, 128–42, 153–54), much originating from overseas. Preston and van de Walle (1978, 275–97) have tested these hypotheses for the nineteenth century in three French urban areas. They concluded that sanitation, especially purified water, was more important than nutritional improvement even in the first half of the nineteenth century, and explained their different finding from that of McKeown in that they had "not chosen to date hygienic improvements from the passage of hygienic laws but rather from the implementation of public works, which often antedated legal changes" (Preston and Van de Walle 1978, 291), noting that McKeown, Brown, and Record (1972, 345–82) had cited 1884 as the critical date for hygienic improvements because of the passage of a major sanitary act in that year. The demonstration by Wrigley and Schofield that there was little correlation in England from 1751 to 1871 between the movement of either real wages or the price of consumables and mortality trends offers support both to Razzel and to Preston and van de Walle. Caldwell (1979, 413), employing findings from African and Indian studies, has also argued that McKeown placed too much emphasis on the maldistribution of food between social classes and too little (or rather none at all) on maldistribution by age and sex within the family.

Most transition theorists are less interested in Western mortality trends during the twentieth than during the nineteenth century. The reason is that by 1900 it was clear that an unprecedented and irreversible mortality decline had occurred: the expectation of life at birth had reached fifty years in Sweden,

Australia, and New Zealand and was close to that in the Netherlands, England, and France. Nevertheless, the major part of the mortality transition still lay ahead: England, after 150 years of decline, had recorded an increase of life expectation at birth little more than half of the gain yet to be achieved in the first eight decades of the twentieth century. Preston has addressed the nature of the Western as well as Third World mortality transition during the present century (Preston 1975, 231–48). He concluded that the Malthusian subsistence ceiling on mortality gains had retreated in a most remarkable way:

> Factors exogenous to a country's current level of income probably account for 75-90 percent of the growth in life expectancy for the world as a whole between the 1930s and the 1960s. Income growth per se accounts for only 10–25 percent. (Preston 1975, 237–40)

He identified the exogenous factors as being mainly medical technology (Preston 1975, 243–44). As a result of the development of the technology the richest countries could secure a national expectation of life at birth around 74 years by the 1960s, more than five years above the level even the greatest wealth could achieve in the 1930s. Indeed by 1963 increases in per capita income above $800—and some countries had achieved over twice that level—secured no further advantages in reducing mortality (Preston 1975, 235).

During the 1930s and 1940s it became clear that mortality was falling faster in a range of colonies than had been the case in the colonial powers themselves when they had achieved the same initial mortality level (Taeuber and Beal 1944, 222—55; Davis 1944, 256– 78; Moore 1944, 279–99; Jurkat 1944, 300–317; Kiser 1944, 383–408; Cleland 1944, 409–23; Notestein 1944, 424–44); Egypt, India, Java and the Philippines were frequently cited. By the 1950s it could be observed that almost the whole developing world was involved in this change (Stolnitz 1955, 24–55). To explain the situation, before the Second World War, stress was placed upon colonial law and order, the carrying out of sanitation projects, and the implementation of action for alleviating famine. By the 1950s medical technology was much more emphasized. George Stolnitz wrote:

> Quantitative application of the concepts of demographic transitions, if made by analogy to Western experience, is apt to be futile or misleading as a guide to the mortality prospects confronting the underdeveloped world today. (Stolnitz 1955, 51)

> The primary role of international rather than national health agencies, the use of antibiotics, the development of cheap yet effective

methods for combating malaria—each of these is very nearly a mid-century innovation. (Stolnitz 1955, 53)

Davis (1956, 305–18) drew upon this new information to attack the Malthusian constraints, arguing that Malthus had overestimated the significance of subsistence and had underestimated the separate impact of disease. He pointed out that E.F. Penrose (1934, 17–19, 36–43) had employed interwar data twenty years earlier to make this case. Thirteen years later, Davis and Eduardo Arriaga employed Latin American mortality data to conclude:

> . . . in recent decades public health measures have exercised a strong influence on death rates, independently of economic development. In the most advanced countries the improvement in mortality has always depended mainly on economic development, because it is this development that supports public health itself. This is why the rate of improvement in those countries has been gradual and amazingly constant throughout their modern history. In the current underdeveloped countries, on the other hand, the rate of gain in mortality during recent decades has been notably accelerated by the importation of public health techniques, personnel and funds from the industrialized countries, regardless of local economic development or non-development. (Arriaga and Davis 1969, 223–42)

Ansley Coale and Edgar Hoover wrote in 1958 that "substantial economic improvement may be a sufficient condition for a decline in mortality, but it is not today a necessary condition" (Coale and Hoover 1958, 14). I. Orubuloye and Caldwell showed that there were very marked differences in the mortality level in rural Nigeria according to whether there was access or not to modern medical facilities (Orubuloye and Caldwell 1975, 259–72).

The argument was essentially one of a global society in which technology, especially that with the emotive connotations associated with saving lives, flowed easily. Inevitably a theoretical counterattack followed, and this too was supported by new data. This reaction took two forms: first, a claim that the Malthusian restraint, as measured by income, had been underestimated; and second, the proposition that the element of social change had been largely ignored both in recent change and in the first mortality transition. As early as 1962 it was pointed out in the United Nations Population Bulletin that "where important gains have been made in the levels of income and education, these also have contributed to the success of efforts to cut down the death rates" (*Population Bulletin of the United Nations*, No. 6, 1962, 10).

Jacques Vallin (1968, 845–68) argued, from a comparative analysis of Third World mortality data, that there was still a close relation between average per capita income and the mortality level and that medical technology alone was likely to encounter a ceiling, perhaps around sixty years, beyond which the expectation of life at birth could not be pushed without major breakthroughs in economic development. Preston (1980, 291) noted that national data might obscure the nature of mortality determinants for "studies of mortality differentials among individuals by social or economic class in countries as disparate as India and the United States consistently reveal lower mortality rates among the upper classes". In 1975 Preston had shown a close relationship between expectation of life at birth and national per capita income for countries with national incomes per head below $500 (constant 1963 dollars)—that is, the great majority of developing countries—and a very sensitive association among the poorest countries (1975, 235). Indeed, the Malthusian effect among the poorest countries appeared to have intensified over the previous thirty years. "Far from becoming dissociated from income, mortality may have become more responsive to it in low-income countries" (Preston 1975, 240). He thought it possible that either the new health measures were exploitable only by countries that had reached a certain level of economic development or that international technical aid had deliberately concentrated on populations likely to respond most rapidly to their assistance. Recently it has been argued by Davidson Gwatkin (1980, 615–44) and by Lado Ruzicka and Harold Hansluwka (1982, 83–155) that a marked deceleration has occurred in mortality decline in many countries of the Third World and that the underlying dependence of health upon economic development has been reasserting itself. Henry Mosley (1983) believes that the role of social and economic change in the postwar mortality decline in developing countries was underestimated and that of medical technology overestimated.

At the same time, evidence has accumulated that economic development may have a different mortality impact according to the type of social change chosen to go with it, and indeed that development may well be an intricate interrelation between technological and social change with further advances in each being dependent to a considerable extent on movements in the other. The clearest demonstration of the significance of the social element in mortality decline has probably been the strong inverse relation shown between the level of parental education, especially that of the mother, and infant and child mortality (Behm 1978, 10; Caldwell 1979; Caldwell and McDonald 1981; Preston 1978). Nevertheless, broader social change is almost certainly involved. Alan Hill, Sara Randall, and Oriel Sullivan (1982, 82–84) explained the striking mortality difference between two Sahelian communities in terms of their differential access to the outside world and hence to imported behavioral patterns. John Caldwell, P.H. Reddy, and Pat Caldwell (1983) showed that the limited impact of modern medicine in a rural area of India was explained by a deficient demand for its services because of alternative traditional explanations of sickness and its cure, and that greater demand depended on externally imported social change leading to concepts of health and cure being progressively transferred from the religious to the secular domain. Furthermore, the reduction of infant and child mortality was to a considerable extent dependent on changes in internal family relationships and emotional and material priorities, which were the very essence of social change and were only partly determined by economic developments.

Recent research on Third World mortality trends has thrown new light on the Malthusian equilibrium. Preston's analysis of the great length of time that is likely to elapse before an increase in income is totally erased by the larger population resulting from the induced decline in mortality—usually a matter of centuries—suggests that, although the low-level equilibrium trap postulated by Leibenstein (1957) and Nelson (1956) may once have been a cause of economic-demographic equilibrium, it has no relevance to the contemporary world (Preston 1975, 240–41). Hill, Randall, and van den Eerenbeemt (1983, 83–85), in a study of different communities in rural Mali, have shown the highest mortality—and presumably once the highest mortality-fertility equilibrium level—in a comparatively well fed community (where half the births resulted in deaths by five years of age although "almost none [of the children] was below standard when assessed in terms of weight for age or weight for height"). Their explanation was a deficiency in specific foods, particularly milk and (more convincingly) relatively high levels of infectious disease arising from more crowded residential arrangements and from the greater densities of permanently settled deltaic riverine agricultural populations in close contact with each other and presumably with high levels of pollution of drinking water. The question of a demographic equilibrium resulting from settlement density and infectious disease, rather than from subsistence constraints, may remain open.

THE IMPACT OF MORTALITY DECLINE ON OTHER DEMOGRAPHIC BEHAVIOUR

Two major questions remain. Does mortality change lead to other demographic change and is mortality transition the necessary and inevitable precursor of fertility transition?

Demographic transition diagrams in their symmetry, often looking like parallelograms, give an appearance of mathematical certainty. Real diagrams usually look very different from each other. When data are first available, births and deaths are never equal, for the transition gap has already opened (at the start of the Wrigley and Schofield [1981, 528–29] series for England, the gap between the birth and death rates for the forty years from 1541 averages not much less than 10 points per 1,000, while over 200 years later the rate for the last half of the eighteenth century is very similar). In few countries has the gap closed again, although the industrialized world shows signs that this may be happening, as it did once before in the 1930s and as it did in France before the First World War. Our belief in a transition from a near-stationary state to that condition once again arises mostly from mathematics and the finiteness of resources. It is sobering to reflect on what estimate might have been made in 1541 (when the population of England was 2.8 million) of the country's ultimate carrying capacity without endangering the achieved standard of living.

Why should fertility fall once sustained mortality transition has been under way for some time? Willcox (1916, 14) gave one answer: "It is the decline in the birth rate, and only that, which has enabled mankind to grip and hold fast the advantages promised by the decline in the death rate." These advantages were a reduced pressure on wealth and food supply and hence a larger share for all. Davis also presented a variant of this theme (although his argument owed much to Arsene Dumont [1890] and his social capillarity theory, which explained why he who was least encumbered by dependants could gain promotion faster in middle-class employment in nineteenth-century France):

> Under a prolonged drop in mortality with industrialization, people in north-west Europe and Japan found their accustomed demographic behaviour was handicapping them in their effort to take advantage of the opportunities being provided by the emerging economy. They accordingly began changing their behaviour. Thus it was in a sense the rising prosperity itself, viewed from the standpoint of the individual's desire to get ahead and appear respectable, that forced a modification of his reproductive behaviour. (Davis 1963, 345–66)

In fact, in his presentation, which he also described as the theory of multiphasic response, Davis did not argue that the response to mortality decline was necessarily fertility decline:

> The process of demographic change and response is not only continuous but also reflexive and behavioural—reflexive in the sense that a change in one component is eventually altered by the change it has induced in other components, behavioural in the

sense that the process involves human decisions in the pursuit of
goals with varying means and conditions. (Davis 1963, 345)

Six years later, employing a multiphasic approach, Dov Friedlander (1969, 359–81) published an analysis of the reaction to mortality decline in nineteenth-century rural England and Sweden, finding support for the hypothesis that fertility decline had been delayed because of the possibility of migration to urban centers and other industrializing areas. This was the first response to mortality decline, and there was a clear implication that fertility decline in Britain as a whole may have been postponed by the possibility of migrating to the United States or to British colonies around the world. Later, William Mosher (1980, 395–412) reexamined the case of rural Sweden and concluded that the description of the demographic sequence for that population was wrong. The primary response in northwestern Europe until the late nineteenth century to declining mortality and resulting increased population pressures and declining real wages has been identified as postponed marriage (Wrigley 1969; Habakkuk 1971). Such postponement modified an already low fertility level in England (with the average age of female marriage over twenty-six years in the mid-sixteenth century) (Wrigley and Schofield 1981, 423) and produced only limited movements in the gross reproduction rate: 2.3 in the latter part of the fifteenth century, down to 2 in the mid-nineteenth century, averaging as low as 1.9 for only three successive quinquennia around the 1670s; finally rising persistently above 2.5 from 1771 (Wrigley and Schofield 1981, 528–29).

All these theories assume that, beyond a certain point, a larger family of surviving children threatens living standards. The problem is that they all deal with northwestern Europe, where there is evidence that the proposition may have held good for centuries, but possibly in conditions of land tenure, inheritance, and family structure that were specific to that society. Most were also based on an analysis of movements once Europe had been transformed by commercial and agricultural change and even when industrialization was occurring. In these circumstances there may well have been new direct pressures on fertility arising from the kind of new social structure described by Dumont and implied by Davis. Notestein's formulation (described above) was universal and implied that the "arrangements" (Notestein's word—"props"—has been used by some of his followers) to keep fertility as high as mortality were necessary because most families would otherwise have had fewer children, presumably because it would have been to their economic advantage to do so. An analysis of Notestein's theory is rendered more complex by the fact that he also wrote of the direct impact of modernization on fertility, possibly to explain why the gap between mortality and fertility decline was not longer in time. He wrote of the "urban and industrial society" as being a major factor in fertility decline, and also specified the development of technology, the erosion of the traditional family and the growth of individualism, concluding: "The more rapid response of mortality than of fertility to the forces of modernization is probably inevitable; the reduction of mortality is a universally accepted goal and faces no substantial social obstacles" (Notestein 1945, 41).[11]

A considerable literature has now come into existence attesting to the lack of economic disadvantage, and usually the positive advantages, of the large family in most pretransitional societies. Caldwell reported from a 1963 survey in Ghana that the old tended to report net lifetime gains from high fertility (Caldwell 1967, 217–38), and later that the Yoruba of Nigeria equated high fertility with prosperity (Caldwell 1976, 193–253; 1977, 5–27).[12] Mead Cain (1977, 201–27) showed how Bangladesh families secured net positive returns over time from their children, while the Chicago New Household Economists argued why this would be so (Schultz 1974). Crimmins, Easterlin, Jejeebhoy, and Srinivasan (1981, 30–35) argued that most pretransitional families were unable to achieve numbers as large as they desired and would find economically beneficial, although, on the first point, others would argue that high-fertility societies with largely uncontrolled fertility do not consciously formulate fertility targets. There is probably a movement toward a theoretical consensus that major social and economic change produced both the mortality and fertility declines with the fact of the mortality decline perhaps bringing the onset of the fertility decline forward in time and certainly steepening it. Cald-well, Reddy, and Caldwell, in rural India, have identified a range of demographic and family changes as having common origins rather than as being multiphasic response (Caldwell, Reddy, and Caldwell 1982, 689–727; Caldwell 1983).

Family size in these discussions is usually that of surviving children. There has been considerable debate, much of it of marginal importance to the theory of demographic transition, about the extent parents replace children who have died.[13] In societies where no fertility control is practiced, the main mechanism would seem to be the biological one whereby an infant death leads to the mother ceasing to lactate and ovulating again earlier than would otherwise have been the case. It is also possible that some women wean children earlier than most, thus on average fitting more births into the reproductive span with higher infant mortality levels and so serving a spurious replacement effect. The danger of drawing misleading conclusions from such analyses has long been stressed (Taylor, Newman, and Kelly 1976, 263–78; Williams 1977, 581–90). John Knodel (1982, 177–200) reported from a study of nineteenth-century German village populations that prior to the practice of a significant level of fertility control no decisive answer could be given as to whether there was any replacement behavior. Once fertility transition began, however, efforts to replace children who had died became clearly evident and "couples with the most favourable child mortality experiences were most likely to adopt family limitation and to reduce their fertility." This last finding provides a clear link between mortality and fertility decline, once both transitions are clearly under way, although it might be noted that Balakrishnan (1978, 135–45), employing macro data, could not establish such a relation in Latin America. Rutstein's (1974, 182–88) analysis of Taiwan data also fails to demonstrate any strong relation.

FINAL NOTE

There is substantial agreement that economic modernization in the West, with its antecedent and succeeding scientific revolutions, produced the onset first of mortality and then of fertility transitions. In the present century, poorer parts of the world have not been forced to follow the same sequence and hence, as the world has become one, have been able to experience relatively fast mortality decline, at least partly because of the export from industrialized countries of modern medical technology. Yet there is growing evidence that subsistence and other material circumstances may be already placing Malthusian constraints on continued mortality declines in much of the Third World so that the abolition of large national mortality differentials may await global industrialization in the generations or centuries to come. Nevertheless, much remains to be done before mortality transition theory can be comprehensive. The following are some of the lacunae.

Social change probably played a major role in mortality decline. The work on the effect of parental education suggests as much (little work has yet been undertaken on the impact of the children's education on their own mortality). Consumer demand for modern health services, parental care, the care of individuals for themselves are vast areas for research and theory. There was probably a complex interrelation between technical change, the rise of education and its changing content, and health behavior. Much remains to be explained.

The onset of mortality decline occurred before the onset of fertility decline but was almost certainly not the major determinant of the latter. What is less frequently noted is that most of the mortality decline occurred after the onset of the fertility decline: four-fifths in England, for instance, even though the mortality transition has so far occupied three centuries in contrast to one century for the fertility transition. Almost certainly, interactions took place. Davis (1963, 345) implies as much in his theory of multiphasic response although he does not subsequently consider the possibility that fertility decline accelerated mortality decline because of the obligations felt to care more for the smaller family and indeed the desire to do so, or because lower fertility reduced maternal mortality and the incidence of child mortality characterized by high birth orders. Yet evidence of relatively very low levels of infant and child mortality among the deliberately achieved small families in Ibadan City, Nigeria (Caldwell and Caldwell 1978, 2–18) and apparently of very low mortality among the children of those who have signed the one-child certificate in China (Xian 1983, 144) suggests that this aspect of transition theory needs more attention. Even here, the interaction may not be simple: work in India suggests that the lower mortality among children, the greater care and the relatively lighter work loads assigned to them may all be part of a reversing of emotional and economic priorities in the family, (Caldwell, Reddy, and Caldwell 1983) a reversing of wealth flows (Caldwell 1982), although interactions undoubtedly also exist.

Finally, far too little has been done to incorporate into both mortality and demographic transition theory the intervention of national governments and international agencies and the accompanying sentiments and ideologies that have made such action possible. They tend to be treated as exogenous, as something artificial and determined, in contrast, to the more natural transitions of the West. Nevertheless, comprehensive theory should aim at embracing the whole picture.

NOTES

1. For England, see Wrigley and Schofield. *Population History of England: A Reconstruction*, London: Edward Arnold, (1981, appendix A.3, 528–29), where an expectation of life at birth of 37.3 years is given for 1791, a level probably reached by India by the late 1950s.

2. An expection of life at birth of 37 years in the 1870s is given in Knodel (1974, 5).

3. Marx, *Capital* (1976, 1:472–73), argues that Malthus said little that was not contained in James Steuart, *Inquiry into the Principles of Political Economy*, 1767; Robert Wallace, *A Dissertation on the Numbers of Man in Ancient and Modern Times*, 1753, and *Various Prospects of Mankind, Nature and Providence*, 1761; and Joseph Townsend, *A Dissertation on the Poor Laws*, 1786.

4. For Ghana back to 1921 with implications for the early period, see Caldwell (1967b, 2:104).

5. The crude birthrate in Ghana has been estimated at 52 per 1,000 in 1921 (Caldwell 1967b, 94), and may have been higher earlier in keeping with an even higher infant mortality rate. Davis (1951, 69) estimated the Indian crude birthrate as 49 per 1,000 for 1911–21 and 46 per 1,000 for 1921–31, although his estimates for the earlier period, the three decades following 1881, were 49, 46 and 48 respectively.

6. It should be noted that where such methods are no longer dangerous, as for instance the shortening of the lactation period, the total fertility rate can exceed 10. See Eaton and Mayer (1954) on the Hutterites in the United States. But these are postequilibrium conditions. The

Hutterite total fertility rate was in fact 9.4 in 1936–40; it would have been higher but for delayed marriage following the twentieth-century American pattern (the total marital fertility rate was over 12).

7. See, for instance, Charbonneau and Larose (1976).

8. See cover illustration of Dublin, Lotka, and Spiegelman (1949).

9. See reviews by John C. Caldwell of: Greenough (1982) in *Population and Development Review* 9 (1983):541–42; and State Family Planning Commission of China (1983) in *Population and Development Review* 10 (1984).

10. "Gin" was a generic name for all spirits.

11. Most of the preceding points are expressed more pointedly in Notestein (1953).

12. Both papers also appear in Caldwell (1982).

13. See the summary in Preston (1975b), especially the editors' "Introduction"; Friedlander (1977, 1:183–204); and Preston (1978a).

11

THE MECHANISMS OF DEMOGRAPHIC CHANGE IN HISTORICAL PERSPECTIVE

John C. Caldwell

It is indisputable that a settled, largely subsistence economy based predominantly on familial production will be one with high fertility (except where there are pathological problems),[1] and that it is inevitable that a capitalist society with a fully developed labor market producing nearly all goods and services would be one where fertility is low. It is not this tautology that is important for our times, but the question whether there can be lags or accelerations in the chain from the material forces of production to the modes of production to such parts of the superstructure as family structure and fertility behavior, and whether, as in the Third World (and parts of the West), imported social concepts can change the local superstructure at a different rate than would have been dictated solely by the movement of the economic base in a culturally autonomous society (and, although it is not necessary for the argument, whether such changes in the superstructure can actually modify the base). The critical change is one which extends so far that high fertility is no longer economic. These quibbles might mean a difference of decades in pinpointing the onset of fertility decline and billions in the estimates of the size of the eventual quasi-stationary global population, as well as significant differences in the interpretation of demographic change in the nineteenth-century West and the contemporary Third World.

A RECAPITULATION AND RESTATEMENT OF THE WEALTH FLOWS THEORY

In terms of its ultimate impact on fertility, the significant aspect of the economy is whether production is based on the familial organization of labor or whether there is a free and monetized labor market (i.e., capitalist production). The long history of familial production is not homogeneous—hunting and gathering bands may have been typified by wealth flows from the younger to the older generation without a specific child-parent flow, and fertility may have been valuable more in terms of numbers and security than in terms of production before the external imposition of greater security—but such production never favored highly controlled fertility. Familial production is not confined to subsistence agriculture but has long typified precapitalist artisan and commercial families, as well as the families of landless laborers—and, in a sense, even the nobility and administrators in such societies can organize their families in this way.

The familial organization of production was maintained even in urban areas because of the strength of the cultural superstructure—based on the needs of subsistence agriculture but working effectively outside it. The central point that must be emphasized is that for most of human history the cultural superstructure has been overwhelmingly concerned with matters that maintain the modes of production—with how people adhere to or stray from the behavior patterns expected in terms of their age, sex, relationship to each other, and so forth.[2] The praise, excitement, and scandal of the village is very largely about such things. Music and art may to some extent have a life of their own, but they usually reinforce these themes, and religion very largely does so. The parallels with our own society are not at first sight so clear, but they are there and are spelled out below.

The superstructure is then very powerful. In a society that is isolated or little affected by outside cultural influences—which has been the situation of the leading segments of the West for a millennium—that power is likely to be a conservative one. Where there are strong external cultural influences, the course of change is much more open.

Some of these points will be clearer after we examine the familial and capitalist cultural superstructures. The need to do so arises because the economic value of children to parents is determined by behavioral patterns monitored by these superstructures. It is also pertinent to consider whether the superstructures are all of a piece or whether parts can be modified (with implications for fertility) without immediately endangering the mode of production.

FAMILIAL PRODUCTION: THE CULTURAL SUPERSTRUCTURE

The fundamental aspect of familial culture is the emphasis on the family itself: on its primacy, on its home as its castle, on its continuity, and on the maintenance of its internal relationships. Continuity is expressed and reinforced by rites of birth, puberty or initiation, marriage, and, above all, death, for the funerary observations link the living with the ancestors, reinforcing continuity and emphasizing the importance of the old (Davis 1977, 93). This is true even where there is no ancestor worship as such (although it should be noted that over great stretches of Asia normally described as adhering to one or another of the major religions, aspects of ancestor worship exist in the village household religious observations while in sub-Saharan Africa such practices are usually maintained even in societies apparently converted to major religions). Stories, pictures, songs, myths, and proverbs tell of good sons and daughters, faithful wives, and the wise and venerable old.

The stabilizing element in familial production, and that which ensures larger returns to its productive and reproductive decision makers, is the segmentation of the family and society by age, sex, marital status and relationship. The fact that the family is a producer as well as a consumer unit means that it is widely typified by patriarchy (Shanin 1972, 28–29). Such rule may not be absolute; Lewis reported of the Mexican village that "the most even-tempered marriages are those which follow a middle course: the wife does little to challenge the authority of the husband and the husband is not too overbearing toward his wife" (Lewis 1960, 55). Indeed, the more powerful may be constrained by the need to behave in accordance with that power; Mandelbaum (1970) stresses the necessity in India for the old to retain their dignity.

The conflict between familial morality, suited to familial production, and extrafamilial morality, suited to the capitalist labor market, can be extreme during periods of transition. Both tourists and development experts who have wandered into a society of family production are likely to decide that the lack of "development" arises from an inadequate morality. At the same time, parents with children tending to obey the new extrafamilial morality are likely to regard them as a testimony to an inadequate upbringing.[3] Until the transition of morality has taken place, the direction of the wealth flow is not likely to reverse.

Early capitalism eagerly accepted the family's willingness to impose a firm upbringing in order to induce the ability to work hard and without complaint. It also appreciated the family teaching its less powerful members that it was good for them to live austerely, and that there should be no resentment of differential treatment and privilege. Indeed, if the family taught honesty and diligence better than the state, it was a good thing. There was no problem in maintaining the sanctity of the family; in fact, the decreasing need for organizing productive relations between its members reduced the internal tensions. However, the fact that the family breadwinner in the labor market had to be of working age meant that the recognition of the head of a family was likely to be extended to the head of the nuclear component even of an extended family. Sometimes the employer placed more emphasis on virtues like thrift and sobriety than had been the case in the traditional family.

This situation in which the traditional family retained its ancient morality and produced obedient employees for a system not based on family production and not fundamentally in need of much of its morality, proved surprisingly stable. There were, of course, reasons also at the family level for maintaining the system. If the young were employed outside the family but handed over most of their earnings, then the patriarchal system could survive almost intact—but the young had to be exhorted more, for no longer were the sanctions such simple ones as denial of access to land and food. If the womenfolk would continue to live modestly and work hard to produce household domestic services, then the household could obtain these products more cheaply than they could be acquired from the outside market—but the family had to emphasize the difference between the things that men were suited for and those that lay in the female sphere. High fertility helped: it emphasized the female role, it kept the mother tied to the home, and it supplied her with extra helpers. Capitalism could hardly do anything but approve; it was able to obtain a man's labor for lower wages than would have been needed by his family to obtain all their needs directly from the market. The parallel is striking with the situation described by Meillassoux where foreign firms in Africa paid low wages in the knowledge that subsistence support would be supplied by the workers' extended families (Meillassoux 1972, 102).

Ultimately, as the labor market expanded in the industrializing West, this stability was undermined. The need for higher levels of skills, and the temptations of relative affluence, meant that children were put into school on a mass scale, with complex and ramifying effects.[4] The school presented children with new authority figures; it undermined the ability of the old to claim greater wisdom; it substituted virtue in being diligent in schoolwork for diligence in household activities; it raised consumption expectations; and ultimately it encouraged parents and children, as well as husbands and wives, to see each other in new lights with an inevitable tendency towards egalitarianism.

At the same time, the position of the wife lost its earlier stability, first in the middle classes. In England (here we seem to be picking up a specific Western thread which probably accelerated global demographic transition) parents had not lived with their married children and intervened between child and spouse for a very long time and mothers-in-law had not kept daughters-in-law in their place (Macfarlane 1978). Over centuries "affective individualism" developed (Stone 1977), spurred by growing wealth and probably by the decline in familial production. The culmination of this process with nineteenth-century affluence has been described well by Ann Douglas in *The Feminization of American Culture* (1978) (even if one disagrees with her distinguishing of the central mechanism). Up to about 1880, in the English-speaking world, almost frantic attempts were made to convince middle-class women that their place was in the home—no longer because of dire need nor even because of a moral imperative, but because they were essentially gay, frivolous, decorative creatures who took dresses more seriously than industry or ideas.[5] By the second half of the twentieth century the market was competing strongly for the labor even of married woman with young children and was increasingly offering to produce most household needs.

Inevitably, morality had changed toward those more suited to a fully developed capitalism. The stress of the rights of the old had almost disappeared and that on male prerogatives was declining. Morality had passed successively from being chiefly the concern of the family to that of the church and ultimately the state. More importantly, in terms of the likely impact on fertility, it was concerned ever less with intrafamilial relations. This meant a declining chance of an economic return from children in later life, which, together with the fact that their productive usefulness when young had crumbled, turned the wealth flow downward and made low fertility inevitable.

CONTRADICTIONS AND CHANGE

Clearly, except in periods of long stability, there is not likely to arise a superstructure that exactly fits the needs of the current state of the modes of production. Although there has been a persistent family mystique, the family—especially that which controlled production—has always been marked by tensions, some inevitable and some equilibrating. Such tensions should be distinguished from the bitterness that marks rapid changes in parts of the Third World during which some family members feel not so much that their position is invidious, but that they have been robbed of age-old rights (Kiray 1976, 261–71). Much of the interest and excitement of village life—the essence which keeps life from being so miserably poor and dreary as outsiders often assume—lies in observing the skill with which some villagers observe the traditional mores and niceties in contrast to the daring with which others bend the rules or the crassness with which some break them. This carries through into life with capitalist production; much of English manners, literature, and humor centers on the degree of skill in noting and observing social class differences.

Nevertheless, there are stress points in the traditional family that are of crucial importance with either evolutionary or imported social change.

One is the incompatibility between the high value placed on the family built up by reproduction and so sustained by full blood ties and the need to maintain a production unit of efficient size in conditions of capricious mortality and accidental subfertility or a sexual imbalance in births. Thus, many of the most family-conscious societies tend to be marked by remarriage, step-parents, half-brothers and sisters,[6] fictive kin, and adoption.

Another is the incongruous position of the patriarch. In order to maintain his position of awesome respect from a distance, and because of the related delegation of authority, he tends to become increasingly isolated. He avoids intimacy, he cannot talk to his sons as he would to other men, and he has to allow his wife to run the household almost as if he were not present. Where segregation is substantial, he may have to spend much of his time out (in coffee shops in Turkey) because the house has become a woman's place.[7] There are difficulties in the father-son relationship; as parents grow older they usually tend to assume more managerial roles (hence the upwardly flowing wealth flow), especially if the family is wealthy,[8] but the real intergenerational strain can come later if an increasingly senile old man tries to maintain his control over a son at the height of his powers. The power delegated to the older women often becomes real in practice, and the alliance formed between her and her son may undermine the ideal family structure and serve as an instrument for change.[9] The problem of senile old men—and the problem of unduly delayed inheritance—is increasingly aggravated by a demographic factor, declining mortality.

The greatest potential for conflict and change arises from the peculiar position of women. Women are a major—and underestimated—part of the workforce. In fact—and this point is rarely taken into account in demographic literature—patriarchs do not distinguish very much between the labor inputs of wives and children (and they can substitute for one another, a potentially important point in the timing of demographic transition). Precisely in those societies, where all respondents tell the researcher that women are of so little value that the birth of a daughter brings no joy, girls are so socialized to obey and to work that they become, when married out, the backbone of the family labor inputs. This is often obscured by emphasis being placed on the managerial role of the mother-in-law or on an artificial analytical division between "productive work" and "household activities."[10] In India, "though the young wife is taken to be a person of little consequence in the family, her role is one of great importance. Few family roles are subject to such close scrutiny and so liable to such quick redressive action" (Mandelbaum 1970, 93). Indeed, her own family is supposed to participate in that process by upbringing, instruction at the time of marriage, and even subsequent intervention if necessary (Mandelbaum 1970, 85).[11] It might be noted that daughters, even though married out, retain certain value by this very fact in that such marriages help create family alliances.

With regard to women, there is one curious parallel between the superstructure of traditional familial production and of two-tiered capitalistic production where women work in the household. In each, the male position is most secure, and stability is most easily maintained, if women are kept divided. There is strong male pressure—and supporting jokes and folk wisdom—against too much "sisterhood" developing.

The peculiarities of women's position stem partly from the delegation of male power to the mother-in-law with a consequent frequent bitterness and even hatred between the older and younger woman that remains a standing threat to the whole family structure. This is reinforced by the fact that the younger woman usually adopts a position which is closer to the real long-term interests of her husband than is the position adopted by his mother. The situation is stable only if the bond between the younger husband and wife is kept weak, partly by emphasizing the husband's prior obligations to his parents and siblings, but necessarily also by downgrading the pleasures of marital sex, reinforced in many societies by an insistence that the wife display little emotion during sexual relations with her husband. The maintenance of this situation depends to a considerable degree on arranged marriage.[12] The maintenance of power by the older generation has important implications for reproduction because it separates reproductive decision making from those biologically involved.

A related issue is the purity of wives. In Mexico this may mean a diminution of all external family contacts (Lewis 1960, 57), the husband's as well as the wife's, and may have direct demographic consequences: "Men feel most secure when their wives are pregnant or have an infant to care for; thus, to have one child follow upon another is a desirable state of affairs from the men's viewpoint" (Lewis 1960, 58).

A weakness of the superstructure generated by familial production is the almost inevitable strain between its morality and that of the major religions which are likely to have strongest hold over its urban or elite populations (one of the distinctions between the Little and Great traditions in India) (Redfield 1955; Redfield and Singer 1954; Marriott 1955). A religion that is not wholly family-based is likely to make some appeal directly to individuals, rather than always through the patriarch, and it is likely to put some stress on individual moralities applying to one and all, rather than on gradations by family position. The same is true of all legal systems, and of most other actions which a state might take.

With economic change, a crucial weakness is the attitude toward instilling, or allowing, competitiveness and individual initiative in children during their upbringing. Traditional childrearing opposes such concepts, which can weaken the traditional family. As capitalism develops, employers are increasingly forced to demand such attributes. Eventually, tempted by the chance of external income, many families allow their children to develop such characteristics so as to compete successfully for jobs in the marketplace. In these circumstances, the direction of the wealth flow changes quickly. The willingness of families to make this change in upbringing depends not only on the economic temptations but also on the stress the culture has traditionally put on children knowing their place.

Most of the discussion has assumed patriarchy and has implied patrilineality and patrilocality—rightly in terms of the great majority of Third World societies. But there are areas, especially in Southeast Asia and parts of tropical Africa, where matrilineality or matrilocality or neolocality are quite common. Such societies may resist change less readily when faced with Westernization (furthermore, Western inheritance and land law codes and attitudes tend to produce confusion and consequent change in matrilineal societies).

PROBLEMS IN INTERPRETING THE COURSE OF WESTERN FERTILITY

The major problems in applying wealth flows theory to the West are (1) the relatively low fertility in western Europe before the final sustained decline; (2) certain populations with an earlier fertility decline; (3) the surprisingly late start of general fertility decline; (4) the sudden beginning of sustained fertility decline in a range of countries during the short period from the 1860s to the 1880s; and (5) the long, slow, and interrupted decline in fertility over the past hundred years.

One point should be made at the outset. The West was the one culture that received no models from other cultures (except—and this may be important—certain models transmitted by Christianity, which, though transmuted and reinterpreted in many ways, originated in the classical world or even in Hebrew society). Hence, there were lags that are unlikely to be seen again, first in creating a superstructure where high fertility disadvantaged reproductive decision makers, and second in substituting easier for more difficult forms of contraception. We are unlikely to witness again a society with as little agricultural production as characterized England of the 1870s without low fertility, and we are unlikely to find in future Third World transitions the level of use of withdrawal as a contraceptive method as was found in a substantial part of the West earlier this century. Neither the Western capitalist development, nor the superstructure, nor the pressures on it to change, were the same throughout the West. Much remains to be discovered about cultural interchange, and the West still has cultural leaders and followers. But in much of the society there was a homogeneity compared with contemporary global society.

The West had for long not maximized upward wealth flows (a fact of fundamental importance in the world demographic transition). Families and households had not generally been multigenerational for centuries. Part of the explanation, at least in England, according to Macfarlane's analysis, may have been a much earlier reduction in familial production than was once assumed (Macfarlane 1978).[13] Part may have been because the complex family is easier to form by arranged marriage, an institution forbidden by canon law (Davis 1977, 106). Macfarlane appears to hint at reasons reaching back through Saxon culture to German tribal patterns, which had never fully adjusted to the conditions of a peasantry. Some of the cause must lie in the nature of the strong post-Conquest state and of the feudal system, but some may well lie in the existence of a strong church with behavioral (superstructural) concepts formed in the urban areas of the Roman Empire at its height, when much production was not familial (the external nature of the church would not have rendered that a crucial point in any case). Certainly, an examination of nineteenth-century Australian society suggests that fertility remained high, at least at that time, not so much because large families added greatly to economic well-being but because they did little to detract from it (Caldwell and Ruzicka 1978; Ruzicka and Caldwell 1977). (Frequent references will be made to the Australian transition, not because it was atypical of the Western tradition but because it seems to have been very typical, and we happen to have done some work on it of a kind that we hope will soon be duplicated in other Western societies.) Yet, marital fertility in the pretransition West was high even in terms of the contemporary Third World.[14] Moderate fertility was achieved largely through the postponement of marriage, and I believe that this will eventually be shown to have had little to do with any effort to restrict the ultimate size of the family (at least before the second half of the nineteenth century) but was concerned almost entirely with the achievement of economic security and a sufficiency to capitalize marriage and its domestic economy.[15]

Nevertheless, there is evidence for the nobility of Geneva and the aristocracy of France of a measurable degree of marital fertility control from about 1700 (Henry 1965, 451–52), and of more general practice accompanied by declining marital fertility in France from the last quarter of the eighteenth century (Bourgeois-Pichat 1965, 482). In contrast, marital fertility did not fall anywhere else in the West (or the world) before the 1860s,[16] and there is no evidence of marital fertility restriction even among the British aristocracy before this date (Hollingsworth 1965, 373).

Now, it is possible that there were downward wealth flows among the French aristocracy by this time (although children were valuable for the delegation of power, but it is unlikely that these mattered financially). Familial production was declining in France, but was not as low as in England, and in any case some of the early falls in fertility appear to have occurred in predominantly family-farming areas of Normandy and the Gironde.

This means that one other factor must be reconsidered: the locus of fertility decision making. In the multigenerational family, whether co-residential or not, that locus was likely to be found in the generation older than that actually involved in reproduction, and, if the flow of wealth was upward (or even close to zero), the result was high marital fertility. The position was much the same in the two-generation family, where it inclined toward male dominance. The remaining case for consideration is where there was a significant degree of female participation in the two-generational family. One reason for this qualification is that in nearly every fertility study of pretransitional populations it has been shown that wives are less likely to favor high fertility than their husbands.[17] Women may well have a material interest in avoiding very high fertility even before the wealth flow changes decisively downward, in that frequent births inconvenience and even immobilize them, as well as tending—especially in premodern societies—to affect their health.[18]

A greater role in female fertility decision making would itself imply an important transition in the superstructure—toward a greater belief in female coparticipation or companionship in work or social activities, and perhaps evidencing and accelerating a decline (perhaps with increasing secularization) in strong moral or religious views on the separate roles of the sexes and the sanctity of maternity. Changes of this kind may well have occurred among the French nobility (described by Sauvy as "that brilliant and corrupt aristocracy which introduced forbidden practices . . . from the world of prostitution into that of irregular unions and adultery, and from there to the marriage chamber") (Sauvy 1969, 362), but were they so likely among the mass of the people? Something very significant had certainly happened in France among the latter where by the mid-nineteenth century, marital fertility levels were probably only around two-thirds of those in other western European countries (Lesthaeghe 1977; Knodel 1974; van de Walle 1974). Nevertheless, what had happened was probably distinct from what was to occur toward the end of the century, when France fully participated (in spite of the demographic myth that France's long slow fall in fertility was a substitute for the later sharper falls in other parts of the West) in the general fertility transition—during the thirty years from 1850 to 1880 French marital fertility fell by 9 percent in contrast to a fall of 32 percent in the next thirty years from 1890 to 1910; for this latter period, a slightly smaller decline than that experienced by Belgium but greater than those in Germany, the Netherlands, and Australia.[19]

My interpretation of late-eighteenth- and nineteenth-century French social history is that there is as yet no convincing demonstration of greater male-female partnership during that period. Evidence may well be forthcoming, for one of the persistent strains in the struggle for greater female rights in England and Australia during the second half of the nineteenth century was the claim that the French woman worked beside her husband instead of being relegated to the nursery.[20]

The real proof that the superstructure can move at a significantly different rate from the modes of production is provided by the fact that marital fertility did not fall decisively until the 1870s or 1880s in any Western country except France. By this date only one-fifth of the British male workforce was in agriculture (Mitchell with Deane 1962, 60) (it had been only one-third half a century earlier), and a much smaller proportion in agricultural familial production or any other type of familial production. The argument put forward here is that the lag in the superstructure in the way of life controlled by the mores and attitudes of the society was so great that children were not an appreciable economic disadvantage (that is, the wealth flow had not turned decisively downward) until this time. Two other explanations can be put forward. The first is that the wealth flow had changed, but that at first the only mechanism for adjustment that was known or countenanced was delayed marriage. This appears not to have been the case. The proportions married had not been falling in western Europe (indeed, they appear to have been rising over the preceding half century),[21] and may well have been at a level typical of Europe for centuries[22]—well back to a period when the wealth flow had certainly been upward. There is no evidence in Australia that before the 1880s delayed female marriage was regarded as a method for containing family size.[23] The second is that there was a specific lag in facing the fact either that children had become uneconomic or that contraception could be used or was acceptable. Here again the Australian evidence for the 1850–80 period is that large families were not felt to be economically oppressive and that family size was not thought to be a factor determining success in life (Caldwell and Ruzicka 1978, 84–86). This was in marked contrast to premature male marriage, which was widely believed to be an economic indiscretion that was exceedingly difficult to remedy subsequently. After high fertility joined early male marriage as an economic indiscretion—from the 1880s—contraceptive practice became increasingly acceptable and marital fertility began to decline rapidly. Something had happened in the 1870s or 1880s—not earlier in the century.

What did happen in the 1870s and 1880s? The contemporary Australian material reveals three significant trends: the enforcement of universal, compulsory schooling; and intensification of the movement for women's suffrage and for more equal rights for women; and an increase in the availability of the goods of the consumption society and their advertisement. In contrast, it did not exhibit a steep decline in infant or child mortality or any marked change in occupational structure (there had never been subsistence agriculture, and familial production made up a very small part of the whole economy). The populace were becoming more worldly but there seems to be little indication that they were becoming less religious until close to the end of the century. Contemporary observers felt that it was schooling that changed the impact of children on the family, and they were almost certainly right. The reason why even free schooling made children costly has been argued elsewhere (Caldwell and Ruzicka 1978, 88–90),[24] and will not be repeated here. What has not been said, but does seem possible, is that there was a complex interaction between husbands, wives, and children. Before compulsory schooling, the domestic workforce had consisted of the wife and the children. Once the latter went to school, more of the household work devolved on the wife, and the specifically female objection to repeated childbirths became more intense. Furthermore, children could hardly live less austerely without their mothers also doing so; this was particularly so, once an increasing proportion of mothers had themselves been to school. Fertility fell at much the same time in a score of countries because the universal schooling was implemented at much the same time in all. This was largely a social decision, based on increasing affluence—the economy at the time was not expanding at so high a rate as to need this sudden rise in educated persons. Fertility within countries also often fell from about the same year across a broad spectrum of society irrespective of the role in the economy played by the parents.[25]

Fertility continued to fall for another hundred years, partly because the traditional family with its segregated roles and its justification of such segregation took so long (and more) to dismantle. As the wealth flow toward children increased, large families were described by all as unbearably expensive. Looking after children became far more emotionally draining, partly because of the extra thought given to their welfare, and partly because of the increasing clash between less restrained children and far more expensive and fragile housing and household possessions. Efficient use of contraception did not occur at once, and its effect was partly negated by the fact that it allowed more universal and earlier marriage. Not all the movement was in the superstructure. Elsewhere the two-tiered structure of production has been described (Caldwell 1978, 568–71). At least as much labor input went into the subsistence production of household goods and services as into production outside the home during most of these hundred years. Slowly the market overcame the complex problems of competing efficiently in producing many of these services. Slowly, too, but faster by the 1950s, the expanding labor market began to tempt women to go outside the home to work. Increasingly the superstructure changed to justify this transformation, inevitably with friction and some bitterness.

PROBLEMS IN INTERPRETING THE COURSE OF THIRD WORLD INFERTILITY

The process in the peripheral areas of the West and in the Third World has not been, and could not be, like that just described. The central fact of our times has been the ability of the dominant western economy to establish a global economy and society. This transformation has been based on the strength of the Western economy. The export of its social arrangements has not been based on similar social strength but on two other features: the ability of the paramount exporting economy to sell its society as well, and the fact that the Western society was ahead in accommodating itself to the more capitalist economy and hence offered a model for change when traditional social relations fitted increasingly badly with new modes of production.

There is a tendency among more economically determinist social scientists of a functionalist persuasion to interpret the parallel between economic change toward a more Westernized model and social change toward the same model as demonstrating the domination of that social change by the economic change. This, I suggest, is a major error leading to a fundamental misinterpretation of what is happening, and what is likely to happen, in the contemporary world. It overestimates the impact of economic change alone, and accordingly tempts researchers to measure demographic and social change with economic indices alone or predominantly. It explains highly significant transformations in family relationships in occupational terms, when even the participants are keenly aware that imported social models have played a major role and even made the acceptance of new occupations possible. It neglects the fact that some Western economies had so changed during the early nineteenth or even eighteenth centuries that the availability of seductive external models of family relations could have changed family relationships to the point of rendering high fertility economically disadvantageous without any faster movement in the economic base (although such family changes may have speeded up the movement). If greater egalitarianism in emotional relationships and in consumption (and possibly production) decisions had developed between parents and children and between husbands and wives, fertility might well have fallen much earlier.

The Western society, and above all the Western family pattern, is not for the Third World merely an external pattern. It is largely imposed. Western richness has been identified with the Western way of life. Missionaries, colonial administrators, imported legal systems, the media, and schools have all taught it. International programs, especially family planning programs, both assume and, almost unconsciously, advocate the Western family. In United Nations statements about the 1975 International Women's Year and the 1979 International Year of the Child no concessions were made to family relationships that were not contemporary-even avant-garde-Western ones. The West has also exported a view of life and a secular skepticism of religion and traditional ways and ethics that has powerfully catalyzed its direct teachings of family change.

Mass schooling has probably had a greater impact on the family than even in the West. There are several reasons for this. First, mass schooling has come in many countries at an earlier stage in terms of the economic and occupational structure than in the West. Second, the message that schooling means an access to Western riches and the Western way of life has been almost universally received. Third, Western schooling assumes and teaches the Western way of life-especially the Western family-almost exclusively. Even teachers who do not live a very Western family life believe that they should not deny the validity of the Western family message when teaching their students. Fourth, traditional families treat educated members quite differently than uneducated members (Caldwell 1979)-invariably educated children cost more and give less. Most demographic and social surveys of the Third World yield measures testifying to the extraordinary impact of formal schooling, even patently poor schooling-but little has been done to investigate the nature of that impact.

The literature on the nature of family change in Third World countries is still limited-there is actually more concentration on the traditional situation-but what exists is instructive, especially in the clarity with which it, usually inadvertently, reveals for many societies that children's economic value ultimately declines with such change. Examples will be taken here from studies of three societies subjected to a substantial amount of external influence: Eregli, a small town in Turkey on the coast of the Black Sea, studied by Mubeccel Kiray in the 1960s (Kiray 1976); Tepoztlan, a highland village in central Mexico, studied by Oscar Lewis in the 1940s and 1950s (Lewis 1960);[26] and K'un Shen, a village on the southwest coast of Taiwan, studied by Norma Diamond in the 1960s (Diamond 1969).

The parallels are striking in spite of the three populations being equidistant around the world, and the differences few and not very significant.

First, the young people, especially the sons, are restless. They have learned of a different way of life. Their clothing is changing somewhat faster than their parents approve, largely, one gathers, because of the implied threat to authority. The children are noisier than they were and a stage known as adolescence can be discerned—a fact not unrelated either to schooling or the media.

There is not only implied challenge but actual challenge. Sons are restless working for their fathers on the family farm or in the family business, partly for the social reason that they resent the imperious paternal authority, and partly for the economic reason that they could earn more money elsewhere than the pocket money they are allowed from the family production. Because of the isolation and pride of the patriarch, the mother often mediates, strengthening her alliance with her son and subtly changing all family relationships.

Daughters are constrained to take their examples from their mothers, but those examples are changing. Indeed, among women, it is the authority that has been given to older women that is allowing change. "As they grow older they become more self-assertive and oppose their husbands' attempts to limit their freedom and their business ventures. . . . The present trend in the village is for the younger women and even the unmarried girls to take on the more independent attitudes of the older women" (Lewis 1960, 56).

Among the young, spousal bonds are tightening. In Taiwan the "love marriage" is appearing; in Mexico the proportion of arranged marriages is declining; while in Turkey, the arrangement of marriages without the consent of the future spouses is now rarely attempted. A potent factor is female education. In Taiwan, "the increasing amount of education as one moves down the age scale . . . gives a woman an advantage over her mother-in-law compared to earlier times" (Diamond 1969, 62). In Turkey, "many [husbands] even stress that they prefer their wives' advice to that of older members of their families who have been unable to keep up with today's fast-changing relationships, institutions and values" (Kiray 1976, 270). There are clearly parallels here with the situation described for sections of Ghanaian and Nigerian society (Caldwell 1968; Caldwell and Caldwell 1978; Caldwell and Caldwell 1976). In all societies, these new balances within the family are increasingly militating against the establishment or maintenance of the multi-generational household—a fact with implications for both emotional relations and for productive ones.

Relationships are changing—sometimes leading to bitterness, as distinct from the stresses and even hatreds of the traditional family. In Taiwan, "K'un Shen recognizes that sons have an obligation to support their parents. . . . Yet allegiance to parents is not sufficient to hold the household together. . . . There is considerable bitterness among some of the older people, who feel that they have no authority over any of their sons' households, and their presence is resented. It is not often that a man over 50 or a widow with a married son can maintain a position as household head. The leadership passes to the next generation and the elders become subordinates" (Diamond 1969, 64). Another account of Taiwan reports "a new uncertainty about relationships within the family, a recognition (though not necessarily an acceptance) of a new emphasis on the husband-wife relationship and its threat to the traditionally more important relationship between parents and sons" (Wolf 1972, 129). In Turkey, "generally a son takes his mother's side in any conflict between her and his wife" (Kiray 1976, 267). Nevertheless, "sons who change their behavior towards their fathers [and this is becoming common] also begin to change in their actions towards their wives and their mothers. Consequently, often a mother can no longer count on supreme power over her daughters-in-law if her son starts to take his wife's side against his mother" (Kiray 1976, 267). Often the extent of change is not faced; in Turkey, "fathers usually do not admit that such conflict exists, and are very reluctant to concede that their rights and duties have changed with the times [read Westernization for times] . . . both parties can usually be led to believe that neither's role has changed and so authority can formally be retained" (Kiray 1976, 265–66).

The unity of the traditional family was also based partly on force, and this, too, is being undermined. In Mexico, "severe punishment is traditional. . . . On the whole, Tepoztecans agree that punishment has become less severe and that there is a greater toleration toward children's faults. This is particularly true among the more permissive and better educated younger generation" (Lewis 1960, 60).

These changes have important economic implications, not least for the value of children (and hence, also, children-in-law). In Mexico, "the custom of having daughters working in the home is a deeply ingrained one. . . . Many mothers exploit their daughters, particularly the oldest" (Lewis 1960, 62–63). In Turkey, a mother, fearing further weakening of her emotional bond with her son, nowadays not only is likely to consent to separate households, but often takes the necessary action to see that it can be arranged, "although she has no desire to see her son leave or be deprived of the help of his bride" (Kiray 1976, 265).

A PROBLEM IN CALCULATING THE ECONOMIC VALUE OF CHILDREN

There is an important and curious problem that often besets the researcher when trying to draw up a balance sheet of the economic gains and losses from children. Its solution has implications for the timing of the reversal of the wealth flow.

In rural or even in poor urban populations, it is often denied that children cost anything, even when long-term benefits gained from them are fairly explicitly recognized. One explanation, which I have stressed elsewhere (Caldwell 1976), is the widespread concept of "more mouths, more hands"—they join their mothers from a young age in helping to grow food. Another is the fact that children's costs are shared—in Africa they wander from one relative's cooking pot to another 's. A third is that the whole process is seen as dynamic and not static; infants grow so quickly into children whose value offsets or exceeds their cost, and their births are so frequently regarded as investments from which gains will shortly flow, that parents without a young child can easily feel economically deprived.

Yet, a reworking of survey results suggests that this explanation is not sufficient and that it is not what many respondents are implying. What some seem to be saying is that there are no costs within a family—that is what a family means. The argument appears to be that there is no parallel between deliberately putting some income aside—putting money in a bank that could be used to buy food or clothing or more frivolous things, or subtracting a greater proportion of food produced for sale in the market—and tightening one's belt a little more as children multiply in order to make the same amount of food or clothing go a greater distance. The latter is regarded as enforced saving, and hence easy to achieve compared with the more difficult voluntary saving represented by the first examples. It is, of course, common that it is the children, or they and their mother, who do most of the belt tightening, and hence there is no real cost to the decision maker. [27] It is also possible that such tightening increases child mortality,[28] but once this is noted as a major problem the chances are that both the emotional and wealth flows have turned decisively downward. Thus, the ensuing benefits from children are received without any appreciated initial outlay. There has been forced saving and investment at no felt cost.

If this calculus is common, then the point where the wealth flow is felt to swing toward the children is clearly displaced to a later date. The calculus probably is common, but the displacement is probably much rarer, because the family and its economy have so changed from the traditional pattern by the time the reversal is near that forced savings are rarely felt. But the calculus may be important in explaining the great stability of high fertility well before that divide is reached.

THE LESSONS

The fundamental point is that the fertility declines of the past century have been one of our most significant indicators of a massive change in the human condition. They are not the product of anything no more deep-seated than change in ideal family size or of acquaintance with contraception or of a sudden and belated recognition that children were contrary to the family's economic interests.

This brings us to perhaps the central mystery of population studies. The statistical techniques are ever more impressive and are both needed and valuable in that they measure the true demographic position and the direction and speed of change. But in themselves they do not tell us anything about the nature of that change. Attempts to apply survey techniques with questions about reproductive attitudes and behavior have told us something about short-term western fertility change, but the findings have often been fairly trivial and the resulting published volumes curiously unexciting even to professionals in the field. The application of the same techniques to non-Western societies has probably been misleading while producing results that are equally unexciting. This is unusual in the social sciences where most fields tend to produce from time to time spates of work that do seem to cast new light on human behavior and the nature of human societies. The lack of excitement is also surprising in view of the historical significance, and the importance to individuals, of the phenomena being investigated.

A correct theory of stable high fertility and of fertility decline will be essentially a theory of social and familial change. The attempt in this paper may often miss the exact mark. Nevertheless, the truth lies somewhere in the general area it has attempted to traverse. High fertility was not uneconomic in the traditional family engaged in familial production, while it is uneconomic in contemporary societies with a dominant nonfamilial labor market. The cost of children, or the balance between gains accruing to parents and losses experienced by them because of having children, depends very greatly on the conventional emotional and economic relations within the family—that is, on the superstructure. This superstructure may lag behind changes in the method of production—nothing else will explain the lateness of the Western fertility decline—or it may move forward surprisingly rapidly, when the relations of production are changing, as a result of imported values and behavioral patterns as is at present occurring in much of the Third World as a global, Westernized society is being created.[29] Certainly there may be lags, but they are lags in family relations which prevent fertility from becoming uneconomic as early as might otherwise be the case. They are not lags in the recognition that children are uneconomic—the "props" of Notesteinian demographic transition theory whereby religion and social creed hide reality from parents. This means that if demographers wish to explain the phenomena they study, they must either become real social scientists or alternatively confine themselves to measuring what other disciplines might be asked to explain. They must also approach fertility causation with a more sophisticated apparatus than the largely tautological one of "intermediate variables" (Davis and Blake 1956), originally an intriguing concept and one that still serves graduate students well as a checklist, but one that also convinces many of the same students that they have done all the explaining that needs to be done.

Such an apparatus will have to give priority to studying families with fundamentally different relations of production. The failure to do this has produced not only Westernized and basically false pictures of fertility behavior in the Third World but also similarly Westernized and unhelpful pictures of the sociology of the family—pictures which suggest that the family structures of the world can be adequately described in terms of continua of such characteristics as inheritance, marriage payments, combinations of relatives living together, and so on, without a prior picture of the relations of these characteristics to the whole, and the varying natures of that whole.[30]

In terms of fertility change in the Third World, the rates of economic growth and of occupational change are relatively easily measured, and predicted with somewhat greater difficulty and inaccuracy. What will determine the timing and speed of fertility decline is the rate at which family relations are Westernized. This is not merely a function of the level of cultural flow from the West. It is also very much affected by the receptivity or opposition of the receiving cultures. The areas of the world where high fertility persists longest will not necessarily be the poorest. It is likely that they will be the Islamic world where Koranic injunction serves to insulate the existing family structure,[31] and sub-Saharan Africa where the lineages retain a surprising amount of their strength even while welcoming Western imports that do not impinge on family relations. It is clear that family planning programs hasten fertility falls in some countries (Mauldin and Berelson 1977) (but not equally clear that they can initiate falls). It would be unwise to assume that this represents a simple case of contraception meeting a recognized need. The existence of such programs and governmental backing for them suggests new spousal relations and tends to legitimize such trends. The use of contraceptives, even with a degree of duress, can also change family relations.

It is also unwise to talk of societies with high child mortality and consequent high and compensating fertility. A central reason for high child mortality is that the direction of the emotional flow has not changed (Caldwell 1979), and stress is still put on the importance and needs of the older generation. It follows that child mortality will be relatively higher than it might otherwise be and that high fertility is not economically disadvantageous and is likely to characterize the society.

The current debate, whether family structures or relations in the West ever resembled those of the contemporary Third World, is almost irrelevant. What is relevant is the impact of contemporary Western patterns on contemporary Third World patterns. Nor is the lack of homogeneity in either the West or Third World of much importance. Clearly, parts of the West have greatly affected other parts.[32] Clearly also, Westernization is a relative concept. Even the West's leading edges are changing rapidly, partly because the labor market is tempting members of the family who have never before been attracted and is increasingly proving to individuals within the family that they need ever less protection from its structure. Nevertheless, the nature and pace of change is not solely directed by the market—the European cultural heritage plays an important role. For instance, the egalitarian ideological element in that heritage has allowed the market demands on individuals to be interpreted in very specific ways. The arguments of women's movements, and those of the younger generations are often conceded, partly because opposition to them would betray much older principles.

These changes can be studied. Even in terms of the empirical base for my own suggestions, Thadani has probably underestimated its size,[33] modest though it may still be. There already exist very substantial findings on the nature of differing societies and their families, and also on change, little used by either demographers or others as yet to interpret fertility levels or fertility trends.

Certain central conclusions should be stressed. The first one is that a society based on familial production cannot but emphasize high fertility or take uncontrolled fertility for granted. Such high fertility provides labor and keeps women in a position where they are family-centered, work hard, and do not demand to compete with their menfolk in consumption. When the emotional and wealth flows are both from young to old (and they must flow in the same direction, except during brief periods of traumatic change), children also work hard and consume relatively little. Any relaxation in the veneration for the old and the male would fundamentally change the production and consumption system and, in a society of predominantly familial production, would be automatically reversed as the system became less efficient from the viewpoint of the older male decision makers. Such societies exhibit high infant and child mortality, not merely because they do not possess adequate modern health services, but also because greater care lavished on children would upset the priorities assigned to different individuals within the family structure, alter the time allocation of labor, change the balance of consumption, and render the young less likely to accept the direction of their labor or to work as hard. A society based on the labor market does not need an upward flow in either veneration or wealth. Ultimately, the need of the employer to appeal directly to all individuals, and of the producer to attempt to maximize consumption among all by direct temptation, and of the strong state necessary to impose the community-based morality means that such a society not only does not require the same family priorities but inevitably causes their erosion. In the end, children become an economic burden, and, with the emotional flow directed toward them, a large number of them become an emotional burden, too.

This change is accelerated by the imposition of mass education systems. This was so in the West. It is much more true in the contemporary Third World, where the arrival of mass education has occurred at a time when the move toward a global economy, together with a more rarely noted but equally important move toward a global society, has meant a major attack on the old family system. That system could not change if the system of production were not altering at the same time, but the external intrusion speeds up the rate of change in the superstructure (which, in turn, as children are more likely to seek work elsewhere or to keep a larger share of their earnings, inevitably accelerates the transformation of the system of production). We will not have an industrialized world by the end of the century, but it is unlikely that there will be any substantial parts of it where fertility is still high and has shown no decline.

This chapter has attempted to demonstrate just how intricate and compelling are the mechanisms that sustain high fertility in pretransitional societies. Those mechanisms are the fundamental sinews of the society and uncontrolled fertility is not merely an aspect of the society but the central aspect of the cultural superstructure that maintains the relations of production. Accordingly, the study of fertility transition is the study of the transformation of familial production into production through the labor market, of traditional society into modern society. There can be no discipline of "population studies" in the area of demographic transition that is not devoted to studying social and economic change in all aspects. Conversely, the failure of theorists of social and economic change to recognize the central role of demographic transition, both in terms of its occurrence and timing, in explaining the transformation of traditional society, is not merely an unfortunate omission in their explanations, but evidence of the basic inadequacy of those explanations. This is being treated more fully elsewhere (Caldwell 1982, 297–332).

NOTES

1. That is, in the low-fertility belt of Middle Africa.
2. The role of conversation in maintaining the modes of production has been investigated during 1979–80 by the author and Pat Caldwell, first in Bangladesh in collaboration with A.K.M. Jalalluddin, and second in South India in collaboration with P.H. Reddy and others in a joint project of the Department of Demography, The Australian National University, and the Bangalore Population Centre.
3. See Wiser and Wiser (1971, 263–67) for an excellent description of a man in rural India who became an exemplary village headman to the disgrace and heartbreak of his parents when it became obvious that he was not placing his family's interests first.
4. So much so that only a few points are being made here; the issue as a whole is being treated in a separate paper, J.C. Caldwell (1980, 6, 225–55).
5. Unpublished file compiled by Pat Caldwell on nineteenth-century Australia from *the Sydney Herald*, *the Sydney Morning Herald*, and *the Australasian*.
6. On premodern France, see Natalie Zemon Davis (1977, 93).
7. Cf., on India, Mandelbaum (1970, 58–61); on Turkey, Fallers and Fallers (1976, 247); on Mexico, O. Lewis (1960, 56–61).
8. Cf., on Bangladesh, Barkat-e-Khuda (1979).
9. Cf., on Turkey, Kiray (1976, 266–67).
10. As in Connell and Lipton (1977).
11. Mandelbaum (1970, 85), with a reference to Ramabai Ranade (1938).
12. Cf., on Mexico, O. Lewis (1960, 58).
13. Macfarlane (1978). His analysis is taken back to the beginning of the thirteenth century.
14. In Australia, an Ig of around 0.7 until the 1880s (J.C. Caldwell and Ruzicka (1977, Appendix A); in Belgium, an Ig of over 0.8 until the 1860s; in the Netherlands, one of over 0.8 until the 1890s (Lesthaeghe 1977, 102); in Germany, one of over 0.75 until the 1870s (Knodel 1974, 39); and, for comparison, an Ig of 0.76 in Mexico in 1960 and 0.66 in Taiwan in 1930

(Coale (1967, 2:209); 0.56 in Korea in 1925 (Coale, Goldman, and Cho, (1979, 13); and 0.55 in Ibadan, Nigeria, in 1973 (J. Caldwell and Pat Caldwell (1980, 19).

15. J.C. Caldwell and Ruzicka (1978, 4:84); and findings from an ongoing project by J. and Pat Caldwell. There is a myth that Ireland was different and marriage was severely delayed at an early date in order to restrict fertility. Actually its Im index in 1870 (immediately before the onset of the Western fertility transition) was 0.42, the same as Sweden and lower than Norway, and its Ig index was 0.67, just below England and Wales and well below Norway and Sweden (see Coale 1967). The postponement of marriage in rural Ireland was a problem of land shortage and land inheritance, and hence of the proper time to marry. By 1900 Ireland's Im was the lowest in Europe, but by 1900 western Europe had changed and the wealth flow was everywhere downward.

16. Between 1860 and 1890 marital fertility began to decline in most western and central European countries and in English-speaking countries of overseas European settlement.

17. Females in India expressed lower family size ideals or a desire for longer birth intervals, or less desire for the last birth or the next one (United Nations 1961, 137–58; Sovani and Dandekar 1955, 105–6); Kenya (Dow 1967, 784–91); East Java (Gille and Pardoko 1966, 514–17); Turkey (D. Kirk 1966, 577); Tunisia (Morsa 1966, 583–84); Sri Lanka (Kinch 1962, 90–91); and Ghana (J.C. Caldwell 1968, 85–91). The exceptions, where the men desired fewer children, were Taiwan (Freedman 1963, 226–28); and Malaysia (Coombs and Fernandez 1978, 57–73), close to or after the beginning of fertility transition, as well as a range of contemporary Western countries.

18. The joint project of the Department of Demography, The Australian National University, and the Bangalore Population Centre, which combined demographic and anthropological approaches, has produced a great deal of evidence for this assertion.

19. All comparisons are in terms of Ig (see Lesthaeghe 1977; Knodel 1974; van de Walle 1974; Ruzicka and Caldwell 1977). The 1880—1919 decline was 41 percent in Belgium, 26 percent in Germany, 21 percent in Australia and 22 percent in the Netherlands.

20. Unpublished file compiled by Pat Caldwell on nineteenth-century Australia from *the Sydney Herald*, *the Sydney Morning Herald* and *the Australasian*.

21. Cf. Lesthaeghe (1977, 102). The Im index for Belgium rose from 0.375 in 1845 to 0.435 in 1880, that for France from 0.516 in 1840 to 0.538 in 1880, that for Germany from 0.454 in 1865 to 0.501 in 1880, and that for the Netherlands from 0.389 in 1850 to 0.469 in 1880 (in each case the first estimate is the earliest available).

22. From the seventeenth century, according to Hajnal (1965); from at least the thirteenth century in England, according to Macfarlane (1978).

23. Ongoing project by J. Caldwell and Pat Caldwell.

24. On the Third World, see Caldwell (1968, esp. 96–114).

25. W. Brass reports (personal communication) that fertility began to decline in every county of England about 1876; Ruzicka and Caldwell (1977, 171–76) reported fertility declines commencing in all Australian occupational groups during the 1880s.

26. The village was also studied by Redfield (1930) in the 1920s.

27. Merrylin Wasson reports that this was the usual case in the poor quarter of old Delhi where she worked for a number of years (personal communication).

28. Evidence for this is the higher child mortality often found in larger families. Cf. Wray (1971, 9).

29. The Soviet Union and China have not been overlooked. It will be argued elsewhere that, in terms of the relations of production, they have been Westernized at least as fast as any other society.

30. See, for instance, Nimkoff (1965).

31. This refers mostly to the Islamic heartland, not to Indonesia or Malaysia.

32. In evidence given to the Royal Commission on *The Decline of the Birth Rate and on the Mortality of Infants in New South Wales,* vol. 1 (Sydney: New South Wales Government Printer, 1904), it was testified on more than one occasion that the leading influence was that of the French.

33. One analysis omitted was J.C. Caldwell and Pat Caldwell (1976, 347–65).

12

HUMAN MIGRATION: A HISTORICAL OVERVIEW

William H. McNeill

Defending hearth and home against strangers, on the one hand, and roving to far places in search of food and excitement, on the other, have always been opposing poles of human experience. They tend to manifest themselves most strongly at different stages of the life cycle: roving being an affair of youth, homekeeping of adulthood as well as of infancy and old age. The roving pattern of behavior has obvious biological advantages: apart from expanding the range of genetic mingling and variation, rovers occasionally discovered new foods and in rare instances even opened up new ecological niches for human occupancy. Their restless movements continually probed for new possibilities and tested old barriers, usually finding nothing of importance to other human beings, but every so often opening the way for critically important technological, geographical, and/or social breakthroughs.

Roving behavior, therefore, had an important role in human (and prehuman) evolution. Humankind could not have become the earth-girdling, dominant species we are without roving and without the migrations that followed successful discovery of new possibilities made manifest by such roving. Human occupation of the Americas and of previously islanded lands of Oceania is only the most recent—and geographically most extensive—example of processes that are as old as humankind.

The earliest phases of prehuman and human evolution are too little known for us to speculate usefully about the importance of roving and migration in those remote ages. But once skilled human hunters had mastered the art of killing big game and had discovered how to maintain a subtropical microenvironment next to their hairless bodies by wearing clothes, a truly remarkable globe-girdling migratory expansion began. Human hunting bands moved across the Bering Straits and all the way south to Tierra del Fuego within a few thousand years, and simultaneously filled up all the other corners of the globe where suitably large-bodied game animals could be found.

About 8000 B.C. this vast migration began to reach inelastic limits. This led many different human communities to intensify their search for food, diversifying diet so that humans again became omnivorous. Intensified food searches soon provoked the invention of agriculture in several different parts of the earth where suitably nourishing plants could be artificially propagated. Early agriculturalists were not necessarily sessile: in the Middle East, for example, where wheat and barley were the principal initial crops, slash-and-burn cultivation required farming communities to remove to new ground every few years; and since suitable new ground could only be found beneath the canopy of a deciduous forest, this meant periodic migration across distances that may sometimes have been considerable. Other styles of early cultivation—in particular the millet cultivation of the Chinese loess soils—do not seem to have required removal to new ground; perhaps for that reason, the Middle Eastern pattern of grain cultivation came to occupy a much larger region of the Old World—from the Atlantic face of Europe and North Africa to northwest India—than was true of other, more sessile early styles of agriculture.

Movement by boat also became significant for human society before cities and civilization appeared. The horizon for this kind of movement in the Mediterranean seems to have been about 4000 B.C. I am not aware of what the best estimates for the beginning of navigation in the southern seas and oceans may be, but coastal movement (and occasional long-range migration by sea) affected human occupancy of the shores of the Indian Ocean long before civilized societies established themselves in those parts.

There are systematic and persistent differences between movement by ship and movement overland; and the cultural reactions to contacts initiated by sea are systematically different from reactions to land contacts. This is not the place to try to define such differences in any detail. Suffice it to say that ships, being capable of carrying men and goods in relatively large quantities for long distances at relatively little cost, may initiate intense but intermittent encounters across cultural frontiers. Contacts overland are likely to be more continuous, and the samples of an alien style of life that can be carried on a man's back or on the back of pack animals are more rigorously selected than are the contents of a ship. The result is a longer lasting, more dilute encounter across cultural boundaries. Consequently, contact overland characteristically produces different reactions from overseas contacts between alien societies.

In this connection, it is interesting to note that the earliest civilization known to archaeologists seems to have arisen as a result of sea-borne migration of the people we know as Sumerians into Mesopotamia from somewhere south, presumably along the shores of the Persian Gulf. The newcomers established themselves as rulers of whoever may have lived in the marshy estuaries of the Tigris-Euphrates before they got there, and soon began to develop new skills and techniques for exploiting the agricultural as well as the fishing and fowling possibilities of that exceptional environment. The result was the emergence of cities and civilization by about 3000 B.C.

Other parts of the globe became seats of early civilizations not very long afterward. The valleys of the Nile, the Indus, and the Yellow River were the most important sites of such early civilizations in Eurasia. Different patterns seem to have prevailed in the Americas and in Africa, party because crops and climates differed, but also—and perhaps chiefly—because epidemiological conditions created by the emergence of civilizations were different in Africa and in the Americas from those prevailing in the temperate zones of Eurasia. In what follows, I endeavor to sketch a pattern of migration that I believe to have been characteristic of traditional Eurasian civilizations: Middle Eastern, Indian, Chinese, and European alike. I do not try to say anything about the Amerindian civilizations nor about the various high cultures that developed in Africa where the Eurasian migration patterns did not, I think, prevail; and if other patterns did, I do not know enough even to guess what they may have been.

My thesis is that from Sumerian times until the latter decades of the nineteenth century—almost throughout civilized history in other words—four currents of migration can be distinguished and were, indeed, necessary for the maintenance of Eurasian civilized society. These four currents of migration divide into movements affecting the unskilled—primarily peasants or ex-peasants—and movements of elites.

First, consider mass migration patterns. My hypothesis rests on the idea that differential patterns of mortality were created by the conditions of city life. This, in turn, permanently drew migrants from their place of birth—into cities, on the one hand, and off toward the frontiers of settlement, on the other. How epidemiology could create and sustain such a double pattern of die-off and compensatory migration requires a little explanation.[1] When comparatively large numbers of human beings began to live in cities, many different infections became more common because proximity multiplied opportunities for parasitic organisms to pass from one human host to another. Not only this: when human numbers attained a critical threshold (sometimes in the hundreds of thousands), entirely new forms of infection that passed directly from human to human with no intermediate host or dormant form of the infectious organism became viable. These infections constitute the array of familiar childhood diseases of the recent past: smallpox, measles, mumps, and the like. Such diseases could survive only within civilized societies, since only there were human numbers and frequency of contact sufficient to allow the infectious organism to find an unceasing succession of new hosts.

This class of infections provokes antibody formation in infected humans so that one exposure to the disease will create immunity for many years, usually for a lifetime. In a disease-experienced population, therefore, only children are suitable hosts for these infections. But among inexperienced populations this is not the case. In such societies, adults are just as vulnerable as children to infection and death. Thus, the impact of these civilized diseases upon disease-experienced populations is entirely different from their impact on virgin populations: a fact of enormous import for human history.

A result of the intensification of infection that urban conditions of life induced was that until the latter part of the nineteenth century cities were population sumps. Eighteenth-century London, for instance, required an in-migration of an average of 6,000 persons per annum simply to maintain itself—a sum of 600,000 for the entire century, which was more than the entire population of the city in 1700.[2] No comparably reliable figures exist for earlier ages; but I believe this necessity for recruiting urban population from the countryside—what we can perhaps call the Dick Whittington syndrome—is about as old as cities themselves.

The reasons for saying this are twofold. Early (ca. 2000 B.C.) Mesopotamian texts such as the Epic of Gilgamesh refer casually to lethal epidemic infection as an evidence of divine power. This shows that conspicuous and demographically significant epidemic infections had become routine aspects of urbanism by 2000 b.c. (i.e., within the first millennium of city living). Second, the language of administration and recordkeeping in the cities of southern Mesopotamia shifted during the third millennium from Sumerian to Akkadian. I believe that this shift registered the result of in-migration to the (initially) Sumerian-speaking cities from the Akkadian-speaking countryside—a pattern of migration that at some point must have assumed such a velocity as to make it unnecessary for the in-migrants to learn the language of the established managers of the city. A modern parallel from European history is the way in which Prague and Budapest ceased to be German-speaking cities when the pace of in-migration from the Czech- and Magyar-speaking countryside assumed an increased velocity in the course of the nineteenth century, partly in response to industrial expansion, and partly as an aftermath of cholera (and other epidemic) die-off of German-speaking urban dwellers. It seems possible, therefore, that the linguistic shift in ancient Mesopotamia (which had no apparent political or military base) attests the existence in remote antiquity of the same rural to urban migration current that played such a prominent role in eighteenth-century London and nineteenth-century Prague and Budapest.[3]

Armies constituted another significant population sump for civilized societies. They assumed demographically significant roles about a thousand years after cities first came into existence. It is, indeed, useful to think of armies as mobile cities, exercising power over the countryside from a movable focus in much the same way that cities were accustomed to exercise power over their rural hinterlands from a fixed location. And like cities, the human density of armies (and of people fleeing before their ravages) induced intensified infections that were far more lethal than weapons. In modern times, when figures become more or less accurate, soldiers' deaths from disease far outranked deaths in action until after the Boer War, 1901–3.

Rural emigrants had, accordingly, two alternative paths of migration available to them: either moving into the city to make their fortunes as chance and aptitude and places opened by die-off of older urban populations might permit, or serving in an army—voluntarily or by conscription—and pursuing a career under arms, where life expectancy was even shorter than in town and the pattern whereby fresh recruits moved into slots vacated by veterans' deaths was a good deal more obvious and immediate—speedier and more massive in other words—than was commonly the case in cities.

A second traditional current of mass migration from the peasant countryside ran in an opposite direction: toward the frontier of settlement. This may perhaps be termed the Daniel Boone syndrome. Lands toward the periphery of civilized styles of living were ordinarily made available for settlement by intensified die-off of partially isolated populations resulting from contacts with disease-experienced city folk. This phenomenon was massively apparent in the Americas, where contacts with white men regularly decimated Indian populations. Similar processes prevailed in the deeper past, at the fringes of other civilized communities, from the time that the characteristic diseases of civilization established themselves in cities and thereby conferred upon disease-experienced civilized communities an epidemiological weapon wherewith to mow down isolated, disease-inexperienced communities.

Innumerable instances of how an unfamiliar infection can play havoc in isolated communities are known from recent times. When measles was first introduced into Fiji, for instance, 25 percent of the population died of the infection within a few weeks; the English doctor who observed these appalling effects published what became a classical account of this sort of virgin-soil epidemic (Squire 1877, 72–74). To give a more recent illustration: when the Alcan highway was opened in 1942, a previously isolated Alaskan community experienced nine different, serious infections within the first nine months that trucks began to move through their community. Had the sick not been spirited away to modern hospitals as soon as a new infection appeared among them, it is impossible to believe that this tiny community of some 130 individuals could have survived the catastrophic exposure to diseases of civilization the Alcan highway meant for them (Marchand 1943, 1019–20).[4]

Obviously, such epidemics opened the way for relatively easy expansion of civilized settlement, if climate and soils and other natural conditions made it possible for familiar ways of exploiting the environment to be applied in the newly emptied landscapes. Indeed, civilized expansion of this kind resembles the growth patterns of bread mold on an agar jelly, whereby the mold excretes a substance—penicillin—lethal to rival forms of life. Civilized communities do the same merely by breathing in the presence of disease-inexperienced human adults.

Thus, while endemic disease in urban centers maintained a flow of migrants from countryside into town, epidemic disease operating toward the periphery of the civilized region sporadically depopulated frontier zones, which thus became available for pioneer settlement by other migrants from the same rural hinterland. An inward flow of relatively low-skilled ex-rural peasants toward cities (and armies) thus matched an outward flow toward unsettled frontiers on the part of the same population.

This, I think, was the fundamental pattern of human migration in China, India, the Middle East, and Europe; and its operation had much to do with the fact that in these regions a single style of civilized life (or closely related variants upon a single style, like the differences between Latin and Orthodox Christendom in medieval times, or between German and French civilization in the nineteenth century) tended to assert itself and maintain recognizable identity across relatively very large times and spaces. In parts of the earth where these two basic patterns of migration did not assert their homogenizing force, high urban cultures exerted a less long-lived and less territorially extensive effect. Their rise and fall could be and apparently were more rapid and may have affected rural life less intimately than was the case in the temperate zones of the Old World.

Two more migration patterns nevertheless also deserve attention though they affected smaller numbers of persons, being an affair of elites and ruling classes rather than of the masses. As before, one such current moved inward toward the centers of urban life and civilization, and a second moved outward toward (and beyond) civilizational frontiers. I wish to consider the latter pattern first, since I believe it manifested itself before the contrary migration of elites inward toward the center of civilization set in.

From the earliest days of the river-valley civilizations of the Near East it is clear that certain important raw materials had to be brought into the emerging cities and court centers from afar. Mesopotamia and Egypt both lacked timber and metals. Mesopotamia also lacked stone. Yet, these commodities played a critical role in early civilized technology. Trade expeditions, often undistinguishable from raids, were necessary to assure a supply of these and other valued raw materials.

This economic motive for penetrating distant regions was supplemented from quite early times by missionary impulses, perhaps sustained by the fact that a missionary, preaching some doctrine valued for religious reasons, might also expect to secure for himself an honored and relatively comfortable status among the barbarian populations who received him and accepted his message. Thus, the spread of the so-called megalithic tomb and other structures around the coasts of western Europe as far as the Baltic during the third millennium B.C. seems to have been accomplished by missionaries of a faith that taught life after death and set great store by accurate astronomical observations. Often, too, trade and conversion went hand-in-hand. Merchants and raiders carried ideas as well as goods; and if those ideas somehow illumined reality as experienced by distant and alien peoples among whom they penetrated, ideational borrowing and adaptation could and did occur in quite the same way that technological traits and skills might also diffuse outward from a civilized center along routes of trade—always within limits set by the receptivity of the distant community to the imports from the civilized center.

Among the skills exported from civilized communities were those of organized violence. As long as human communities did not produce more than was needed to keep alive, raiding and robbery were relatively unrewarding. Moral inhibitions against seizing what one had not himself labored to make available for human consumption must, I think, have been very strong in early agricultural communities; and in the absence of food surpluses, a community that tried to live by robbery and pillage would speedily kill off its victims and thus find itself unable to live any longer by rapine. Only when populations came into existence that habitually produced more than they themselves consumed did a predatory pattern of life become practicable. And it was only when urban elites had come into being and learned how to feed themselves by extracting foodstuffs from agriculturalists that populations that habitually produced more food than they needed for their own use came into existence.

Eventually, however, dwellers-round-about discovered that they could rival city elites in preying upon the rural peasantry, seizing food and other commodities on a hit-and-run basis. With luck, a raiding party could expect to get in ahead of civilized tax and rent collectors or armies living off the countryside. As militarization of the barbarian world proceeded, such raiders became rivals and potential heirs to civilized ruling classes. In Eurasia, the main reservoir of barbarian prowess established itself on the grasslands of the steppe, with a secondary center in the drier zone that shades off into desert south of the steppe. Recorded political history largely turns upon how one wave of barbarian invaders after another coming off the steppe or in from the deserts of the Middle East and Central Asia conquered civilized lands and established themselves as rulers. Successful conquerors, of course, set out as best they could to prevent others from following directly in their rear, overthrowing their power. Diplomatic missions, tribute payments, punitive military expeditions, elaborate border defenseworks to shelter standing armies or, alternatively, local self-defense of civilized landscapes by peasant militias or by professionalized warrior classes living in the countryside: all these and more were tried. And all, sooner or later, failed to check fresh invasion and conquest from the barbarian fringes. This Genghis Khan syndrome, therefore, matched and opposed the Marco Polo/Dr. Livingstone trade-missionary syndrome, each affecting relatively small elites, and pulling them in opposite directions.

The historical importance of these patterns of elite migration seem very considerable. Efforts at defense and no less persistent efforts at raid and conquest provided a fertile stimulus to administrative and technical innovation, from the time the war chariot burst upon civilized communities with initially irresistible force until the present. In addition, the far-ranging movements of warrior, trading, and missionary elites spread familiarity with a considerable variety of high skills across otherwise unbrideable distances. Skills of China could and did seep westward along paths of communication, just as Roman or Middle Eastern and Indian skills and ideas could move in the opposite direction along the same communication paths.

Whenever established institutions and ideas of a particular civilization failed to function satisfactorily, the possibility of taking alien notions and skills seriously arose. Much of the cultural history of civilized societies in the Eurasian world turned upon such sporadic receptivity on the part of one civilization for things imported (and in the process normally also distorted) from an alien, distant civilized center. From this point of view, the massive interaction between Western civilization and the various other high cultures of the earth that has been a conspicuous feature of the last two or three centuries is not more than the most recent (though perhaps the most dramatic and drastic) such process.

Intercivilizational exchange and stimulus provided a major—perhaps *the* major—stimulus to change within civilized communities ever since the plurality of civilized cultures became knowable to suitably located and strategically situated individuals. The ancient Greeks' encounter with the Orient, so tellingly recorded in Herodotus' pages, and the initial Chinese encounter with the Middle East, more briefly recorded in the historiography, have the advantage of being accessible to us through surviving texts. Other similar encounters ran all the way back to the time when predynastic Egyptians met ideas and skills emanating from Sumer and saw that they were good, some time before 3000 B.C. Such stimuli drastically altered patterns of cultural growth and often accelerated developments or turned them into new paths. Or so I argued in *The Rise of the West: A History of the Human Community* (1963), which, with its emphasis upon cultural diffusion, may be read as a paean to the world historical significance of elite migration.

Two observations about these migration patterns seem worth making. First, mass migration was not always a matter of a more or less free individual or group response to their perceptions of the world and its opportunities.

Obviously, the existence of civilization and cities, with the patterns of human migration these communities created, put extraordinary strain upon the rural food-producing peasantry. Their efforts sustained the city folk in a most direct fashion by raising the food the citizens consumed. They also supported cities and rulers by exporting a portion of their offspring after having borne all the costs of raising them from infancy to adolescence. It follows that high rural birthrates, as well as the regular production of a lot more food than the village population of working age itself required, were preconditions for the maintenance of civilized patterns of life.

If one reflects on the hardships and difficulties such requirements placed on the peasantry, it is not surprising that population shortages in the countryside could and sometimes did threaten the survival of city life and civilization. In such cases, legal enactment often sought to assure fulfillment of vital functions by assigning individuals to specific jobs and roles in society. A second possibility was to recruit labor by organizing slave raids aimed at bringing additional manpower to bear on tasks for which an adequate supply of local personnel was not available. Slave soldieries and household servants were sometimes more prominent in the past than slave cultivators; but since slaves seldom reproduced themselves, all three kinds of slavery depended on the availability of a supply of enslaveable people somewhere at a distance.

Wherever such pools of enslaveable population were discovered and exploited—whether in Africa or on the Turkish steppes or in Russian villages—they constituted a sort of auxiliary reservoir of labor for civilized societies, supplementing the peasant labor resources available closer at hand, which had proved insufficient to fill all the posts and perform all the functions the civilized ruling classes wanted or needed to have performed.

Second, it made a good deal of difference whether the circulatory patterns of migration I have described were entered upon by isolated individuals and small family groups that left their native place and moved to the city, into an army, or to the frontier as a result of individual decision or whether such channels of migration were instead entered upon by larger social groups—whole tribes or villages—that entered into the circulatory system of civilized society as organized communities, so that they could maintain, for example, a linguistic identity of their own in novel situations, and perpetuate distinctive cultural characteristics even after they had entered into the very heart and core of civilized society. The Jews who wept by the waters of Babylon in the time of Nebuchadnezzar and the Visigoths and Vandals who sacked Rome in the fifth century a.d. sufficiently illustrate the difference that migration in organized groupings can make to the historic role such migrants may play as against anything possible for isolated individuals and small family groupings.

Finally, I should point out that the fourfold pattern of civilized migration in Eurasia that I have sketched did not exclude other remarkable migratory movements during the historic age. Among peoples but little affected by acquaintance with the skills of civilization, some quite extraordinary migratory dispersals are known to have occurred. The Indonesian migration from Borneo to Madagascar, the Polynesian migration through the islands of the central Pacific, the Eskimo circumpolar migration and the Bantu migration within Africa each allowed human communities to penetrate and exploit in new ways hitherto uninhabited or very thinly inhabited landscapes. As such, they partook of the process described in my first pages—pushing human occupancy ever closer to absolute geographic limits.

From about 1700 the patterns of civilized migration outlined above began to encounter fundamentally new circumstances. It can be argued, indeed, that the world of our own time is only beginning to come to grips with the changed conditions of migration that began to manifest themselves in the eighteenth century and became massive human realities in the course of the nineteenth.

What were the new circumstances? First and most widely experienced was a change in population dynamics that resulted in an unprecedentedly massive and prolonged population growth, approximating to a rate of about 1 percent per annum. In many parts of the world, reception of American food crops—maize, potatoes, peanuts, etc.—played a part by expanding available food supplies. Diminution of local violence as a result of easier monopolization of superior force that the invention and spread of cannon involved may have diminished deaths from human agency. But by all odds, the most powerful disturber of older balances was surely the increasingly effective homogenization of civilized infections. This meant that in city after city and in one rural community after another in contact with such cities, epidemic was succeeded by endemic forms of disease. As wider and wider territories were merged into a more nearly homogeneous disease pool by a heightened frequency and range of communications, the conditions that in earlier times had allowed a ring of rural communities close by city disease-centers to produce a population surplus on a regular basis for the replenishment of urban numbers began to apply to larger territories. As all important lethal infections became endemic within the limits set by climate and other natural conditions, the possibility of epidemic die-off of adult populations diminished. Consequently, human communities, traditionally adjusted to withstand sporadic epidemic die-offs, found themselves multiplying incontinently. In practice, this meant that the major civilized regions of Eurasia all witnessed the first phases of the modern population explosion during the eighteenth century, though in some lands the effect was quickly dampened by food shortages or political disorder.

Correspondingly, the epidemiological process whereby previously isolated peoples were exposed to death-dealing civilized infections accelerated, since the same intensified pattern of communication that assured homogenization of diseases in civilized lands also increased the risk of exposure to infections for populations without previous experience of the disease in question.

Thus, from about 1700 onward, an accelerated rate of epidemiological destruction of primitive communities accompanied an accelerating rate of civilized population growth. At first, Europeans were by far the best situated to take advantage of this new circumstance. They sailed the ships that plied the high seas, carrying infections as well as goods and ideas. Since they controlled the ships, it was relatively easy for Europeans to initiate settlements overseas in lands emptied or partially emptied of their previous inhabitants by the action of civilized infections. This process had of course begun in the sixteenth century with the European discovery of America; it expanded to South Africa (first Dutch settlement 1652), Australia (first English settlement 1788), New Zealand (first European settlement 1790s, but organized British colonization only from 1840), and to many lesser islands and shore stations in other remote regions of the earth. Overseas European colonial settlements, in turn, built up trade and intensified exchange patterns across the oceans, thus accelerating epidemiological destruction of remote populations while forwarding the general process of European expansion—economically, technologically, and demographically all at once.

On top of this already sharply disbalanced world situation, Europeans began to pioneer the discovery and administration of effective public health measures. Two horizons seem especially significant here: the development of vaccination against smallpox at the very end of the eighteenth century, and the introduction of an arterial-venous system of water supply and waste disposal, beginning in the 1850s. Urban water supplies that were guarded against amebic and bacterial contamination sharply diminished infectious disease transmitted through drinking water. Sanitary sewage disposal inhibited yet other infections propagated by contact with feces. Soon afterward came the discovery of disease-causing germs, and of ways to check the chain of infection by scientifically tested and often not very expensive forms of prophylaxis. Such revolutionary changes in public health meant that Europeans were abruptly freed from a long series of previously significant diseases—smallpox, dysenteries, diphtheria, plague, and others—while relatively effective means were simultaneously devised to keep more stubborn infections at least partially in check, tuberculosis and malaria chief among them.

Such a population surge was further complicated by the changed demographic regime in the cities and along the frontiers of civilized lands. As infectious disease circulation became more nearly worldwide and more nearly uniform (within climatic limits), the phenomenon of marginal die-off became trifling. By the beginning of the twentieth century only a few tiny and remote communities remained to be mowed down by an initial exposure to the infectious diseases of civilization; and the regions in which such populations lived—the Arctic north and the Amazon jungle, for instance—are not regions easily available for occupancy by migrating peasants, however crowded they may find themselves in their native land.

Similarly, as urban concentrations of humanity ceased to be lethal through the implementation of elementary public health measures, city folk became capable not merely of reproducing themselves, but of sustaining natural increase. Thereby, opportunities for migrants from the countryside to enter urban communities had to compete with a far greater number of persons born and bred in the city, whose skills were often better adapted to city existence than those of uprooted peasants could be. To be sure, cities could and do continue to grow and migrants from crowded countrysides do continue to move into town—or at least to the ring of squatters' shanties that surround many, perhaps most, of the world's cities. Such areas constitute a sort of visual evidence of the increased difficulty rural migrants face in insinuating themselves into the tissues of urban society, thanks to the cessation of an age-old pattern of urban die-off that has resulted from the new practices of public health administration.

Hence, the peoples of Asia, Africa, and Latin America face a fundamentally altered circumstance as they move toward the cresting of their population explosions. Absorption of rural migrants has begun to require far more intensive applications of capital investment—educational investment as well as material investment in machines and the like that alone can render their labor usable in urban settings.

The magnitude of the problem boggles the mind, so much so that I find it hard to imagine any peaceable, happy resolution of the current population explosion. For the foreseeable future it seems sure that overcrowded and impoverished lands, in which traditional patterns of migration and modes for utilizing (and consuming) rural surplus populations have been interrupted, will share the earth with far less densely populated lands, in which the standard of living is immensely higher; and the gap between such regions is more likely to widen than to narrow in the immediate future. This in turn means, I think, that pressures for migration into the richer, emptier lands will mount, and only an increasingly ruthless application of force is likely to prevent such movements.

I freely confess that I do not see the path of wisdom in such a situation. Free migration across, as well as within, state boundaries would speedily result in catastrophic collisions between migrants and older populations—collisions that would dwarf the recent problems of American cities where in-migrant blacks have confronted older immigrant classes in what remains an only precariously peaceful fashion.

Closed frontiers do not appeal to me either, for they can remain closed only by resort to brutal police methods or some kind of Big Brother supervision of every individual person within state boundaries.

Whether any intermediate policy can be formulated whereby some concept of optimal rates of migration from poor to richer lands could be defined so as to permit migration only on such a scale as to minimize damages to all the parties concerned seems to me dubious. And even if such a policy could be defined in the abstract, application in detail would open the way to extraordinary acts of arbitrary judgment by those officials entrusted with its administration. For, if hundreds wish to migrate and policy dictates that only scores shall do so, who decides which applicants should be preferred?

Contemplating the world situation, who can say confidently that intelligent management and deliberate policy will be able to alleviate the problems of migration arising from the extraordinary differences of wealth that currently exist between different parts of the earth? Instead, I suspect that age-old controls on humanity are likely to assert their sovereign power so that some combination of violence, famine, and disease will again, as so often in the past, reduce the extremes of contrast that today exist.

Yet, I do not despair of the possibility of using intelligence to mitigate an intractable and probably insoluble problem. To understand better may not permit control and resolution of all difficulties; it may, nevertheless, allow us to navigate the current of contemporary world history a bit more skillfully, dodge some of the rocks, and perhaps soften some of the sharpest hurts that current conditions inflict and seem likely to inflict in time to come. Intelligence has never done more than that in human affairs; to do less would be unworthy of our humanity.

NOTES

1. For a fuller discussion, see McNeill (1976).

2. This calculation is based on the famous London Bills of Mortality. Cf. Brockington (1968, 99).

3. For instructive details regarding the severity of urban die-offs in early modern times in Europe see Mols (1954–56). Until I read this work I had no idea how severe were plagues and other epidemics in European cities of the early modern age. The loss of up to half a city's population in a single season was a routine disaster that called for no more than ordinary ritual prophylaxis and an accelerated in-migration from the countryside for a few years to restore things to normal.

4. In fact, only seven persons died: three from measles and four from meningitis.

13

FROM SEX RATIOS TO SEX ROLES

Marcia Guttentag and Paul F. Secord

Imagine two societies, EROS and LIBERTINIA. In both, women's behavior and that of the men with whom they interact seems strange and absurd. In EROS, men are romantic love objects and enjoy staying home and taking care of the children. The double standard of morality is more strict for men, who have weaker sex drives. Women dominate the business world and government as well, and many prefer their husbands to stay at home, while they provide for them. In LIBERTINIA, women and men have roles similar to those in EROS but families are much less stable. Divorce, illegitimacy, and abortion rates are all high. Standards of sexual morality are low for both sexes, and men, in particular, are often exploited as sex objects by women.

These imaginary societies seem impossible to us, and the reason for this is that they dramatically reverse certain core features of the role identities of women and men. These features, in their normal form, have been so unvarying throughout history that they are taken for granted, and most of us have come to think of the behaviors they represent as stemming from the biological natures of men and women. The key elements depicting men and women have been reiterated countless times in history, literature, drama, and in our daily lives. No other human roles have been so constant.

EROS and LIBERTINIA were constructed with a purpose, namely, to show what would logically follow if an underlying condition that has pervaded all of human history were to be changed. This condition is the key to understanding the sex roles and identity of men and women. In EROS and LIBERTINIA, the usual prevailing condition has been reversed—there, women, not men, hold what we term *structural power*. This power derives from their superior economic, political, and legal position in society, as well as from the sheer weight of the social values and practices that implement these powers. This alone could account for all of the strangeness of these two societies when compared with more familiar ones. There, men are like women, and women are like men. But men in EROS are different from men in LIBERTINIA, and the same is true of women. This occurs because EROS has a low sex ratio, with men in short supply, and LIBERTINIA a high ratio, with a surplus of men. These ratios alter the *dyadic power* of women and men, combining with the existing balance of structural power to produce different overall effects.

The central question here concerns the means by which sex roles are generated and maintained. We have a particular interest in explaining the means by which an imbalance in sex ratios combines with the prevailing imbalance in structural power to produce changes in the attitudes and behaviors of men and women in relation to each other and, with sufficient time, to produce changes in the associated sex roles and institutional structures, such as the family. Our thesis would be more complete if we could detail the various links between the demographic conditions and the psychological and social effects. At this point in our knowledge, however, no final explanation can be provided. All that can be done is to sketch some plausible mechanisms and look for evidence that might support or reject them. Such an approach should increase our understanding and sharpen further research so that definitive answers might ultimately be provided.

Explanations such as we are seeking are bound up with questions about human nature itself, and with the value positions taken on human nature by social scientists and others. Issues arise, such as the biological differences between men and women and their consequences for sexual and other behaviors; the nature of love between men and women; parental behavior and attitudes, especially commitment to children; and the relative contributions of economic, cultural, and societal factors to relations between the sexes. For these reasons, many diverse, impassioned views about man-woman relationships have strong effects on the manner in which such relationships are conceptualized and explained. Consequently, it should be no surprise that many different and contrasting mechanisms could be proposed to explain the social effects of imbalances in sex ratios. Our reaction will be to thread our way through this maze of contradictions by sticking to the main lines of argument and evidence and avoiding lines of explanation that seem implausible or illogical, or that are contrary to the facts as we see them.

In what follows, we outline our argument in sharp profile. To clear the ground, several assumptions must first be made explicit.

SOME BASIC ASSUMPTIONS

To deal more sharply with the arguments and evidence, we will put aside for now the issue of the biological natures of men and women. In spite of the advances that have been made in understanding the biology of gender, no definitive conclusions can yet be drawn about the effects of biological properties or conditions on *behavior*. This is true not only for differences between male and female behavior, but also for variations in the behavior of different individuals of the same sex. We do not have any firm evidence that some biological condition or constitutional property makes one individual more sexually active, more aggressive, more emotional, or more perceptive than another, nor do we know of any such biological conditions that account for the other behavior differences that are usually imputed to males and females. For the present, we assume that males and females are not biologically different in ways that produce important behavioral differences, in order to better zero in on the societal and social differences that might account for the different behaviors of males and females.

Another basic assumption that we make here is that men and women need each other. Obviously, this is partly biological and specifically sexual, although the variety of forms that sexual behavior takes under various social conditions makes it clear that sexual biology is not simply and directly expressed in a narrow band of sexual behavior, nor even exclusively toward the opposite sex. Moreover, the needs of men and women for each other are obviously not solely sexual; companionship, nurture, play, maintaining a home and family, and a great variety of other forms of expression characterize male-female transactions. Once again, to focus on the societal and social determinants of relationships, we assume no difference between men and women in the strength of their needs, sexual or otherwise. In the absence of strong evidence, making the assumption that men have stronger sex needs than women—or the reverse assumption—would simply beg the question we are trying to answer.

A key condition that must be stressed is the unequal division of structural power that has prevailed from the earliest recorded history and that is deeply embedded in the background of current societal structure and sex-role identities. The balance of this power has been overwhelmingly in the hands of males, and this has had a profound effect on the roles and identities of men and women, the forms that relationships between them have taken, and the social institutions, such as the family, that have evolved to maintain such relationships in keeping with the accepted value systems of society.

It is men who have been lawmakers, business executives, entrepreneurs, heads of families, judges, police officers, presidents, governors, dictators, and generals. This imbalance of power has been so pervasive and ever-present that it has often been taken for granted and simply ignored when the natures of men and women have been considered. Quite possibly, many of the differences between men and women that are taken to be natural or biological are in fact consequences of the unequal distribution of structural power between the sexes. Since an unequal distribution has been virtually always present, it could well be that what we see as "natural" differences between men and women are simply due to this ever-present difference. We will examine this possibility.

THE ORIGIN AND MAINTENANCE OF SEX ROLES

Social scientists take for granted that social roles are shaped through socialization. Age-sex roles, for example, are shaped by parents and others from infancy onward, in the kinds of behaviors they encourage and approve of in a child, depending on its gender. Socialization is more than conscious shaping; adults and others often serve as role models that children may copy on their own. This socialization process continues throughout adult life, whenever individuals assume new role positions (such as becoming a husband or wife, a soldier, a minister, or a newly retired person).

But role socialization in this sense is of little help in explaining how particular roles emerge in a society in the first place, or how these roles change over time. It only shows how the new generation gets recruited into old ways of doing things, and how an individual in society progresses from one role to another. Much less attention has been given to how particular roles change (for instance, why mothers today behave differently from their grandmother or even from mothers of twenty years ago), and to the twin problem of why roles stay the same over time. Only in more recent years have social scientists come to think of social roles as dynamic, in the sense that they must be constantly renewed by the individuals enacting them if they are to survive, and further, that a full explanation requires identification of the origination, and sustaining forces, as well as of the pressures toward change. We detail some of these forces in connection with sex roles, with special attention to the effects of imbalanced sex ratios.

Adult sex roles are shaped, maintained, or changed through what can be thought of as two relatively independent sources: the social exchanges of the role partners, and the task demands that bear on those roles. These two sources are not, of course, completely independent; task demands may influence social exchanges, and vice versa. But the interactions between two role partners, such as husband and wife, and the task demands that bear on each role, can only be understood in the larger context of the society in which they occur. That men hold the balance of economic and political power in society has profound effects on the nature of the exchanges between any two role partners, as well as on the task demands that each partner bears. The society itself specifies what kinds of exchanges and task demands are appropriate for each role actor, at least within limits, and these have been accepted for the most part by the two parties.

Task demands originate partly in the physical and social setting of the role position, sources that are often beyond the power of the role actors to alter. In early America, for example, frontier women in the midwestern region were thrust into the role of farm wife, which automatically imposed upon them all of the domestic and farm chores necessary for maintaining the farm, and further, because they were female, they would bear many children as a matter of course.

The task demands of a social role are relatively fixed by physical or societal conditions, whereas social exchanges are more subject to negotiation between the role partners. Task demands are partly social, in the sense that they derive in part from the structure of society. For example, if we think more broadly of an adult woman's role (as contrasted with that of wife/mother) in the midwestern frontier, we can see that frontier society provided little in the way of alternative roles for an adult unmarried woman. With few exceptions, women had no means of supporting themselves and were apt to be dependent on relatives for shelter and means of subsistence. Thus, in a sense we can think of this midwestern frontier society as providing a rather narrow, single set of task demands for its adult women—always recognizing a few exceptions, of course. The importance of this concept of task demands as imposed by the physical and social setting of a role cannot be overestimated.

SOCIAL EXCHANGES AND DYADIC POWER

Sex-ratio imbalances produce their effects by disturbing the balance of social power between the two sexes. How this comes about can be conceptualized in terms of a theory of social exchange that has been generated by adapting the economic model of exchange to the social realm. We will provide a brief, informal sketch of the theory and then discuss it in more detail, particularly in association with imbalanced sex ratios.[1]

Dyadic power in a relationship between two persons derives from the psychological resources that one partner has for satisfying the needs of the other partner. The more such resources a person has and the stronger the needs of the partner for those resources, the greater the dyadic power. This effect is tempered by the extent to which the weaker person is dependent specifically on one partner for satisfaction. For example, when the weaker party in a relationship can gain satisfaction outside of the relationship, the power of the stronger party is weakened. We refer to this social power deriving from dependencies in a two-person relationship as dyadic power.

In relationships between members of the opposite sex that are open to change or dissolution, demography is linked with dyadic power in the following way: When one gender is in short supply, it becomes more difficult for the opposite sex to find a partner. Moreover, relationships are apt to be less satisfying for the gender in oversupply. This follows because the scarce gender has more sources of satisfaction alternative to the partner, while the partner has fewer. These conditions generate more dyadic power for the party with more alternative sources of satisfaction because of the way they affect the exchange of resources. This party is less dependent on the partner and can turn elsewhere for satisfaction. The partner, on the other hand, has fewer options and thus must provide a level of satisfaction sufficiently above the first party's alternative sources in order to keep the relationship alive.

This is the substance of the argument, but it needs fleshing out to be fully understood. In an economic exchange, each party experiences costs and benefits in a transaction with another party. Further, competition and supply and demand all bear on the exchange. In like manner, the focus of *social exchange theory* is on the social transactions in a relationship between two persons as they take place in the context of the larger set of options that each party has in other relationships. The relationship may be initial or temporary, or it may be of long duration.

As in economic exchange, interactions between a man and a woman can be viewed as exchanges where each party experiences certain benefits and costs. The benefits and costs are largely psychological, including not only sexual pleasures but enjoyment of intimacy, companionship, feelings of self-worth, or whatever. Costs are also psychological, such as "spending" one's time, embarrassment or rejection, guilt or deception, and so on. These benefits and costs, taken together over a period of time, yield each party's outcomes.

The degree of satisfaction yielded in an exchange depends both on the resources of one's partner to benefit one, and the intensity of one's need for such benefits. For example, the ability to carry on a good conversation is a resource if one has a partner who likes to participate in such conversation. A person may be beautiful or handsome, sexy, fun to be with, emotionally supportive, able to take charge of a situation, a good listener—these are common resources that most people enjoy in a partner—but clearly, whether they are valuable resources depends on what one wants from a partner. For example, some would rather take charge of a situation themselves, or do the listening instead of the talking. The beauty of a woman may be a resource desired by the man she is with, but if she is with a woman, it may be a liability.

The extent to which resources and needs determine the level of satisfaction in the outcome of social exchanges depends on yet another important condition that varies with prior experiences in and out of the relationship. Outcomes by themselves neither tell us about satisfaction with a series of exchanges nor whether further exchanges will take place. The model of economic exchange makes this clear. Whether or not a woman who has just purchased something thinks that she has just made a good buy depends on what she thinks the going price is. Similarly, satisfaction with the outcome in a social relationship depends on the level that is expected.

In economic exchange, the going price is the expected level. Just as this is based on other transactions of the same kind from the past, on tentative pricings from other sellers, and even on prices that one thinks might be obtained, the level of expectation for a social transaction is based on similar transactions in the past and on the alternative transactions that a party perceives as available. A desirable man may be accustomed to highly satisfying interactions with women; he expects more and would be less satisfied with or even disappointed by some actions than would a less desirable man. The concept of *alternatives* is crucial: human satisfactions are always relative; their evaluation depends on what might have been experienced instead. These potential experiences may be estimated from past experiences or from optional alternatives, real or imagined.

From these concepts of outcomes, expectations, and alternative options follow implications about the relative satisfactions of each party, the relative dependencies of each on the other, the relative power each has over the other, and the desire to continue or discontinue the relationship.

Worth noting in passing is the point that the most common objection to this application of exchange theory is that it makes friendship and love appear calculating and self-serving. In answer to this objection, it should be clear that social exchange theory does not require a conscious weighing of costs and benefits in a relationship—that would indeed belie the very meaning of friendship and love. Exchange theory does not even make any assumption of "equitable" exchanges between partners because each partner's satisfaction depends on his or her own expectations and outcomes. The viewpoint taken in social exchange theory is quite different—namely, that the *feelings* of satisfaction, warmth, love, rejection, or bitterness are often all that is consciously experienced, but that these feelings result nevertheless from an unconscious assessment of the balance between outcomes, expectations, and alternatives.

While a calculus may enable prediction or explanation of the kinds of emotional reactions that will occur, it need not imply a deliberate, self-conscious calculation of benefits and costs by people in a relationship. An analogous situation may help here. Consider the case of a child who has received too little attention. He is apt to engage in exhibitionism, attention-getting tactics, and even unpleasant or inappropriate behavior. This does not mean that he has consciously calculated the amount of attention he has received and compared it with some expected level, yet he reacts as if he had such knowledge and responds to the lack of attention. Innumerable human behaviors are based on quantitative assessments that occur below the level of awareness. This is obviously true of skilled movements, such as those in piano playing or touch typing. We may safely assume that complex quantitative assessments also underlie some social behaviors.

A further complication that must be understood is the interplay between resources and needs and the shaping of these by societal structures and processes. A simple example is beauty. Patterns of physical attributes that are seen as beautiful, and thus as a resource of their possessor, are socially determined. This is clear from the wide cultural variations in what is considered beautiful. In the same way, more complex attributes such as status and power constitute resources only by virtue of societal processes. What conveys status depends on central social values. Constraints on freedom to negotiate are socially conditioned in a similar way. Some features of a relationship are not negotiable because society rigidly defines them, and deviation from the rules results in disaster for the perpetrator. In some societies, for example, if a young woman loses her virginity, her identity is permanently spoiled and she cannot achieve a good marriage. Finally, we noted earlier that the task demands stemming from the physical and social setting of the sex role in question are in many respects independent of the social exchange process within a given relationship.

Social exchanges are seen in clearest outline where both participants in a relationship have maximum freedom to behave in a variety of ways, including leaving the relationship. There are two sources controlling this freedom. One is the extent to which the social roles of the participants have been prescribed and limited by society, and the other is the stage of the relationship. Thus, the exchange process is most dramatically demonstrated in relationships that are tentative or new, or in an early stage, and where the roles are not narrowly prescribed. Even though they are strangers to each other, the exchanges that might take place between a bank teller and a customer are strictly limited by the narrow prescriptions of their respective roles. On the other hand, two strangers meeting at a cocktail party might have a wide range of exchanges that they could engage in. This is directly analogous to free market conditions under sufficient demand, where both buyer and seller have the freedom to reject or accept an exchange, and have available alternative sources of exchange.

The subtleties involved in constraints on social exchanges may be illustrated by another example. Consider the "sex game," as played through encounters at singles bars. It might appear at first that such encounters are open to a wide variety of exchanges. In fact, though, only the usual constraints on sexual intercourse between strangers are lifted: most other social exchanges unrelated to this outcome are not available in such encounters. Indeed, perhaps this is the reason why many single people find encounters at singles bars distasteful. The unwritten but clearly understood rules constrain the participants to a rather narrowly prescribed set of acts that end in sexual intercourse. Freedom to interact in alternative, nonsexual but satisfying ways is mostly ruled out by the mutually shared expectations that singles bar frequenters hold. Thus, while the usual constraints on sex between strangers are lifted by such games, behaviors that fall outside of the game theme are ruled out.

In contrast to brief encounters, when a relationship between two persons is long-standing and has many personal and institutional commitments, certain types of exchanges are no longer available. Examples are provided by the perennial concerns about losing their freedom experienced by single men or women when contemplating marriage. But it should also be recognized that long-term relationships, like friendships and marriages, also open up and facilitate kinds of social exchanges that are not available in the early stages of such relationships.

Finally, a society that is stable and that has long-standing traditions places more constraints on the forms that relationships may take, thus limiting the exchanges that are open to negotiation. For example, when women are strictly limited to the traditional domestic role of wife/mother, they have fewer choices in the way they relate to a man and in the life "career" that they may adopt. This interlocking of exchange processes with societal structures and contexts is a theme that will recur, and it is crucial to understanding how sex-ratio demography affects relationships between men and women.

ATTRACTION, DEPENDENCY, AND DYADIC POWER

From the viewpoint of social exchange theory, two elements are of foremost importance in any relationship between a man and a woman: attraction of each to the other and the dependency of each on the other. Attraction has to do with the level of outcomes that each experiences in transactions with the other, relative to what each party expects, and dependency, with the alternative options that each party has. Let us consider attraction first, and dependency second.

A simple principle is that the level of attraction to the other party in a relationship is a function of the level of outcomes experienced in relation to the level that is *expected*. The expected level is relatively stable and has become established as a result of the outcomes experienced in past exchanges with the same party, in similar exchanges in other relations, and in optional exchanges in alternative relations. The more the actual outcomes exceed the expected level, the more attraction will be experienced. Put simply, a strong liking or attraction for another person results from rewarding exchanges with the person that appreciably exceed those ordinarily experienced.

The other component of social exchange theory, dependency on the relationship, is at the heart of our thesis concerning imbalances in sex ratios. Staying in or leaving a relationship depends on the extent to which outcomes in the relationship exceed those that are available in alternative relationships. It is this fact that brings in competition and supply and demand in social relationships, and it is this fact that alters the balance of power within the relationship when sex ratios are out of balance. If the outcomes in alternative relationships are perceived by an individual to be highly satisfying (whether they actually are or not), this perception will raise the level of what is expected within the existing relationship. This makes it less attractive because the outcomes are then closer to the expected level. At the same time, this party is less dependent on it for satisfaction. Remember that we are discussing tentative or early-stage relationships, for alternatives loom larger in this phase and often become more psychologically remote when a mutual commitment has taken place.

SEX RATIOS, DEPENDENCY, AND ALTERNATIVES

If the number of single men only slightly exceeds the number of single women, the number of alternative options in finding a partner will be approximately equal for both partners. The age and social-class constraints on pairings of men and women require this slight excess of eligible males. But let us consider the situation where there are appreciably more single women than men. Under these circumstances, men have, on the average, more alternative relationships than women. This provides more freedom of choice for men, as well as a sense of control over the way they relate to a woman. Of crucial importance is their level of expectation for optional relationships, particularly that alternative relationship that carries the highest expected outcomes. In a relationship without commitment, the outcomes must exceed those in the best alternative relationship if the man is to stay in the existing relationship. In fact, only if a woman can maintain her partner's outcomes at a level above those of alternative relationships will he remain. The more alternatives he has, the less dependent he is on the relationship. Consider now the position of the woman in this precommitment relationship, in a context where women outnumber men. She may have no visible alternatives at all, except the one of being alone; therefore, unlike her male partner, she is highly dependent on him. She is in the position of having to provide high outcomes for him, but whether she receives them or not, she has to continue the relationship or risk being alone. In fact, if she particularly dislikes the alternative of being alone, she may stay in the relationship even though it provides outcomes that are well below what she would ordinarily expect. Outcomes below the level of expectation produce dissatisfaction and feelings of rejection, yet she remains in the relationship. This effect of alternatives helps to explain the common but puzzling observation that couples often remain together even when they both seem very unhappy with each other. In that instance, the alternatives to staying in the relationship appear worse to both parties.

Vis-à-vis her partner, the woman in a low alternative situation feels powerless, while her partner has a feeling of power over the relationship. She may have to put up with various behaviors on his part that she finds distressing or obnoxious. She may have to provide outcomes for him that are psychologically costly for her, while he can easily balk at providing outcomes for her if they are costly to him. From a theoretical viewpoint, he will not engage in exchanges that are costly for him and which thus produce net outcomes for him that are below his level of available options. Thus, he has the power to control her behavior so as to maximize his own outcomes without at the same time having to make sacrifices that would keep her outcomes at a high level.

If, in spite of her efforts, he abandons her for another woman, her feelings of rejection and her resentment are apt to be multiplied by the uneven exchange in which she has given more than he has. She will have a strong sense of having been unfairly treated, which may intensify her feelings of being impotent and powerless. She put forth extra effort and yet was rejected.

What is important to understand here is that it is not necessary for men or women to be directly aware of the imbalance in the relative numbers of men and women who are available. It is not a matter of directly perceiving the sex ratio. Rather, as a result of continuing experiences in encounters with the opposite sex, the average individual whose gender is in the minority occasionally has more alternatives in terms of actual or potential partners, whereas the opposite sex has fewer such alternatives. From time to time, this manifestation produces a one-up, one-down situation that leads the party whose gender is in the minority to have higher expectations for outcomes in an existing relationship and less willingness to commit oneself, while the individual of the opposite sex feels a greater dependency on the existing relationship and is willing to give more. When the sex ratio is considerably out of balance, the widespread effects increase the visibility of desirable alternatives for the scarce gender, and the injustices and exploitations undergone by the gender in oversupply become more salient.

COMMITMENT AND INSTITUTIONALIZED RELATIONSHIPS

An important concept in relationships is commitment. Perhaps the most formal commitment in our society between a man and a woman is marriage, but we can also conceive of commitments that are progressively weaker until they reach the point of no commitment. Most relationships have some degree of commitment. Even voluntarily spending one's time with another person on only one occasion may set up at least a weak anticipation that one might see him or her again. Commitments need not be formal. They amount to an expectation on the part of both parties that they will continue to see one another and behave toward each other as they have in the past; in other words, a commitment has to be shared or mutually understood. At some point the commitment may be made explicit, perhaps when the couple decides to share the same residence, or to get married. But a commitment could become quite strong through mutual understanding without even being explicitly discussed. With this understood, let us now leave the precommitment stage of a relationship and assume that it has continued to the point where making an exclusive commitment to each other is being considered. Again, our discussion continues to focus on the exchange process as it would occur in modern Western societies, where both parties would have some freedom of choice. Whether a commitment involves marriage or not, living together or separately, such a commitment usually carries with it an agreement not to engage in intimacies outside of the relationship, and sometimes additional constraints are placed on relating to third parties. It involves commitment of a considerable block of one's time, at the very least, much of one's recreational or spare time is shared with the other party. Along with it comes an implication of emotional support and caring on the part of the other party, who becomes someone to depend on in time of need or trouble. But at the same time it implies an agreement to take the bad with the good; one puts up with the other's tantrums, quirks, or obnoxious habits. Both parties receive some benefits from the commitment. They feel more secure; they no longer need to try to impress, or to always be on their best behavior; they can relax and be more comfortable. Note particularly that a joint exclusive commitment implies a kind of sharing, a give-and-take attitude on the part of both parties. These various positive and negative features combine to yield an outcome for each party that results from the commitment. Each party must feel that he or she will be better off with the arrangement—again, not necessarily a conscious calculation, since the only tangible manifestation of it may be a desire for the commitment—than without it. Where such a desire exists, both parties value each other highly, and this in turn raises the outcomes of both.

IMBALANCED SEX RATIOS

Now consider the decision to make an exclusive commitment where the prevailing sex ratio involves a considerable excess of unattached women. Remember the core principle: dependency on a relationship is a function of the extent to which outcomes in that relationship are above the level of expectation for alternative relationships. Generally, it is the level of expectation in the best alternative relationship that counts as the basis for comparing outcomes in a current relationship.

When there are many unattached women to whom a man can relate, his level of expectation in the best alternative relationship is apt to be considerably higher than it would be when the sex ratios were equally balanced and his choices limited. This means that he will be less dependent on the current relationship. Moreover, it means that he is less likely to make a commitment because its outcomes do not appreciably exceed what he could attain in multiple relationships. The existence of any alternative relationships with high outcomes means that a commitment would carry the cost of giving them up. In a word, when unattached women are available, men are reluctant to make a long-term commitment to one woman.

What about exclusive commitment from the point of view of the woman in the current relationship? Her alternatives are low when sex ratios are low, since few unattached men are available. This means that she is highly dependent on the relationship. Because of this dependency, a lack of commitment on the part of her male partner will be experienced as psychologically costly; it may even mean that she has to bear feelings of jealousy, the pain at times of being slighted, or being alone, or occasionally being rejected by her male partner. All this means that she will be especially eager for and desirous of a mutual commitment. Her outcomes in the relationship, even with their costs, are still above what she could expect in alternative relationships that are either nonexistent or not very attractive. But above all, an exclusive commitment would greatly reduce or even eliminate her heaviest costs, thus markedly raising her outcomes.

Under different circumstances, where the alternatives available to two lovers are limited, both could easily experience highs as the result of a mutually exclusive commitment, which is self-enhancing—a special recognition of self-worth. In the case described here, however, the male partner is unlikely to anticipate a euphoric state resulting from an exclusive commitment, and thus may either decide against it or immediately regret having made it. The regret follows from the costs experienced in having to give up alternative relationships.

Finally, staying with the circumstances where male alternatives are plentiful, let us look at those relationships where a mutual commitment has taken place, either in the form of marriage, living together, or simply exclusive intimacy. Once firm commitments are made, there is a considerable cost in breaking them. Leaving a mate involves inflicting pain, facing accusations, and raising questions of fairness, breach of trust, and guilt. All of these are costs that reduce the outcomes of an alternative relationship. Some costs perhaps may be of temporary duration; others may endure for years. Where alternative relationships are more potential than actual, both parties are apt to stay in the current relationship. But under the circumstances where male alternatives are abundant, the constant possibility of alternative relationships remains a threat to the woman and an opportunity for the man.

It may well be that for many men who are committed to a relationship with a woman the alternatives are not psychologically real or salient. But for those men for whom the alternative seems real enough and attractive enough, the commitment may be threatened or actually broken. At the very least, a man who perceives potential alternative relationships may feel less dependency on the existing relationship and have a feeling of greater power in it. Obviously, this is much less likely to happen where sex ratios are more balanced; moreover, where sex ratios are high, involving many alternatives for women and few for men, commitments are also apt to last longer.

EFFECTS OF STRUCTURAL POWER ON EXCHANGES

So far we have focused on the generation of dyadic power through social exchanges, ignoring the impact of larger societal processes on two-person relationships. Obviously, the roles of men and women in the larger society and the relative power they have there also have profound effects on the form that exchanges in relationships take. We have referred to economic, political, and other powers that derive from societal structures as structural power. The relative structural power of men and women also has profound effects on the form that exchanges in relationships take. It should be clear that such power can restructure psychological resources and each party's dependence on them. This is accomplished by putting limits and constraints on what is negotiable, by defining resources in ways that are favorable to men and unfavorable to women, and by generating moral values that work to the advantage of men. The unequal division of these powers between the two sexes is responsible for the characteristic forms that sex-role identities have taken throughout history.

We can put the matter this way: When structural power is in the hands of the gender that is on the low side of the sex ratio, that power is augmented by dyadic power. Under these circumstances, exchanges are most favorable to the stronger party. When the sex ratio is the other way around, the dyadic power at the disposal of the party whose gender is scarce may serve as a counter to structural power.

More specifically, since men always have the structural power, when they are also fewer in number than women (low sex ratio), their structural power is augmented by dyadic power and thus constitutes a potent source of change in sexual and other relationships between men and women. Even when women are scarce (high sex ratio), the structural power of men may, under some circumstances, provide some advantages in relation to women. Whether or not this occurs depends on the degree of imbalance in structural power and in the sex ratio; extreme shortages of women have sometimes failed to create better conditions for them and, on occasion, even made matters worse.

Two factors create asymmetries in power imbalances, and quite different situations prevail, depending on whether men or women hold particular kinds of power. In the first place, men have virtually always held the balance of structural power. Thus, this asymmetry is a constant. Our descriptions of EROS and LIBERTINIA have shown how different sex-role identities could be if women held this form of power. The second factor creating asymmetry is also important. The psychological resources that each sex provides for the other are very different. Of course, these are socially determined, and we could envision a very different distribution, yet certain features have been common to men and women in most societies. When women are scarce, the ability of individual men to provide high outcomes for women becomes more important. This usually means that men who possess status, income, and power will be more apt to have female partners than men without these attributes.

When men are scarce, it is often beauty, youth, and more intangible womanly attributes that give a woman an advantage in attracting a man. In this latter situation contradictory pressures shaping women's roles are apt to be prominent. On the one hand are pressures toward adopting a role much despised by feminists, one that emphasizes a woman's sexual attraction for and complementariness to a man as reflected in extreme form in such magazines as *Cosmopolitan*, or in books like *Total Woman* (Morgan 1973). This role may also emphasize motherhood and homemaking. The direction taken includes doing things specifically to please a man such as dressing according to his tastes, participating in activities that he enjoys, and catering to his needs. Family activities centering on the children may also have a central place.

This move is one kind of response to the background competition for men in a situation where they are scarce. But an entirely different set of pressures also follows from our analysis and may coexist with the former. The difficulties that women face under these competitive circumstances and the low outcomes that many women have in interaction with men, including successive rejections or abandonments, create pressures toward lessening their dependence on men and toward attempts to increase women's structural power—either social, economic, or political, as reflected in the current feminist movement. The direction taken here emphasizes being oneself instead of being what some man wants one to be, giving some attention to one's own needs, and developing an independent identity as a person.

These two directions are essentially incompatible, and presumably the same woman would not attempt to move in both of them at the same time. In fact, to the extent that these reactions to overdependency and the lack of dyadic power are organized into group actions, the groups would be expected to be in opposition to one another. Roughly speaking, the feminists and antifeminists among women fit these directional movements. In connection with group organization it is worth noting that the more imbalanced the sex ratio, the larger the number of individuals who get the short end of social exchanges, and the greater the possibility that these individuals will interact to form organizational efforts at correcting the situation. This is one of the reasons why low sex ratios give impetus to feminist movements. Concerted action by men when sex ratios are too high is not without precedent either. Recall attempts by legislative bodies to limit the bride-price when it had been driven very high by the scarcity of women in the medieval period, or the fact that the Chinese-American tongs put many of their women into brothels when sex ratios were astronomically high.

Those women who already have a satisfactory relationship with a man, involving mutual commitment, may possibly remain unaware of or unconcerned with the lack of marital opportunities for women. On the other hand, direct threats to their own relationship may stimulate active efforts on their part to improve it. Unfortunately these may take the form of emphasizing a subordinate feminine role instead of making an effort to achieve a more meaningful relationship. If they are in a relationship that is more transient, where commitment is uncertain, women may even be more active. Most women cannot fail to observe what happens to their close female friends and acquaintances in their relationships with men. They may be called on to provide emotional support for those female friends who experience difficulties or rejection in their relationships with men, and sometimes this may lead them to give more attention to their own relationship with a man.

Some women move, instead, in the direction of more independence and a separate identity. A series of rejections and failed relationships may lead to consciousness raising, to a redefinition of self and of one's relationship to men. Social, economic, and sexual independence apart from men may become goals. But this does not mean that all feminists, or even a majority of them, have had or currently have inadequate relationships with men. Marked inequities and inequalities experienced by women in most spheres of life may be sufficient motivation for changing the existing state of affairs. Moreover, a woman may have a successful and satisfying relationship with a man but still be exercised by inequality in her career situation or by the unfortunate experiences of her women friends in relation to men.

It is important to keep in mind that the primary condition to which women are reacting is the unequal balance of dyadic power in relationships with men which results from the shortage of men as marital partners, and as aggravated by the fact that men also possess superior structural power. A shortage means that an appreciable number of women will have emotionally disturbing experiences with men; moreover, the surplus of women will lead men to value women less, to be less committed to any one woman, and to deemphasize traditional relationships between men and women and the traditional roles that accompany them. But when the situation is the other way around, when sex ratios are high and there is a shortage of women, men value women more and treat women very differently, though on their own terms. They emphasize and reinforce traditional relationships in which women have a subordinate role. This is possible despite the shortage of women because men possess superior structural power.

We have considered social exchange processes mostly in the context of low sex ratios, where men are in short supply, and here we add some additional comments within the other context, where sex ratios are sufficiently high (say, above 125), so that for most men, unattached women are not at all easy to find. We need not discuss in detail all of the features of exchanges and alternatives. Obviously, they resemble those outlined for low sex ratios, except that here they are reversed for the two sexes. In addition, some features are different and require discussion.

Let us assume that in love relationships, most of the initiative remains with the male. While this has been weakening in modern times, it is doubtful whether initiative is equally divided yet between male and female. At any rate, when male alternatives are plentiful, male initiative is an advantage to men; it makes it less costly for them to sample optional alternative relationships because the probability of rejection is lower. Male initiative, combined with low female alternatives, makes it doubly costly for women to try out alternative relationships.

We are now discussing a different situation from the earlier one—a situation where female alternatives are plentiful and male choices few. Under these circumstances, male initiative is more costly because the probability of rejection is high. Beyond this, the male is now in the position of having to offer more: if he is to maintain a relationship with a woman, he either has to create high outcomes for her or find a way to limit her alternatives. This latter path more readily leads him to make a mutually exclusive commitment. But much more is involved. Typically, men have more structural power than women; they are in a better position to shape social practices. Hence, the ways in which men raise the outcomes of women differ sharply from the ways in which women raise the outcomes of men when the reverse circumstances prevail. Moreover, men can and do use their power to limit women's alternatives.

One example is the creation of the romantic tradition in which women are highly valued as sweethearts, wives, and mothers. This tradition also emphasizes mutually exclusive, monogamous commitments in the strongest form. Thus, at one stroke, women's outcomes are raised, and at the same time their alternatives are limited. Strong family values are favored: virginity becomes prized. If society considers women who have lost their virginity to have spoiled identities, men have succeeded in controlling female alternatives, at least with respect to sexual intercourse. Women who bear children are often exalted as mothers; the family and the home are cherished. Men give enough to women under these circumstances and make strong commitments so that women often accept the morality that is imposed upon them and support it themselves. Like men, they too believe in virginity, monogamy, motherhood, and family.

In those societies where men have sufficient power, many other customs may arise to control the alternatives that women have in relation to men and to make them the exclusive "property" of one man. Woman's activities and roles are limited; in some societies they may be extremely cloistered. Keeping women from the world of work, preventing them from gaining economic independence, from owning property, from having rights of various sorts, and from gaining an education that might prepare them for a career makes them more dependent on men because it maintains the advantage that men hold in structural power.

In modern industrial societies, a new factor arises to alter the balance of power: Women gain economic power through working. This lessens the structural power of men over them, and men are less able to dictate the forms that relationships between men and women will take. As a larger and larger proportion of women work for a living, the structural power of men vis-à-vis women weakens. Women become able to live apart from men and to relate to them on their own terms. Their greater independence permits them to turn to pursuits other than in the home, such as politics or professional careers. Since women seem to be moving increasingly in this direction, we should anticipate that the marked changes in the relative structural power of the two sexes will bring about profound changes in their roles and identities.

Finally, we have been arguing that men have used their favorable balance of power to shape women's roles to their own advantage. One objection that might be raised is that many women not only accept these roles, but even defend and support them, and are happy with them. This is true even when sex ratios are low. In effect, those women who defend traditional roles do not see their relationship to men as having unfavorable outcomes. Why don't they? If a social exchange perspective is to provide maximum understanding, this circumstance requires explanation.

This condition might be reconciled with social exchange theory in several ways. In the first place, the value to be placed on rewards and costs in an exchange is partly an individual matter. How much a particular outcome is worth depends on the individual's psychology. Some features of the traditional role are valued more highly by some women than by others. For example, they may especially enjoy children, or the leisure that comes from being supported by a husband, or even doing things just to please their male partner. So they may perceive the outcomes in their relationship with a man as meeting their expectations, even if the relationship is a traditional one.

Still another aspect of social exchange theory may be invoked to explain how women might be satisfied with traditional roles. Females acquire their values by growing up in a society controlled largely by men. Central values and the social practices that reflect them are acquired through socialization, and these values and practices in turn play a part in defining the outcomes experienced in social exchanges. Consider, for example, the Muslim woman in Morocco who, from our (American) perspective, has a social role far inferior to that of a man.

More than two dozen elements demonstrating this inferiority have been identified (Dwyer 1978). They include the following: adult men can marry on their own decision, while women must obtain the consent of a male authority; polygyny is permitted to a man, but not to a woman; husbands may divorce as they wish, but wives are required to have substantial grounds; virginity is required for a woman's first marriage, but not for a man's; a husband can withhold conjugal sex, but a wife cannot; extramarital sex is prohibited by law for both sexes, but men are not punished, while women are; in case of divorce, children legally belong to the husband; for management of property belonging to children, a male representative is nearly always required; women must observe a curfew from sunrise to sunset, while adult men are not restricted; women must be secluded, but men have no restrictions; husbands select the household of residence, since women have no say; mosques are completely open to men, but women must use women's prayer rooms; women may not make eye contact with strangers, but men may; women must dress so as to cover all but the eyes and fingertips, while men may expose their faces and lower arms; brides have restrictions on visiting their family and friends, but men do not; women cannot work without the consent of their husband or father, unless they are widows or divorcees; in inheritance, a female generally gets one-quarter, while a male gets three-quarters; most property in a marriage belongs to the husband, since the wife owns only her personal possessions; women are generally excluded from the courtroom, while men are not; women are restricted from holding such offices as judge, prayer leader, and sultan; adult women can vote, but typically do not because of modesty.

While Muslim women in Morocco often protest some of these restrictions, it is clear that many of them not only accept most of them but also consider them appropriate and right (Dwyer 1978). Obviously, their outcomes are defined by them in a manner very different from how an American woman might see them. This situation presents no problem for social exchange theory. Remember that satisfaction with a relationship is a function of the degree to which outcomes exceed the level that is expected. Moroccan women come to expect to enact certain roles in relation to men; and these expectations are more or less in line with what is accepted by their society. Thus, there is no reason to expect them to be more dissatisfied with their role than American women are with theirs.

Another point here is that social exchange theory does not require the assumption that exchanges be "equitable." No set of concepts common to both parties permits the calculation of equity. Each role actor expects to be treated in certain ways by the partner. These are the "role rights" that are the partner's "role obligations," and exchanges in role settings go on most smoothly when both parties share each other's definitions of rights and obligations. Still, these are separate for each social role; they are not measured in a common frame of outcomes by the partners themselves or by some concept of "equity."

Instead, in exchange theory, each individual's satisfaction or dissatisfaction with a relationship depends on his or her outcomes in relation to their level of expectation—always remembering that the latter is influenced not only by one's previous experiences in and outside of the relationship but also by potential alternative relationships. Dissatisfaction with a relationship is brought about either by changes in the level of what is expected or by changes in outcomes. Thus, if consciousness raising leads women to expect more from men, they can readily become dissatisfied with relationships that were formerly satisfying. Or, when potential alternative relationships appear more attractive, dissatisfaction may arise. Of course, potential alternative relationships may change one's level of expectation in an existing relationship. For example, a woman might perceive that her friends relate to their husbands in a way that permits them to have a satisfying career in the workplace, and she might imagine a potentially satisfying relationship with a man that would permit her to do so as well.

To sum up this last argument, from the perspective of a participant in social exchanges with a partner, outcomes may be seen as satisfactory or unsatisfactory, depending on whether they are above or below the participant's level of expectation. But since each party's own expectations and outcomes are qualitatively different from the other's, the two sets of outcomes are not usually seen within a single framework as matching each other or as equitable. It is only from the perspective of observers outside of the relationship that this type of comparison can be made, and it is only from this viewpoint that we can make the assertion that women's roles have been shaped to the advantage of males.

This is why many women in the United States today do not understand the feminist position. They see their own role as qualitatively different from that of a man, and they have no desire to compete with him in the workplace, so long as they can find a man who will partially or wholly support them in exchange for their performance of the homemaking/mother role. Given their perspective, it is impossible for them to perceive such arrangements as inequitable, since inequity can only be seen from a perspective that is outside of the relationship.

A final comment. The emphasis on outcomes, power, and dependency in social exchanges between men and women as a function of alternative relationships available to one or the other party is apt to appear cynical. It may well give the impression that the track to happiness is best traveled by the jockey who is most skilled at maneuvering to achieve a dominant position. But this would be a gross misreading of our position. Under this misinterpretation, men (or women) would be happiest when women (or men) are widely available and when one refrains from anything but half-hearted commitments. Such a view would overlook the core value of human relationships: the social bond of commitment. A mutual commitment between two persons is a bond of trust, faithfulness, and sometimes love; each party cherishes the interests of the other as his or her own. The outcomes of exchanges in such a relationship are usually immeasurably higher than in relationships where commitment to each other is low.

NOTE

1. Social exchange theory has its origins in social psychology, economics, and sociology. Among the large literature on the topic are the following major works: J.W. Thilbaut and H.H. Kelly, *The Social Psychology of Groups*, New York: John Wiley, 1959; P.M. Blau, *Exchange and Power in Social Life*, New York: John Wiley, 1964; G.C. Homans, *Social Behavior: Its Elementary Forms*, rev. ed., New York: Harcourt Brace Jovanovich, 1974; G.C. Becker, *The Economic Approach to Human Behavior*, Chicago: University of Chicago Press, 1976; H.H. Kelly and J.W. Thilbaut, *Interpersonal Relations: A Theory of Interdependence*, New York: John Wiley, 1978.

Part IV

SOCIAL MOVEMENTS AND REVOLUTIONS

14

NEW SOCIAL MOVEMENTS AND RESOURCE MOBILIZATION: THE EUROPEAN AND THE AMERICAN APPROACH

Bert Klandermans

In Europe as well as in the United States, important social movements have arisen in the past decades. The two continents show remarkable similarities in this. Student movements, environmentalist movements, women's movements, and peace movements developed on both sides of the Atlantic Ocean. In Europe they were successors to large prewar movements such as the suffrage movement, the workers' movement, and more generally, socialism, communism and fascism. In the United States the civil rights movement was their most important predecessor.

These movements not only influenced politics but also left their mark on the literature: quantitatively, in an explosive growth in the number of publications; qualitatively, in new theoretical approaches. The people in the movements that had grown up starting in the 1960s were generally not from the most deprived groups of society. And this cast a measure of doubt on the leading theories. Researchers in Europe and the United States were faced with the question: where, if not from deprivation, did these movements come from?

It is quite remarkable that, despite these similar developments, the direction in which answers were sought differed on the two continents. While in the United States resource mobilization theory shifted attention from deprivation to the availability of resources to explain the rise of social movements, in Europe the "new social movement approach" focused attention on the growth of new protest potentials resulting from the developing postindustrial society.

Each of these approaches shows but one side of the matter. Taken separately, each of them offers an inadequate explanation for the rise of the movements of the 1960s.

I discuss and contrast resource mobilization and the new social movement approach. I show how both are necessary to understand social movement participation. While leaving in-depth study of why the respective approaches developed as they did on the two continents to the sociology of knowledge, I conclude by offering a few hypotheses on this.

RESOURCE MOBILIZATION

Resource mobilization theory rejects the traditional social movement approach according to which social movements came about as a result of grievances due to relative deprivation. It was argued that grievances as a result of structural conflicts of interests are inherent in every society. The formation and the rise of social movements depend on changes in resources, group organization and opportunities for collective action (Jenkins 1983). Whether or not a group takes action depends on the availability of resources.

The resource mobilization approach has been most fruitful in the analysis of mobilization processes. It emphasizes the importance of existing organizations and networks. The mobilization potential of a group is determined by the extent to which it is organized. Existing organizations and networks not only increase the chance that persons will be confronted with a mobilization attempt but also make "bloc recruitment" possible.

Costs and benefits of participation play an important role in the analysis of mobilization processes. This part of the theory leans heavily on Olson's (1968) logic of collective action. The introduction of costs and benefits of participation into the analysis of recruitment made possible a more sophisticated approach to differential recruitment. Different sorts of incentives could be distinguished. Although the terms differed, collective (or purposive) benefits were distinguished from selective incentives, and selective incentives were divided into social and nonsocial incentives (Klandermans 1984; Oberschall 1980; Wilson 1973). A distinction was made between different forms of action, and it could be shown that moderate and militant action (Klandermans 1984) and low- and high-risk activities (McAdam 1984) appear to entail differences in participation because of a divergent cost-benefit ratio, and that a certain category of incentives appeals more to one social group than to another.

Organization

According to the research mobilization approach, organization is an important resource for a social movement. Organization decreases the costs of participation (Morris 1981), is important in the recruitment of participants (Oberschall 1973, 1980) and increases the chances of success (Gamson 1975;

but see Piven and Cloward 1979 for the opposite argument). Its emphasis on organization as a resource meant a rejection of the traditional view that a low level of organization was a distinguishing feature of social movements. Gerlach and Hine (1970) remarked in this connection that the impression of disorganization could easily be aroused by the specific organization form of social movements, which is a collectivity of groups and organizations with a mutual network of relations but without centralized decision making and leadership. Expectations of success play an important role with respect to the collective incentives of participation. Expectations of success are related to several other concepts that the resource mobilization theory has brought to the foreground. The political systems in which social movement organizations operate vary in vulnerability to political pressure. The presence of third parties and alliances considerably increases the chance of success (Fireman and Gamson 1979). The discovery of a new tactic sometimes inaugurates a protest cycle (McAdam 1983; Tarrow 1983). As long as the opponent does not know how to respond to the new tactic, the chances of success are higher. After a while this changes, because the opponent learns how to react.

To summarize, resource mobilization theory explains cycles of protest from the combined influence of changes in the availability of resources and in the perceived chances of success. When a societal group with certain grievances has more resources at its disposal and when the chances of success of a protest movement increase, the protest activity increases.

NEW SOCIAL MOVEMENTS

In contrast to the resource mobilization orientation, the new social movement approach sought the explanation for the rise of the social movements of the past decades in the appearance of new grievances. It stresses that the new movements (such as the environmental movement, the women's movement, and the peace movement) differ from the old movements (such as workers' movements) in values, action forms, and constituency. It attempts to relate the growth of these movements and their essence to developments in Western industrialized societies. New social movements are taken to be a reaction to modernization processes in such societies (Brand 1982; Melucci 1980; Van der Loo et al. 1984). In this respect the new social movement approach is related to Smelser's (1982) theory of collective behavior. Structural strain in his theory is akin to new grievances as a consequence of modernization processes in the new social movement approach.

The literature mentions the following characteristics typifying new social movements. Values: new social movements are antimodernistic. They no longer accept the premises of a society based on economic growth. They have broken with the traditional values of capitalistic society. They seek a different relationship to nature, one's own body, the other sex, to work and to consumption. In other words, their interests lie in issues involving the superstructure, the sphere of reproduction. Matters that previously belonged to the private sphere are becoming topics of political discussion. This is sometimes referred to as the politicization of private life.

Action forms: new social movements make extensive use of unconventional forms of action. One of their chief characteristics is a profusion of single-issue groups and organizations. They take a dissociative attitude towards society, one expression of which is their antagonism to politics. They prefer small-scale, decentralized organizations, are antihierarchical, and have an antipathy for the principle of representation. The emphasis lies on self-help and self-organization.

Constituency: Two population groups are particularly predisposed to participation in new social movements. First, groups that are affected by problems resulting from modernization. These groups are not composed of social classes or ranks because the problems with which they are confronted (for instance, the construction of a nuclear reactor or the location of cruise missiles) are not limited to particular social strata. Second, there are groups that, owing to a more general shift in values and needs, have become particularly sensitive to problems resulting from modernization. These groups are primarily found in the new middle class—the well-educated young people working in the service sector. In reality, the picture turns out not to be as simple as the theories about new social movements present it (Brand et al. 1983; Van der Loo et al. 1984).

The new social movements literature sets out to answer the question, "Where do these new values, action forms and constituencies (or protest potentials, as they are called) come from?" The answer has been sought in various directions, although all explanations see a connection between modernization and continuing economic growth.

New Aspirations

A great many authors ascribe the rise of new social movements to changed values. They fall back on Inglehart's theory about postmaterial values. In 1977, Inglehart described the silent revolution as he felt it was taking place in Europe. By this he meant a dramatic and continual change from materialist to postmaterialist values. Seeing that postwar youth could be assured of the satisfaction of material needs, nonmaterial needs such as self-actualization, participation, etc., had a chance to flower. In an international comparative study among young people from sixteen to twenty-nine years, Inglehart found that

28 percent of them in the Netherlands, 17 percent in the United States, 15 percent in West Germany, 13 percent in the U.K. and 9 percent in Austria favored postmaterialist values (Inglehart 1979). Other research has also established changes in values: the erosion of conventional middle-class values, the decline of the traditional achievement ethic, a changed attitude toward work and career. Supporters of postmaterialist values come into conflict with a political and social system that is chiefly materialist. Their preference for unconventional action forms can be explained both by the pattern of values they favor and by the fact that they are in a minority position.

Another group of authors sees a reaction to the welfare state in the new social movements. Because the welfare state permeates more and more reaches of life, it is held responsible for the ensuing problems. At the same time it has created new entitlement needs with respect to government services. Furthermore, increased prosperity has caused the demand for scarce goods to grow. Many of them are positional goods (for instance, pleasant living surroundings, a car, education that gives access to attractive professions.) When used extensively, however, these can be an obstruction to the satisfaction of needs (traffic jams, the little boxes of suburbia). The result is heightened competition, which leads to more disappointments. Briefly, the welfare state has created new needs that can no longer be satisfied.

Satisfaction of Needs Endangered

In contrast to authors who explain the rise of new social movements by "new aspirations" (Klages 1980), there are Marxist and non-Marxist authors who seek an explanation in the increased strain related to the problems resulting from industrialization and bureaucratization.

According to non-Marxist explanations, industrialization and bureaucratization have resulted in a loss of identity. Loss of identity leads to the loss of traditional ties and loyalties. People become receptive to new utopias and different commitments, thus creating a breeding ground for new social movements. Young people are said to be particularly vulnerable to this. The negative effects of economic growth, industrialization, and technological development on the satisfaction of important needs have also been held responsible. Self-destructive aspects of Western society are pointed to (the exhaustion of natural resources, the growing number of conflicts between industrialized countries, between East and West and North and South), the decreasing efficiency of production (rising economic, social, psychological, and ecological costs), and the decreasing problem-solving capacity of highly industrialized societies. These developments, in conjunction with the evolution of postmaterial values, are seen as the breeding ground for new social movements. According to these authors, postmaterial values and the related protest movements primarily arise among professional groups that are not directly tied to market mechanisms, and groups that are better educated. It is among these groups that protest movements then flourish.

Marxist-oriented scientists emphasize the intervention of both the state and the capitalistic economy in ever more reaches of life as the chief explanation for the rise of the new social movements. This leads to a network of regulatory, ministering, supervisory, and controlling institutions, and increases the danger of loss of legitimacy. As long as people can find adequate compensation for the unfavorable results of industrialization and modernization, and as long as traditional ties and normative structures maintain a private sphere the state cannot touch, loss of legitimacy can be avoided. But it is precisely the private sphere that is becoming more and more the domain of state intervention. As a result of these developments, traditional ties break down. In addition, because of the economic recession, compensation for the negative results of industrialization is often no longer certain. The new social movements fight for the "reappropriation of time, of space, and of relationships in the individual's daily experience" (Melucci 1980, 219). This is the reason they demonstrate for freedom of choice in matters relating to the private sphere, such as abortion, death, gender roles, and the reason for the emphasis on autonomy and independence.

Touraine on New Social Movements

In conclusion, a brief comment on the views of Touraine (1981; Rucht 1985). Although some say he introduced the term new social movements, his views are quite different from those discussed above. According to Touraine, we are presently in a transition from an industrial to a postindustrial society. Such profound transitions are marked by social movements: the workers' movement accompanied the transition to an industrialized society.

Nowadays, according to Touraine, the role played by the workers' movement is nearly over. In the postindustrial society, new social movements will join battle with the ruling class for control of society. The new social movement that will take over the historical role of the workers' movement is not now recognizable as such. Sociological analysis must prove whether protest movements that manifest themselves are indeed the precursors of new social movement. Touraine once took the student movement to be a herald of the new social movement (1978), later the environmental movement (1980). But in both cases he changed his mind.

The new social movement approach relates the location of new protest potentials to processes of modernization in the highly developed Western societies. The new protest potential has two parts: (1) Groups that are affected by the results of industrial modernization. These are primarily groups that have gotten behind as a result of marginalization processes: youths, women, the elderly, and groups that threaten to be disqualified by automation. (2) Groups that have a specific sensitivity to the problems resulting from modernization processes. These are groups whose material needs are satisfied, and who are increasingly confronted with the negative results of economic growth in the competition for positional goods; groups working in the service sector whose profession makes them particularly sensitive to post-materialist values and vulnerable to the negative results of industrial development; and the postwar generation, which grew up under favorable material circumstances.

INTERMEDIATE BALANCE

Resource mobilization and the new social movement approach complement one another. In Melucci's (1984) view, the new social movement approach explains why, but not how, a movement is set up and maintains its structure. It formulates hypotheses about the rise of protest potentials without saying anything about concrete actions and actors. The resource mobilization theory does the reverse. It pays a great deal of attention to the how of collective action, but not to the why. In this sense, the "European" models are the obverse of American resource mobilization theory. I would like to illustrate this by showing how each of the two approaches contributes to the explanation of the willingness of individuals to participate in activities of a social movement.

MOBILIZATION POTENTIALS, RECRUITMENT NETWORKS, AND MOTIVATIONS TO PARTICIPATE

The concept of participation in a social movement is too abstract to work with in theory and research. Particularly if we start looking into the motivations to participate, we cannot get around the fact that an individual associates very different costs and benefits with various activities. Klandermans (1984) demonstrated this for moderate and militant union action, McAdam (1984) for low- and high-risk activities in the civil rights movement, and Briet et al. (1987) for high- and low-threshold activities in the women's movement. Furthermore, different activities make different demands of the recruitment process. McAdam (1984) assumed that in the case of low-risk activities, little more is needed than contact with a recruiting agent, but that high-risk activities require much more intensive approaches. Briet et al. (1987) showed that this was also true for low- versus high-threshold activities. Participation must thus be specified into participation in specific activities.

Participation in social movements is something that takes place in the context of the formation of mobilization potentials, the formation of recruitment networks, and the arousing of the motivation to participate. It is important to distinguish these processes because they require very different activities of social movement organizations, and different theories are needed to analyze them. In the formation of mobilization potentials, a social movement must win cognitive, attitudinal and ideological support. In the formation of recruitment networks, it must increase the chance that people who belong to the mobilization potential are reached. In arousing the motivation, it must favorably influence the decision of people who are reached by a mobilization attempt.

Mobilization Potential

Mobilization potential refers to the potential of people in a society who could theoretically be mobilized by a social movement. The mobilization potential of a social movement does not coincide with the groups whose relative deprivation the movement is concerned with and/or who will benefit by the achievement of the goals of the movement, although such groups can easily be added to the mobilization potential. The same is true of groups that have lost confidence in the authorities. The mobilization potential of a social movement describes the limits within which a mobilization campaign can be successful. People who are not part of the mobilization potential will not consider participating in activities of the movement, even if they are reached by a mobilization attempt. The mobilization potential is the reservoir from which the movement can draw. This reservoir is not formed spontaneously. It is the result of consensus mobilization, that is, the often lengthy campaigns in which the movement propagates its view that certain states of affairs are unacceptable (Klandermans 1984). Although widespread relative deprivation or lack of trust in the authorities are important factors, consensus mobilization is needed to convert it into mobilization potential (cf. Gurney and Tierney 1982; Schwartz 1976; Turner 1969).

The distinction between proactive movements, which want change and claim new rights, and reactive movements, which defend the existing order, is interesting in this connection (Tilly, Tilly, and Tilly 1975). Proactive movements need to do more in the way of consensus mobilization than reactive movements. The former must first legitimize new beliefs, while the latter simply uphold the existing ideology, which requires no legitimacy as long as its hegemony is not violated (Ferree and Miller 1985).

Recruitment Networks

The part of the mobilization potential that is the target of mobilization attempts tells us about a movement's organization and recruitment networks. The further the branchings of a movement reach, the more they are interwoven with other organizations, the greater will be the number of people who are reached by a mobilization attempt. However successful a movement may be in mobilizing consensus, however large its mobilization potential may be, if it does not have a recruitment network to reach people, its mobilization potential cannot be put to use.

The importance of networks for reaching potential participants has been pointed up in various ways in the literature. Gerlach and Hine (1970) found that people were much more inclined to join religious movements if they were approached by people whom they trusted on other grounds. Bolton (1972) showed how new members of peace groups were recruited in circles with a high proportion of people who were already members. Orum (1974) and Wilson and Orum (1976) pointed out the importance of friends or relatives who were already involved in a movement as a factor in the explanation of participation. The introduction of network analysis in this field made possible more systematic analyses.

The formation of recruitment networks involves both extending the reaches of the organization, particularly at a local level, and forming coalitions with other organizations (Ferree and Miller 1985; Klandermans and Oegema 1984; Wilson and Orum 1976). During the mobilization campaign itself, a movement organization will have to mobilize persons who hold positions in the recruitment network. It can then seek to reach sectors of the potential via a mobilization attempt. When such persons back out, a recruitment channel becomes a dead end. The chance of this happening is greater the more centralized and hierarchical a social movement organization is (Klandermans 1985).

The density of the recruitment network also influences the method of recruitment. Using face-to-face recruitment, a social movement organization can reach many people only if it has a dense network. If it does not, it can turn to indirect forms of recruitment. McCarthy (1983) and Mitchell (1984) showed how American environmental organizations managed to make effective use of direct mail for the recruitment of participants. But indirect recruitment seems most likely to work in cases of low-risk or low-threshold participation (cf. Briet et al. 1987; McAdam 1984).

Motivation to Participate

Using the idea of costs and benefits of participation, various authors have attempted to specify the motivation to participate (Fireman and Gamson 1979; Klandermans 1984; McAdam 1984; Mitchell 1979; Muller 1980; Oberschall 1973, 1980; Opp 1985; Pinard 1983; Wilson 1973). Most of them give a prominent role to Olson's logic of collective action (Olson 1955). Fundamental to this is the distinction between collective and selective incentives.

Theories that assume participation in a social movement derives from a consideration of costs and benefits of participation must consider Olson's analysis. All of them see the motivation to participate as a function of collective and selective incentives. But they reject Olson's statement that collective incentives make no difference at all. They assume an additive relationship between the two sorts of incentives, implying that they can reinforce or compensate one another. With respect to the collective incentives, a multiplicative relationship is assumed between the value of the collective good and the expectancy of success. Basically, the various elaborations show important similarities. The common building blocks are the value of the collective good, the expectancy of success, social and nonsocial incentives. Elements of this basic model have been further elaborated by various authors. Klandermans (1984) distinguished between the goals of a specific collective action and the social changes that a movement favors. The perceived instrumentality of specific goals for intended social changes and the attitudes toward these changes determine the value of specific goals. In his view, deprivations, aspirations, moral obligations, attitudes and ideologies make people a part of the mobilization potential of the movement. These cognitions are linked to participation in collective action by the perceived instrumentality of specific goals for social changes.

Oberschall (1980) and Klandermans (1984) elaborated the expectancy of success. Both of them linked the expectancy of success to the number of participants. From a hypothesized relationship between the number of participants and the probability of success, the individual contribution as a function of the number of participants can be derived (see also Oliver, Marwell, and Teixeira 1985). Klandermans (1984) added to this that persons have to decide to participate at a point when they do not know whether others will participate. Their decisions have to be based on their expectations about the behavior of others. The expectation that participation helps to produce the collective good was categorized as follows:

1. Expectations about the number of participants
2. Expectations about one's own contribution to the probability of success
3. Expectations about the probability of success if many people participate.

Muller (1980), Opp (1980), and McAdam (1984) elaborated the social incentives. Both Muller and Opp made a distinction between reactions of approval and disapproval of significant others and normative justifications of collective action. The latter may be considered generalized expectations about the reactions of the environment. McAdam (1984) showed that structural factors such as being integrated in activist networks, prior contact with a recruiting agent, and ties with other participants are important determinants of participation. The social psychological explanation of this is simple. It is not so much the positive reactions that participation will yield in such networks, but the social costs of nonparticipation that play a role. For people who have many ties with such networks, nonparticipation would mean that they would have to justify to other people in those networks why they did not take part.

SYNTHESIS

We are now in a position to indicate how resource mobilization and the new social movement approach complement one another. Besides that, there are some themes both of them ignore. The new social movement approach has clearly concentrated on the factors that determine the mobilization potential of modern social movements. Developments in postindustrial societies effect deprivations and aspirations among the societal groups who most immediately experience their unfavorable consequences and among groups that are extrasensitive because of the development of postmaterial values. But it has not answered the question how these new potentials are activated. In resource mobilization theory we see the reverse: a great deal of attention to the mobilization of resources, to the significance of recruitment networks, to the costs and benefits of participation and to the factors that influence them, but no attention at all to the formation of the mobilization potentials movements draw from in mobilization campaigns.

One thing both approaches overlook is the importance of consensus mobilization. The new social movement approach too easily assumes that mobilization potentials form spontaneously through societal developments. It overlooks the fact that social movement organizations themselves have an important share in defining the situation. Seeing that resource mobilization theory does not concern itself with the formation of mobilization potentials, it, too, largely disregards the importance of consensus mobilization. An important part of consensus mobilization is defending and propagating the instrumentality of special goals for social changes which would do justice to the deprivations and aspirations of people who belong to the mobilization potential of a movement. Resource mobilization theory simply assumes the existence of mobilization potentials. The new social movement approach does not make an issue of mobilization for specific collective actions. As a result, neither of them studies their tangent point: the instrumentality of goals of collective action for the solution to the problems that define the mobilization potential and the mobilization of consensus for this. An essential element of every mobilization campaign thus escapes the attention of both approaches.

IN CONCLUSION

The question now is why theory formation took such a different course on the two continents. Although I do not have the final answer to this question, some assumptions may be formulated. But first let me emphasize that I have not intended to leave the impression that the European and the American literature stand in absolute contrast. This is certainly not true. As early as 1969, Turner surmised in a neglected article that a new social movement form had appeared. Turner thought (and this somewhat resembled Touraine's line of thinking) that, after the liberal humanitarian movement and the socialist movement, things were taking a new turn. The key concepts of the new movement would be personal values and alienation. The movement's adherents would be young people. Ten years later Perrow (1979) suggested explanations for the movements of the 1960s in the United States with his terms "the greening" and "the graying" of America. These concepts showed remarkable similarities with the "rising expectations" and "need defense" of the new social movement literature. The resource mobilization approach was applied in Europe as well. Klandermans used it in a study of participation in union action (Klandermans 1984), the women's movement (Briet et al. 1987) and the peace movement (Klandermans and Oegema 1984). In the same period, Opp (1985) applied it in research of participation in the antinuclear movement in West Germany. And resource mobilization theory has recently started to gain interest in Europe, as shown by such publications as Rucht (1984), Melucci (1984), and van Noort (1984).

But why were developments so divergent, at least initially? A number of assumptions may be formulated. To start with, the movements may have been of a different nature. There is something to be said for this, particularly in the case of West Germany as compared to the United States. The American movements were less anti-establishment and more institutionalized than the West German ones. Yet there were important similarities. Neither in the Netherlands nor in West Germany were all segments of the modern movements antiestablishment, and the modern movements in the United States comprised radical groups as well. Differences in historic developments in the social movement sector might also be the explanation. The modern social movements in the United States succeeded the civil rights movement in a more or less unbroken line. There was also a smooth transition with respect to action repertoire. But the modern movements in Europe were the first great cycle of movements since World War II. They had no direct forerunners, and could only be compared with the workers' movement and the prewar women's movement or peace movement. They quite clearly formed a break with the past, both in constituency and in action repertoire. Perhaps students in Europe concentrated more on the break with the past, while continuity was more emphasized in the United States.

In the third place, differences in scientific tradition may have played a role. The resource mobilization orientation fit into the pragmatic tradition of the American social sciences, while the new social movement approach found its place alongside the Marxist, Weberian social scientific tradition in Europe.

Again, the personal experience of a generation of scientists may have played a role. Many of the present generation of students of social movements in the United States were personally involved in the civil rights movement and there they learned the importance of organizing, of mobilizing resources, etc. Perhaps they gave precedence to questions related to this in their own research and theory formation. European social scientists had no such training school.

Before raising the question "Where will this go in the future," I would like to point out the probably unintended political implications of the blind spots of both approaches. With its argument that there are always grievances in a society and that the rise of new social movements cannot be explained by the aggravation of grievances or the growth of new frustrations, the resource mobilization approach turns social movement organizations into a few of the many actors who must compete for scarce resources in a pluralistic society. The presence of resources rather than indignation over injustice explains the rise of protest movements; resources moreover that often must be made available by outsiders. The grievances themselves, the injustice at the root of it all, became subordinate. Protest movements were thus stripped of their political significance.

The new social movement approach definitely does not put the grievances that generate protest movements in second place. On the contrary, the weaknesses of highly developed societies are enlarged upon and new social movements are interpreted as reactions to derailments in and of those societies. But in all its analytic power the approach is not very helpful to movement activists. Many analyses excel in detailed descriptions of the problems of postindustrial society. At the same time they seem to imply that these developments are inevitable. Protest movements may well be understood in this framework as an expression of discontent, but they cannot prevent things from happening or alter the march of time. In this way, too, protest movements are stripped of their political significance. A synthesis of the two approaches would be a step in the direction of acknowledging the political significance of social movements. Will theorizing on the two continents continue to diverge or will there be a move toward integration? There are signals of a growing interest in both approaches in Europe and the United States as well. Some publications have tried to bridge the gap (cf. Melucci 1984) between the new social movement approach and resource mobilization theory. There also have been meetings between scholars from the two continents (Klandermans and Tarrow 1985). This is as is should be, for as I have argued, the European and American approaches complement rather than exclude each other. Such integration not only could enhance the field by improving theoretical frameworks, it could also mark the beginning of a tradition of comparative and cooperative research on social movements.

15

SILENCE, DEATH, AND THE INVISIBLE ENEMY: AIDS ACTIVISM AND SOCIAL MOVEMENT "NEWNESS"

Josh Gamson

Shea Stadium is packed. As the Mets play the Astros, New York AIDS activists scream and shout along with the rest of the fans. Their cheers are somewhat unusual: "ACT UP! Fight back! Fight AIDS!" Their banners, unfurled in front of the three sections they have bought out, shout plays on baseball themes: "No glove, no love," "Don't balk at safer sex," "AIDS is not a ball game." The electronic billboard flashes some of their messages as well. The action gets wide coverage the following day. Later, in a Newsweek (1988a) article on the activist group ACT UP, a baseball fan complains, "AIDS is a fearful topic. This is totally inappropriate."

The fan is right, on both counts; in fact, I would suggest, he inadvertently sums up the point of the action. He also calls attention to the oddities: Why fight AIDS at a baseball game? Why mix fear and Americana? Who or what is the target here?

Susan Sontag and others have noted that the AIDS epidemic fits quite smoothly into a history of understanding the disease through the "usual script" of the plague metaphor: originating from "outside," plagues are visitations on "them," punishments of both individuals and groups, they become stand-ins for deep fears and tools for bringing judgments about social crises. "AIDS," Sontag (1988) suggests, "is understood in a premodern way."

Yet the plague of AIDS has brought with it understandings and actions that are hardly "premodern": civil disobedience at the Food and Drug Administration protesting the sluggish drug approval process, guerrilla theater and "die-ins," infiltrations of political events culminating in the unfurling of banners protesting government inaction, media-geared "zaps," illegal drug research and sales, pickets and rallies. AIDS has given rise to a social movement. This is not, in fact, part of the usual script.

Silence, Death, and the Invisible Enemy 239

Perhaps, then, AIDS can be understood as part of a different script as well. Much has been written about "new social movements" (NSMs); perhaps AIDS activism follows an outline particular to contemporary movements. This classification presents its own difficulties: social movement literature has a hard time clarifying exactly what is "new" about contemporary social movements and can, through its fuzziness, easily accommodate yet another social movement without shedding new light.

In this chapter, I examine AIDS activism—by which I mean an organized "street" response to the epidemic—through the activities of ACT UP (the AIDS Coalition to Unleash Power), its most widespread and publicly visible direct-action group.

ACT UP, which began in New York, has chapters in Chicago, Boston, Atlanta, Los Angeles, Houston, Rochester, Madison, Nashville, San Francisco, and a number of other cities. The groups are loosely federated under the umbrella of the AIDS Coalition to Network, Organize and Win (ACT NOW). New York is by far the largest ACT UP, with weekly meeting attendance in the hundreds and membership estimated at nearly 3,000, while the others are smaller. San Francisco, with a membership of over 700, averages 50 people at general meetings. My comparisons between ACT UP in San Francisco and chapters in New York and other cities are based on a national conference in Washington, D.C., internal publications, informal discussion and interviews, and newspaper reports.

Using data from six months of participant-observation research (September 1988 through February 1989) in San Francisco's ACT UP, coupled with local and national internal documents and newspaper writings about the group, I develop an analysis intended both to sharpen focus on the struggle over the meaning of AIDS and to challenge some of the hazy understandings of social movement newness. The analysis here treats ACT UP not as an exemplar but rather as an anomaly, asking what unique conditions constitute the case and how the case can aid in a reconstruction of existing theory. Micro- and macro-level analyses are linked through seeking out an "explanation for uniqueness" such that "we are compelled to move into the realm of the 'macro' that shapes the 'micro' that we observe in face-to-face interaction" (Burawoy 1989, 7).

In the first part of the chapter I briefly review approaches to contemporary social movements, locating ACT UP within this literature. I then turn to ACT UP's activities and internal obstacles, looking at their response to the plague script, the alternative scripts they propose and their strategies for doing so, and the difficulties they face in this process. I argue that asking "who is the enemy?" provides a fruitful direction for making sense of these dynamics because ACT UP members often have trouble finding their "enemies." The chapter continues with an examination of why this may be so, and what light it may shed on contemporary movements. Borrowing from Michel Foucault (1979), I turn to an examination of the forms of domination to which ACT UP members respond. I argue that in addition to visible targets such as government agencies and drug companies, much of what ACT UP is fighting is abstract, disembodied, invisible; control through the creation of abnormality. Power is maintained less through direct force or institutionalized oppression and more through the delineation of the "normal" and the exclusion of the "abnormal." I suggest that this "normalizing" process, taking prominence in a gradual historical shift, is increasingly unlocked from state oppression in recent decades. State figures and institutions—though certainly still deeply involved in this domination—are now less apt to contribute to the production and dissemination of labels, making the process itself, abstracted, the hazy focus of protest. The chapter then traces how responses to normalization play themselves out in ACT UP activities; activists use the labels to dispute the labels, use their abnormality and expressions of gay identity to challenge the process by which this identity was and is defined. Finally, I suggest directions this framework provides for analyzing contemporary movements.

THE THEORETICAL CONTEXT: WHAT'S NEW?

Among the shifts provoked by the rise of massive social movements in the 1960s and 1970s was a rupture in theorizing about social movements. Until that time, the dominant paradigm of collective behavior theory treated noninstitutional movements as essentially nonrational or irrational responses by alienated individuals to social strain and breakdown (for example, Smelser 1963). Many 1960s activists did not fit the mold. Neither anomic nor underprivileged nor responding to crises with beliefs "akin to magical beliefs" (Smelser 1963, 8), they in fact came together largely from the middle class, with concrete goals and rational calculations of strategies. The predictions of classical social movement theory regarding who made up social movements and how they operated had broken down (see Cohen 1985; McAdam 1982).

In the past two decades, attempts to retheorize social movements have moved in two major directions. North American resource mobilization theory accounts for large-scale mobilizations by emphasizing rational calculations by actors, focusing on the varying constraints and opportunities in which they operate and the varying resources on which they draw (see McCarthy and Zald 1977; Oberschall 1973; Tilly 1978; Jenkins 1981). This paradigm, directly challenging the assumptions of collective behavior theory, insists on the rationality of collective action. European theorists, in contrast, have argued that rational-actor models are inappropriately applied to new groups seeking identity and autonomy. The movements of the 1960s and their apparent descendants—the peace movement, for example, or feminist, ecological, or local-autonomy movements—have been taken together by theorists as "new" phenomena to be accounted for; it is their nonrational focus on identity and expression that these theories emphasize as distinctive. They attempt to outline the characteristics shared by contemporary movements and to discern the structural shifts that might account for new dimensions of activity (see Kitschelt 1985; Cohen 1985; Eder 1985; Habermas 1981; Offe 1985; Touraine 1985).

With some exceptions (see, for example, Doug McAdam's 1982 study of black insurgency), American theory, with its insistence on instrumental rationality, tends to pass over these distinctive characteristics—feminist attention to "consciousness," for example, and black and gay "pride"—to which European theories of "new social movements" (NSMs) direct attention. The European literature, then, in that it attempts to explain these apparently new characteristics found also in AIDS activism, provides the stronger conceptual tools with which to approach ACT UP. Yet what is actually "new" according to European NSM theory is both disputed and unclear. Most agree that a middle-class social base is distinctive (see Eder 1985; Kriesi 1989); indeed, the fact that NSMs are not working-class movements focused primarily on economic distribution seems to be a characteristic on which there is clarity and agreement. From here, the range of characteristics expands and abstracts; NSMs claim "the sphere of 'political action within civil society' as [their] space"(Offe 1985, 832); they use different tactics from their predecessors (Offe 1985); their conflicts concern not "problems of distribution" but "the grammar of forms of life," arising in "areas of cultural reproduction, social integration and socialization" (Habermas 1981, 33); they "manifest a form of middle-class protest that oscillates from moral crusade to political pressure group to social movement" (Eder 1985, 879); they are "both culturally oriented and involved in structural conflicts" (Touraine 1985,766), involve a "self-limiting radicalism" that "abandons revolutionary dreams in favor of the idea of structural reform, along with a defense of civil society that does not seek to abolish the autonomous functioning of political and economic systems" (Cohen 1985, 664).

Common to this list is a recognition that the field of operation has shifted, broadly put, to "civil society" and away from the state; that culture has become more of a focal point of activity (through "lifestyle" and "identity" movements, for example); and that this shift has to do with broad changes in the "societal type" to which movements respond and in which they act. Common to the list is also an unclear answer to the question of how new the shift really is; as Jean Cohen (1985, 665) points out, the theme of defending civil society does not in itself imply something new—the question "is whether the theme has been connected to new identities, forms of organization, and scenarios of conflict." New social movement theorists—even those like Touraine and Cohen, who address these questions directly—seem to be unclear on what these shifts and changes really are: What exactly is the "cultural field" of "civil society" and what do these movements actually do there? What is it that is different about contemporary society that accounts for the characteristics of new social movements? When and how did these changes take place?

ACT UP AS A NEW SOCIAL MOVEMENT

ACT UP provides an opportunity both to examine some of these issues concretely and to offer new hypotheses. The AIDS activist movement appears to share the most basic characteristics of "new social movements": a (broadly) middle-class membership and a mix of instrumental, expressive, and identity-oriented activities. Rather than exclusively orient itself toward material distribution, ACT UP uses and targets cultural resources as well. What, this examination asks, does ACT UP do on the cultural terrain? What light does their activity shed on the question of "newness"? How can a study of this group contribute to an understanding of shifts in the nature of social movements and in the nature of the social world in which they operate?

The answer begins with the group's overall profile. ACT UP/San Francisco grew out of the 1987 San Francisco AIDS Action Pledge, becoming ACT UP in the fall of that year after New York's ACT UP began to gain recognition. In addition to planned and spontaneous actions, the group meets weekly in a church in the predominantly gay Castro neighborhood. ACT UP/San Francisco is made up almost exclusively of white gay men and lesbians, mostly in their twenties and thirties. The core membership—an informal group of about thirty-five activists—draws from both established activists (gay rights, Central American politics, etc.) and those newly politicized by AIDS.[1] Some, but by no means all, of ACT UP's membership has either tested positive for HIV antibodies or been diagnosed with AIDS. As one member said, "I'm here because I'm angry and I'm tired of seeing my friends die." The membership is typically professional and semiprofessional: legal and health care professionals, writers, political organizers, students, artists with day jobs. ACT UP/New York and ACT UPs in other cities exhibit similar profiles (Green 1989).

Self-defined in their flyers and media kits as "a nonpartisan group of diverse individuals united in anger and committed to direct action to end the AIDS crisis" (ACT UP 1988a), ACT UP pushes for greater access to treatments and drugs for AIDS-related diseases; culturally sensitive, widely available, and explicit safe-sex education; and well-funded research that is "publicly accountable to the communities most affected" (ACT UP 1988a). Moreover, the group pushes for the participation of people with AIDS (PWAs) in these activities (ACT UP 1989). The idea here is to change the distribution of resources and decision-making power; the principle guiding actions is strategic, aimed at affecting policy changes. "People have been fighting for social justice in this country for centuries," says one member (September 1988). "We're going to get aerosol pentamidine [a treatment drug for pneumocystis pneumonia] a lot quicker than we're going to get social justice."

ACT UP is also often involved in actions, however, whose primary principle is expressive. They focus inward on "building a unified community" (the gay and lesbian community and, increasingly, a subcommunity of PWAs and the HIV-infected), and on the "need to express the anger and rage that is righteous and justified" from the community outward. They organize at times around actions in which AIDS is not the central issue or in which AIDS activism is incorporated into the project of "recreating a movement for gay and lesbian liberation." This orientation toward identity and expression, while not excluding older-style strategic action, is one key characteristic cited by students of post-1960s social movements.

Most interestingly, though, one hears and sees in ACT UP a constant reference to theater. ACT UP operates largely by staging events and by carefully constructing and publicizing symbols; it attacks the dominant representations of AIDS and of people with AIDS and makes attempts to replace them with alternative representations. At times, ACT UP attacks the representations alone; at times, the attack is combined with a direct one on cultural producers and the process of AIDS-image production.

Another action principle weaves through ACT UP. As *Newsweek* (1988a) puts it, ACT UP has often "deliberately trespassed the bounds of good taste": throwing condoms, necking in public places, speaking explicitly and positively about anal sex, "camping it up" for the television cameras. This trespassing or boundary-crossing—and we can include in it the infiltration of public and private spaces (the Republican national convention, for example, where activists posing as participants unfurled banners)—both uses and strikes at the cultural field as well. In this case, rather than react to images of AIDS, activists use a more general tactic of disturbing "good taste"—and, in a point *Newsweek* quite characteristically misses, calling attention to the connection between cultural definitions and responses to AIDS. Boundary-crossing, along with theatrical and symbolic actions, makes clear that ACT UP operates largely on the cultural field where theorists situate new social movements.[2] It also suggests that an examination of the specific pattern of culturally oriented actions may be especially revealing. By focusing on the cultural activities of AIDS activists as a key distinctive element, I by no means want to suggest that this activism is primarily cultural. In fact, treatment issues, needle-exchange programs, and access to health care, for instance, are all common subjects of action. Pursuing this examination via ACT UP's peculiarities, I hope to generate possibilities for grounding and developing social movement theory.

ACT UP'S INTERNAL OBSTACLES

The examination turns, then, to ACT UP's distinctive characteristics. ACT UP's strong cultural orientation has already been noted. In addition, buried in its various strategies are three fundamental confusions. First, ACT UP's orientation toward theatrics suggests a clear delineation of performer from audience, yet actions are often planned by ACT UP members without an articulation of whom they're meant to influence. If one wants to affect an audience—for example, by invoking a symbol whose meaning is taken for granted and then giving it a different meaning—one clearly needs a conception of who that audience is. In ACT UP planning meetings, there is often an underlying confusion of audiences, and more often the question of audience is simply ignored. When activists in New York infiltrated a Republican women's cocktail party and later unfurled banners ("Lesbians for Bush," read one), the response of the cocktail partiers, a defensive singing of "God Bless America" (reported in "Workshop on Creative Actions," ACT NOW Conference, Washington, D.C., October 8, 1988), was important not for what it showed about the Republicans' AIDS consciousness, which came as no surprise. Instead, it was important for what it showed the activists about their own power. They were, in effect, their own audience, performing for themselves and making others perform for them. In "brainstorms" for new actions, there is almost never a mention of audience, and action ideas with different audiences proliferate. ACT UP protested Dukakis, for example, with no media coverage, Dukakis nowhere in sight, and no one to witness the protest but passing cars (San Francisco, September 30, 1988). In the meetings I observed, I commonly heard suggestions for actions that bypassed any actual event, heading straight for the at-home audience through "photo opportunities," mixed in with suggestions for actions that almost no one would see. Much of this confusion is exacerbated by an openness of exchange and decentralized decision making born of ACT UP's democratic structure (in San Francisco, decisions are made consensually). The loose organizational structure acts against focused planning and action. I argue, however, that the roots are deeper.

A second point of confusion is that, while ACT UP professes to be inclusive, and ideas are often brought up that target nongay aspects of AIDS (issues of concern to intravenous drug-users, for example, or access to health care for those who cannot afford it), there are few signs that ACT UP in fact succeeds at including or actively pursues nongay members. This does not mean that the membership is exclusively gay men; in fact, a good portion of the activists are women.[3] The formation of coalitions is sometimes brought up as a good idea—"we need to join with others in solidarity around common suffering and common enemies," said the keynote speaker at the ACT NOW conference in October 1988—but generally not effected. Cooperative actions with other groups generate little excitement in San Francisco meetings. Actions are aimed mainly at targets with particular relevance to lesbians and gays; there are few black or Hispanic members, gay or straight. Despite the goal of inclusiveness, ACT UP continues to draw from and re-create the white, middle-class gay and lesbian community.

A third and related problem is perhaps even more fundamental: AIDS politics and gay politics stand in tension, simultaneously associated and dissociated. ACT UP is an AIDS activist organization built and run by gay people. Historically, this is neither surprising nor problematic; among the populations first hit hardest by AIDS, gay people were alone in having an already established tradition and network of political and self-help organizations. Still, this tradition has meant that "AIDS groups have found it very difficult to establish themselves as non-gay, even where they have deliberately presented themselves as such" (Altman 1986, 90). AIDS activists find themselves simultaneously attempting to dispel the notion that AIDS is a gay disease (which it is not) while, through their activity and leadership, treating AIDS as a gay problem (which, among other things, it is).

While this dilemma in part reflects the course the disease itself took, how it plays itself out in ACT UP is instructive. For some, particularly those members who are not newly politicized, ACT UP is gay politics, pure and simple, a movement continuous with earlier activism. They emphasize the need for "sex positive" safe-sex education, for example, linking AIDS politics to the sexual liberation of earlier gay politics. The main organizer of a November 1988 election night rally in San Francisco's Castro district for the gay community to "Stand Out and Shout" about results, envisioned it as a return to the good old days of gay celebration. In planning speakers for the rally, he and others quickly generated a long list of possibles—from the gay political community. Here, AIDS issues often get buried.

For others, it's important to maintain some separation, albeit a blurry one, between the two sets of issues. In New York, for example, when a newspaper calls ACT UP a "gay organization," ACT UP's media committee sends out a "standard letter" correcting the error ("Media Workshop" at ACT NOW Conference in Washington, D.C., October 8, 1988). The ACT UP agenda, when the balance is toward distinctive AIDS politics, often focuses more narrowly on prevention and treatment issues as in, for example, a San Francisco proposal for an "AIDS treatment advocacy project" which argued that "whether it is an entire family with AIDS in Harlem or an HIV+ gay man in San Francisco, treatment is ultimately the issue they are most concerned with" (ACT UP 1988b,1). More commonly, though, ACT UP actions don't fall on one side or the other, but combine an active acceptance of the gay-AIDS connection with an active resistance to that connection.

VISIBLE AND INVISIBLE ENEMIES

Why do these particular confusions occur? They eventually will come to make sense as the particularities of ACT UP's actions are examined. These three confusions with ACT UP, which seem to give its action a somewhat unfocused character, in fact will prove to be core elements of the group's being. Explaining ACT UP's confusions, and those of social movements like it, hinges on the answer to a pivotal question: who is the enemy? Asking this question of ACT UP, one often finds that the enemies against which their anger and action are directed are clear, familiar, and visible: the state and corporations. At other times, though, the enemy is invisible, abstract, disembodied, ubiquitous: it is the very process of "normalization" through labeling in which everyone except one's own "community" of the denormalized (and its supporters) is involved. At still other times, intermediate enemies appear, the visible institutors of the less visible process: the media and medical science.

This second enemy forms the basis of my core theoretical claim: that ACT UP is responding to a gradual historical shift toward a form of domination in which power is maintained through a normalizing process in which "the whole indefinite domain of the non-conforming is punishable" (Foucault 1979, 178). Through labeling, or socially organized stigmatization, behaviors and groups are marked as abnormal; in the last two centuries, the norm has largely replaced the threat of violence as a technique of power. As Michel Foucault (1979, 183) argues, individuals are differentiated

> in terms of the following overall rule: that the rule be made to function as a minimum threshold, as an average to be respected or as an optimum towards which one must move. It. . . hierarchizes in terms of values, the abilities, the level, the "nature" of individuals. It introduces, through this "value-giving" measure, the constraint of a conformity that must be achieved. Lastly, it traces the limit that will define difference in relation to all other differences, the external frontier of the abnormal.

In this process, the dominator becomes increasingly abstracted and invisible, while the dominated, embodied and visible (and, importantly, "marked" through stigmatization), becomes the focus of attention. In effect, people dominate themselves; instead of being confronted with a punishment (physical, material) as a mechanism of control, they confront themselves with the threat of being devalued as abnormal.

These ideas are not incompatible with those put forward by the sociology of deviance and discussions of stigmatization (e.g., Lemert 1967; Goffman 1963), which, of course, call attention to the process of labeling and its impact on the "deviant." The various forms of labeling theory, however, have also been challenged by collective action since the 1960s. Those theories, by studying how one "becomes deviant," and the defensive reaction of "deviants" to an identity defined for them—the "management of spoiled identities" (Goffman 1963) and "secondary deviation" as a "means of defense" against the "problems created by the societal reaction to primary deviation" (Lemert 1967, 17) are ill-equipped to explain the organization of the stigmatized into social movements. As John Kitsuse (1980, 5) argues, the accommodative reactions analyzed by deviance sociology (retreat into a subculture, nervously covering up or denying aberrations) do not "account for, nor do they provide for an understanding of, the phenomenal number of self-proclaimed deviant groups that have visibly and vocally entered the politics" of recent decades. Earlier theories are hard pressed to account for historical change, and for the assertive building of collective movements based on self-definitions that reject the dominant definitions. Foucault, in contrast, treats pressure for conformity not as a given problem for the "deviant" but as a technique of power with a variable history.

Identity strategies are particularly salient and problematic within this domination form. When power is effected through categorization, identity is often built on the very categories it resists. ACT UP's expressive actions, in this light, are part of a continuing process of actively forging a gay identity while challenging the process through which it is formed for gay people at a time when the stigma of disease has been linked with the stigma of deviant sexuality. ACT UP members continue to organize around the "deviant" label, attempting to separate label from stigma. Identity-oriented actions accept the labels, and symbolic actions disrupt and resignify them.

Identity actions and representational strategies thus stand in awkward relationship: they are increasingly linked in the attack on the normalization process itself. In a simpler identity politics—in the celebration of gay liberation, for example—labels are important tools for self-understanding. That sort of politics involves what John Kitsuse (1980, 9) calls "tertiary deviation," the "confrontation, assessment, and rejection of the negative identity . . . and the transformation of that identity into a positive or viable self-conception." ACT

UP members, however, push past this "new deviance" to use stigmas and identity markers as tools against the normalization process. The representation of oneself as abnormal now becomes a tool for disrupting the categorization process; the labels on which group identity is built are used, in a sense, against themselves.

Why, though, is this response to normalizing power coming into its own now? Stigmatization is certainly not new. Foucault, in *Discipline and Punish*, traces a shift in the eighteenth and nineteenth centuries, a shift that takes place primarily in technologies of control: the rise of surveillance techniques and the constitution of the subject by "experts" and scientific discourse. This shift has arguably solidified in this century in Western societies. Yet, while state institutions and actors in the twentieth century certainly have still been involved in the normalization process (as well as in direct repression), they have evidently been less involved in the latter half of this century (or, stated less strongly, less visibly involved). One sees this in the history of civil rights: racism continues while state-sponsored racism and racist policies become less acceptable (see Omi and Winant 1986, 89ff). Similarly, state definitions of women's "roles" have been liberalized, as the state has withdrawn somewhat from prescribing "normal" female behavior. One sees this as well in the response to AIDS; the federal government, while conservative or split in its policies, has over time become somewhat more liberal in terms of labeling. Public health officials advertise AIDS as an "equal opportunity destroyer"; the Surgeon General warns against treating AIDS as a gay disease and argues in favor of protections against discrimination; the Presidential Commission calls for "the reaffirmation of compassion, justice, and dignity" and indicts, among other things, "a lack of uniform and strong antidiscrimination laws" (Johnson and Murray 1988). State institutions increasingly refuse to "discriminate," that is, to set policies based on social labels. As the state becomes less directly involved in normalization, the process itself necessarily becomes more an independent point of attack by the denormalized and resisted as a process. It is within this overall historical shift in methods of domination, this study proposes, that ACT UP's social movement activity makes sense.

ACT UP AND NORMALIZATION

How does this resistance play itself out? What is the link between enemies and actions? Let's begin with the old forms of domination, which are very much still at work. The state is certainly involved in the domination of people with AIDS, as it is in the repression of sexual minorities. For example, the Federal Food and Drug Administration approves drugs and has been sluggish in approving AIDS-related drugs; it is perceived as allowing bureaucracy to get in the way of saving or prolonging lives (*Newsweek* 1988b). In October 1988 ACT NOW organized a conference, teach-in, rally, and day of civil disobedience in Washington, D.C., to "seize control of the FDA" (Okie 1988; Connolly and Raine 1988). The Reagan and Bush administrations were notoriously inattentive to the AIDS epidemic. Reagan first mentioned AIDS publicly at a time when over 36,000 people had already been diagnosed and over 20,000 had died from the disease. While subsequently calling AIDS "America's number one health problem," the administration consistently avoided initiating a coordinated, adequately financed attack on that problem (see Shilts 1988). Reagan and Bush became common targets of ACT UP "AIDSgate" signs and T-shirts, of "zaps," of posters charging that "the government has blood on its hands," of disruption and protest during campaign speeches. In this case, specific state institutions and actors were targeted, mostly through conventional protest actions and media-geared actions. In these cases, it is quite clear who was responsible for needless death and who controlled resources, and ACT UP functions as a pressure group to protest and affect policy decisions. Here, AIDS politics and gay politics were quite separable and separated.

Similarly, pharmaceutical companies are manifest enemies; they control the price of treatment drugs and make decisions about whether or not to pursue drug development. That drug company decisions are guided by considerations of profit (Eigo et al. 1988) is a direct and visible instance of oppression and represents an embodied obstacle to the physical survival of people with AIDS. ACT UP attacks these targets with pressure tactics: boycotting AZT manufacturer Burroughs-Wellcome, zapping that company and others with civil disobedience actions, publicizing government-drug company relations (Eigo et al. 1988). In this example, again, the focus is specifically on issues of relevance to all people with AIDS.

Yet AIDS has also been from the outset a stigma, an illness constructed as a marker of homosexuality, drug abuse, moral deficiencies—stigmas added to those of sexual transmission, terminal disease, and, for many, skin color.[4] AIDS has

> come to assume all the features of a traditional morality play: images of cancer and death, of blood and semen, of sex and drugs, of morality and retribution. A whole gallery of folk devils have been introduced—the sex-crazed gay, the dirty drug abuser, the filthy whore, the blood drinking voodoo-driven black—side by side with a gallery of "innocents"—the hemophiliacs, the blood transfusion "victim", the new born child, even the "heterosexual." (Plummer 1988, 45)

Associated most commonly with the image of the male homosexual or bisexual AIDS "victim" or "carrier" who is vaguely responsible through deviant behavior for his own demise, AIDS has been appropriated to medicalize moral stances: promiscuity is medically unsafe while monogamy is safe; being a member of certain social groups is dangerous to one's health while being a member of the "general population" is dangerous only when the un-general contaminate it. As Simon Watney (1987, 126) notes, in AIDS "the categories of health and sickness. . .meet with those of sex, and the image of homosexuality is reinscribed with connotations of contagion and disease, a subject for medical attention and medical authority."

The construction and reconstruction of boundaries has been, then, an essential aspect of the story of AIDS. The innocent victim is bounded off from the guilty one, pure blood from contaminated, the general population from the AIDS populations, risk groups from those not at risk. Those who span the boundaries arguably become the most threatening: the promiscuous bisexual, the only one who can "account for and absolve the heterosexual majority of any taint of unlawful desire" (Grover 1987, 21) and the prostitute, with her long-standing position as a "vessel of disease" (Grover 1987, 25).

Who achieves this demarcation of boundaries? Who has made AIDS mean what it does? Who is the enemy? Two manifest producers of stigmas appear (in addition to certain public figures who disseminate them): the mass media, on whose television screens and newspaper pages the stigmatized are actually visible, and medical science, which translates the labels into risk-group categories. ACT UP thus challenges the medical establishment, largely by undermining the expertise claimed by them. Activists keep up to date on and publicize underground and foreign treatments (e.g., Eigo et al. 1988), sell illegal treatment drugs publicly, yell the names of known AIDS-illness drugs in front of the FDA ("Show them we know!" the organizer calls). They wear lab coats and prepare a "guerrilla slide show" in which they plan to slip slides saying "He's lying" and "This is voodoo epidemiology" into an audiovisual presentation by a health commissioner.

ACT UP also sets up challenges to the media. An ongoing San Francisco battle had ACT UP shutting down production and members negotiating with producers over the script of an NBC drama, "Midnight Caller." In that script a bisexual man with AIDS purposely infects others and is shot and killed in the end by one of his female partners. It was objected to by ACT UP members as playing on "the great fear of the 'killer queer'"[5] and implying that, as an ACT UP representative put it, "basically it's justifiable to kill a person with AIDS" (Ford 1988). A similar response has been discussed for the San Francisco filming of Rand Shilts's And the Band Played On, a controversial history of the American AIDS epidemic. The media are usually treated by ACT UP as allies in the public relations operation of garnering coverage. As one New Yorker put it (October 1988), "the media aren't the enemy, the media are manipulated by the enemy, and we can manipulate them too." When actively involved in the labeling of people with AIDS as murderers, however, the media become the enemies to be fought. This ambivalence makes sense: the media, as the institutional mechanism through which normalization is most effectively disseminated, are both a visible enemy and a necessary link to a more abstract form of domination.[6]

The question of who is behind the generation and acceptance of stigmas, though, for the most part doesn't get asked as activists plan and argue, perhaps because the answer is experienced daily: everyone and no one. No one actually does it and everyone participates in it—your family and your neighbors as well as the blatant bigots far away. It's a process that appears usually as natural, as not-a-process.

PLAYING WITH LABELS, CROSSING THE BOUNDARIES

Fighting this largely hidden process calls for different kinds of strategies, mostly in the realm of symbols. Examining the symbolic maneuvering of ACT UP, we can begin to see how fighting the process calls for particular strategies. ACT UP's general strategy is to take a symbol or phrase used to oppress and invert it. For example, ACT UP makes explicit challenges, guided by other AIDS activists and particularly PWAs, on the kind of language used to discuss AIDS. In place of "AIDS victims," they speak of "people with AIDS" or "people living with AIDS." In place of "risk groups," they insert the category of "risk practices." They talk about blood and semen rather than "bodily fluids," and they challenge the exclusionary use of "general population" (see Grover 1987).

The strategy runs much deeper than speech, however. The visual symbol most widely publicized by American AIDS activists—"SILENCE=DEATH" written in bold white-on-black letters beneath a pink triangle, the Nazi emblem for homosexuals later coopted by the gay movement—provides a snapshot look at this process. Here, ACT UP takes a symbol used to mark people for death and reclaims it. They reclaim, in fact, control over defining a cause of death; the banner connects gay action to gay survival, on the one hand, and homophobia to death from AIDS, on the other. ACT UP's common death spectacles repeat the inversion. In AIDS commentary death is used in a number of ways (Gilman 1987); it is either a punishment (the image of the withered, guilty victim), an individual tragedy (the image of the lonely, abandoned dying), or a weapon (the image of the irresponsible "killer queer"). A "die in," in which activists draw police-style chalk outlines around each other's "dead" bodies, gives death another meaning by shifting the responsibility: these are deaths likened to murders, victims not of their own "deviance," but shot down by the people controlling the definition and enforcement of normality. You have told us what our deaths mean, their actions say, now we who are actually dying will show you what they mean.

A similar shift of responsibility takes place around the symbol of blood. In popular discussions, blood is talked about in terms of "purity" and a benevolent medical establishment working to keep "bad blood" out of the nation's blood supply. In many ACT UP activities, "blood" is splattered on T-shirts (San Francisco, October 3, 1988) or doctor's uniforms (Washington, D.C., October 11, 1988). Members want to shoot it out of squirt guns, blood-balloon it onto buildings, write "test this" with it on walls ("Creative Actions" workshop, Washington, D.C., October 8, 1988). Here, on one level, they use the established discourse of purity against its users as an angry weapon: "infected" blood is everywhere. On another level, though, the frame is shifted from purity (in which the blood supply is "victimized") to crime (in which PWAs are victimized). The blood becomes evidence not of infection, but of murder; the activists are blood-splattered victims, as was made explicit in posters originally directed at Mayor Koch in New York and later translated into an indictment of the federal government. "The government has blood on its hands," the sign says, "One AIDS death every half hour." Between the two phrases is the print of a large, bloody hand. In a San Francisco rally against Representative William Dannemeyer's Proposition 102 (October 3, 1988), which would have required by law that doctors report those infected and those "suspected" of infection, require testing at the request of doctors, employers or insurers, and eliminate confidential testing, ACT UP carried a "Dannemeyer Vampire" puppet. The vampire, a big ugly head on a stick, with black cape and blood pouring from its fangs, was stabbed with a stake later in the action. Here, ACT UP activates another popular code in which blood has meaning—the gore of horror movies—and reframes blood testing as blood sucking. It is not the blood itself that's monstrous, but the vampire who would take it. By changing the meaning of blood, ACT UP activists dispute the "ownership" of blood; more importantly, they call attention to the consequences of the labels of "bad" blood and "purity" and implicate those accepting the labels in the continuation of the AIDS epidemic.

Boundary-crossing, though tactically similar, goes on the offensive, while inversions are essentially reactive. The spectacle of infiltration and revelation runs through real and fantasized ACT UP actions. Members speak of putting subversive messages in food or in the pockets of suit jackets, of writing messages on lawns with weed killer, of covering the Washington Monument with a giant condom, of replacing (heterosexual) bar ashtrays with condom-shaped ashtrays. They place stickers saying "Touched by a Person with AIDS" in phone booths and stage a mock presidential inauguration through the San Francisco streets during rush hour (January 1989). The idea, as one activist put it, is to "occupy a space that's not supposed to be yours," to "usurp public spaces." San Francisco's underground graffiti group, specializing in "redecorating" targeted spaces, sums up the principle in its humorous acronym, TANTRUM: Take Action Now to Really Upset the Masses.

The ideas that charge brainstorming sessions and the eventual choices for visual and theatrical activity at actions are not arbitrary. The selections are revealing. Spaces and objects are chosen that are especially American (that is, middle American—lawns, cocktail parties, baseball games, patriotic symbols, suits) and presumably "safe" from the twin "threats" of homosexuality and disease. ACT UP here seizes control of symbols that traditionally exclude gay people or render them invisible and takes them over, endowing them with messages about AIDS; they reclaim them, as they do the pink triangle, and make them mean differently. In so doing, they attempt to expose the system of domination from which they reclaim meanings and implicate the entire system in the spread of AIDS.

It is important to notice that ACT UP's identity-oriented actions often revolve around boundary-crossing and label disruption. These are strategies for which these mostly white, middle-class gay people are particularly equipped, largely because their stigma is often invisible, unlike, for example, the stigmatized person of color. They can draw on a knowledge of mainstream culture born of participation rather than exclusion and, thus a knowledge of how to disrupt it using its own vocabulary. Here the particular cultural resources of ACT UP's membership become important; they are resources that other movements (and gay people from other races or classes) may not have to the same degree or may not be able to use without considerable risk.

Gay campiness, raunchy safe-sex songs in front of the Department of Health and Human Services, straight-looking men in skirts wearing "Fuck Me Safe" T-shirts (Washington, D.C., October 1988), lesbians and gay men staging "kiss-ins," a general outrageousness that "keeps the edge"—these actions simultaneously accept the gay label, build a positive gay identity, challenge the conventional "deviant" label, connect stigmatization to AIDS deaths, and challenge the very process of categorization. This is the power of the pink triangle and "SILENCE=DEATH"; the building of an identity is linked with the resistance of a stigma as the key to stopping the AIDS epidemic. "We are everywhere," says the sign at a D.C. ACT NOW rally, a sign common at gay political demonstrations, and the noisy expressions of collective anger and identity add up to the same claim. Here, the gay "we" and the AIDS "we" are melded; the destabilizing effect of the suddenly revealed homosexual is joined with the fear that suddenly no space is safe from AIDS. A chant at several San Francisco protests captures the link between asserting an identity and challenging the labels: "We're fags and dykes," the activists chant, "and we're here to stay." Meaning: we are what you say we are, and we're not what you say we are. "We're here," they chant, "we're queer, and we're not going shopping."

What exactly is being challenged in these symbolic inversions? Certainly, in symbols like the Dannemeyer vampire and the bloody hand attributed to the government, the old and consistent enemy, the state, is mixed in; but it isn't exclusive. ACT UP disrupts symbolic representation, heeding the call to "campaign and organize in order to enter the amphitheater of AIDS commentary effectively and unapologetically on our own terms" (Watney 1987, 54). It does so, moreover, often through symbols that are not tied to the state but to "mainstream" American culture. In the case of inversions, AIDS and gay labels are not necessarily linked: any oppressive marker is taken over. In the case of boundary-disruption, AIDS and gay labels are connected; the fear of gay people and the fear of AIDS, now linked in the normalization process, are used to call attention to themselves. In both cases, the process of stigmatization, by which symbols become markers of abnormality and the basis for decisions about "correcting" the abnormal, is contested.

STRATEGIES AND OBSTACLES REVISITED

The mix of strategies, then, can be seen in terms of the visibility of enemies. More familiar, instrumental pressure-group strategies attempt to change the distribution of resources by attacking those visibly controlling distribution. Identity-forming strategies are particularly crucial and problematic when the struggle is in part against a society rather than a visible oppressor. Label disruption—contained in identity-forming strategies, and the core of symbolic strategies—is a particular operation on the cultural field. It is made necessary by a form of domination that operates through abstractions, through symbols that mark off the normal. (I am not suggesting, of course, that these are discrete types in concrete actions; actions are always mixed exactly because the forms of domination are simultaneous.)

We can also make sense of ACT UP's internal obstacles through this lens. It is not surprising that the question of audience becomes a difficult one to address. First of all, the audience often is the group itself when identity formation becomes a key part of struggle. Yet at the same time, we have seen that identity struggles involve pushing at the very labels on which they are based, and here the audience is the entire society. Actions are thus often founded on a confusion of audiences. More commonly, the question of audience is simply lost because the underlying target of action is the normalization process. While it might be more "rational" for ACT UP activists to try to spell out the particular audience each time they design an action, the struggle in which they are involved makes the particularity of an audience difficult to see. When stigmatization is being protested, the audience is the undifferentiated society—that is, audience and enemy are lumped together, and neither is concretely graspable.

Understanding that ACT UP is attacking this particular form of domination, we can also see why ACT UP is caught between the association and dissociation of AIDS politics from gay politics. Clearly, PWAs and gay people are both subject to the stigmatization process; this process, as it informs and supports responses to AIDS, has become literally lethal for PWAs, gay and nongay, and dangerous for those labeled as "risk group" members, gay men (and often by an odd extension, lesbians), drug users, prostitutes, blacks, and Hispanics. Socially organized labels that, before AIDS, were used to oppress, are now joined with the label of "AIDS victim." This form of domination is experienced by ACT UP members as a continuous one. AIDS is a gay disease because AIDS has been made to attribute viral disease to sexual deviance. Separating AIDS politics from gay politics would be to give up the fight against normalization.

Yet joining the two politics poses the risk of losing the fight in that it confirms the very connection it attempts to dispel. This is a familiar dilemma, as Steve Epstein (1987, 19) points out, and one that is not at all limited to the gay movement: "How do you protest a socially imposed categorization, except by organizing around the category?" Organizing around a resisted label, in that it involves an initial acceptance of the label (and, in identity-oriented movements, a celebration of it), can tend to reify the label. Identity politics thus contain a danger played out here: "If there is perceived to be such a thing as a 'homosexual lifestyle'" (Epstein 1987, 48). The familiarity of the dilemma, though, should not obscure its significance. This is neither a dilemma attributable simply to the random course of AIDS nor to mistakes on the part of activists, but to the form of domination to which social movements respond.

In this light, it is not surprising that ACT UP has difficulty including nongays and forming coalitions. In some ways, ACT UP is driven toward inclusiveness since AIDS is affecting other populations and since the fight includes more broad-based struggles over resources. But, as we have seen, resistance to labeling involves accepting the label but redefining it, taking it over. Group identity actions are bound up with this resistance. This drives ACT UP strongly away from inclusiveness. The difficulty in walking these lines—between confirming and rejecting the connection between gay people and AIDS, between including and excluding nongays—is built into the struggle against normalization in which ACT UP is involved.

BODIES AND THEORIES

I have argued that ACT UP responds to the script of the AIDS plague by undermining that script, resisting the labeling through which contemporary domination is often effectively achieved. This seems to be missed by most observers of AIDS, who interpret the politics of AIDS on the model of conventional politics. Randy Shilts's 1988 best-seller, for example, ignores the development of grassroots AIDS activism even in its updating epilogue. AIDS serves as a particularly vivid case of disputed scripts in American politics in that the epidemic of disease, as others have noted, has occurred simultaneously with an "epidemic of signification"; AIDS exists "at a point where many entrenched narratives intersect, each with its own problematic and context in which AIDS acquires meaning" (Treichler 1987, 63). ACT UP illustrates this, treating the struggle over the narratives opened and exposed by AIDS as potentially lifesaving.

ACT UP also illustrates major effects of an historical shift. If, as I have proposed in drawing on Foucault, domination has gradually come to operate less in the form of state and institutional oppression and more in the form of disembodied and ubiquitous processes, it is hardly surprising that diseased bodies become a focal point of both oppression and resistance. As the enemy becomes increasingly disembodied, the body of the dominated—in this case, primarily the diseased, gay male body—becomes increasingly central. The AIDS epidemic itself fits this process so well as to make it seem almost inevitable: the terror of the disease is that it is an enemy you cannot see, and, like the labels put to use in normalizing power, it is spread invisibly. AIDS activism in part struggles against this disembodied type of power by giving that body—its death, its blood, its sexuality—new, resistant meanings. The plague script meets here with the script of new social movements.

But what does this tell us about theorizing new social movements? First, it calls into question the value of "newness" as a reified category of analysis. In suggesting that the history of enemies and types of domination is central to understanding ACT UP, this study points to a gradual shift rather than a radical break in movement activity; "newness" militates toward a focus on a moment (the 1960s) rather than a history that reaches back into, for example, the eighteenth and nineteenth centuries (as in the historical transformation that Foucault describes). It obscures what may be instructive continuities across time. Second, this study points toward ways of distinguishing among contemporary movements. To assert that ACT UP exemplifies contemporary movements would clearly be to overstate the case; rather, this analysis demonstrates the insufficiency of analyzing different movements as like phenomena simply because of a shared cultural and identity focus. Operating on the "cultural field" means something more specific than focussing on problems that "deal directly with private life" (Touraine 1985, 779) or even targeting and using narrative and artistic representation. ACT UP's cultural strategies reclaim and resignify oppressive markers. Orienting actions towards identity formation means something more specific than "defend[ing] spaces for the creation of new identities and solidarities" (Cohen 1985, 685). Identity assertions in ACT UP point up boundaries, using the fear of the abnormal against the fearful. These are specific operations that may be shared by other contemporary social movements—those subject to stigmatization, for example, and which are also in a position to "shock"—and not by others. Stigmatization, moreover, may take different forms and give rise to different types of movement activity. Whether in Shea Stadium or at the FDA, discerning the types of enemies to whom movements are responding is a task for analysts of social movements as well as for activists within them.

Acknowledgements: This paper would not have been possible without the thoughtful comments, challenges, and support of Michael Burawoy and Steven Epstein. I'm also grateful for comments on an earlier version of the article from the members of the UC-Berkeley Participant-Observation seminar and David Kirp, Kim Voss, Tomas Almaguer, Bill Gamson, Zelda Gamson, and the Social Problems reviewers. Thanks also to the members of ACT UP/San Francisco.

NOTES

1. Unless otherwise noted, quotations and descriptions of actions are drawn from the author's field notes from September 1988 through January 1989 (ACT UP weekly general meetings; Media Committee weekly meetings and activities, and other committee meetings; ACT NOW AIDS Activism Conference, October 8-11, 1988, Washington, D.C.; ACT UP/San Francisco actions). For a sampling of published reporting on ACT UP, see Green (1989); *U.S. News & World Report* (1989); Linebarger (1989); Tuller (1988); Ford (1988); Johnson (1988); Okie (1988); Connolly and Raine (1988); Morgan (1988).

2. By way of comparison, it is important to notice that most AIDS politics does not operate according to this description, but according to a more conventional political model. "Most AIDS politicking," as Dennis Altman (1986, 105) describes it, "has involved the lobbying of federal, state and local governments. . . . [This] has meant dependence upon professional leaders able to talk the language of politicians and bureaucrats."

3. Why so many women are attracted to the AIDS movement is an interesting question to which I have accumulated only brief, speculative answers: some because their friends are dying, some because of a history of working in health politics through women's health issues. One woman suggested an answer that seems to run deeper and along the lines suggested by this study. Oppression through AIDS, she said, is the most severe end of a spectrum of violence to which "all gay people are subject." For her, while silence might not mean literal death, it would mean a symbolic death (not being allowed to live as "me").

4. The activist response of black communities to AIDS has, though, differed greatly from that in gay communities, and this merits careful examination not allowed for here. The lag in

black and Hispanic activism has been attributed by one observer to a combination of lack of material and political resources (minority PWAs are disproportionately lower class or underclass) and "denial" on the part of minority leadership (because of the dangers posed by feeding racism with the stigma of disease, and because of strong antigay sentiments in black and Hispanic cultures) (see Goldstein 1987).

5. The figure of the irresponsible killer-victim was popularized by Randy Shilts in the character of Gaetan Dugas, an airline steward Shilts labels "Patient Zero." Shilts charges that Dugas knowingly spread the virus throughout the continent. For a critique of Shilts, see Crimp (1987b).

6. The mass media clearly play a very central and complex role in contemporary activism (see, for example, Gitlin 1980), an examination of which is unfortunately beyond the scope of this chapter. It is quite likely that much of the escalation of symbols comes from the need by social movements to compete for attention in an increasingly message-dense environment; this does not explain the content of those symbols, though, nor does it explain why the media at times become explicit enemies.

16

REVOLUTIONS OF THE LATE TWENTIETH CENTURY: COMPARISONS

Ted Robert Gurr and Jack A. Goldstone

The modern concept of revolution was formed two centuries ago in France, and the political relationship between rulers and ruled has never been the same since. The compelling example established by the French Revolution of 1789 was that a nation's people, by concerted political struggle, could fundamentally transform the political order that governed their lives and, with it, the social and economic structure of society. The revolutionary impulse has far more often been suppressed or diverted into reform than it has succeeded. Of the forty-eight civil and revolutionary wars being fought in the early 1960s, only nine ended with victory or major concessions for the rebels, compared with thirty-five military defeats and one protracted struggle that was still going on in 1995 in northern Burma. In 1989, the success of popular revolutionary movements in central Europe was counterbalanced by the brutal suppression of democracy movements in Burma and China. Revolutionary seizures of power often accomplish only limited, sometimes temporary reforms, as happened in Bolivia and Egypt after their 1952 revolutions, in Iraq after the Ba'thist revolution of 1958, and in South Korea after the student-led revolution of 1960. The Philippine revolution of 1986 is going the same way. Nonetheless, the essential idea that rulers are ultimately accountable to their people has persisted and, in uncommon circumstances, has led to political upheavals that profoundly changed for all time the character of the societies in which they occurred.

ORIGINS OF REVOLUTIONARY CRISES

The specific conditions that generate revolutionary crises and shape the processes of revolutionary conflict are highly diverse. Nevertheless, revolutionary movements since the end of the era of the world wars have, in general, differed in three aspects from those that preceded 1945. First, the geopolitical setting has changed. Recent revolutions have occurred in relatively small, often fairly urbanized countries with semimodern colonial or dictatorial governments, rather than in large and predominantly rural nations with long-standing traditional governments, such as formed the setting for the "classic" social revolutions of France (1789), Russia (1917), and China (1911–49). Second, recent revolutionaries have been more often animated by opposition to local colonial, racial, or superpower domination, and by specific ethnic or religious claims, than by the quest for universal ideals that motivated most eighteenth- and nineteenth-century European and Latin American revolutions. And third, late-twentieth-century revolutions unquestionably have been more shaped and constrained by international intervention than most of their predecessors.

Nonetheless, these changes seem to reflect more changes in the makeup of the international order than changes in the processes governing the development of revolutionary situations. At the most general level of analysis, we argue that all revolutions proceed through three phases, beginning with a state crisis, followed by a struggle for power, and efforts by the eventual victors to reconstruct the state. Moreover, no revolutionary crisis occurs until there is a conjunction of three necessary conditions: a crisis in the old state, alienation of a significant segment of the elite, and mass mobilization. In Table 1 we summarize the principal sources of these conditions in each of ten cases, as well as the factors that shaped each revolutionary struggle and its outcomes.[1]

State Crises

Some scholars have argued, after studying the classic revolutions that occurred before 1950, that international competition (Skocpol 1979) and fiscal crisis (Goldstone 1991) are the essential or most important sources of state crisis. We find that serious economic problems beset many of the ten prerevolutionary regimes seen in the table, including excessive debt (Iran, Poland), economic stagnation and decline (in the Philippines, both African cases, Poland again), and the high costs of fighting internal wars (Nicaragua, Afghanistan, Zimbabwe, Israel). But many other contemporary regimes have confronted similar problems without succumbing to revolutionary pressures.

Examination of the ten cases reveals a much more diverse set of internal and international conditions that can lead to a crisis which weakens state authorities' grip on power. We think now that a state crisis should not be defined as a specific objective condition but rather as a situation in which significant numbers of elites and popular groups believe that the central authorities are acting in ways that are fundamentally ineffective, immoral, or unjust.

Table 1. Summary of Cases

	IRAN	NICARAGUA
Sources of State Crisis	• Excessive debts • Inability to control inflation • Loss of nationalist credentials • U.S. pressure to reduce oppression of regime opponents	• Inability to avoid economic damage from rebellion • Loss of nationalist credentials • U.S. pressure to reduce oppression of regime opponents
Sources of Elite Alienation	• State attacks on *ulema*, landlords, bazaaris • Exclusion of middle classes from power • Corruption • High inflation, uneven development	• State attacks on opposition politicians • Increasing exclusion of middle classes from power • Corruption • Decline of business climate
Sources of Mass Mobilization	• Population growth and urbanization exceeding economic opportunities • Service and support by *ulema* and mosques • Uneven economic growth with lagging traditional sector • Inconsistent persecution by SAVAK • Mobilization by nationalist/Islamic ideology	• Population growth and urbanization exceeding economic opportunities • Service and support by FSLN • Inconsistant persecution by the National Guard • Mobilization by nationalist/Sandinista ideology
Shape of Revolutionary Struggle	• Coalition of traditional and Westernized elites against the shah • Conflict between traditional and Westernized elites	• Coalition of FSLN and church and business leaders against Somoza • Conflict between FSLN and church and business leaders
Outcome	• Triumph of religious elite • Radical Islamization • Regional rebellions and war with Iraq • Gradual normalization of relations with states other than the U.S.	• Initial triumph of FSLN • Limited socialization of economy, covert aid to revolt in El Salvador • War against U.S. backed contras • Business elite-backed party wins in 1990 but government crippled by political rivalries and lack of resources

Table 1. Summary of Cases (continued)

	VIETNAM	CAMBODIA
Sources of State Crisis	• Excessive dependence on U.S. • Loss of nationalist credentials • Unfavorable commodity price shifts	• Excessive dependence on U.S. (Lon Nol) • Loss of nationalist credentials • Costs of war incursions from Vietnam war
Sources of Elite Alienation	• Factional conflicts • Corruption • Anti-imperialism	• Factional conflicts • Corruption • Anti-imperialism
Sources of Mass Mobilization	• Population growth and urbanization exceeding economic opportunities • Population service and support by Vietcong • Persecution by U.S./RVN armed forces • Mobilization by nationalist, anti-imperialist, Communist ideology	• Population growth exceeding economic growth • Population mobilization by Khmer Rouge • Costs of Vietnam war excursion • Mobilization by nationalist, Communist-inspired ideology
Shape of Revolutionary Struggle	• Coalition of rural peasants and middle-class nationalists against U.S.-backed political elites and urban bourgeoisie • Conflict between nationalist/Communist leaders and urban bourgeoisie	• Coalition of Khmer Rouge and Prince Sihanouk against U.S.-backed elites • Conflict between Khmer Rouge and Sihanouk-connected traditional and bourgeois elements
Outcome	• Military triumph of North Vietnam-supported nationalist/Communist elites • War with China, Cambodia • Gradual economic liberalization and international recognition	• Genocidal overhaul of Cambodian society • Vietnamese armed intervention, overthrow of Khmer Rouge, installation of pro-Vietnam regime • UN-installed democratic government still challenged by Khmer Rouge rebels

Table 1. Summary of Cases (continued)

	PHILIPPINES	AFGANISTAN
Sources of State Crisis	• Economic decline • Loss of nationalist credentials • U.S. pressure to reduce oppression of regime opponents	• Separation of the state from rural/tribal support • Excessive dependence on Soviet aid • Loss of nationalist credentials (Communists)
Sources of Elite Alienation	• Growing exclusion of middle classes from power • Corruption • Attacks on opponents (Especially B. Aquino)	• Attacks on traditional elites • Corruption • Factional conflicts among the Communists
Sources of Mass Mobilization	• Population growth and urbanization exceeding economic opportunities • Urban mobilization by electoral and labor organizations • Rural mobilization by the NPA (Communists)	• Rural mobilization by tribal and religious leaders • Persecution and legal disorientation resulting from Communist policies • Mobilization by nationalist, Islamic ideologies
Shape of Revolutionary Struggle	• Coalition of military reformers and traditional bourgeois/landed elites against Marcos • Conflict of traditional bourgeois/landed elites with both military reformers and rural Communists	• Coalition of tribal and religious leaders against Soviet-backed Communist regime • Conflicts between tribal/religious factions
Outcome	• Triumph of traditional bourgeois/landed elites in people power revolution • No rural reforms; conflicts continue with rural ethnic and Communist movements; repeated coup attempts by military reformers	• Soviet intervention to aid regime, sustained guerilla war • Soviet withdrawal yields a stalemated war, with severe factional conflicts along regional and ethnic lines

Table 1. Summary of Cases (continued)

	ZIMBABWE	SOUTH AFRICA
Sources of State Crisis	• Excessive costs of war, inability to end violence, international sanctions • Economic decline • International (chiefly British) pressure to achieve majority rule	• Excessive costs of war, inability to end violence and international sanctions • Economic decline • International pressure to achieve majority rule
Sources of Elite Alienation	• Black elites: exclusion from power, persecution • White elites: divisions over policy	• Black elites: exclusion from power, persecution • White elites: international opprobrium, divisions over policy
Sources of Mass Mobilization	• Black population growth exceeding economic opportunities • Black population growth reducing relative weight of the white population • Rural mobilization by nationalist leaders (ZANU, ZAPU)	• Black population growth exceeding economic opportunities • Black population growth reducing the relative weight of the white population • Urban mobilization by ANC, Inkatha, AZAPO, COSATU, etc.
Shape of Revolutionary Struggle	• Coalition of opposition groups against white-led state • Conflicts between political-ethnic factions (mainly ZAPU vs. ZANU)	• Lack of opposition coalition: scattered struggles against white-led regime • Conflicts among opposition movements: ANC, Inkatha, AZAPO, etc.
Outcome	• Negotiated settlement under international auspices, bringing majority rule and protection for white rights • Triumph of ZANU-PF over all tribal opponents; incorporation of ZAPU; movement toward a one-party state	• Negotiated constitutional agreement on free elections leading to majority rule • Continuing challenges to ANC rule, some violent, from Inkatha and rightwing white organizations

Table 1. Summary of Cases (continued)

	POLAND	PALESTINE
Sources of State Crisis	• Excessive Western debts and dependence on the USSR • Loss of nationalist credentials • Economic collapse	• Israel: very mild, chiefly costs of war, dependence on the United States • PLO: loss of Lebanese base, creating power vacuum in contiguous areas
Sources of Elite Alienation	• Exclusion of technical elites from power in favor of party • Failure of Poland to keep pace with Western Europe • Corruption	• Israeli: divisions over policy • Palestinian: exclusion from power and economic opportunities; persecution • Palestinian: continued economic stagnation • Palestinian: articulation of nationalist ideology
Sources of Mass Mobilization	• Rapid population growth and urbanization exceeding economic opportunities • Support and services by the church • Urban and rural mobilization by Solidarity	• Population growth far exceeding economic opportunities • Popular support and services through nationalist/ethnic, anti-Zionist ideology
Shape of Revolutionary Struggle	• Coalition of church, intelligentsia, workers, and peasants against the Soviet-backed Communist regime • Military coup, followed by renewed struggle • Withdrawal of Soviet support, followed by negotiations for limited but free elections	• Coalition of external PLO and internal struggles against Israeli occupation
Outcome	• Solidarity victory in elections • Solidarity-led government • Continued conflicts over economic policy between left and center urban, rural, and varied political groups • Search for economic organization and political stablization	• Negotiated agreement for limited autonomy for occupied territories • Terrorist attacks by Hamas aimed at sabotaging implementation of autonomy agreement • Hardening of Israeli attitudes against accommodation

State crises are, in other words, crises of legitimacy. And standards of legitimacy vary widely across cultures, so we cannot say a priori which actions or failures by authorities will lead to crisis.

A key failing in almost every case is the inability of the state to accomplish major tasks it sets for itself: to promote growth, maintain internal order, defend itself against foreign intrusion. The immediate source of ineffective government usually lies in its administrative structure. Most, but not all, the prerevolutionary states seen in the table were hampered by bureaucratic ineptitude and corruption, most clearly in (South) Vietnam, Cambodia, Nicaragua, Iran, Poland, and the Philippines. Afghanistan is a case in which the revolutionary Marxist regime that seized power in 1978 was even more inept than its monarchist predecessor. In three contrasting instances—Zimbabwe, South Africa, and Israel—the political will and bureaucratic capacity of the regime were high at the onset of conflict, but internal and external pressures escalated so sharply that they exceeded the capacity of the state to resist without change. The major source of internal pressure in these three countries was the rejection of authorities' legitimacy by subordinate ethnic majorities (in the African cases) or large minorities (in the case of Israel). The critical external pressures have been applied by international supporters of these subordinate peoples. In many cases, demographic factors affected the state's ability to meet goals or maintain effectiveness. The rapid urbanization of Poland, Iran, Nicaragua, and South Africa created problems of social control over dense working-class neighborhoods. The rapid growth of nonwhite populations in Zimbabwe and South Africa and of the Arab population in the Israeli-occupied territories made sustaining economic systems based on those populations' subordination and exclusion increasingly difficult. Also, rapid population growth in all the countries analyzed has made it more difficult to maintain per capita economic growth or has contributed to sharp regional and sectoral income inequities.

In addition, in every contemporary revolution, international factors have contributed directly or indirectly to state crisis. Economic penetration and exploitation were critical factors in Iran, Nicaragua, and Poland, whose ruling elites were widely perceived to be serving and benefiting from foreign economic interests. The presence of foreign advisers and troops in support of prerevolutionary regimes in (South) Vietnam and Cambodia and in revolutionary Afghanistan undercut their rulers' nationalist credentials. In appearance, and soon enough in fact, these rulers were the local agents of superpower rivalries rather than defenders of their countries' own interests. Foreign economic and political penetration played a critical role in undermining the nationalist credentials of the ruling elites in most of the ten cases.

Foreign economic and military presence are the result of deliberate policies that national leaders can in principle resist; not so the transnational inspiration provided by African decolonization in the 1960s and 1970s, which gave great impetus to African nationalism in Rhodesia and South Africa. It is generally true that dramatic political movements, successful revolutions above all, help convince people in similar situations elsewhere that they are the victims of injustice at the hands of dominant groups. International support for a subject people—Palestinians under Israel occupation, blacks in white-ruled southern Africa—helps translate the sense of injustice into political action.

Elite Alienation

At least some of the political and economic elites supporting an old regime must be sufficiently alienated that they seek revolutionary alternatives. All the sources of state crisis just enumerated have the potential for alienating some of the elite, that is, people whose skills and positions are such that they are able to influence large numbers of others. Some of the elite are disgusted by corruption and inefficiency, some are responding to economic crisis, many become convinced that their rulers have sold out the country or their class. The crucial added factors are conflicts over culture and ideology and conflicts over the distribution of power.

We consider first the cultural dispositions of the elites supporting the old regime. It is quite clear, for example, that some state authorities have undermined the bases of their legitimacy by undertaking actions and policies that violate fundamental elite cultural precepts. The shah of Iran alienated the religious elite by his policies of secularization. In Afghanistan, the communist regime alienated religious and tribal elites by its socialist policies. For Cambodians, the state was personified and legitimized by the royal family, in the person of Prince Sihanouk, but he was deposed in 1970 by his premier, Lon Nol—an act that led many Cambodians to support Sihanouk's new nationalist movement or the Khmer Rouge counterelite.

In many contemporary societies, particularly those most affected by global political and economic changes, there are multiple ideological streams of influence on elites. In the face of crisis, growing numbers of the elite, especially younger, university-educated people, are likely to reach for other ideological lenses to interpret their world and find pathways out of crisis. The policies of the discredited old elite often shape, by reaction, the ideology of opposition. Superpower intervention may push radicals into the arms of an opposing ideological camp (the Sandinistas embrace Marxism, Solidarity endorses capitalism) or toward xenophobic rejection of any foreign influence (the Khmer Rouge). Secular materialism in an old regime can stimulate a reaffirmation of religious faith, such as that of Islam in Iran and Afghanistan and of Catholicism in Poland.

Ethnic self-determination is one kind of alternative worldview that has had a natural constituency among the leaders and spokespeople for subordinate majorities in Rhodesia and South Africa, and for the Palestinians in the Israeli-occupied territories. But there are few places left in the world where this kind of self-determination can attract a countrywide following because only a handful of countries are still ruled by ethnic or ethnoreligious minorities. Ethnic self-determination in the twenty-first century is more likely to fuel civil wars—among the Karen and Kurds, the Tamils and Abkhaz, nations fighting to establish their own state—than to motivate revolutionary movements.

Nevertheless, political nationalism—asserting national integrity and self-determination against foreign occupation or influence—has played a key role in many revolutionary struggles. In Iran, Nicaragua, Vietnam, and Cambodia, political nationalism helped bind diverse elites into coalitions against authorities who were believed to be too subservient to the United States; in Poland and Afghanistan, elite nationalist coalitions similarly formed to oppose regimes that were considered subservient to the Soviet Union. Strong national religious traditions—such as Iranian Shi'ism and Polish Catholicism—may then emerge as the basis for nationalist organizations with political aims.

Although ethnic self-determination and political nationalism have played increasing roles in recent revolutionary movements, universalizing ideologies still retain considerable force. Marxism, though fading in Europe and most of Latin America, remains a potent agent in mobilizing popular groups to revolutionary causes in the Philippines and Peru. Nor should we overlook the persisting influence of Western humanism and political egalitarianism, which led Great Britain to put pressure for change on Rhodesia and which weakened the willingness of ruling elites in Zimbabwe, Poland, South Africa, and Israel to continue to rule by force in the face of popular challenges under the banner of political democracy. The same humanist doctrine, when pressed strongly by the Carter administration on U.S. client states, constrained the repressive actions of the shah of Iran, the Somoza clan in Nicaragua, and Marcos in the Philippines. Arguably, it also helped to ensure their defeat.

Alienated members of the elite do not necessarily act politically on their views. Inertia is a powerful force, especially for people with safe and comfortable positions, and fear of reprisal is an equally strong force, ensuring outward loyalty to an old regime. Widespread, passive alienation within an elite nonetheless weakens an old regime because, in the public sphere, it increases careerism and corruption and thus further reduces efficiency. This situation is precisely what crippled the party and state bureaucracies in communist Poland and other East European regimes.

The second, more active route of elite alienation is conflict over the distribution of power. To the extent that authorities adopt a policy of narrowly confining political power and participation, and excluding or marginalizing religious, technical, business, and labor leaders, they create active opposition, as such marginal elites often take leadership roles in mobilizing opposition against the authorities. Limited attacks on marginal elites by leaders seeking to cow, but not eliminate, opposition—such as the murders of Pedro Joaquin Chamorro in Nicaragua and Benigno Aquino in the Philippines, or the attacks on bazaar merchants and religious elites in Iran—often backfire, increasing and unifying elite opposition. The increasing narrowness and exclusivity of rule by the shah in Iran, Somoza in Nicaragua, and Marcos in the Philippines helped to antagonize and push into active opposition formerly supportive elements of these states' elites. Similarly, the efforts of the Khalq faction in Afghanistan, the Thieu regime in Vietnam, the Lon Nol clique in Cambodia, and senior Communist Party elites in Poland to exclude systematically all people opposed to the regime's policy from power; the racial exclusiveness of the regimes in Rhodesia and South Africa; and the exclusion of Arabs in the Israeli-occupied territories from effective political participation—all these actions forced educated and influential opponents of regime policies into revolutionary roles.

Elite alienation has its greatest potential effect in the armed forces. Most students of revolution agree that a determined ruling class can rely on force to remain in power, even in the face of revolutionary challenges, so long as it has the unquestioned loyalty of the officer corps and troops. The defection of part of the military to the revolutionary side is usually a fatal blow to an old regime. The two clear-cut examples among our cases are Iran and the Philippines, where key officers decided to disobey orders from threatened autocrats, thus opening the way to revolutionary victory. In three other instances—Cambodia, South Vietnam, and Nicaragua—prolonged combat eroded officers' loyalty and soldiers' willingness to fight, but there was no precipitous shift in support from one side to the other.

Mass Mobilization

In principle, revolutionary change can be attempted "from the top down" by determined leaders committed to using all the instruments of the state to engineer social and economic transformation (Trimberger 1978). Ataturk took such a course in Turkey in the 1920s, making it the most modern and secular state in the Islamic world; Lenin and Stalin imposed revolutionary changes in the Soviet Union by force and at great human cost. In practice, most would-be revolutionaries in the late twentieth century have had to mobilize mass followings as part of their strategy for seizing power and reconstructing state and society. The only exception among the ten cases is Afghanistan, in which urban Marxist revolutionaries took power through a coup and then, in a grotesquely misguided attempt to engineer revolutionary change, inspired mass resistance by a conservative rural population under the banner of Islamic fundamentalism.

A wide and deep sense of grievance among ordinary people is a necessary condition for counterelites who seek to mobilize a mass following. There was no shortage of grievances in the prerevolutionary societies we have studied: widespread dissatisfaction over economic conditions, especially among urban peoples; frustration about the lack of opportunities for real political participation, especially among students and the middle classes; widespread anger about foreign intervention and official corruption; and rural hostility toward the predatory and repressive policies of urban-based regimes.

One of the most striking features of our cases is the frequency with which the old regimes followed policies that intensified grievances and focused popular anger on the state. In virtually every instance, threatened governments used force and violence in ways that increased popular resentment and active support for revolutionary movements. In the Philippines and Nicaragua, the government's assassination of respected spokesmen for the liberal opposition—Senator Benigno Aquino in 1983, editor Pedro Chamorro in 1978—was the catalyst for coalition building and mass mobilization among disaffected urban Filipinos and Nicaraguans. In Cambodia and Vietnam, the government's punitive strikes against villagers suspected of supporting rebels pushed many peasants, out of fear or anger, into the ranks of revolutionary armies. In Iran, a turning point in the revolutionary crisis came in September 1978 when the government used gunships and commandos to kill some 4,000 protestors—an appalling act of repression that, far from deterring opposition, intensified it and simultaneously undermined the loyalties of some of the military. The South African and Israeli governments used the less deadly tactics of restricted movement, imprisonment, and harassment to discourage black and Palestinian activists. The legacy of these tactics is deep-rooted hostility and resistance to authority among an entire generation of young people that post a long-term challenge to governance by the new black-majority government in South Africa and the emergent Palestinian Authority in the West Bank and Gaza.

The opportunities for revolutionary mobilization vary widely, depending on where grievances are concentrated and which aggrieved groups are most accessible to the potential revolutionary leaders. Three patterns of revolutionary mobilization are discernible among our cases. In the Maoist pattern, seen in Vietnam, Cambodia, and Zimbabwe, a cadre party of revolutionaries followed a long-term strategy of political and organizational buildup, mobilizing a mass base of support before challenging the people in power. In the Leninist pattern, seen in Nicaragua and Iran, a vanguard party built up a disciplined opposition organization, positioned itself to take advantage of a spontaneous upsurge in mass opposition, and briefly allied itself with other regime opponents. Once the revolutionary struggle had begun, the vanguard leaders sought to mobilize their followers to dominate the revolutionary struggle and shape the revolution's outcome. In the third, pluralist, pattern, seen in Poland, the Philippines, and the antiCommunist phase in Afghanistan, a number of distinct counterelites joined in mobilizing their followers against the old regime, but they sought to maintain a coalition or pluralist settlement of the revolutionary struggle rather than having one party embark on purges to eliminate all other elements from the postrevolutionary regime. The South African and Palestinian nationalist movements in their middle phases showed elements of both Maoist and Leninist strategies, as nationalist leaders sought both to build revolutionary organizations and to take advantage of spontaneous popular mobilization, with different factions vying to dominate each revolutionary movement. In South Africa the pluralist model eventually prevailed, as most Africans, Asians, coloreds, many white liberals, and the South African Communist Party formed a coalition against the Afrikaner elite that held together from the mid-1970s through 1995. The nationalists of the PLO, however, have not yet been able to coalesce with or attract supporters of Hamas and other militant opponents of compromise with Israel.

The mass bases of revolutionary power may be urban or rural or both. All ten of our revolutionary (and counterrevolutionary) movements developed in countries with a disproportionately large number of marginal young people—numerous because of high population growth and marginalized by a relative lack of economic opportunities. In Iran, Poland, and South Africa, mobilization was most effective in the rapidly growing urban areas. In Afghanistan, Cambodia, Vietnam, and Rhodesia, the revolutionaries were recruited mainly in the countryside, and in the remaining three cases—Nicaragua, the Philippines, and the West Bank and Gaza—mobilization cut across the urban-rural division.

The social bases for mobilization vary markedly among our cases. In the classic revolutions envisioned by Marxists, economic class is the only conceivable basis for mobilization, though the possibility of cross-class coalitions is granted. Few of our cases fit this classic ideal. Only the Cambodian and Vietnamese revolutionaries followed Marxist precedents, by using the Chinese Maoist precepts for mobilizing a mass peasant following. Religion and ethnicity, which in Marxist thought are supposed to be only vestigial social forces, have both proved to be potent bases for contemporary revolutionary action. The religious-based mobilization of Poles, Iranians, and Afghans has already been mentioned. The Roman Catholic church also played a supporting role in Cory Aquino's people power revolution; reform-minded Catholic activists, energized by Liberation Theology, were one of the pillars of Sandinista support in the war against the Somozas; and Islam reinforces Palestinian nationalism in the West Bank and Gaza. Thus, religious commitments and connections played a major role in six of the ten cases.

Ethnically based revolutionary movements developed in the two African cases. Ethnicity is the obvious basis for mobilizing opposition when an old regime has held power on behalf of a dominant ethnic group, as in Rhodesia and South Africa, but ethnic loyalties are not a guarantee of revolutionary solidarity in such societies. Nationalist politics in Rhodesia/Zimbabwe have been often split along the faultline that divides Ndebele from Shona. In South Africa during the final stages of Afrikaner rule some coloreds and Asians cooperated with the Afrikaner government, some whites worked for the African nationalist cause, and black nationalists divided into several hostile camps, particularly the feuding African National Congress and the more narrowly based Zulu Inkatha movement.

The specific interactions among state crisis, elite alienation, and mass mobilization affect the timing and character of state breakdown. They also help shape the subsequent process of coalition building and constrain in many ways the outcomes of a revolution.

PROCESSES OF REVOLUTIONARY CONFLICT

The necessary condition for the successful revolutionary overthrow of an incumbent government, even if it is in a state of crisis, is the emergence of a broad coalition among its challengers. Such a coalition typically includes significant elements of the elite and mobilized mass support. Without such a coalition, a seizure of power is unlikely to have revolutionary effects, whatever its leaders claim. They may have to give up revolutionary pretensions as the price of holding on to power or face a counterrevolution in reaction to their policies. The latter was the fate of the Afghan Marxists' attempt to impose a revolution from above.

Democratic Coalitions

Probably the most striking development in contemporary revolutionary practice, as distinct from doctrine, is the emergence in several of our cases of new political coalitions that mobilized a cross-section of mainly urban people on behalf of democracy, economic growth, and social justice. Professional, business, and white-collar groups played a major role in these movements, along with intellectuals, students, and a broad spectrum of blue-collar and service workers. Such alliances brought down the Somoza dynasty in Nicaragua and Ferdinand Marcos in the Philippines and ended Communist Party rule in Poland, East Germany, Hungary, and Czechoslovakia. The success of the ANC in building a multiracial coalition and sustaining it during the difficult negotiations with the Afrikaner government contributed greatly to the largely-peaceful transition to black majority rule in 1994.

It may be objected that such coalitions are merely alliances of convenience among people whose main bond is opposition to a repressive old regime. This possibility is belied by the fact that in the examples cited above, supporters tended to agree on general principles of civil and political rights and on the need for social and economic reform. Moreover, they have accomplished at least seven successful revolutions since 1979—more than Marxists have managed to accomplish in twenty-five years.

Prodemocratic revolutionary coalitions are subject to stress and breakdown like any others. Nondemocratic elements in a coalition may be able to dominate and drive out their coalition partners, as the *ulema* did in revolutionary Iran. The Polish revolutionary coalition broke up in the early 1990s in part because the intellectuals and middle classes supported economic restructuring, the costs of which fell disproportionately on blue-collar workers in inefficient, state-protected industries. As a consequence, the remnants of a shrinking Solidarity movement fragmented into blue-collar, white-collar, and rural segments, and a succession of short-lived coalition governments have held power in Warsaw.

Coalition Breakdown and Stalemated Revolutions

Revolutions seldom have neat endings. Often they get bogged down in factional strife among erstwhile coalition partners, abetted by international intervention. The revolutions in Afghanistan, Cambodia, and Nicaragua were stalemated for varying lengths of time because of fragmentation among elites and attempts by foreign powers to manipulate their outcomes. In Afghanistan, a Marxist revolutionary elite headquartered in Kabul, well-supplied by the Soviet Union, opposed a fractious coalition of Islamic revolutionary leaders, some of them in exile, who were amply supported by the United States and the Pakistan military. No coherent political program could be pursued by either party. The Marxist regime was defeated in 1992 and the tenuous alliance among the mujaheddin quickly fell apart. Since then Afghanistan has been rent by civil war among contending ethnically and regionally based factions. The Marxist revolution is dead but no group or coalition has been able to concentrate enough power even to reconstitute a government, much less to establish a revolutionary Islamist society.

The first phase of the Cambodian revolution was engineered by the Khmer Rouge leadership, which violently eliminated all potential challengers to its rule until forced out of Phnom Penh by invading Vietnamese forces in December 1978. The Vietnamese withdrew in 1989, in the face of strong U.S., Soviet, and ASEAN pressures, but sporadic warfare continued until a peace accord was reached in October 1991. The accord provided for a UN Transitional Authority in Cambodia (UNTAC) with a large force of international peacekeepers and technical and administrative personnel. During the next two years UNTAC, the largest UN operation ever organized, guided the political reconstruction of Cambodia, including the drafting of a constitution, national elections, and the inauguration in 1993 of a new democratic regime led by a coalition of Prince Sihanouk's followers and pro-Vietnamese political figures. The Khmer Rouge boycotted the process and thus were sidelined. Recent reports of widespread corruption in the new government and resurgent Khmer Rouge activities suggest that Cambodia's transition to democracy also is stalemated.

The Nicaraguan revolution affords another illustration of the process of revolutionary stalemate: The Sandinista coalition encompassed representatives of virtually all social sectors when it seized power in 1979, but the Marxism of the populist Sandinistas soon drove the middle-class moderates out of the coalition, and some of them went shopping for foreign support to strengthen their hand. The Sandinistas, meanwhile, lacked the instinct for the jugular that would have enabled them, like the Bolsheviks in revolutionary Russia, to terrorize their opponents into submission.

These three cases illustrate vividly that protracted conflict is the price of the failure to build and hold together a coalition that encompasses the revolutionary elite and a broad popular base. Narrowly based coalitions may be sufficient, but only if they are ruthless enough to eliminate or drive into powerless exile all potential rivals and schismatics. All three stalemated revolutions demonstrated the crucial role of international support and intervention in shaping revolutionary strategies and outcomes. Each of the revolutionary parties, once in power, had foreign champions prepared to supply material and military support, and groups that opposed or defected from the revolutionary coalition found competing foreign powers who were ready to support counterrevolutionary challenges. Thus, the protracted postrevolutionary struggles in Afghanistan, Cambodia, and Nicaragua were jointly the result of fractures in the revolutionary coalition and competition among foreign supporters of elite factions. In all three countries, the people on behalf of whom the revolutions were fought ended up as victims rather than victors. More than 1 million noncombatants have died and continue to die in Afghanistan; as many as 3 million died in Cambodia.

Coalitions in Ongoing Revolutions

The ongoing efforts to bring about revolutionary changes in South Africa, in the Philippines, and by the Palestinians also can be characterized in terms of coalitional politics within the revolutionary leadership. In South Africa, the Afrikaner government in 1990 acknowledged the African National Congress as the representative of black South Africans, but what looked at first like a move that strengthened the revolutionary coalition led instead to a sharp increase in factional fighting between ANC supporters and the Zulu-based Inkatha. There are other, so far less visible, fracture lines that threaten to divide the leadership of the newly empowered ANC from some of the colored and Asian elites and to divide the nascent black bourgeoisie from more radical and less privileged groups in the urban townships.

The Palestinian nationalists have had a dominant coalition headed by Yasir Arafat since 1969, though significant factions have remained outside the umbrella of the PLO. The *intifada* threatened to disrupt the coalition because it gave rise to a new, militant local leadership in the occupied territories. The PLO had limited success in accommodating and incorporating this grassroots leadership in the dominant coalition. The threat posed by their militant rivals, Hamas, helped prod the Israeli government into negotiations with the PLO. But the violent efforts of Hamas to sabotage negotiations and implementation of the 1994 autonomy agreement have hardened the divisions within the Palestinian elite and intensified conflict within the Israeli elite. Now the Israeli political leaders—the inheritors of what was once a highly cohesive revolutionary elite—are also in disarray, divided against themselves over how to respond to opponents who simultaneously wage terrorist war on Israeli civilians and campaign for greater autonomy.

Equally great disarray has been evident among the Filipino revolutionaries. The popular movement that brought Cory Aquino to power represented the reforming impulses of the urban middle and professional classes. Efforts to extend the ruling coalition to incorporate significant elements of the left subsequently failed. The Marxist and populist leadership of the New People's Army are still committed to insurgency, and neither the middle-class reformers nor the revolutionary insurgents have much to offer to the Muslim separatists of the southern Philippines. It is now evident that the Aquino revolution of 1986 was simply one dramatic phase of a revolutionary conflict that can be expected to continue indefinitely.

The Role of Violence in Revolutionary Conflict

The use of violence for political ends is central to most definitions of revolution, but the evidence of our ten cases suggests that this is a misplaced emphasis. Events of the 1980s and early 1990s demonstrate that in some circumstances, revolutions occur without substantial resort to deadly force and that when violence is an intrinsic part of the revolutionary struggle, it is not necessarily of high magnitude. Revolutionary conflicts are, on average, less deadly than civil wars and politicides—the mass murder by the state of its political opponents; the most deadly of our ten revolutionary conflicts are those that attracted foreign military intervention. Finally, the cases provide no consistent evidence that any one kind of armed struggle, or armed defense of an old regime, is likely to be successful.

The communist win in Vietnam and the Khmer Rouge triumph in Cambodia illustrate the classic revolutionary model of military victory following a protracted period of revolutionary political mobilization and armed struggle. African nationalists in Rhodesia were on the same course when the Smith regime decided to negotiate a settlement. This kind of armed struggle is still a plausible model in predominantly rural, peasant-based societies.

The 1979 overthrow of the shah of Iran was regarded at the time as signaling a new model of revolutionary action, but historically minded scholars could equally well have evoked parallels with events in Paris that led to the French Revolution of 1789. What happened in Iran was an urban-based revolution in a modernizing society in which the peasantry played no significant role. The revolutionaries relied mainly on street demonstrations rather than armed force, and the Iranian regime's attempt to restore order by using violence against unarmed demonstrators illustrates the principle that repression in revolutionary situations is a double-edged sword. As we noted above, that decision widened and intensified support for the revolutionary coalition and led to crippling defections in the Iranian military.

Although elites who command an old regime seldom give up without a fight, the struggle is not necessarily a violent one. The communist regime in Poland gave up power to Solidarity after a protracted political contest in which there was virtually no violence, and Poland provided a scenario for more rapid transitions from communist to multiparty democracy elsewhere in central Europe. The Aquino people power revolution in the Philippines, incomplete though it has proved to be, is another example in which the revolutionary drama was played out in nonviolent street confrontations. In both these situations, though, some members of the old regime were disposed to make a bitter and bloody fight of it—as the shah did for a while in Iran and Ceausescu in Romania. The Filipino and most central European transfers of power were nonviolent because of policy shifts by the United States and the Soviet Union. It was made clear to Marcos and the old-line communist rulers of central Europe that they no longer had the political or military support of their foreign patrons. So they chose not to fight.

South Africa offers a still more dramatic example of a nonviolent revolutionary transition from the white minority regime to a black-majority ANC government. Much political violence occurred during the process, but virtually none was targeted at white South Africans. International economic sanctions and diplomatic pressures played significant roles in inducing the Afrikaner elite to seek accommodation. Equally or more important was the calculation of far-sighted Afrikaner leaders that they could best protect their economic advantages by negotiating a constitutional transfer of power.

We might wish that the Philippines, central European, and South African examples are the bellwether of future revolutionary struggles, but the bloody suppressions of China's democracy movement in June 1989 and of a similar movement in Burma the same year demonstrate that older methods of responding to revolutionary pressures are still part of threatened elites' repertoires of action. Neither the Chinese nor the Burmese regime was susceptible to foreign pressures or withdrawal of support, and both were willing to use overwhelming, unrestrained violence against unarmed demonstrators.

In two of our cases, Zimbabwe and Nicaragua, international pressures were crucial in bringing about a negotiated resolution of what had been militarized revolutionary conflicts. In the Nicaraguan case, the United States and other Central American countries pressured the Sandinista regime into an electoral process that ended in its unexpected defeat in 1990. In Rhodesia, pressure from Great Britain and the United States, reinforced by international sanctions, led the white-settler regime headed by Ian Smith to accept the transfer to majority rule in 1978–79. Violence was instrumental to both outcomes. It is unlikely that the Rhodesian regime would have made the crucial concessions it did without the escalating pressures caused by the guerrilla warfare of African nationalists. Similarly, the costs of fighting the U.S.-backed *contra* guerrilla insurgency were instrumental in the Sandinista's decision to put that government to the electoral test.

These comparative observations indicate how diverse the revolutionary process and its immediate outcomes can be, but four general observations can be made. First, the process of revolutionary struggle is largely one of coalition formation and maintenance or breakdown. Second, the extent and duration of violence in the revolutionary process is a function of the decisions and tactics of both (perhaps one should say, all) parties to the conflict. Revolutions are not intrinsically or inevitably violent.

Third, there is a detectable trend away from militarized revolutionary conflict, as in Vietnam and Cambodia, Nicaragua and Afghanistan, toward confrontational tests of political will between revolutionary political movements and old regimes. The alternative winning strategy for modern revolutionaries is to mobilize enough political force and international support, with credible threats of disruption and violence, so that the old leaders are persuaded that the costs and risks of resistance are greater than the costs of power-sharing or early retirement.

The fourth observation, already made but worth repeating, is that international involvement is critical in shaping the revolutionary process and its outcomes. The waning of the Cold War has been accompanied by increased reliance in the international community on peaceful means of managing local conflicts that threaten regional stability. In revolutionary situations, this change is manifested in a shift away from military intervention by the superpowers and regional powers toward reliance on pressures and persuasion to bring about negotiated settlements and nonviolent transfers of power. Vietnam, Afghanistan, and Cambodia are examples of the old pattern. The new pattern is exemplified by the course of events in Zimbabwe in 1978–79, central Europe in 1989, and Nicaragua in 1990. We observed above that public and private international pressures, economic and political, were instrumental in weakening the commitment of the South African government to apartheid. International pressures were equally important in inducing the Israeli government to negotiate an autonomy agreement with Palestinian nationalists.

CONSEQUENCES OF REVOLUTION

The revolutionaries' seizure of power is the necessary precondition for any kind of directed revolutionary change. Their objectives are not necessarily clearly formulated, but they usually face the immediate imperative of consolidating political power. The ten revolutions summarized in the table include nine in which revolutionaries took power but only three that are complete as of late 1994, in the sense that the new leadership has consolidated power by either coopting or eliminating all potential competitors (Vietnam, Iran, and Zimbabwe). Two ended in counterrevolutions that ousted the original revolutionary leaders (Afghanistan and Nicaragua), while the UN-backed Cambodian regime still confronts a Khmer Rouge insurgency.

Whatever the fate of the revolutionary coalition, the longer-term question is how effective the new leaders are in implementing their revolutionary program. Most of our cases are too recent to permit an assessment of these long-term achievements, but their relative progress can be judged along four general dimensions: reconstruction of the state, socioeconomic structure, international position, and prospects for political democracy.

Reconstruction of the State

All nine of the revolutionary transfers of power considered here occurred in states paralyzed by crisis. The question is whether, how, and to what extent the new leaders can create state institutions that are more resilient than those they replaced. The clearest cases of enhanced state capacity are in Vietnam and Iran, both of which have dealt more or less successfully with international challenges and the postrevolutionary succession of new leadership. Both also have survived considerable economic hardship. Zimbabwe has faced no great internal or external challenges, and Poland's new government confronts serious economic challenges with a state apparatus that is still undergoing substantial changes. The postrevolutionary state in Cambodia has been rebuilt on the democratic model with a massive infusion of UN assistance, but its long-term viability following the late 1993 UN withdrawal is uncertain. The greatest failures of state making occurred in Afghanistan and Nicaragua, where the potential legitimacy of the new institutions was quickly (in Afghanistan) or slowly (in Nicaragua) undermined by the disastrous policies pursued through those institutions. There is no Afghan state now nor is anyone likely to rebuild it in the near future. The post-Sandinista government in Nicaragua is democratic, like that in Cambodia, but is in chronic fiscal crisis.

Socioeconomic Structure

Revolutions invariably are built on popular grievances over socioeconomic issues harnessed to elite ambitions for societal change. This statement suggests two test questions to be asked about the social and economic consequences of revolutionary seizures of power:

— To what extent do the revolutionary leaders remain committed to their original program of revolutionary change?
— To what extent do revolutionary changes address the causes of the popular grievances, and at what cost?

We must recognize that the contents of revolutionary programs virtually always change along the way, not primarily because leaders "sell out" the revolution, but because shifting domestic and international circumstances require "mid-course adjustments." The Vietnamese, Iranian, and Zimbabwean leaders seemingly have remained loyal to their revolutionary ideals. Poland's new leaders continue to adhere to democracy but are at odds about economic and social policies. There have been few allegations of corruption about the leaderships of Vietnam and Iran and fewer than the African norm in Zimbabwe—one possible indicator of the continuing authenticity and legitimacy of the revolutionary leaders in these states. Nonetheless, the solution of fundamental social and economic problems has largely eluded leaders in all countries. In Afghanistan, Iran, Nicaragua, and Poland, majorities are worse off materially than before the revolution. In the Philippines, most people are no better off, and the traditional landholding elite still dominates the rural areas. Only in Zimbabwe have economic grievances been even partly met, and the white commercial farming elite there still exercises a disproportionate economic influence.

The Sandinista leadership in Nicaragua enthusiastically pursued a program of socioeconomic change, but it was hampered by external (military) and internal (social) resistance and eventually was voted from office because of economic ruin. Analogously, the Khmer Rouge leaders followed what was unquestionably the most radical program of social and economic reconstruction of the contemporary era, including the virtual annihilation of the old urban and middle classes, and the results were far short of the autarchic and egalitarian, agrarian utopia to which they aspired. They created instead a nightmare that alienated most of the presumed beneficiaries and even many of their own cadres. In Nicaragua and Cambodia, the failures of policies of revolutionary change helped discredit the revolutionary leadership in each country and contributed to their replacement by new leaders. The same fate befell the Marxist government in Kabul.

One positive but intangible outcome is common to all the revolutions, including the revolution in progress among Palestinians: the revolutionary leaders or their successors all reasserted national identity and autonomy.

International Position

One issue is whether any postrevolutionary regime has substantially improved its international standing. The revolutionary governments of Afghanistan, Cambodia, and Nicaragua declined in international standing because through international intervention, they lost much of their old regimes' limited freedom of political action. Vietnam can claim the greatest gains. Its revolutionary forces stalemated the United States, defeated the Saigon regime, and later bloodied the Chinese army in a 1979 border war. By managing to consolidate its two peoples and establishing regional dominance over Laos and Cambodia, this regime has unquestionably gained in international stature. U.S. recognition of the regime in 1995 can only enhance its international position. But its war involvements, and hostility toward China, have badly hurt the country's prospects for development. South Africa's initial gains seem the most substantial. It is no longer a pariah state and once again attracts foreign investment. And the new ANC regime is beginning to use its prestige to assert leadership, both political and economic, of other states in southern Africa.

Revolutionary Iran has established its credentials among Muslim fundamentalists throughout the world by asserting the primacy of Islamic principles in social and political life and by distancing itself from Western and Marxist influences. On the down side, the costly war with Iraq and hostility toward Western countries precluded most technological and developmental assistance during the 1980s. Since 1991, however, Iran has gained materially and politically by tacitly siding with the West and conservative Arab states against Iraq in the Gulf War.

Zimbabwe has joined the ranks of respectable independent African states and has succeeded in maintaining reasonably satisfactory relations with Great Britain and with South Africa, even during the apartheid era. But the international stature of independent, European-dominated Rhodesia could scarcely be lower. Poland also has improved in international standing. Its revolutionary politics have been widely praised throughout Europe and the West and emulated in other central European countries. Its radical and abrupt shift toward a free-market economy also has been closely scrutinized by policymakers from Moscow to Prague and Bonn to Washington, D.C. Looking back from 1995, the Poles are to be admired for undertaking a massive economic experiment affecting 39 million people with material success and second only to that of Hungary. But the aggregate economic gains have been achieved at the cost of shredding the social safety net and stripping the once-proud Polish working class of most of its status, earning power, and political influence.

PROSPECTS FOR POLITICAL DEMOCRACY

The most significant revolutionary gains enumerated thus far are political ones: dictators deposed, more effective state institutions founded, national identity reaffirmed, international stature enhanced. One or more such gains can be claimed in eight of the nine countries where revolutionaries now or formerly held power. The final question is whether and under what circumstances revolution can improve the prospects for Western democratic insitutions and the protection of civil and political rights. The revolutions in Zimbabwe, Poland, the Philippines, and South Africa had prodemocracy outcomes. The same can be claimed for Nicaragua, following the electoral counterrevolution of 1991, and Cambodia after the UN-supervised installation of an elected government in 1993. The remaining three completed or stalemated revolutions have had very different outcomes. The successful revolutions in Iran and Vietnam spawned authoritarian and repressive regimes that are the antithesis of democracy, while none of the contending factions in the Afghan civil war are in any sense proponents of democracy.

Three circumstances and conditions of revolution jointly determine the chances for revolutions to have prodemocratic outcomes. One is whether the prerevolutionary society has any democratic experience. Democratic values and institutions are far more likely to take root in societies with some democratic traditions, like Poland and the Philippines, than in societies like Vietnam, Iran, and Afghanistan whose political traditions are almost wholly autocratic.

Second are the ideological commitments of the revolutionaries and their supporters, domestic and international. Most of the new leaders in central Europe and the Philippines are serious about democracy and are strongly encouraged in their commitment by the United States and West Europeans. So are Nicaragua's and South Africa's new leaders. Palestinian nationalists have more conditional attitudes about democracy: the PLO'S supporters are prepared to accept democracy if and when it helps maintain popular support, but they may abandon it when it is expedient to do so. In the Palestinian instance, external support and the policies of the Israeli government can make or break the prospects for a democratic future. There is no discernible elite support for democracy whatsoever among the revolutionary elites of Iran, Afghanistan, or Vietnam. Cambodia is a question mark whose regime in summer 1995 began to suspend political rights in ways reminiscent of autocracies elsewhere.

The most inimical condition for democracy is a protracted and violent revolutionary conflict. Intense conflict hardens attitudes on all sides and convinces the victors that they must rely on force to suppress potential opponents. It takes a full political generation or more to overcome the battle-hardened revolutionaries' habit of relying on force to maintain power. We know of no clear exceptions to this principle in this century, and certainly there are none among the ten cases surveyed.

In Poland and elsewhere in central Europe, the present prospects for democracy are on the positive side of the ledger, provided that their revolutions are not discredited by economic collapse. In South Africa the prospects for survival of democracy depend on two conditions: maintaining multiethnic cooperation and improving the economic and social conditions of the black majority. The revolution in the Philippines and the electoral counterrevolution in Nicaragua initially seemed to improve the chances for democratic outcomes, but these countries' economic problems are so severe that they are at serious risk of more conflict, and intensified conflict can be expected to lead to authoritarian solutions. Aside from the Philippines and Cambodia, none of the Asian revolutions, from Iran to Vietnam, show any potential for democratic political developments in the foreseeable future. Prospects for a democratic outcome in the revolutionary conflict under way in Palestine hang in the balance. The longer and more bitter the conflict over implementation of the autonomy agreement, the more disillusioned the participants and the less the chances are for consolidation of a Palestinian government that will maintain democratic institutions and rights.

NOTE

1. This selection is the revised and abridged final chapter of *Revolutions of the Late Twentieth Century*, Jack A. Goldstone, Ted Robert Gurr, and Farrokh Moshiri, Boulder, Colo.: Westview Press, 1991. It draws on the ten case studies presented in that book: H. John LeVan, "Vietnam," 52–87; Devora Grynspan, "Nicaragua," 88-115; Farrokh Moshiri, "Iran," 116–35; Jaroslaw Piekalkiewicz, "Poland," 136–61; Anwar-ul-Haq Ahady, "Afghanistan," 162–93; Richard J. Kessler, "The Philippines," 194–217; Barbara Harff, "Cambodia," 218–34; James R. Scarritt, "Zimbabwe, 235–71; C.R.D. Halisi, Patrick O'Meara, and N. Brian Winchester, "South Africa," 272–97; and Joshua Teitelbaum and Joseph Kostiner, "The West Bank and Gaza," 298–323.

17

WOMEN IN EASTERN AND CENTRAL EUROPE

Jo Brew

Women in the former Soviet bloc are losing out in the transition from socialism to capitalism. They are being forced out of work, out of public life, back into the home. Women are made redundant before men and make up the majority of the unemployed. Childcare facilities are being shut, leaving women no choice but to rear young children at home. In some places, shopping is difficult with shortages and long queues. There are growing attacks on women's right to reproductive choice and concurrently the number of elected or selected female decision makers is tumbling, reducing the chances for women to influence new legislation.

The widely held assumption that the transition in the former Soviet bloc has opened new possibilities and opportunities for women is a myth. Only a small group of younger skilled women have better prospects. For the vast majority of women, life is becoming harder, and the future is looking bleaker. The devastation of the economy, the dismantling of the welfare state, and the loss of legal protection for women is a step in the wrong direction for women. This transition is not liberating women. It is adding to their oppression.

HISTORY

Since the 1917 Bolshevik revolution in Russia, communist and capitalist women have had somewhat different experiences. "The Woman Question" in the Soviet bloc was informed by two key texts: Engel's *Origins of the Family, Private Property and the State*, and Lenin's *On the Emancipation of Women*. Engels said capitalism caused the oppression of women and that women would be liberated by socialism. Like other Marxists, he played down the biological differences between the sexes and said that nurture, not nature, divided men and women.

Marx had called the family "bourgeois." Lenin went on to say that the kitchen was the center of household slavery. Lenin's solution was to draw women into paid work and to reduce their domestic burden.

Alexandra Kollontai, the Bolshevik spokeswoman on the "Woman Question," went further and outlined a utopia in which the site of women's oppression, households themselves, would become redundant and wither away. Domestic tasks would be reorganized and replaced with collective laundries, mending shops, household crews, central kitchens, public restaurants, and childcare institutions. Children would be brought up by the collective, not the family (Mulholland 1992).

Immediately after the 1917 revolution the Bolsheviks passed a series of proequality laws, legalizing abortion and giving women the vote. Lenin was partially justified when in a 1919 speech to the Fourth Moscow City Conference of Non-Party Working Women, he said "apart from Soviet Russia, there is not a country in the world where women enjoy full equality" (Lapidus 1978).

But in the war-devastated Union of Soviets, practical help for women was less forthcoming. Kollontai's utopia proved too expensive, and the first Bolshevik legislation on the home, the 1918 Family Code, did nothing to relieve women's domestic burden. In fact, it strengthened the "bourgeois" family (Lapidus 1978).

The new Soviets did, however, find it useful to draw women into the workforce. In 1920, Universal Labor Conscription obliged all healthy adults to work for the state. Kollontai applauded this new law, hoping it would force awareness on women and contribute to the downfall of the patriarchy. Women's liberation would come through participation in the workforce.

In practice, Soviet socialism never got very far with liberating women. It was too busy building heavy industry. During seventy years of communism women were, however, more protected than women under capitalism.

Communist efforts toward equality hinged around the workplace, with legal guarantees to equal wages and employment. This fitted nicely with the communist full-employment policy—everyone should be working, building socialism.

The USSR's full-employment policy started with the industrialization drive in the 1930s (Eberhardt and Heinen 1992). The policy was taken up in central and eastern Europe after the Second World War when they became communist. Labor market participation of women was between 70 and 90 percent, much higher than the 25–50 percent in the West.

Hungary, for example, became socialist in 1948 and instituted a full-employment policy immediately (Eberhardt and Heinen 1992). The Second World War had been so devastating that everyone was needed to rebuild the country; men and women, young and old, worked and participated in building socialism. In the 1949 census, 64 percent of women between the ages of fifteen and fifty-five were registered as "housewives." According to the 1984 microcensus, the term "housewife" was used by a mere 15 percent of women. In 1989, 77 percent of Hungarian women were employed (Eberhardt 1991).

To facilitate women's entrance into the labor force, a series of domestic services (cheap transport, food stores open sixteen hours a day, workplace canteens, school meals, health care, nurseries, and kindergartens) were institutionalized in the early 1950s. But by the end of the 1960s, less importance and less resources were given to these services and standards declined (Eberhardt and Heinen 1992).

Labor market participation was high but women were concentrated at the bottom of the hierarchy and were paid about 30 percent less than men.

Women started moving into the labor market in the late 1950s under a state program touted as "emancipatory feminism" (Mulholland 1992). An "equal status" program changed the constitution and removed obstacles to women's access to work. Creches and childcare facilities were improved, and unemployment became acceptable only in cases of disability, pregnancy, or care of infants.

Unemployment

Economic restructuring has worsened women's lot. Privatization has meant layoffs—women first. "We have many unemployed. Seventy-five percent of those out of work are women and they are first in line for redundancy," said Polish Supreme Court Judge Sylvia Tapelska in June 1992. "It is very hard to change attitudes. Women's standing in society and their employment opportunities are not given a high priority in parliament. If there is a contest between a male and female candidate for a job, the male applicant will invariably be chosen" (*The European* 1992). The idea that the male "breadwinner" needs a job more than a woman is predominant.

In a Polish opinion poll at the end of 1990, 45 percent of working women's husbands thought that women should not work outside their homes. The same opinion was shared by 53 percent of men whose wives did not work professionally, 35 percent of working women, and 47 percent of housewives (Kuratowska 1991).

"The State can no longer be the good nanny," say the authorities, to justify cuts in social services. Unemployment in the former German Democratic Republic is estimated at 30–40 percent in cities and regions dependent on a single industry (Eberhardt and Heinen 1992). Unemployment is the most pressing problem for Russian women. In May 1992, 80 percent of the 2 million jobless were women.

There has also been a dramatic increase in pornography and prostitution. "I earn more in one hour than my mother does in a month," said one young girl working on the Czech-German border (Greenberg 1992).

Christine Schidler, an East German economist, reported to a conference of European Socialist Feminists in October 1992 that two-thirds of the unemployed in her "annexed" country are women. "Women are facing permanent expulsion from the labor market. They are learning what it means to be disposable." They resent this; 97 percent want to go out to work. In 1991 only half as many children were born as in 1989. "There is a child strike," said Schidler, which is "the sum of individuals' refusal to go along with the policy of banning women from the labor market."

Under communism, unemployment was "a horrible punishment, a removal of identity for crimes against the state" (Mulholland 1992). This explains why some women resist it.

Women are felt to be unreliable workers. They take time off to care for sick relatives, and take maternity leave. In 1992 the European Parliament's Committee on Women's Rights heard gruesome stories of young East German women undergoing voluntary sterilization in order to make themselves more employable. A sterilization certificate proves a woman will not get pregnant and leave work to look after the child.

There is systematic discrimination against women looking for work. At the end of 1989 in Hungary, 31,750 of 46,609 (68 percent) available jobs were reserved for men (Eberhardt 1991, 41). Some Hungarian joint ventures openly state a preference for men in their advertisements (Lado 1991). In the Slovak Republic there were 77,570 unemployed and the number of vacant posts was 7,563. Only 29 percent of these were for women (Okruhlicova 1991). Since the beginning of restructuring, the number of jobs on offer for Polish women has been only one-third of that for men.

Western Aid

Aid from the European Community to the restructuring East is unmonitored for sex bias, but members of the European Parliament suspect aid is being commandeered by men. A sizable amount of European Community money is going to a major Polish training college for Catholic priests, according to Marijke Van Hemeldonck MEP. She wanted to visit a "so-called agricultural college" near Auschwitz, to see for herself how it fulfilled European Community funding priorities of training managers and developing agriculture. Though she encountered resistance, she succeeded. She found a religious education college for priests with its own farm. (The Polish church is a big landowner.) One wing of the building has been renamed an "agricultural college," and despite the fact that much of Poland's agriculture is run by women, women are excluded because they cannot train to be Catholic priests. "It has been remarkably inefficient and it's an improper use of money," said Van Hemeldonck (European Parliament Women's Committee, Summer 1992).

Back to the Home

Women have been called a "reserve labor force"—drawn out of the home when labor is in demand and sent back when unemployment rises. Once in the home, the state wants them to take on the caring services it used to provide.

Not all women are averse to domestication. In Hungary and Romania, surveys show women are welcoming the opportunity to stay at home with their children (Eberhardt 1991, 9). According to a 1986 survey, 12 percent of economically active Hungarian women said that on working days, apart from sleeping, they had no free time. Sixty-four percent said that they had only one or two extra hours a day (Eberhardt 1991).

Working conditions before the fall of the wall were harsh, which helps explain why in Poland, for instance, staying at home is seen as "new and progressive". Zofia Kuratowska describes women textile workers in Lodz, Poland:

> When they leave the mill after the night shift, their faces are gray, they are poorly dressed, their hair is ruined by the conditions in which they have to work and it lacks style. They are overweight because of an unbalanced diet and it is hard to define their age. These women are always burdened with heavy bags containing the day's shopping, for which until recently, they had to wait for hours in lines. They hurry home in crowded buses and trams in order to prepare meals for their family. No wonder they look the way they do. They do not have the time to take care of themselves properly. (Kuratowska 1991)

Polish women are attracted to domestic life. According to recent polls, 60 percent would like to return to the home. That's just as well because 60 percent of childcare facilities have been closed since 1989. In addition, divorces are harder to get since the transition—new laws require travel to a regional court instead of a local one. Czech women have also been experiencing forced domestication.

Domestic Work

The crux of women's problem in the transition to capitalism is that women are less adaptable than men. They have not got time to change because they are too busy reproducing. Women are specialist reproducers—of new labor (children), and existing labor (feeding the family, caring, mending, and so on). Women "generally carry out three-quarters of all domestic duties and more than half their time is spent buying food and preparing meals. In the ex-USSR, this is the equivalent to a working week—including domestic tasks—of 76.3 hours for women and 56.4 hours for men" (Eberhardt and Heinen 1992).

So, men have around twenty hours per week more than women to adapt to capitalism. Men produce; women reproduce. Capitalism generally manages not to pay labor for reproducing. Reproduction is an external cost for which women pay. Women spend most of their waking hours reproducing—supporting the weak (children, sick people, the old). Unburdened men (apart from the odd ones like the two Czechoslovakian men who took parental leave in 1990) have more time to learn new skills and can afford to take more risks.

The *ex-communist bloc* was noted for its good social security system which helped women reproduce labor. Women could rely on a network of childcare facilities and maternity benefits far better than in the West. In Romania, for instance, a fully paid maternity leave was granted for four months, followed by another six months of reduced working schedule for breast-feeding (Kuratowska 1991).

In the drive to profit, benefits are being cut and childcare facilities, once the responsibility of enterprises, are being shed. One hundred thirty-seven local creches were closed in Poland in 1990—a loss of 15,000 places. Increased fees mean that many women can no longer afford childcare. In Saxony, East Germany, the government recently tried to charge 100 deutsch marks per child per week, as opposed to the 35 pfennige per day parents previously paid toward the cost of meals. Other social security support measures, like the system of pregnancy checks are being dissolved in favor of private medical practices (Miller 1991).

Almost all the company-run creches and most of the nursery schools in Poland, Romania, and ex-Yugoslavia have been shut. Many canteens in Bulgaria have been closed.

Lenin, who said that the kitchen was the center of household slavery, would be horrified to see women cooking at home.

Women's domestic work means that women seldom have time to take on a second job; in this transition period second jobs are an important way to switch careers, for instance by setting up an independent company. There are almost no women setting up private companies. In June 1992 Olga Ticha, a forty-nine year-old computer software specialist from Prague, explained to a Congress of business and professional women why Czech women have such problems setting up independently. "Under the small business law they need to have 'appropriate qualifications.' Even with those qualifications they must also have three years' 'relevant experience'—difficult for newly trained women or those who have raised a family" (*The European* 1992).

Gone are the days of 1949–55, when it was not just the Polish woman's right to work but her duty. Posters showed a girl driving a tractor, and songs praised the brave tractor drivers who took part in the so-called work competition and the Six Year Plan. Twenty years later, when the birthrate fell at an alarming rate, official propaganda encouraged women to have at least three children and a famous slogan urged "Irena go home" (Kuratowska 1991).

According to feminists in Russia, the state policy of *perestrokia* (restructuring) has been replaced with *domostroika* (homebuilding)—a policy of forcing women out of public life and into the home. Draft laws on "the protection of the family, maternity, fathering and childhood" pose the first legislative threat to abortion rights, suggest reducing women's working hours and propose that men should be officially recognized as the head of the family (speech at the conference of European Socialist Feminists 1992).

Marriage and Poverty

Russian women earn only 60 to 75 percent of men's income and are 80 percent of the unemployed. In these conditions, husbands are premium, if only for their second income. But "Russian husbands are reputed to be drunkards and philanderers who don't lift a finger at home," according to Susan Poizner (1992). "One survey showed that while the average woman interviewed spent 31.7 hours per week on childcare and household chores (which are even more arduous without modern conveniences such as washing machines and cars), men spent only 13.6 hours a week doing housework. This unequal distribution of labor, along with the high rate of alcoholism among Russian men, has been connected to Russia's high divorce rate—and hence to the number of single mothers. Russian men are also three times more likely to remarry than their wives" (Poizner 1992).

Some women do not marry in the first place. Ten percent of children born in the former USSR are born to single mothers, who are having a particularly difficult transition to capitalism. Although aid for single mothers has increased since the Russian price reforms began in January 1992, prices have risen faster. Things are expected to deteriorate following the federal government's decision to pass social security to the impoverished localities.

"Theoretically, a new mother can return to her old job within three years," according to Anastasia Posadskaya, director of the Institute of Gender Studies at the Academy of Sciences of Russia. "In fact, that rule is violated all the time because either the job doesn't exist anymore, or the enterprise has been privatized and the new owners feel no responsibility to take the woman back" (Poizner 1992).

Hungarian women are becoming poorer due to the drop in the real value of the childcare grant. The largest group in poverty are women who are looking after their children at home on this grant (Eberhardt and Heinen 1992). The situation of women in Lithuania/Latvia/Estonia is similar to that of women in the former USSR with regard to food shortages, unemployment, and domestic work. In these northern Baltic states infant mortality is twice as high as in the other republics. Seventy-five percent of expectant mothers are ill (Eberhardt and Heinen 1992).

Reproduction

Privatization might be taking over from central planning in the economic sphere, but governments still want to control female fertility. Rather than "privatize" or liberalize reproduction rights, the states are strengthening their grip, particularly in Poland.

In May 1990, the Polish ministry of health passed regulations requiring women seeking abortions in state hospitals to get approval from three doctors. There was no parliamentary debate and little public notice. In May 1991, the same ministry banned several types of oral contraceptives. The minister hoped condoms would share the same fate and that following a Catholic way of life would protect Poles from AIDS (*The Economist* 1992). In May 1992, a new code of ethics drafted by the National Doctors' Guild went into effect. Although not a law, the result was Guild suspension of doctors performing abortions except in cases of rape or threat to a woman's life (*The Economist* 1992). Abortion has been the main form of birth control with approximately 600,000 performed a year, but since the spring of 1992, there have been virtually no abortions performed in Polish hospitals (Eberhardt and Heinen 1992).

The Polish public routinely declares itself 60 percent in favor of abortion, but to no avail. An attempt by Poland's ombudsman to challenge the ethics code as unconstitutional had little support among politicians (*The Economist* 1992). In February 1992, a group of Polish MPs were praying to save the "unborn child" of a fourteen-year old Irish rape victim whom the Dublin Supreme Court had allowed to leave the country for an abortion. Almost half the members of parliament supported a bill that would replace the 1956 law on abortion[1] (*The Economist* 1992).

Lech Walesa explained to a member of the European Parliament in 1991 why the Poles are clamping down on abortion. "Christianity is our business. Poland would not exist without the Church. The Church and the State had a close symbiotic relationship for centuries" (answer to a question asked by Jean-Pierre Cot MEP [Socialist, France]).

Religious teachings have been reintroduced in Polish schools. Women are supposed to copy Jesus' mother, Mary: mother, wife, and virgin. The present antiabortion law has been personally endorsed by the pope, and Catholics who refused to sign antiabortion petitions were threatened with denial of sacraments.

In Hungary, too, religious and right-wing tendencies have been attempting to restrict abortion since the election of the new government in 1990. The Feminist Network and the Green Party Women's section have responded by collecting signatures to support women's right to legal abortion. (These independent bodies are significant because no autonomous women's organization came into existence before 1990) (Eberhardt and Heinen 1992). Before the change of government, abortion was legal up until twelve weeks into pregnancy. In 1989 there were 87.1 abortions per 1,000 women; doctors performed 90,000 abortions in 1991. In late 1991 the highest court ruled that Hungary's liberal abortion regulations were unconstitutional and gave parliament until the end of 1992 to change them (*The Times* 1991).

Proposals have been made in Czechoslovakia to restrict the current abortion law by giving the doctor the right to refuse the termination of a pregnancy or the right to increase the price of an abortion to the equivalent of an average salary (Eberhardt 1991). While there are similar attacks in Slovenia and Ukraine, Russian women have retained their right to abortion and improvements have been made in Romania.

Russia has seen abortions skyrocket since the end of the Cold War. In 1988 there were 106 abortions for every 100 live births. By 1991, this had increased to 137 abortions. Soviet women have long had the right to abortion on demand. Since the supply of contraceptives has always been woefully inadequate, abortion is necessarily a major form of birth control.

Abortions are currently legal in Romania. Immediately after Ceausescu fell, the Romanian constitution and the abortion ban were changed. The "demographic policy" of 1967 had put an absolute ban on abortions, which had previously been free. Contraceptive devices and products disappeared. Doctors and patients faced prison if caught performing abortions. Emergency wards and operating rooms in gynecological clinics were put under police surveillance. Periodically, these measures were reinforced and extended through such practices as compulsory gynecological examinations to detect nondeclared pregnancies for working women between the ages of sixteen and forty-five. These rules have been loosened since the revolution (Celac 1991).

Elected Representatives

The number of women in decision-making positions in eastern and central Europe is tumbling. In the past, women made up 20 to 33 percent of parliamentarians, thanks to a strict but much criticized communist quota system. As a result of the free elections held in 1990, in Romania the women in parliament fell from 34.3 to 3.5 percent, in Czechoslovakia from 29.5 to 6 percent, in Hungary from 20.9 to 7 percent, and in Bulgaria from 21 to 8.5 percent (The Division for the Advancement of Women 1991). In the USSR, the pre-Gorbachev quota system meant that 33 percent of the deputies elected to the Supreme Soviet in 1984 were women. Relaxation of the system resulted in women making up only 15 percent of those elected to the USSR Congress of People's Deputies in 1989 (Eberhardt and Heinen 1992).

There are only five Polish women on the National Solidarity Committee of 90 members. In Hungary's 1990 election only 28 out of 386 seats were won by women (7.2 percent), compared with 80 (21 percent) in the 1985 one-party state elections.

Feminism

After 1917, nonparty activism was curtailed in all spheres in the Soviet Union as the communists established a monopoly on power. The most important women's organizations were the all-Union Soviet Women's Committee and, at the local level, women's councils (*zhensovety*). Communist Party domination and comprehensive censorship (denial of access to key feminist texts produced in the West) made it impossible for women to criticize the sexual division of labor and power in ways which challenged the party line (Greenberg 1992).

According to Valentina Konstantinova, a senior fellow at the new center for Gender Studies of the Russian Academy of Sciences, "The Soviet Women's Committee was an organ of the Communist Party. It was just window dressing to make propaganda about the supposed status of Soviet women under Socialism" (Erlanger 1992).

"In this second revolution, which began in 1985 and which continues, women and women's issues have played a very small part." Younger men are a little more inclined to help around the house, but "most men take little or no household responsibilities; they make a career only, or drink, or play soccer, or only watch it on television" (Konstantinova, quoted in Erlanger 1992).

"Women are still not ready to defend their rights to decent deliveries, to contraception. There are still many taboos. (Examination of) rape and sexual harassment is taboo, and it's getting no better these days, it's even getting worse" (Konstantinova, quoted in Erlanger 1992).

On the bright side, independent feminist activity is on the increase. March 1991 saw a women's forum held in Dubna, near Moscow, attended by 172 women representing forty-eight organizations from twenty-five cities (Ashwin 1991). Russian feminist women held the second Russian women's conference in November 1992. In 1992, St. Petersburg women formed a movement called Survival, whose aims were to fight against commercialization of creches and kindergartens, price increases, and unemployment, which the group says is especially high among female workers (RFE/RK 1992).

Getting established as a legally recognized feminist group in Russia poses problems. The first feminist group to be legally recognized was *Transfiguration*. In 1988, seven Moscow friends gathered around Dr. Dian Medman's kitchen table. According to Dr. Medman, a biochemist and the group's president, "We began to dream that it might be possible to organize officially, to have a special forum for women" (Barry 1992).

The vice president of Transfiguration, Zoya Boguslavska, defines feminism as "having a choice."

> For years, women were expected to do hard labor—laying asphalt, for example—and still shoulder all the burdens at home; buying food, cooking, raising the children. If feminism means anything, it means having some choices about balancing home and work. (Barry 1992)

The estimated fifty to seventy-five members of Transfiguration (which include scientists, economists, speech therapists, writers, poets, translators, artists, zoologists, music teachers, a businesswoman, a stockbroker, and a lawyer) pay 25 rubles (about 25 cents) a year for membership. The group decided early on that, given the level of need in Russian society, they should take a practical approach. They are the sole support for two schools: one for autistic children and another for retarded children (Ashwin 1991).

There are some stirrings of feminism in Prague, including a women's studies course at Charles University, set up by the former Charter 77 figure, Jirina Siklova. But the feminists are isolated and unconfident, like Pavla, a Prague punk with orange hair, member of an all-women's rock band. She was amazed to hear that rape could be considered serious enough in the United States to merit the heavy sentence given boxer Mike Tyson in spring 1992 (Barry 1992).

"Feminism is still a bad word. Under the communists it was seen to be bourgeois, now under the new right it is seen to be too leftist," according to Czechoslovakian Dana Branova. "Only a handful of intellectual women identify themselves as feminist."

War

Civil war is the biggest problem for women in the former Yugoslavia. At the seventh European Forum of Socialist Feminists in October 1992, Serbian Maja Korac reported one Serbian man as having said in description of the current conflict, "In this war, the most interesting things are shooting and fucking." Three women from the warring communities of former Yugoslavia spoke from one platform. Croatian Jasmina Kusmanovic told horror stories of systematic rape of women and girls by Serbian soldiers. Serbian Korac confirmed them, and said Serbian women have seen their men brutalized by war and are suffering a 100 percent increase in domestic violence.

The capitalist disrespect for human life is showing grotesque distortions in the Balkan war, placing a higher price on female life than male. Serb snipers are paid for their killings: $500 for a Western journalist, 400 deutsch marks for male civilians, but double for women and children and even more for pregnant women.

REASONS FOR WOMEN'S LOSSES IN THE TRANSITION TO CAPITALISM

Why are women losing out in this transition period? Why can't they protect their position? Why isn't the burden shared more evenly between women and men?

The key problem for women is that they have almost total responsibility for childcare and looking after the weak. This burden makes it difficult for many women to defend themselves. They do not have time to set up businesses, learn new skills, or enter politics. The first imperative is to survive, to feed the family.

Marxists argue that the position of women is based on society's wealth. Liberation is a function of society's level of productivity and not merely its social structures. Only rich countries will pay women to reproduce labor. Women's desire to be liberated is meaningless in a poor country. When a country has enough money, women might get liberation.

The truth about this Marxist argument is that no country ever says "Yes OK, we are now rich enough to liberate our women." They say, "Women wait, there's no money for equality." That is what the 1990s central and eastern European men are saying—"There's a world recession, times are hard, we've got to compete. . . ." It is especially severe in the former communist bloc because of years of distorted production patterns, specifically an overconcentration on the military/industrial complex. The debt-ridden state says it cannot afford to run a welfare system and is looking to women to run a replacement welfare system, at home, for free. The corresponding ideology promotes the caring mother in the home, the backbone of the family.

These are the economic reasons for the backlash against women. The Marxists believed that ideology follows economics, but the seventy-year Marxist experiment indicates that there are other guiding principles at work.

Soviet socialism was an attempt to run society based on egalitarian philosophy, yet new manifestations of sexism emerged almost immediately. Economic reorganization did not change sexual inequality. The "bourgeois" family was not eradicated and women were not freed from the domestic burden. Socialism did not liberate women. "Under socialism we were taught that capitalism means the rich exploit the poor, but socialism means the government exploits the women," said Libuse, fifty, a math and physics teacher in a Prague secondary school (Mulholland 1992).

Admittedly, the failure of socialism, because of its commitment to equality, is a setback for anyone wanting equality. But is it necessary to take one step backward in order to take two forward? Maybe.

Just as the enfranchisement of women showed that if voting changed anything, they'd abolish it, the Soviet socialist experiment has taught us that mass participation in the paid labor market does not necessarily reduce women's oppression. An economic revolution (albeit corrupted to serve state, military, and nationalistic ends) achieves little for women.

The transformation process that has been under way since 1989 shows that economic disruption is bad for women. A drop in production hits women (the weaker) hardest. When unemployment rises, a woman's place is in the home. The old "nature" arguments come out, and women's subordination is justified through science and religion. When men feel threatened, they attack the weak: women, immigrants, outsiders.

Capitalism will not relieve women. Western capital repeatedly forgoes efficiency and profit in order to conform to the sexist norms of society. It is not "profitable" to underuse women's skills, to overlook women's talents, but it is usual. There are too many examples of sexism overriding capitalist economic logic to believe that women's oppression is caused by capitalism.

Only a deep and genuine sexual revolution will liberate women.

CONCLUSION

The great expectations of 1989 have come to nothing. The first tastes of capitalism are bitter, not sweet. Women have not found liberation in the new free market. They have merely changed masters and are finding the shiny capitalist whip more stinging than the communist one.

At least women under communism had creches, night shops, maternity allowances, and jobs. At least they had formal equality; at least the state professed to support equality. At least they had quotas to ensure they were represented in parliament and in the party.

Under capitalism women are losing their protections. They are learning what it is like to be the losers in capitalist competition, and with the communists gone, there is no one around to pick up the pieces. The creches are closing. The maternity payments are frozen while inflation soars, thus phasing out state aid to mothers. It's harder to look after children, and it's becoming harder to plan families, because in many countries, authorities are tightening up on the main form of birth control, abortion.

There is a noticeable swing to the right all over central and eastern Europe, and women are among the victims. Sexism, racism and nationalism are on the rise. In some countries, especially Poland, the Catholic church is making great headway promoting the traditional view of women as mothers, wives, and virgins. Freedom to divorce and abortion are under threat.

Women are being forced out of the labor markets and into the home. Selective redundancies of women have led to glaring inequalities—in Russia 80 percent of the unemployed are women. This serves only to make women more dependent on men.

There are some feminist groups forming, but they are few and far between; furthermore, they tend to focus on the immediate alleviation of poverty, rather than the attainment of equal rights in general. They are patching the society, not demanding its transformation. It is often argued by Western feminists that women's self-organization is a key to liberation. Therefore, much attention has been given to the fledgling feminist forums in the former Soviet bloc.

But while feminist groups are positive, they constitute only a minute proportion of the population: intellectuals and academics. They might be the vanguard of the revolution, but not when their efforts patch, rather than change, society.

Perhaps a more hopeful sign comes from the masses of women on child strike. Many East German women have decided to stop having children. There has been a 50 percent drop in the birthrate. If the state and men are going to exclude women from jobs, from money, from prestige when they have a baby, then the women will not reproduce.

But in the end neither child strikes nor feminist groups will solve women's problems in eastern Europe. Only a change from a society based on competition to cooperation will liberate women. Unfortunately, capitalism glorifies competition and heaps prizes on the winners. And even more unfortunate, in the foreseeable future central and eastern Europe will be capitalist and the winners will be men.

NOTE

1. A Polish law stating that "each human being has a right to life starting from conception," and prohibiting abortion went into effect in March 1993. Doctors (but not the women getting the abortions) are subject to two years of imprisonment for causing "the death of [the] conceived child." See Valentine M. Moghadam, "Gender and Revolutionary Transformation: Iran 1979 and East Central Europe 1989," *Gender and Society* (1995): 350–51.—Editor's Note.

18

THE FUTURE OF EASTERN EUROPE: LESSONS FROM THE THIRD WORLD

Ziauddin Sardar and Merryl Wyn Davies

A new world has been made by the disintegration of the communist bloc. The patterns of the past no longer apply. This is a common argument. Change is often a fickle illusion, however, that masks tenacious continuities. The citizens of Eastern Europe may soon join the ranks of those who have had to learn that their brave new world is a perilous place.

Today, eastern European states are in a similar position to numerous Third World countries during their independence in the late 1940s and early 1950s. Although they have a slightly more developed, if somewhat obsolete and redundant, technological infrastructure, their position in the global economic order is not much different from many large developing countries such as India, Brazil, and Egypt. The parallels between these developing countries and the newly liberated eastern European states is the only appropriate analogy for understanding the challenges that face the emerging nations of the East. There are significant differences, no doubt. Yet the similarities are the surest key to the questions that need to be debated. For this reason it is most likely that the matter will be brushed aside. It is far too embarrassing—politically as well as academically—for all concerned.

Liberation, or independence, as the states of eastern Europe are learning to their cost, is not a cure-all; it is simply the assumption of a new set of problems and constraints. Soon, they will come to realize—as Third World countries have already realized—that reform is as much required by Western capitalism as it was by Stalinist communism. And, like so many thinkers in developing countries have known for so long, they may even come to terms with the knowledge that the language to discuss humane solutions is elusive in the *realpolitik* of both systems.

There are three strong parallels, and one major difference, between the emergence of Third World countries after World War II and the present situation of eastern European states. Both groups are a product of a colonial history which, though different in it ideological makeup, is singularly homogeneous in its legacy—dependency. Both groups gained their "independence" within a world order with well-established rules of economic and commercial behavior. Both groups are totally marginalized from the centers of political, economic, technological, and cultural power. And the difference: unlike the Third World states, eastern European countries can legitimately claim to be part of the dominant global civilization—they are essentially Western by possession of common roots in Western civilization and culture. Whether this will mark a point of departure between the development in the Third World over the past five decades and the possible future of eastern Europe is a debatable point. Certainly, the "common ground" between the Third World and eastern Europe will be the major decisive factor shaping the future of former Soviet satellites.

THE NEW OLD WORLD ORDER

Eastern Europe has the same periphery-to-center relationship with the existing economic powers as the Third World. The Third World countries gained their independence in an international economic order that is also the chief inheritance of the newly liberated eastern European states. The framework of this economic order was set up at the end of World War II by the Bretton Woods conference, held at the town of that name in the United States. It set up the World Bank and the International Monetary Fund. At the Bretton Woods conference, the Western nations, having lost their empires, made institutional arrangement for continuing their domination and exploitation of the newly emerging nations. The Third World itself was not a party to the negotiations nor has it benefited from the results. Instead, it has discovered, to its cost and dismay, that the system was designed to discriminate against it and to ensure its dependence on the established power blocs in the industrialized countries. To this day, even though there have been some minor changes, the voting power in key institutions like the IMF reflects the world of the 1940s and 1950s. The eastern European states are set to suffer the same injustice from the existing world economic order as the Third World.[1]

The Third World nations have realized that all new worlds are founded on continuity. It is the continuity of the old international economic order that is shaping the "newness" of a world transformed by the collapse of communism. As the Third World has found to its cost, you can swap one master for another and still remain slaves. What this means for eastern Europe is that communism has been replaced by a new form of economic slavery: that of IMF, World Bank, and multinational corporations' monopoly capital. The iron curtain will soon be replaced by a poverty curtain, at least for the more southern of the former Soviet satellites. Hungary, Poland, and Czechoslovakia may eventually be allowed to enter the EU (although, as we argue below, this could in itself be a new form of colonialism), but others—Albania, Bulgaria, Romania, and Yugoslavia—are most likely to be in the same position as Turkey, and the doors of the EU are unlikely to open for them. Thus, eastern Europe is set to follow the old patterns of underdevelopment in the new order of the postcommunist world.[2]

More specifically, the future course of "development" in eastern Europe will have the following Third-World-type characteristics.

1. The IMF and World Bank will enforce the classical, top-down, capitalist model of development on eastern European states. This will induce the newly liberated states into becoming satellites of industrialized nations. The material gains of this development will come through loss of autonomy, politically and morally, and expropriation of local control of resources, and will accrue to a tiny portion of the population that will become the new elite. As the Third World knows, material gains from IMF- and World Bank-backed development strategies take a long time to trickle down to the mass of the population, if at all. A tiny group of "haves" will thus dominate a vast majority of "have-nots"; and a new breed of elite will run eastern European states while the mass of the people will find themselves with few opportunities for betterment.
2. Eastern European nations are being given preferential treatment in the rescheduling of their debt burden to Western banks. But they, like the Third World, are trapped in the debt syndrome. They will find their room for manuver and choice curtailed by the agenda of what is good and necessary set by remote and faceless money men. As aid flows to eastern Europe, its constituent states will find themselves in a similar debt trap to that of so many Third World countries: what this will mean in practical terms is that real resources will flow from eastern Europe to the West, inducing deeper and deeper dependency with all the attendant consequences such as poverty, unemployment, and social degradation.
3. The only economic edge of eastern Europe, like so many developing countries, is cheap and abundant labor. Eastern European states will thus end up supplying western Europe with an internal pool of cheap labor with all the fragility that this gives to economic development. This is the "Catch 22"[3] that so many Third World nations have suffered. The problem is not getting foreign investment to come into the country, but getting it to stay so that it can generate locally sustainable growth and direct this investment in an appropriate and desirable

direction. Multinational companies are not interested in investing in a technology that is useful or desirable for a developing nation; their concern is to find the cheapest labor for the manufacture of the individual components of their consumer goods, which are actually put together at a totally different location. With such a new pool of labor clamoring for jobs there is no reason why multinational corporations should not have a bonanza while the economies of eastern Europe show little benefit from the hyperactivity.

4. Just as in the Third World, communism in eastern Europe placed industrialization as a first priority in essentially agricultural and rural nations. The basic health of their economies has been deformed as has that of Third World nations by the neglect of agriculture and the failure to make a balance between urban needs for cheap food and adequate remuneration of rural labor. Adjusting that balance has proved an irreconcilable problem for Third World nations. Once the imbalance occurs it is virtually impossible to adjust it without provoking social unrest either in the city or the countryside. IMF- and World Bank-induced strategies will further enhance this imbalance in eastern Europe, generating increasing social strife and unrest.

THE OLD NEW NATIONALISM

At independence, many Third World countries discovered that the departing, or not-so-departing, colonial powers had created purely artificial nation-states. Thus, for example, Pakistan was divided into "West" and "East" with a thousand miles of Indian territory between them; the Kurds were scattered between Iran, Iraq, and Turkey; and the Sudan was put together from a "Muslim north" and a "Christian south." The Third World nation-states were *designed* to be unstable, to fall apart, and to provide continuous and constant tensions to enable the newly independent states to be locked into a particular socioeconomic framework.[4] Eastern European states also find themselves to be purely artificial entities: nationalism in itself is an insufficient rationale for creating a homogeneous state and is always subject to constant subdivision, as Yugoslavia and Czechoslovakia are learning to their cost and as many other emergent eastern European nation-states may soon demonstrate.[5]

Moreover, soon after independence, Third World countries discovered that colonialism simply froze the old rivalries into history. Once the colonial structures had disappeared, the old ethnic and minority questions returned to the fore. Similarly, communism did not solve national and minority disputes in eastern Europe, it merely locked them away in the ice chest of the police state.

Eastern Europe is the Balkans, origin and cauldron of Balkanization. Its history of the past 500 years has been one of a consistent battle among nationalities, cultures, and language groups. The very model that was held up to impel both reified nationalism and the horror of disintegration for artificially created Third World states was derived from the historic experience of eastern Europe, whose instability has bedeviled Europe for centuries. The continuity of the problem is a stark reminder of the limits of human ingenuity; there still is no answer to the urgent questions of plural nations within the ethos of the modern national state.

The process of gaining independence for the Third World was momentous, every bit as much as the overthrow of totalitarian control is for eastern Europe. The emergence of a new, sustainable political order proved far more problematic. Given the fact that central Europe is the birthplace of nationalist rebellion, where it acquired its mystique, Third-World-style independence movements, with all that entails in terms of violence and terror, are surely on the cards in the near future for many eastern European countries. A recent U.S. *Times-Mirror* poll on European attitudes confirms the trend: "In every country sampled in eastern Europe, at least 40 per cent felt hostile to the main national minority. Most Poles, Hungarians and Bulgarians felt that part of their country lay within another country, and resented the fact: a substantial proportion of Lithuanians, Czechs and Slovaks and Germans felt the same."[6]

In Germany, there has been a shocking upsurge of nationalism and racism—indeed, the incidents of racism have reached an all-time high since the collapse of the Third Reich. Moreover, the exponential rise in racism is not limited to former East Germany: in the prosperous cities of the West firebombings and stabbings of Romanians, Poles, and Turks have become commonplace. Such developments, by introducing political instability, will not only strengthen the trends for underdevelopment in eastern Europe and ensure its dependent status, but also say something about the desire of eastern European countries to join the EU.

DOES THE EUROPEAN UNION (EU) MAKE A DIFFERENCE?

When eastern European countries speak of the "European home," state their goals as "the return to Europe," they define "Europe" first and foremost as the EU. As noted above, the European roots of ex-Soviet satellites are the single most important difference between them and the Third World. But it is not just the common history that is so attractive. For the leaders of the eastern European states, the EU exerts a tremendous attraction, because it symbolizes a coveted economic success, but above all it constitutes for them a successful "security community" and a veritable *état de droit* which has been able to overcome old antagonism and imbalances of power. . . . In the economic and strategic vacuum which has characterized Central and Eastern Europe after the failure of COMECON and the dissolution of the Warsaw Pact, they believe that accession to the EC will be a guarantee of economic development, a safeguard against a return to the old system and a warranty enabling them to avert the probable resurgence of nationalism and the resulting conflict.[7]

The EU is therefore seen as a panacea for all problems—economic development, rise of nationalism and consequent Balkanization—that the Third World has continuously faced and which eastern European states are set to encounter in the near future. But a return to Europe, however desirable it may be, is not going to be an easy task. The present harsh reality is that as a market the EU is closed to eastern European states, while the eastern European states themselves are totally open markets for the EU countries. This is a privileged and advantageous situation for the member states of the EU, who, when it comes to the real crunch, will not be too disposed to a more equitable situation. Western Europe is competing with an increasingly powerful, more organized, and more technologically advanced threat from Japan: it needs captured markets to offset the considerable advantages of Japan. In such a climate, the most realistic, and pessimistic, scenario is that eastern Europe, like the Third World, will become a dumping ground for EU consumer goods and services. In an increasingly shrinking world, this is what the "free market forces" dictate.

There is also the "hopeful syndrome" best exemplified by Turkey. Turkey becomes increasingly dependent and devoid of autonomy in order to fulfill the basic criteria for membership—political stability, implementation of aggressively monetarist policies, reduction of its agricultural base. Given its present status and political structure, however, it can never attain the stability that is required. This suits the EU rather well as it has a dependent satellite without the cost of admitting it to membership. Eastern European states may find themselves having the same status. Furthermore, there is the racist dimension: the questions asked of Turkey (is it really European?) could well be raised in the case of certain eastern European countries. Hungary, Poland, and Czechoslovakia are the vague boundary line where the question arises. Moreover, it is the horror of what the process of Balkanization did to the stability of Europe—being integral to the cause of the last two world wars—that is the major rationale for the existence and maintenance of the EU. The question would be raised: how can we allow these countries into the EC until they have resolved being the Balkans?

There is, however, a definite probability, however small, that east European states will be integrated within the EU. This development, too, could produce equally disastrous results for the weak economies of eastern Europe. Suppose, for the sake of argument, hurdles such as the Common Agriculture Policy can be overcome, and the EU is benevolent enough to allow the eastern European states into the club. Would that mean that the eastern European states would suddenly be on a sure path to development and that nationalism would be curbed? The most likely outcome of the sudden blast of competition from the EU's more established and vastly more powerful economies would be to destroy much of the infant private industry in eastern Europe. The exercise would be similar to East Germany being taken over by West Germany; and the consequences will be almost exactly the same. And if there were some economic gains to be made from the exercise, could the inner drive for autonomy and cultural expression and authenticity among ethnic minorities—which is surely the hallmark of the 1990s—be brought with economic gains? The key question to ask here is: is there or has there ever been an eastern European ethos? And if there is a distinct eastern European identity, or a number of identities, how will it/they respond to being once again submerged, especially if rising material standards fulfill Drucker's dread promise of making nationalism the "ism" of the bourgeoisie?[8]

The point is that the EU is a club for the privileged few; these privileges can be retained only by the EU's acting as a fortress against the rest of the world and operating in the old Bretton Woods economic order. Enlarging this club to bring in poverty-stricken and politically unstable eastern European states would surely mean the loss of these privileges; no club behaves against its own best self-interests. The EU option is not open to eastern European states, at least not in the near future.

CONCLUSION

We cannot see the liberation of Eastern Europe as simply a result of the failure of the Marxist system—as the ultimate triumph of capitalism. This would be too naive a response. It was, like the liberation of Third World countries, essentially a long-delayed process of decolonization. Like the British and French empires of the past, the Kremlin had to learn the limits of its power.

Moreover, the wholesale rejection of communism in eastern Europe was not purely pragmatic. It was not just that communism vaunted utopia and delivered economic malaise. Communism, like colonialism, dehumanized through its routine bureaucratic indignities, suppressed cultural expression, negated the history of ethnic minorities, and trampled on the dignity of the individual. It was not just the physical and material necessity of standing in a bread queue that killed communism. It was what standing in a bread queue did to people and made them feel about themselves and the state in which they lived that spelled the death knell of communism.

Those who revolted in the bread queues will soon find that replacing them with a scramble for a share of material plenty has its own set of indignities. The dole queue is as soul-destroying as the bread queue. The West may have the capacity to generate tremendous wealth and conspicuous consumption, but it has never devised the means of ensuring equitable distribution and genuine equality of access and opportunity. It is the citizens of the Third World who have the greatest experience of the consequences of this lack in the ideological matrix of capitalism. Eastern Europe may have returned to democracy; but democracy is not the empowering of the majority but the fake consultation of the mass by a system dominated and run by an entrenched elite that holds the levers of power. That is the conundrum of the Western democratic ideal out of which the Third World has been unable to break and which looks set to bedevil eastern Europe. It is therefore natural for eastern European states both to learn from the experience of the Third World and to make common cause with them, to add new and significant Western voices to the agenda for genuine structural change in the international economic order.

Quite simply, Third World nations have got used to the awful truth: however laudable democratic ideals may be, they are almost impossible to realize when the aspirations of the state are (1) to develop on established Western models; (2) to accommodate the pressure of dependence; and (3) to overcome the legacy of nonindependent growth. The result has been a diversity of forms, and shades of totalitarianism, authoritarianism, military regimes and persistent, all-pervading elite domination. In 1989 the dominoes in eastern Europe fell in the direction of democracy. But, as the experience of developing countries teaches us, tomorrow they could just as easily fall again another way.

A stark set of questions now faces eastern Europe: The end of ideology is the beginning of what? Now that communism no longer exists, is capitalism the only option? Is the process created and envisioned at Bretton Woods now complete? Can the ideals of pluralism be sustained within the concept of the modern nation as instrumental rationality? What will provide national aspirations and inclusion? What will ensure genuine freedom, including cultural and ethnic freedom, and participatory democracy, including economic democracy, for all? The answers could lead eastern European countries to retrace the disastrous development paths of Third World states or toward their own unique roads to self-reliance and self-sufficiency and the creation of new models of "state" that allow cultural fulfillment for all minorities and give them equal participation in governance.

NOTES

1. For a more detailed analysis, see Sardar (1981,334–41).
2. See Amin, (1990).
3. See Heller, (1962).
4. See Toffler, (1990); Hinsley, (1986).
5. See Brzezinski, (1989–90,1–25).
6. See Ascherson, (1991).
7. See de la Serre, (1991,739–46).
8. See Drucker, (1990).

19

CONCLUSION: OF RIVERS AND SOCIAL CHANGE

Charles Tilly

None of us—either students nor teachers nor anyone else—can escape social change. The world will not stand still for any of us. The collapse of regimes in eastern Europe, the massacre of refugees in Central Africa, the spread of AIDS throughout the world, the rise of multinational corporations, the decline in American birthrates, the expansion of computerized work and communication arrive not just as daily news but also as personal problems or opportunities. Few students or teachers of sociology will react to any of the dramatic news by leaping up instantly and rushing to the main sites of action. Yet all of us will feel the impact of these changes in the form of taxes we pay, political choices we make, products we buy, sexual relations we establish or avoid, jobs we hold—or, for that matter, jobs we fail to get because they have disappeared. Studying social change sensitizes us to how momentous shifts in social organization affect our individual lives, and other people's as well.

Nor can we ignore social change outside our own country on the ground that it is someone else's problem. The entire world impinges on us, and we impinge on the entire world. Here are some signs of our world's increasing connectedness:

1. In 1990, Exxon's $90.5 billion of worldwide foreign sales exceeded the gross national products of European countries Albania, Bulgaria, Czechoslovakia, Greece, Hungary, Iceland, Ireland, Luxembourg, Malta, Norway, Poland, Portugal, Romania, Turkey, and Yugoslavia—not to mention that of most countries in Asia, Africa, and South America (UNCTAD 1993, 26; Sivard 1993, 43–44).
2. Kuwait citizens constituted 55 percent of Kuwait's population in 1957, and a mere 40 percent in 1985, when 78 percent of the Kuwaiti labor force were noncitizens (Shah 1986, 815). Other Gulf oil states likewise hosted majorities of foreign workers.

3. From 1970 to 1991, outflows of foreign direct investment increased worldwide at a rate of about 13 percent per year, while real gross domestic product rose at a declining rate averaging in the vicinity of 4 percent (UNCTAD 1993, 92–93).
4. The estimated annual human contribution to global warming of major greenhouse gases ran roughly six times higher during the 1980s than it had over the 1765–1960 period; the vast majority of this increase resulted from the burning of fossil fuels and the use of chlorofluorocarbons, both originating chiefly in urban-industrial areas but spreading their effects throughout the world (Stern, Young, and Druckman 1992, 47–51).
5. "IBM (United States) has alliances with Thomson-CSF (France) to market microprocessor chips, with Toshiba (Japan) to cooperate in the development of static random access memory chips, with Siemens (Germany) for work on advanced dynamic random access memory chips, and with Toshiba and Siemens to develop a new 256 megabyte chip" (UNCTAD 1993, 143)
6. Although the first recognized AIDS epidemic occurred in North America, by 1990 the world contained an estimated 8.8 million carriers of HIV, 5.8 million of them in sub-Saharan Africa (World Bank 1993, 33, 99).
7. Of the $1.95 trillion in worldwide foreign direct investment as of 1992, $1.17 trillion came from the United States, the United Kingdom, Japan, or Germany; about three-quarters of the total was invested in already "developed" countries, but that still left almost $500 billion of American, British, Japanese, and German investments for poorer countries (UNCTAD 1993, 14).
8. At the end of 1990, the world harbored about 17 million officially designated refugees, people displaced from their native countries by state action and/or natural disasters. About 5.7 million of them were then sojourning in Africa, another 7.9 million in Asia (United Nations 1993, 20–21). By 1994, the estimated total had increased to 19 million (New York Times, March 20, 1994).

These news items reveal intercontinental influences of great, increasing scope. Current trends in flows of workers, diseases, plants, pollutants, weapons, drugs, technology, information, commodities, political practices, and cultural forms do not pack as neatly into compact statistical wrappers, but in general they too give evidence of increasing world connectedness. To explain such changes stands high on the agenda for students of social change. Merely to recognize them makes the study of social change urgent.

Social critic and sociologist C. Wright Mills once called for the sociological imagination "to grasp history and biography and the relations between the two within society" (Mills 1959, 4). "The first fruit of this imagination," he declared,

> is the idea that the individual can understand his own experience and gauge his own fate only by locating himself within his period, that he can know his own chances in life only by becoming aware of those of all individuals in his circumstances. In many ways it is a terrible lesson; in many ways a magnificent one. We do not know the limits of man's capacities for supreme effort or willing degradation, for agony or glee, for pleasurable brutality or the sweetness of reason. But in our time we have come to know that the limits of "human nature" are frighteningly broad. We have come to know that every individual lives, from one generation to the next, in some society; that he lives out a biography, and that he lives it out within some historical sequence. By the fact of his living he contributes, however minutely, to the shaping of this society and to the course of its history, even as he is made by society and by its historical push and shove (Mills 1959, 5–6; as a bit of evidence for social change over the last few decades, notice how in 1959 even a progressive scholar unself-consciously used "he" and "his" for all humans).

Mills located sociological analysis at the intersection of biography and history in social structure. That formulation nicely captures a major reason for pursuing the study of social change: for self-knowledge, to figure out what in the world is going on around us, and how it is intervening in our own lives. But it also identifies another equally compelling reason: for empathy, to understand what is happening to fellow humans elsewhere in their individual lives. Self-knowledge and empathy complement each other, and the study of social change can enlarge both of them.

As earlier chapters in this book show, sociology offers a set of tools for disciplining the enlargement of self-knowledge and empathy. The tools include demographic analysis, opinion surveys, participant observation, historical reconstruction, and much more. Most of them involve gathering information on a larger scale and by more disciplined means than most of us adopt in everyday life. None of us needs a survey to find her or his way to work or school, but only the largest survey of all—a national census—provides a comprehensive picture of a national population's distribution and change. Censuses have become indispensable tools for students of social change. So have on-the-spot observation, historical comparison, and reconstruction of demographic transformations.

Essential tools also include concepts for ordering the information, concepts such as ideology, class, culture, and industrialization, each needing careful definition before it does us much good. In order to work on a large scale in a disciplined way, we must use comparable categories that correspond to coherent phenomena we can observe reliably. One of the most troublesome concepts, it turns out, is the basic one: social change itself. The social world does not come to us nicely wrapped as history, biography, social structure, and social change, much less as ideology, class, culture, or industrialization. It comes to us as particular short-run messages, conversations, encounters, obligations, and other interactions with other people. It comes to us as an onrushing profusion of episodes.

Since that world never stands still, "social change" sometimes seems to mean everything that happens to people, that great river in which all humans swim. Some social analysts have even tried to capture that sense of comprehensiveness in general theories of progress, social evolution, cycles, or decay. (For example, nineteenth-century French thinker Auguste Comte, who coined the words "sociology" and "positivist," divided all of human history into three progressive phases: theological, metaphysical, and positive. Sociology's discoveries, in his view, would cap the science of the positive age.) A successful theory of this kind would amount to a theory of everything. Although we can learn much about the social world's connections from the most intelligent of such theories, all of them fail because they assume a unitary master process determining all changes in social experience. They assume a single stream.

Does the unitary stream exist? Does social change in general actually run like a river? Can we map its direction, measure its depth, identify its contents, and gauge its impact? In fact, we cannot. The phrase "social change" simply labels certain aspects of a great many diverse social processes, each of which follows its own distinct logic. Those particular social processes do resemble rivers. A river has a well-marked course, a clear direction of flow, and rules of its own. The river's rules depend, furthermore, on the climates that touch the river, the terrain through which it runs, and the creatures that live in its depths. A kayaker can learn its rapids, a flycaster its best fishing spots, a hydrologist its physics, an ecologist its systems of life, a steamboat captain its entire course. Social change in general does not resemble such a river. We can learn particular social changes, for example, recent alterations in American immigration, as we learn a nearby stream. But we cannot learn social change as a whole.

The notion of social change in general more closely resembles the abstract idea of a current. Currents include all sorts of continuous onward movements in fluids. We can certainly chart a particular river's flows, but the general idea of a current averages over a wide variety of swirls, eddies, and backwaters. We can, in fact, apply the same idea to any fluid body, searching out the dominant directions of movement and calling them its currents. Even then, however, the idea does not apply neatly everywhere: some fluid bodies lie so still that we can detect no current, while others undergo so much turbulence that the very idea of directionality loses its meaning. Only in between does the broad, abstract idea of current help us order our observations.

The analogy works reasonably well for social change. Examining any particular set of social changes, we can reasonably ask about their relationship to time. We can, among other things, ask about covariation, directionality, and recurrence:

> *Covariation*: changes move together in time, as the birthrate and the marriage rate tend to? Partly because recently married couples have more children than anyone else and partly because the same conditions that favor marriage also favor conceptions and births, rising or falling rates of marriage predict, with appropriate lags, parallel changes in birthrates.
>
> *Directionality*: do they head in one direction over long periods, as levels of literacy have often done? Unlike the stock market, which zigzags from day to day, once the proportion of a large population that can read and write starts rising it commonly continues to rise for years or even decades. People do not ordinarily lose their literacy from one day to the next.
>
> *Recurrence*: or are they instead cyclical, returning regularly to their points of departure, as seems to be the case with women's hemlines, men's lapels, and many other fashions? Recurrent patterns sometimes link to natural cycles such as the seasons, and sometimes to limits built into social processes such as international migration or expenditure on new housing.

As the word "current" implies questions about directions of movement in contained fluids, the words "covariation," "directionality," and "recurrence" state abstract questions about particular processes of change.

We can ask general questions about many particular social changes without supposing that the answers will always come out the same, without assuming that all the questions have meaningful answers in every case, and without imagining that there is a general, lawful phenomenon called social change of which the particular changes are simply special cases. Our overall knowledge of social change will then consist, not of stock answers, but of urgent questions. We can also reverse the angle of observation, bringing

Conclusion: Of Rivers and Social Change   313

many different bodies of knowledge to bear on a single case; just as hydrologists, ecologists, navigators, public health specialists, and geologists all have important, distinctive things to say about any particular river, different branches of social analysis bring different perspectives to the analysis of any particular stream of social changes.

Demographers, economists, psychologists, political scientists, and sociologists properly select their own aspects of a complex reality. Confronted with the declining employment in manufacturing that has marked most Western economies since the 1950s, for example, demographers often stress the population's aging as well as distinctive demographic features of workers in the expanding service sector, while economists stress productivity gains in manufacturing that reduce the demand for labor and shifts of manufacturing to low-wage countries. In short, social changes are occurring all around us, and one of social science's most important tasks is to help explain them, but social change in general is not a coherent phenomenon whose laws we can discover. It does us little good to ask whether social change as a whole is accelerating in our time, but a great deal of good to ask whether gender relations or social movements or manufacturing technology are changing faster now than they did before World War II. That is the sort of question this book asks. Think of the book as a tool kit of questions to ask about social changes that matter to your life.

The study of specific social changes involves the location of cause-effect chains in time. Cause-effect relations sometimes recur in a wide range of conditions. Take the chapter on gender inequality by Janet Saltzman Chafetz, earlier in this book. When Chafetz analyzes changes in gender inequality between the sexes, for example, she lays out a very general set of ideas about the influence of work on other areas of social life, but then closes in rapidly on connected changes of work and gender inequality in the United States and similar countries. She points out that on the large scale (for reasons she does not try to explain) men almost always dominate the overall division of labor, and use their domination to forward changes promising to sustain their dominant positions. (For general explanations of gender differences in these regards, I suggest looking closely at the genetic facts (1) that males, on the average, grow stronger than females and (2) that women bear children, as well as the social fact (3) that men make war, which creates all sorts of power structures including governments themselves.)

The male-dominated division of labor fosters a wide range of inequalities outside of work, as well as ideologies and rules of conduct that support the inequalities. The nature of those inequalities, Chafetz argues, changes roughly in step with the division of labor. Nevertheless, no human being— male or female—can anticipate all the consequences of acting one way or another. Sometimes the changing division of labor generates unexpected but genuine opportunities for women's gains, collective action by women consolidates those gains, and women struggle successfully to defend gains they have already won. The male-dominated division of labor generates its own contradictions. Chafetz applies her reasoning especially to the period since 1850 or so, in which work moved massively from households and small shops to big organizations; that enormous change, in her view, created demands for female labor that men could not anticipate or contain. Work outside the home, in its turn, gave women leverage in many other areas of life. Chafetz stresses changes in women's childbearing, education, and political rights. Thus she locates a very general set of cause-effect relations in the specific time of Western industrialization. We can, in fact, check the validity and generality of her reasoning by:

1. Examining what happens when women who previously worked in factories or offices take up computer- and-telephone-assisted jobs at home (by her reasoning, work at home should reduce their power).
2. Investigating whether similar changes occur in different countries when women's outside employment grows (by her reasoning, women's power should usually grow with outside employment).
3. Determining if the massive unemployment of women in eastern Europe since 1989 (described elsewhere in the book by Jo Brew) has diminished women's power more than men's, as Chafetz's analysis indicates it should have.

We study proposed cause-effect chains in different circumstances to learn how valid and general they are.

Like Chafetz, sociologists who specialize in the study of major social changes usually concentrate on cause-effect chains that (1) cover a considerable time span, (2) have a definable direction, (3) touch many people at the same time, (4) make a significant difference to those people's lives. This book emphasizes changing ideologies, technologies, divisions of labor, demographic structures, social movements, and revolutions, all of which arguably meet the four tests. In principle, however, the same approaches should help us understand changes that do not meet these tests: changes within a single family, changes that keep spiraling instead of moving mainly in one direction, changes that occur very quickly, and so on. The point of social change analyses is to identify valid chains of cause and effect, placing them firmly in time.

Not that any such analysis comes easy; in social change's tangle, clear strands of cause and effect always resist separation. Consider a relatively straightforward change: the multinationalization of automobile production. When manufacturers first started producing automobiles in the 1890s, a few workers in a single shop typically assembled the entire machine from parts they often fashioned themselves, making one part and then one machine at a time. In the 1910s and 1920s, Henry Ford and his competitors set up assembly lines with minute divisions of labor, but still produced their cars from parts they manufactured themselves or procured from local suppliers. Overseas, other automobile manufacturers did the same. Since World War II, however, an enormous internationalization of automobile manufacturing has occurred. The entry of Japanese and Korean vehicles onto the world market has shaken American dominance and competed strongly with European manufacturers as well. In recent years, furthermore, the distinction between one country's production and another's has blurred, as Asian investors have bought into American and European plants, two-country collaborations have become common, and supply of parts has become a worldwide business. In the 1980s, for example, a Ford Escort assembled in Halewood (United Kingdom) or Saarlouis (Germany) for the European market included components from much of the capitalist world:

> *United Kingdom*: carburetor, rocker arm, clutch, ignition, exhaust, oil pump, distributor, cylinder bolt, cylinder head, flywheel ring gear, heater, speedometer, battery, rear wheel spindle, intake manifold, fuel tank, switches, lamps, front disc, steering wheel, steering column, glass, weatherstrips, locks.
> *France*: alternator, cylinder head, master cylinder, brakes, underbody coating, weatherstrips, clutch release bearings, steering shaft and joints, seat pads and frames, transmission cases, clutch cases, tires, suspension bushes, ventilation units, hose clamps, heater, sealers, hardware.
> *Germany*: locks, pistons, switches, front disc, distributor, rocker arm, fuel tank, cylinder head gasket, front wheel nuckles, rear wheel spindle, weatherstrips, speedometer, transmission cases, clutch cases, clutch, steering column, battery, glass.
> *Spain*: wiring harness, radiator and heater hoses, fork clutch release, air filter, battery, mirrors.
> *Sweden*: hose clamps, cylinder bolt, exhaust down pipes, pressings, hardware.
> *Japan*: starter, alternator, cone and roller bearings, windscreen washer pump.
> *Italy*: cylinder head, carburetor, glass, lamps,defroster, grilles.
> *United States*: EGR valves, wheel nuts, hydraulic tappet, glass.
> *Switzerland*: underbody coating, speedometer gears.
> *Belgium*: tires, tubes, seat pads, brakes, trim.
> *Austria*: tires, radiator and heater hoses.

Netherlands: tires, paints, hardware.
Norway: exhaust flanges, tires.
Canada: glass, radio.
Denmark: fan belt. (Dicken 1986, 304)

Sharp-eyed readers of this list have noticed that some items (for example, tires) came from more than one country, which underlines the point: the car assembled in Halewood and Saarlouis could hardly be more international. The basic fact, then, follows easily. From an entirely local production, the automobile has become the focus of flows from all over the world. It remains difficult, however, to sort out causes and effects: What importance should we attribute to sheer technology? To the internationalization of capital? To shifts in markets for automobiles? To the collaboration of governments with capitalists? What effects does this internationalization have? Does it displace jobs, make production more efficient, enrich Europeans, drive down the cost of transportation, clog highways, deplete oil supplies, raise the death rate from automobile accidents? Merely asking all these questions makes two things clear: (1) even for a dramatic change such as the internationalization of automobile production, the causal chains intertwine in great complexity; (2) without guiding questions, concepts, and models, we will get nowhere in sorting out cause and effect.

Is the quest hopeless? No, little by little we gain some grasp of causes and effects in social change. J.C. Caldwell's two articles in this volume on population change, for example, state cautious but firm conclusions about the conditions under which large populations undergo major declines in fertility and why. Because of a wide variety of socially imposed limits (deliberate contraception, abortion, ritual abstinence from sexual intercourse, periodic separation of men from women through war or hunting, temporary sterility due to nursing, and so on), no population produces children at the rate that would be physiologically possible, and agrarian populations vary considerably in fertility levels. (Fertility is simply the rate at which a population is producing children.) Still, populations living on subsistence agriculture in family units, who until recently constituted a majority of the world's population, uniformly produce far more children than populations depending on wages in market economies. Such agrarian populations have not swamped the world because their children have also died off at tremendous rates. But in recent years public health measures and improved nutrition have reduced the devastating death rates of poor agricultural populations. High fertility plus declining mortality mean increasing rates of population growth. As a result, what causes the demographic differences between subsistence agrarian economies and market nonagrarian economies, not to mention the movement from one to the other, nowadays attracts great attention from sociologists and policymakers alike. Caldwell summarizes forcefully what is at issue in current debates.

Although what makes the difference has stimulated bitter controversy since the time of T.R. Malthus, Caldwell makes a strong case that (1) whatever else is going on, where children become a major and visible economic burden on their parents, fertility declines; (2) under those conditions, cohabiting couples adopt deliberate limitations on fertility with the approval, often the active encouragment, of kin and friends; (3) mass education, wage-labor, and women's wage employment outside of their own households increase both the burdensomeness of children and willingness to limit fertility. The causal chain remains incomplete; we can still argue, for instance, about relations among women's employment opportunities and the availability of efficient contraceptives—which causes which, and how?—not to mention their relative importance. Almost certainly, as Caldwell suggests, their relations and importance vary from one population to another. But the historical and contemporary work of demographers has made the general path from high to low fertility fairly clear.

Knowing about valid chains of cause and effect helps a student of social change deal with real-life problems. First comes the problem of identifying the forces impinging on each of our individual experiences; to what extent, for example, does technology set the rhythms of our lives and determine our futures? Second, most of us want explanations of why the larger world, with all its problems and injustices, works the way it does; why do wars and massacres continue, for instance, when so few people seem to want them? Third, we face the challenge of coping with change—or even producing it—through intelligent identification of causes and effects; does it make any sense, we can reasonably ask, to seek greater equality by political means? What kinds of jobs can we reasonably expect to be available to us ten years from now? Finally, understanding of particular change processes helps us sort out valid from invalid moral reasoning, as in deciding whether to blame declining religious belief, and therefore unbelievers, for rising divorce rates, or judging whether Martin Luther King (as Alfred McClung Lee tells us in his chapter) was right to declare that "violence brings only temporary victories; violence, by creating many more social problems than it solves, never brings permanent peace."

In the first case, we can explore the relationship between religious belief and divorce by studying the processes that lead to particular divorces, by following the later experiences of newly married couples who vary in religiosity, or perhaps by comparing the histories of whole countries to see whether declines in religious commitment regularly precede increases in divorce rates. In the second case, we can try to construct balance sheets for violent revolutions: over the long run, do they cause more suffering than they alleviate?

Sorting out causes and effects in such complicated matters is never easy, but neither is making sound moral judgments; disciplined study of how social changes occur can help in both regards.

A careful reader of the book can, furthermore, turn its logic back against its own arguments. Most of the book's authors, for example, assume that large categorical inequalities in wealth, power, and privilege either cause serious injustice or constitute serious injustice in themselves. (I happen to agree with them, but that does not matter here.) Traditional arguments for capitalism, on the other hand, state two principles that contradict the book's viewpoint: first, that concentrations of capital facilitate productive investments, which in the long run make everyone better off; second, that unequal rewards motivate people to innovate and work harder, while equal rewards promote lethargy. Students of social change should be able to identify tests and make comparisons of major changes that will make those assertions more or less plausible. As of the late 1980s, the ratio of the income of the average firm's chief executive officer to that of the average production worker, for example, varied quite a bit among industrial countries:

Germany 6.5 to 1   *Italy* 7.6 to 1
France 8.9 to 1   *Canada* 9.5 to 1
Japan 11.6 to 1   *United Kingdom* 12.4 to 1
United States 17.5 to 1

In the United States, that is, the average CEO received almost 18 times as much income as the average production worker, while in neighboring Canada the multiple was 9.5, in Germany only 6.5. The gap in salaries between CEOs and ordinary workers was almost three times wider in the United States than in Germany. Does higher inequality, by this measure, correspond to higher productivity? Not very closely; Germany, a high-productivity country, has a much lower average ratio than the United Kingdom, which in the 1980s was having serious problems with productivity. Obviously we could use a deeper comparison, several points in time, and more information about categorical differences by gender, race, ethnicity, and age between chief executive officers and production workers. Thus the inquiries in this book lead to new inquiries.

I do not claim, then, that reading this book alone will give every student perfect understanding and peace of mind. But I do claim that it will help almost anyone to start sorting out the complexities of contemporary social changes. The study of social change can enrich your imagination. It can also enrich your life.

REFERENCES

Abrams, Ray
    1933   *Preachers Present Arms*. New York: Round Table Press.
ACT UP/San Francisco
    1988a   "Our Goals and Demands." Informational flyer.
    1988b   "The AIDS Treatment Advocacy Project." Proposal drafted for ACT NOW Conference. September.
    1989   "ACT UP PISD Caucus." Informational flyer.
Adler, E.
    1982   "A Cultural Theory of Change in International Political Economy: Science, Technology, and Computer Policies in Argentina and Brazil." Ph.D. dissertation, Department of Political Science, University of California, Berkeley.
Ahady, Anwar-ul-Haq
    1991   "Afghanistan: State Breakdown." Pp. 162–93 in *Revolutions of the Late Twentieth Century*, ed. Jack A. Goldstone, Ted Robert Gurr, and Farrokh Moshiri. Boulder, Colo.: Westview Press.
Ahluwalia, I.J.
    1985   *Industrial Growth in India: Stagnation Since the Mid-Sixties*. Delhi: Oxford University Press.
Allan, William
    1965   *The African Husbandman*. Edinburgh: Oliver and Boyd.
Almquist, Elizabeth M.
    1975   "Untangling the Effects of Race and Sex: The Disadvantaged Status of Black Women." *Social Science Quarterly* 56:129–42.
Altman, Dennis
    1986   *AIDS in the Mind of America*. Garden City, N.Y.: Doubleday/Anchor.
Amin, Samir
    1990   *Maldevelopment: Anatomy of a Global Future*. Tokyo: UNU.
Andersen, Margaret L.
    1983   *Thinking About Women: Sociological and Feminist Perspectives*. New York: Macmillan.
Andolsen, Barbara H.
    1986   *"Daughters of Jefferson, Daughters of Bootblacks": Racism and American Feminism*. Macon, Ga.: Mercer University Press.
Anglin, D.G.
    1985   "SADCC after Nkomati." *African Affairs* 84:335.
Aptheker, Bettina
    1982   *Woman's Legacy: Essays on Race, Sex and Class in American History*. Amherst: University of Massachusetts Press.
Aptheker, Herbert
    1963   *American Negro Slave Revolts*. 2nd ed. New York: International Publishers.

Ardrey, Robert
    1966   *The Territorial Imperative.* New York: Atheneum.
Aron, Raymond
    1957   *The Opium of the Intellectuals,* trans. Terence Kilmartin. London: Secker & Warburg.
    1967   *The Industrial Society: Three Essays on Ideology and Development.* London: Weidenfeld and Nicolson.
Aronowitz, Stanley
    1984   "When the New Left was New." In *The Sixties without Apology,* ed. Sayres, et al. Minneapolis: University of Minnesota Press.
Arriaga, Eduardo E., and Edgar M. Hoover
    1958   *Population Growth and Economic Development in Low-Income Countries: A Case-Study of India's Prospects.* Princeton: Princeton University Press.
Ascherson, Neal
    1991   "Old Wounds Exposed by Post-communist Thaw." *The Independent on Sunday,* October 6.
Ashwin, Sarah
    1991   "Development of Feminism in the Perestroika Era." *Society,* August 30.
Austin, D.
    1964   *Politics in Ghana, 1946–1960.* London: Oxford University Press.
Balakrishnan, T.R.
    1978   "Effects of Child Mortality on Subsequent Fertility of Women in Some Rural and Semi-Rural Areas of Certain Latin American Countries." *Population Studies* 32:135–45.
Balser, Diane
    1987   *Sisterhood and Solidarity: Feminism and Labor in Modern Times.* Boston: South End Press.
Barkat-e-Khuda
    1979   "Labor Utilization in a Village Economy in Bangladesh" Ph.D. thesis, Department of Demography, The Australian National University, Canberra.
Barnes, Frances
    1970   "The Biology of Pre-Neolithic Man." Pp. 1–18 in *The Impact of Civilization on the Biology of Man,* ed. S.V. Boyden. Canberra: Australian National University Press.
Barnes, H.E.
    1927   *The Genesis of the World War.* 2nd ed. New York: Knopf.
    1929   *The Twilight of Christianity.* New York: Vanguard.
    1938   *An Economic History of the Western World.* New York: Harcourt, Brace and World.
    1939   *Society in Transition.* New York: Prentice-Hall.
    1940   "The World War of 1914–1918," Pp. 39–99 in *War in the Twentieth Century,* ed. Willard Waller. New York: Dryden Press.
Barron, R.D., and G.M. Norris
    1976   "Sexual Divisions and the Dual Labour Market." Pp. 47–69 in *Dependence and Exploitation in Work and Marriage,* ed. Diana Leonard Barker and Sheila Allen. London: Longman.
Barry, Cynthia
    1992   "Women's Group, a First in Russia." *Christian Science Monitor,* May 19.
Bates, Marston
    1962   *The Prevalence of People.* New York: Scribner.

Beale, Frances
1979 "Double Jeopardy: To Be Black and Female." Pp. 90–100 in *The Black Woman: An Anthology*, ed. Toni Cade. New York: New American Library.
1981 "Slave of a Slave No More: Black Women in the Struggle." *Black Scholar* 12:16–24.

Beard, C.A.
1913 *An Economic Interpretation of the Constitution of the United States*. New York: Macmillan.
1932 *The Navy: Defense or Portent?* New York: Harper & Brothers.
1939 *Giddy Minds and Foreign Quarrels*. New York: Macmillan.

Becker, G.C.
1976 *The Economic Approach to Human Behavior*. Chicago: University of Chicago Press.

Behm, H., et al.
1976- "Mortalidad en los primeros anos de vida en los paises de la America Latina."
1977 Series A, No. 1024 a 1032. Santiago: CELADE.

Bellah, Robert N.
1968 "Meaning and Modernization." *Religious Studies* 4.

Bell, Colin, and Howard Newby
1976 "Husbands and Wives: The Dynamics of the Deferential Dialectic." Pp. 152–68 in *Dependence and Exploitation in Work and Marriage*, ed. Diana Leonard Baker and Sheila Allen. London: Longman.

Bell, Daniel
1960 *The End of Ideology: On the Exhaustion of Political Ideas in the Fifties*. Glencoe, Ill.: Free Press.

Bendix, Richard
1964 *Nation-Building and Citizenship: Studies of Our Changing Social Order*. New York: Wiley.

Benn, D.M.
1971 "Conceptual and Methodological Problems in the Study of Ideology." Graduate Research Seminar, Department of Government, University of Manchester.

Bennett, Evelyn Brooks
1978 "Nannie Burroughs and the Education of Black Woman." Pp. 97–108 in *The Afro-American Woman: Struggles and Images*, ed. Sharon Harley and Rosalyn Terborg-Penn. Port Washington, N.Y.: Kennikat Press.

Berch, Bettina
1982 *The Endless Day: The Political Economy of Women and Work*. New York: Harcourt Brace Jovanovich.

Berg, E.J.
1964 "Socialism and Economic Development in Tropical Africa." *Quarterly Journal of Economics* 78(4).

Berger, P.L., and Thomas Luckman
1966 *The Social Construction of Reality*. Garden City, N.Y.: Doubleday.

Berry, Mary Frances
1986 *Why ERA Failed: Politics, Women's Rights, and the Amending Process of the Constitution*. Bloomington: Indiana University Press.

Bhalla, P.
1980 "North-South: A Programme for Survival." Brandt Commissions Report. London: Pan Books.
1988a "Asean: A Study in Regional Cooperation," Manchester Discussion Papers in

Developmental Studies No. 8803. International Development Centre, University of Manchester.
1988b "Regional Cooperation: Can South Asia Meet the Challenge?" Manchester Discussion Papers in Developmental Studies No. 8804. International Development Centre, University of Manchester.
1990 "Regional Groupings in Asia: Should SAARC Follow the ASEAN model?" *Journal of International Development* 2(3):285–309. Brandt Commissions Report.

Bianchi, P., M. Carnoy, and M. Castells
1988 *Economic Modernization and Technology Transfer in China: An Exploratory Study*. School of Education Research Monograph. Stanford: Stanford University.

Black Studies/Women's Studies Faculty Development Project
1983 "Black Studies/Women's Studies: An Overdue Partnership." Women's Studies, University of Massachusetts-Amherst. Mimeograph.

Blau, P.M.
1964 *Exchange and Power in Social Life*. New York: Wiley.

Bluestone, B., and B. Harrison
1982 *The Deindustrialization of America*. New York: Basic Books.

Blumberg, Rae Lesser
1978 *Stratification: Socioeconomic and Sexual Inequality*. Dubuque, Iowa: William C. Brown.
1984 "A General Theory of Gender Stratification." Pp. 23–101 in *Sociological Theory*, ed. Randall Collins. San Francisco: Jossey-Bass.

Bodart, G.
1916 *Losses of Life in Modern Wars*. Oxford: Oxford University Press.

Bolton, C.D.
1972 "Alienation and Action: A Study of Peace Group Members." *American Journal of Sociology* 77:537–61.

Bornstein, L.
n.d. "Technological Policy and the Computer Industry in Brazil." University of California, Berkeley, Institute of International Studies.

Borrus, M.G.
n.d. *Chips of State: Microelectronics and American Autonomy*. University of California, Berkeley. Manuscript.

Boserup, Ester
1965 *The Conditions of Agricultural Growth: The Economics of Agrarian Change under Population Pressure*. Chicago: Aldine.

Bourgeois-Pichat, J.
1965 "The General Development of the Population of France since the Eighteenth Century." In *Population in History: Essays in Historical Demography*, ed. D.V. Glass and V.E.C. Eversley. London: Edward Arnold.

Braibanti, Ralph and Joseph J. Spengler, eds.
1961 *Tradition, Values, and Socio-Economic Development*. London: Cambridge University Press for the Duke University Commonwealth-Studies Center.

Brand, K.W.
1982 *Neue soziale Bewegungen, Entstehung, Funktion und Perspektive neuer Protestpotentiale, eine Zwischenbilanz* (in German). Opladen: Westdeutscher Verlag.

Brand, K.W., D. Busser, and D. Recht
1983 *Aufbruch in ein andere Gesellschaft, neue soziale Bewegungen in der Bundes-*

republik (in German). Frankfurt/New York: Campusverlag.
Brett, E.A.
 1988 "Adjustment and the State: The Problem of Administrative Reform." *IDS Bulletin* 19(4):4–11.
Briet, M., B. Klandermans, and F. Kroon
 1987 "How Women Become Involved in the Women's Movement of the Netherlands." In *The Women's Movements of the United States and Western Europe*, ed. M. Katzenstein and C. Mueller. Philadelphia: Temple University Press.
Brockington, Fraser
 1968 *World Health*. 2nd ed. Boston: Little, Brown.
Brooks, Harvey
 1965 "Scientific Concepts and Cultural Change." In *Science and Culture*, ed. G. Holton. Boston: Houghton Mifflin.
Bruland, T.
 1982 "Industrial Conflict as a Source of Technical Innovation: Three Cases." *Economy and Society* 11:91–121.
Bruyn, S.T. and Paula Rayman
 1979 "Introduction." Pp. 1–10 in *Nonviolent Action and Social Change*, ed. S.T. Bruyn and Paula Rayman. New York: Irvington.
Bryant, Barbara Everitt
 1977 "American Women: Today and Tomorrow." National Commission on the Observance of International Women's Year. Washington, D.C.: Government Printing Office.
Brzezinski, Z.K.
 1960 *The Soviet Bloc. Unity and Conflict*. Cambridge: Harvard University Press.
 1989-90 "Post-communist Nationalism." *Foreign Affairs* 68(5):1–25.
Burawoy, Michael
 1989 "The Extended Case Method." Manuscript.
Burnham, Linda
 1985 "Has Poverty Been Feminized in Black America?" *Black Scholar* 16:14–24.
Cahill, Spencer
 1987 "Reexamining the Acquisition of Sex Roles: A Symbolic Interactionist Approach." *Sex Roles* 9:1–15.
Cain, Mead T.
 1977 "The Economic Activities of Children in a Village in Bangladesh." *Population and Development Review* 3:201–27.
Caldwell, John C.
 1967a "Fertility Attitudes in Three Economically Contrasting Rural Regions of Ghana." *Economic Development and Cultural Change* 15:217–38.
 1967b "Population Change." In *A Study of Contemporary Ghana*, vol. 2, *Some Aspects of Social Structure*, ed. Walter Birmingham, I. Neustadt, and E.N. Omaboe. London: Allen and Unwin.
 1968 *Population Growth and Family Change in Africa: The New Urban Elite in Ghana*. Canberra: The Australian National University Press.
 1976a "Fertility and the Household Economy in Nigeria." *Journal of Comparative Family Studies* 7:193–253.
 1976b "Toward a Restatement of Demographic Transition Theory." *Population and Development Review* 1:321–66.
 1977 "The Economic Rationality of High Fertility: An Investigation Illustrated with Nigerian Survey Data." *Population Studies* 31:5–27.
 1978 "A Theory of Fertility: From High Plateau to Destabilization." *Population and*

	Development Review 4:553–77.
1979	"Education as a Factor in Mortality Decline: An Examination of Nigerian Data." *Population Studies* 33:395–413.
1980	"Mass Education as the Major Determinant of the Timing of Fertility Decline." *Population and Development Review* 6:225–55.
1982a	"The Failure of Theories of Social and Economic Change to Explain Demographic Change: Puzzles of Modernization or Westernization." Pp. 297–332 in *Research in Population Economics,* vol. 4., ed. Julian Simon. Greenwich, Conn.: JAI Press.
1982b	*Theory of Fertility Decline*. London: Academic Press.
1983a	"In Search of a Theory of Fertility Decline for India and Sri Lanka." In *Population Dynamics*, ed. K. Srinivasan. Bombay: International Institute of Population Studies.
1983b	Review of Paul R. Greenough, *Prosperity and Misery in Modern Bengal: The Famine of 1943–1944*. New York and Oxford: Oxford University Press in *Population and Development Review* 9:541–42.
1984	Review of State Family Planning Commission of China, *An Analysis of a National One-per-thousand Population Sample Survey of the Birth Rate*. Special Issue, *Population and Economics*. Beijing, in Chinese with a list of contents in English, in *Population and Development Review* 10.

Caldwell, J.C., and Pat Caldwell
1976	"Demographic and Contraceptive Innovators: A Study of Transitional African Society." *Journal of Biosocial Science* 8:347–65.
1978	"The Achieved Small Family: Early Fertility Transition in an African City." *Studies in Family Planning* 9:2–18.
1980	"Cause and Sequence in the Reduction of Post-Natal Abstinence in Ibadan City, Nigeria." In *African Traditional Birth Spacing,* ed. Hilary Page and R. Lesthaeghe. London: Academic Press.
1983	"Factors Other Than Nuptiality and Contraception Affecting Fertility." Paper presented at World Fertility Survey Seminar on Collection and Analysis of Data on Community and Institutional Factors, London, June 20–23.

Caldwell, J.C., and Peter McDonald
1981	"Influence of Maternal Education on Infant and Child Mortality: Levels and Causes." *International Population Conference, Manila, 1981, Solicited Papers*. Liege: International Union for the Scientific Study of Population, vol. 2, 79–96.

Caldwell, J.C., P.H. Reddy, and Pat Caldwell
1982	"The Causes of Demographic Change in Rural South India." *Population and Development Review* 8:689–727.
1983	"The Social Component of Mortality Decline: An Investigation in South India Employing Alternative Methodologies." *Population Studies* 37:185–205.

Caldwell, J.C., and L.T. Ruzicka
1977	"Australian Fertility Transition: Destabilizing a Quasi-Stable Situation." Working Papers in Demography, no.7. Department of Demography, The Australian National University, Canberra.
1978	"The Australian Fertility Transition: An Analysis." *Population and Development Review* 4:81–103.

Cammack, P., et al.
1988	*Third World Politics. A Comparative Introduction*. London: Macmillan.

Carnoy, M.
1985 "Foreign Debt and Latin American Domestic Policies." Paper delivered at the Institute of the Americas Conference, San Diego, Calif., November 21–22.
1987 "Diffusione Internationale Della Tecnologia e Politiche Nazionali." In *Crescita e competitivita: Strategie nazionalie di Spagne. Brasile e Corea.* Bologna, Nomisma Research Institute, Laboratorio di Politica Industriale. May.

Carson, Clayborne
1981 *In Struggle: SNCC and the Black Awakening of the 1960s.* Cambridge: Harvard University Press.

Castells, M.
1988a *Information Technology, Economic Restructuring, and Urban-Regional Development.* Oxford: Basil Blackwell.
1988b "The Developmental City-State in an Open World Economy: The Singapore Experience." BRIE Working Paper, University of California, Berkeley. Forthcoming.
n.d. *State Intervention and Economic Development in Hong Kong.*

Castells, M., L. Goh, and R.Y.W. Kwok
1988 *Economic Development and Housing Policy: A Comparative Analysis of Hong Kong, Singapore, and Shenzhen.* Institute of Urban and Regional Development Research Monograph Series. Berkeley: University of California.

Castells, M., and R. Skinner
n.d. "The Strategic Defence Initiative as Technologial Policy." University of California, Berkeley. Institute of International Studies.

Celac, Mariana
1991 "Romania." Document prepared for the UN regional seminar of the Impact of Economic and Political Reform on the Status of Women in Eastern Europe and the USSR.

Cerny, P.G.
1982 *Social Movements and Protest in France.* New York: St. Martin's Press.

Chabal, P.
1983 *Amilcar Cabral. Revolutionary Leadership and People's War.* Cambridge: Cambridge University Press.

Chafetz, Janet Saltzman
1984 *Sex and Advantage: A Comparative, Macro-Structural Theory of Sex Stratification.* Totowa, N.J.: Rowman and Allanheld.
1988a *Feminist Sociology: An Overview of Contemporary Theories.* Itasca, Ill.: F.E. Peacock.
1988b "The Gender Division of Labor and the Reproduction of Female Disadvantage: Toward an Integrated Theory. *Journal of Family Issues* 9 (July):108–31.

Chafetz, Janet Saltzman, and A. Gary Dworkin
1986 *Female Revolt: Women's Movements in World and Historical Perspective.* Totowa, N.J.: Rowman and Allanheld.
1987a "In the Face of Threat: Organized Antifeminism in Comparative Perspective." *Gender & Society* 1:33–60.
1987b "Action and Reaction: An Integrated, Comparative Perspective on Feminist and Antifeminist Movements." Paper presented at the annual meetings of the American Sociological Association, Chicago.
1989 "Action and Reaction: An Integrated, Comparative Perspective on Feminist and

Antifeminist Movements" (revised and expanded from the oral paper). In *Cross-National Research in Sociology*, ed. Mel Kohn. Beverly Hills, Calif.: Sage.

Chapman, S.H.
    1956   "The Spirit of Cultural Pluralism." Pp. 103–112 in H.M. Kallen et al., *Cultural Pluralism and the American Idea*. Philadelphia: University of Pennsylvania Press.

Charbonneau, Hubert, and Andre Larose, eds.
    1976   *The Great Mortalities: Methodological Studies of Demographic Crises in the Past*. Liege: International Union for the Scientific Study of Population, Ordina Press.

Cherlin, Andrew, and Pamela Waters
    1981   "Trends in United States Men's and Women's Sex-Role Attitudes: 1972–1978." *American Sociological Review* 46:453–60.

Chodorow, Nancy
    1978   *The Reproduction of Mothering: Psychoanalysis and the Sociology of Gender*. Berkeley: University of California Press.

Cimoli, M., G. Dosi, and L. Soete
    1986   "Innovation Diffusion, Institutional Differences, and Patterns of Trade: A North-South Model." Paper delivered at a Conference on Innovation Diffusion, Venice, March 17–22.

Chen, E.K.Y.
    1985   *The Newly Industrializing Countries in Asia: Growth Experience and Prospects*. Hong Kong: University of Hong Kong, Centre for Asian Studies.
    1987   "Industrial Development, Foreign Direct Investment and Economic Cooperation: A Study of the Electronics Industry in the Asian Pacific." Paper presented at the Seminar on Economic Cooperation through Foreign Investment among Asian and Pacific Countries, Bangkok, May 19–22.

Clapham, C.
    1970   "The Context of African Political Thought." *Journal of Modern African Studies* 8(1):8–13.

Clark, Colin
    1967   *Population Growth and Land Use*. London: Macmillan.

Clark, K.B.
    1965   *Dark Ghetto*. New York: Harper & Row.

Clecak, Peter
    1973   *Radical Paradoxes: Dilemmas of the American Left: 1945–1970*. New York: Harper & Row.

Cleland, W. Wendell
    1944   "A Population Plan for Egypt." *Milbank Memorial Fund Quarterly* 22:409–23.

Coale, A.J.
    1967   "Factors Associated with the Development of Low Fertility: An Historic Summary." *United Nations, World Population Conference, 1965*. New York: United Nations.

Coale, A.J., Noreen Goldman, and L.J. Cho
    1979   "Nuptiality and Fertility in the Republic of Korea." *IUSSP, Seminar on Nuptiality and Fertility,* Bruges.

Coale, Ansley J., and Paul Demeny
    1966   *Regional Model Life Tables and Stable Populations*. Princeton: Princeton University Press.

Cockburn, C.
1983 *Brother: Male Dominance and Technological Change.* London: Pluto Press.
1985 *Machinery of Dominance: Women, Men and Technical Know-How.* London: Pluto Press.
Cohen, Jean L.
1985 "Strategy or Identity: New Theoretical Paradigms and Contemporary Social Movements." *Social Research* 52:663–716.
Cohen, S., and J. Zysman
1987 *Manufacturing Matters.* New York: Basic Books.
Cohn, B.S.
1965 "Anthropological Notes on Disputes and Law in India." *American Anthropologist* 67:82–122.
Cole, L.A.
1975 *Blacks in Power: A Comparative Study of Black and White Elected Officials.* Princeton: Princeton University Press.
Combahee River Collective
1986 *Combahee River Collective Statement: Black Feminist Organizing in the Seventies and Eighties.* New York: Kitchen Table Press.
Conklin, Nancy, et al.
1983 "The Culture of Southern Black Women: Approaches and Materials." University of Alabama Archives of American Minority Cultures and Women's Studies Program, Project on the Culture of Southern Black Women.
Connell, J., and M. Lipton
1977 *Assessing Village Labor Situations in Developing Countries.* Delhi: Oxford University Press.
Connolly, Mike, and George Raine
1988 "50 AIDS Activists Arrested at FDA." *San Francisco Examiner*, October 11, A1.
Constantinople, Anne
1979 "Sex-Role Acquisition: In Search of the Elephant." *Sex Roles* 5:121–33.
Cook, P., and C. Kirkpatrick
1988 *Privatisation in Less Developed Countries.* Brighton: Wheatsheaf Books.
Cook, P., and M. Minogue
1990 "Waiting for Privatization in Developing Countries: Towards the Integration of Economic and Non-economic Explanations." *Public Administration and Development* 10:390–94.
Coombs, Lolagene, and Dorothy Fernandez
1978 "Husband-Wife Agreement about Reproductive Goals." *Demography* 15:57–73.
Coser, Rose Laub
1986 "Cognitive Structure and the Use of Social Space." *Sociological Forum* 1:1–26.
Costa Souza, P.R.
1985 "Los Impactos Economicos y Sociales de las Nuevas Tecnologias en Brasil." FUNDESCO Seminar on New Technologies in Industrialized Countries, Madrid.
Cox, Harvey
1968 "Tradition and the Nature," pts. 1 and 2. *Christianity and Crisis.* 27:218–20, 227–31.
Cramer, James C.
1980 "Fertility and Female Employment: Problems of Casual Direction." *American Sociological Review* 45:167–90.

Crimmins, Eileen M., et al.
    1981   "New Perspectives on Demographic Transition: A Theoretical and Empirical Analysis of an Indian State, 1951–1975." Pp. 30–35 in *Dynamics of Population and Family Welfare 1981*, ed. K. Srinivasan and S. Mukerji. Bombay: Himalaya Publishing House.

Crimp, Douglas, ed.
    1987a   *AIDS: Cultural Analysis/Cultural Criticism*. Cambridge: MIT Press.
    1987b.   "How to Have Promiscuity in an Epidemic." Pp. 237–71 in *AIDS: Cultural Analysis/Culural Criticism*, ed. Douglas Crimp. Cambridge: MIT Press.

Crompton, R., and G. Jones
    1984   *White-Collar Proletariat: Deskilling and Gender in Clerical Work*. London: Macmillan.

Crook, Nigel R.
    1978   "On Social Norms and Fertility Decline in India." *Journal of Development Studies* 14:S198–S210.

Curtis, Richard
    1986   "Household and Family in Theory on Inequality." *American Sociological Review* 51: 168–83.

Cutler, J.E.
    1985   *Lynch-Law*. New York: Longmans, Green.

Davie, M.R.
    1929   *Evolution of War*. New Haven: Yale University Press.
    1949   *Negroes in American Society*. New York: McGraw-Hill.

Davis, Angela
    1971   "Reflections of the Black Woman's Role in the Community of Slaves." *Black Scholar* 3:2–16.

Davis, K., and Judith Blake
    1956   "Social Structure and Fertility: An Analytical Framework." *Economic Development and Cultural Change* 4:211–35.

Davis, Kingsley
    1944   "Demographic Fact and Policy Decline in India." *Milbank Memorial Fund Quarterly* 22:256–78.
    1951   *The Population of India and Pakistan*. Princeton: Princeton University Press.
    1956   "The Population Specter: Rapidly Declining Death Rate in Densely Populated Countries—the Amazing Decline of Mortality in Underdeveloped Areas." *American Economic Review* 46:305–18.
    1963   "The Theory of Change and Response in Modern Demographic History." *Population Index* 29:345–66.

Davis, Natalie Zemon
    1977   "Ghosts, Kin, and Progeny: Some Features of Family Life in Early Modern France." *Daedalus* 106 (Spring).

de la Serre, Francoise
    1991   "The Integration Dilemma: Enlarging and/or Deepening the Community." *Futures* 23(7):739–46.

Deutsch, Karl W.
    1961   "Social Mobilization and Political Development." *American Political Science Review* 55:493–514.

Deyo, F.C., ed.
    1987   *The Political Economy of the New Asian Industrialism*. Ithaca, N.Y.: Cornell University Press.

Diamond, Norma
    1969   *K'un Shen: A Taiwan Village*. New York: Holt, Rinehart and Winston.
Dicken, Peter
    1986   *Global Shift: Industrial Change in a Turbulent World*. New York: Harper & Row.
Donovan, Josephine
    1985   *Feminist Theory: The Intellectual Traditions of American Feminism*. New York: Ungar.
Dosi, G., and L. Soete
    1983   "Technology Gap and Cost-Based Adjustment: Some Explorations on the Determinants of International Competitiveness." *Metroeconomica* 35:197–222.
Douglas, Ann
    1978   *The Feminization of American Culture*. New York: Avon.
Dow Jr., T.E.
    1967   "Attitudes toward Family Size and Family Planning in Nairobi." *Demography* 4:784–91.
Drucker, Peter F.
    1990   *The New Realities*. London: Mandarin.
Dublin, Louis I., Alfred J. Lotka, and Mortimer Spiegelman
    1949   *Length of Life*. New York: Ronald Press.
DuBois, E.C.
    1978   *Feminism and Suffrage*. Ithaca, N.Y.: Cornell University Press.
Dumont, Arsene
    1890   *Depopulation et civilisation. Etude demographique*. Paris: Lecrosnier et Babe.
Dwyer, D.H.
    1978   *Images and Self-Images: Male and Female in Morocco*. New York: Columbia University Press.
Eaton, Joseph W., and Albert J. Mayer
    1954   *Man's Capacity to Reproduce: The Demography of a Unique Population*. Glencoe, Ill.: Free Press.
Eberhardt, Eva
    1991   "Women of Hungary." *Women of Europe Supplement*. Published by the Commission of the EuropeanCommunities. January.
Eberhardt, Eva, and Jaqueline Heinen
    1992   "Central and Eastern Europe: Women Workers in the Transitional Phase." *Report for the International Union of Food and Allied Workers*. Switzerland. May.
The Economist
    1992   "May Poles." May 16.
Eder, Klaus
    1985   "The 'New Social Movements': Moral Crusades, Political Pressure Groups, or Social Movements?" *Social Research* 52:869–90.
Eichelberger, Brenda
    1977   "Voices on Black Feminism." *Quest: A Feminist Quarterly* 4:16–28.
Eigo, Jim, et al.
    1988   "FDA Action Handbook." Manuscript prepared for October 11 action at the Food and Drug Administration.
Eisenstadt, S.N.
    1966   *Modernization: Protest and Change*. Englewood Cliffs, N.J.: Prentice Hall.
Eisenstein, Zillah R., ed.
    1979   *Capitalist Patriarchy and the Case for Socialist Feminism*. New York: Monthly Review Press.

Elger, T.
    1987   "Review Article: Flexible Futures? New Technology and the Contemporary Transformation of Work." *Work, Employment and Society* 1:528–40.
Epstein, Steven
    1987   "Gay Politics, Ethnic Identity: The Limits of Social Constructionism." *Socialist Review* 17:9–54.
Epstien, Scarlett T.
    1962   *Economic Development and Social Change in South India*. Manchester: Manchester University Press.
Erlanger, Stephen
    1992   *New York Times,* March 9.
Ernst, Dieter, ed.
    1980   *The New International Division of Labor, Technology, and Underdevelopment: Consequences for the Third World*. Frankfurt: Campus Verlag.
    1985   "Automation and Worldwide Restructuring of the Electronics Industry: Strategic Implications for Developing Countries." *World Development* 13(3): March.
    1987   *Innovation, Industrial Structure and Global Competition: The Changing Economics of Internationalization*. Frankfurt: Campus Verlag.
The European
    1992   "Bringing Down the Other Iron Curtain." June 4–7.
European Parliament Women's Committee
    1992   Summer.
European Socialist Feminists
    1992   Speech, October.
Evans, P.B.
    1979   *Dependent Development: The Alliance of Multinational, State and Local Capital in Brazil*. Princeton: Princeton University Press.
    1985   "The Development of the 'Electronics Complex' and Government Policies in Brazil." *World Development* 13(3).
Evans, Sara
    1980   *Personal Politics: The Roots of Women's Liberation in the Civil Rights Movement and the New Left*. New York: Vintage.
Fallers, L.A., and Margaret C. Fallers
    1976   "Sex Roles in Edremit." Pp.243–60 in *Mediterranean Family Structures*, ed. J.G. Peristiany. Cambridge: Cambridge University Press.
Fanon, Frantz
    1966   *The Wretched of the Earth*. Trans. Constance Farrington. New York: Grove Press.
Fanzylber, F.
    1986   "Las Economias Neoindustriales en el Sistema Centro-Periferia de los Ochenta." *Pensamiento Iberoamericano*. No. 9.
Feldman, Arthur S., and Christopher Hurn
    1966   "The Experience of Modernization." *Sociometry* 29:378–95.
Fenner, Frank
    1970   "The Effects of Changing Social Organisation on the Infectious Diseases of Man." Pp. 48–68 in *The Impact of Civilization on the Biology of Man*, ed. S.V. Boyden. Canberra: Australian National University Press.
Ferguson, Kathy
    1980   *Self, Society, and Womankind*. Westport, Conn.: Greenwood Press.

Ferree, M.M.
 1987 "Equality and Autonomy: Feminist Politics in the United States and West Germany." In *The Women's Movements of the United States and Western Europe*, ed. M. Katzensteln and C. Mueller. Philadelphia: Temple University Press.
Ferree, M.M., and F.D. Miller
 1985 "Mobilization and Meaning: Toward an Integration of Social Psychological and Resource Perspectives on Social Movements." *Sociological Inquiry* 55:38–61.
Fireman, B., and W.A. Gamson
 1979 "Utilitarian Logic in the Resource Mobilization Perspective." Pp. 8–44 in *The Dynamics of Social Movements*, ed. M.N. Zald and J.D. McCarthy. Cambridge, MA: Winthrop Publishers.
Fishlow, A.
 1986 "Brief Comparative Reflections on Latin American Economic Performance and Policy." Paper prepared for WIDER/United Nations University Conference, August 12–14.
Fishman, Pamela
 1982 "Interaction: The Work Women Do." Pp.170–80 in *Women and Work: Problems and Perspectives*, ed. R. Kahn-Hut, A.K. Daniels, and R. Colvard. New York: Oxford University Press.
Foner, Philip S.
 1976 *Organized Labor and the Black Worker, 1619–1973*. New York: International Publishers.
 1980 *Women and the American Labor Movement: From World I to the Present*. New York: Free Press.
Ford, Dave
 1988 "'Midnight Caller' Script Provokes Gay Activists' Ire." *San Francisco Sentinel*, October 21, 4–5.
Fosdick, H.E.
 1931 Quoted by C.H. Ward, *Builders of Delusion*. Indianapolis: Bobbs-Merrill.
Foster, George M.
 1962 *Traditional Cultures and the Impact of Technological Change*. New York: Harper.
Foucault, Michel
 1979 *Discipline and Punish*. New York: Vintage Books.
Fox, Mary Frank, and Sharlene Hesse-Biber
 1984 *Women at Work*. Palo Alto, Calif.: Mayfield.
Frank, Andre Gunder
 1990 "Revolution in Eastern Europe." *Third World Quarterly* 12:36–52.
Freedman, R., et al.
 1963 "Fertility Trends in Taiwan: Tradition and Change." *Population Studies* 16 March.
Freeman, Jo
 1975 *Women: A Feminist Perspective*. Palo Alto, Calif.: Mayfield Press.
Fried, M., M. Harris, and R. Murphy
 1968 *War: The Anthropology of Armed Conflict and Aggression*. Garden City, N.Y.: Natural History Press.
Friedl, Ernestine
 1975 *Women and Men: An Anthropologist's View*. New York: Holt, Rinehart and Winston.

Friedland, E.A.
  1985 "The Southern African Development Coordination Conference and the West." *Journal of Modern African Studies* 23(2):290–93.
Friedlander, Dov
  1969 "Demographic Responses and Population Change." *Demography* 6:359–81.
  1977 "The Effect of Child Mortality on Fertility: Theoretical Framework of the Relationship." International Union for the Scientific Study of Population, *International Population Conference Mexico, 1977*, vol. 1. Liege.
Frobel, F., J. Henricks, and O. Kreye
  1980 *The New International Division of Labor*. Cambridge: Cambridge University Press.
Gale, Richard
  1986 "Social Movements and the State: The Environmental Movement, Countermovement, and Government Agencies." *Sociological Perspectives* 29:202–40.
Gallup Polls
  1979 London: Social Surveys Ltd.
Game, A., and P. Pringle
  1983 *Gender at Work*. Sydney: Allen & Unwin.
Gamson, W.A.
  1975 *The Strategy of Social Protest*. Homewood, Ill.: Dorsey.
Garrow, D.J.
  1981 *The FBI and Martin Luther King, Jr.* New York: Norton.
Geertz, C.
  1964 "Ideology as a Cultural System." Pp. 47–76 in *Ideology and Discontent*, ed. D.E. Apter. New York: Free Press.
Geertz, Clifford
  1963 *Agricultural Involution: The Process of Ecological Change in Indonesia*. Berkeley: University of California Press.
George, S.
  1988 *A Fate Worse than Debt*. London: Penguin.
  1989 "Third World Debt." *Community Programme Unit*. London: BBC-TV.
Gerlach, L.P., and V.C. Hine
  1970 *People, Power, Change: Movements of Social Transformation*. Indianapolis: Bobbs-Merrill.
Gibbon, Edward
  1845 *The History of the Decline and Fall of the Roman Empire*. Philadelphia: Porter and Coates.
Giddings, Paula
  1983 *When and Where I Enter: The Impact of Black Women on Race and Sex in America*. New York: Morrow.
Giele, Janet Zollinger
  1978 *Women and the Future: Changing Sex Roles in Modern America*. New York: Free Press.
Gilkes, Cheryl Townsend
  1979 "Black Women's Work as Deviance: Social Sources of Racial Antagonism within Contemporary Feminism." Working Paper No. 66. Wellesley, Mass: Wellesley College Center for Research on Women.
  1985 "'Together and in Harness'; Women's Traditions in the Sanctified Church." *Signs* 10:678–99.
Gille, H., and P.H. Pardoko
  1966 "A Family Life Study in East Java: Preliminary Findings." Pp. 514–17 in

Gilman, Sander
    Family Planning and Population Programs: A Review of World Developments, ed. B. Berelson. Chicago: University of Chicago Press.

Gilman, Sander
    1987   "AIDS and Syphilis: the Iconography of Disease." Pp. 87–107 in *AIDS: Cultural Analysis/Cultural Criticism*, ed. Douglas Crimp. Cambridge: MIT Press.

Gitlin, Todd
    1980   *The Whole World Is Watching: Mass Media in the Making of the New Left*. Berkeley: University of California Press.

Goffman, Erving
    1963   *Stigma: Notes on the Management of Spoiled Identity*. Englewood Cliffs, N.J.: Prentice Hall.
    1977   "The Arrangement between the Sexes." *Theory and Society* 4:301–31.

Gold, T.
    1986   *The State and the Economic Miracle in Taiwan*. Armonk, N.Y.: Sharpe.

Goldstein, Richard
    1987   "AIDS and Race." *Village Voice*, March 10, 23–30.

Goldstone, Jack A.
    1991   *Revolution and Rebellion in the Early Modern World*. Berkeley: University of California Press.

Goldstone, Jack A., Ted Robert Gurr, and Farrokh Moshiri, eds.
    1991   *Revolutions of the Late Twentieth Century*. Boulder, Colo.: Westview Press.

Gouldner, Alvin W.
    1976   *The Dialectic of Ideology and Technology: The Origins, Grammar and Future of Ideology*. London: Macmillan.

Grant, Jacqueline
    1982   "Black Women and the Church." Pp. 141–52 in *But Some of Us Are Brave: Black Women's Studies*, ed. Gloria T. Hull, et al. Old Westbury, N.Y.: Feminist Press.

Gray, R.H.
    1981   "Birth Intervals, Postpartum Sexual Abstinence and Child Health." Pp. 93-109 in *Child-Spacing in Tropical Africa: Traditions and Change*, ed. Hilary J. Page and Ron Lesthaeghe. London: Academic Press.

Green, Jesse
    1989   "Sticks and Stones." *7 Days*, February 8, 21–26.

Greenberg, Susan
    1992   "Greer Cheers on Scowling Shopgirls." *The Guardian,* August 8.

Greenough, Paul R.
    1982   *Prosperity and Misery in Modern Bengal: The Famine of 1943–1944*. New York and Oxford: Oxford University Press.

Grieco, J.M.
    1982   "Between Dependency and Autonomy: India's Experience with the International Computer Industry." *International Organization* 36(3).

Grimshaw, A.D., ed.
    1969   *Racial Violence in the United States*. Chicago: Aldine.

Groneman, Carol, and Mary Beth Norton, eds.
    1987   *"To Toil the Livelong Day": America's Women at Work, 1780–1980*. Ithaca, N.Y.: Cornell University Press.

Grover, Jan Zita
    1987   "AIDS: Keywords." Pp.17–39 in *Aids: Cultural Analysis/Cultural Criticism*, ed. Douglas Crimp. Cambridge: MIT Press.

Grynspan, Devora
    1991   "Nicaragua: A New Model for Popular Revolution in Latin America."

Pp. 88–115 in *Revolutions of the Late Twentieth Century*, eds. Jack A. Goldstone, Ted Robert Gurr, and Farrokh Moshiri. Boulder, Colo.: Westview Press.

Guile, B.R., and H. Brooks, eds.
1987 *Technology and Global Industry: Companies and Nations in the World Economy*. Washington D.C.: National Academy Press.

Gump, Janice
1975 "Comparative Analysis of Black Women's and White Women's Sex-Role Attitudes." *Journal of Consulting and Clinical Psychology* 43:858–63.

Gurney, J.N., and K.J. Tierney
1982 "Relative Deprivation and Social Movements: A Critical Look at Twenty Years of Theory and Research." *Sociology Quarterly* 23:33–47.

Gurr, Ted Robert, and Jack A. Goldstone
1991 "Comparisons and Policy Implications," in *Revolutions of the Late Twentieth Century*, eds. Jack A. Goldstone, Ted Robert Gurr, and Farrokh Moshiri. Boulder, Colo.: Westview Press.

Guttman, Herbert
1976 *The Black Family in Slavery and Freedom, 1750 to 1925*. New York: Random House.

Gwatkin, Davidson R.
1980 "Indications of Change in Developing Country Mortality Trends: The End of an Era?" *Population and Development Review* 6:615–44.

Habakkuk, H.J.
1971 *Population Growth and Economic Development Since 1750*. New York: Humanities Press.

Habermas, Jürgen
1981 "New Social Movements." *Telos* 49:33–37.

Hagen, Everett E.
1962 *On the Theory of Social Change: How Economic Growth Begins*. Homewood, Ill: Dorsey.

Hajnal, J.
1965 "European Marriage Patterns in Perspective." Pp. 101–143 in *Population in History*, eds. D.V. Glass and V.E.C. Eversley. London: Edward Arnold.

Halisi, C.R.D., Patrick O'Meara, and N. Brian Winchester
1991 "South Africa: Potential for Revolutionary Change." Pp. 272–97 in *Revolutions of the Late Twentieth Century*, ed. Jack Goldstone, Ted Robert Gurr, and Farrokh Moshiri. Boulder, Colo.: Westview Press.

Harff, Barbara
1991 "Cambodia: Revolution, Genocide, Intervention." Pp. 218–234 in *Revolutions of the Late Twentieth Century*, eds. Jack A. Goldstone, Ted Robert Gurr, and Farrokh Moshiri. Boulder, Colo.: Westview Press.

Harding, Vincent
1980 *The Other American Revolution*. Los Angeles and Atlanta: University of California, Los Angeles, Center for Afro-American Studies, and Institute of the Black World.

Harley, Sharon, and Rosalyn Terborg-Penn, eds.
1978 *The Afro-American Woman: Struggles and Images*. Port Washington, N.Y.: Kennikat Press.

Harris, Louis
1987 *Inside America*. New York: Vintage.

Harris, N.
1986 *The End of the Third World: Newly Industrializing Countries and the Decline of an Ideology.* London: Penguin Books.
Hartmann, Heidi
1984 "The Unhappy Marriage of Marxism and Feminism: Toward a More Progressive Union." Pp. 172–89 in *Feminist Frameworks: Alternative Theoretical Accounts of the Relations between Women and Men*, eds., Alison Jaggar and Paula Rothenberg. New York: McGraw-Hill.
Hartmann, H., R. Kraut, and L. Tilly, eds.
1986 & *Computer Chips and Paper Clips: Technology and Women's Employment.*
1987 Vols. 1 and 2. Washington D.C.: National Academy Press.
Hawthorn, G.
1978 "Introduction." *Journal of Development Studies* 14.
Hegel, G.W.F.
1858 *Lectures on the Philosophy of History.* Trans. J. Sibree from 3rd German ed. London: George Bell and Sons.
Heller, Joseph
1962 *Catch 22.* London: Jonathan Cape.
Hemmons, Willa Mae
1960 "The Women's Liberation Movement: Understanding Black Women's Attitudes." Pp. 285–99 in *The Black Woman*, ed. La Frances Rodgers-Rose. Beverly Hills, Calif.: Sage.
Henderson, J.
1986 "The New International Division of Labor and American Semiconductor Production in Southeast Asia." In *Multinational Companies and the Third World*, eds. D. Watts, C. Dixon, and D. Drakakis-Smith. London: Croom Helm.
1987 "The Internationalization of American Semiconductors Industry." Ph.D. dissertation, Department of Sociology, University of Warwick.
Henry, L.
1965 "The Population of France in the Eighteenth Century." In *Population in History: Essays in Historical Demography*, eds. D.V. Glass and V.E.C. Eversley. London: Edward Arnold.
Hentoff, Nat, ed.
1967 *The Essays of A.J. Muste.* New York: Simon and Schuster.
Herbst, J.
1990 *State Politics in Zimbabwe.* Berkeley: University of California Press.
Hershey, Marjorie
1978 "Racial Differences in Sex-Role Identities and Sex Stereotyping: Evidence Against a Common Assumption." *Social Science Quarterly* 58:583–96.
Herskovitz, M.J.
1939 "Ancestry of the American Negro." *Opportunity* 17:22,23,27–31.
Hertz, Rosanna
1986 *More Equal than Others: Women and Men in Dual Career Marriages.* Berkeley: University of California Press.
Hill, Allan G., Sara C. Randall, and Oriel Sullivan
1982 "The Mortality and Fertility of Farmers and Pastoralists in Central Mali, 1950–1981." Centre for Population Studies Research Paper 82-4. London: London School of Hygiene and Tropical Medicine.

Hill, Allan G., Sara C. Randall, and Marie-Louise van den Eerenbeemt
    1983   "Infant and Children Mortality in Rural Mali." Centre for Population Studies Research Paper 83-5. London: London School of Hygiene and Tropical Medicine.

Hill, Robert
    1972   *The Strengths of Black Families.* New York: Emerson Hall.

Hill, Robert A., ed.
    1983   *The Marcus Garvey and Universal Negro Improvement Association Papers.* Vols. I and II. Berkeley: University of California Press.

Hinojosa, R.A., and Morales, R.
    1986   "International Restructuring and Labor Market Interdependence: The Automobile Industry in Mexico and in the United States." Paper presented at the Conference on Labor Market Interdependence, Mexico D.F. El Colegio de Mexico, September 25–26.

Hinsley, F.H.
    1986   *Sovereignty.* Cambridge: Cambridge University Press.

Hofsten, Erland, and Hans Lundstrom
    1976   "Swedish Population History: Main Trends from 1750 to 1970." *Urval.* Stockholm: National Central Bureau of Statistics.

Hollingsworth, T.H.
    1965   "A Demographic Study of the British Ducal Families." In *Population in History: Essays in Historical Demography*, eds. D.V. Glass and V.E.C. Eversley. London: Edward Arnold.

Holloway Jr., R.E.
    1968   "Human Aggression," Pp. 29–48 in *War: The Anthropology of Armed Conflict and Aggression*, eds. Morton Fried, Marvin Harris, and Robert Murphy. Garden City, N.Y.: Natural History Press.

Homans, G.C.
    1974   *Social Behavior: Its Elementary Forms.* New York: Harcourt Brace Jovanovich.

hooks, bell
    1981   *Ain't I a Woman.* Boston: South End Press.
    1984   *Feminist Theory: From Margin to Center.* Boston: South End Press.

Horowitz, D.L.
    1985   *Ethnic Groups in Conflict.* Berkeley: University of California Press.

Huber, Joan A.
    1991   "A Theory of Family, Economy, and Gender." In *Gender, Family, and Economy: The Triple Overlap*, ed. Rae Lesser Blumberg. Newbury Park, Calif: Sage.

Huber, Joan, and Glenna Spitze
    1983   *Sex Stratification: Children, Housework, and Jobs.* New York: Academic Press.

Inglehart, R.
    1977   *The Silent Revolution: Changing Values and Political Styles among Western Publics.* Princeton: Princeton University Press.
    1979   "Value Priorities and Socio-Economic Change." Pp. 305–43 in *Political Action, Mass Participation in Five Western Democracies*, eds. S.H. Barnes and M. Kaase, et al. Beverly Hills, Calif: Sage.

Inkeles, Alex
    1969   "Making Men Modern: On the Causes and Consequences of Individual

Change in Six Developing Countries." *American Journal of Sociology* 75:208–25.
Inkeles, Alex, and David H. Smith
    1974   *Becoming Modern: Individual Change in Six Developing Countries.* London: Heinemann.
Janiewski, Dolores
    1987   "'Seeking a New Day and a New Way': Black Women and Unions in the Southern Tobacco Industry," in *"To Toil the Livelong Day": America's Women at Work, 1780–1980,* eds. Carol Groneman and Mary Beth Norton. Ithaca, N.Y.: Cornell University Press.
Jeffries, Vincent, and H. Edward Ransford
    1980   *Social Stratification: A Multiple Hierarchy Approach.* Boston: Allyn & Bacon.
Jenkins, J. Craig
    1981   "Sociopolitical Movements." Pp. 81–153 in *Handbook of Political Behavior,* ed. Samuel Long. New York: Plenum Press.
    1983   "Resource Mobilization Theory and the Study of Social Movements." *Annual Review of Sociology* 9:527–53.
Johnson, Chalmers
    1982   *MITI and the Japanese Miracle.* Stanford: Stanford University Press.
Johnson, Clarence
    1988   "Gays Attack KRON Building." *San Francisco Chronicle,* December 12. A2.
Johnson, Diane, and John F. Murray
    1988   "AIDS without End." *New York Review of Books,* August 18,57–63.
Johnston, A., and A. Sasson
    1986   *New Technologies and Development.* Paris: UNESCO.
Jones, Jacqueline
    1985   *Labor of Love, Labor of Sorrow: Black Women, Work and the Family, From Slavery to the Present.* New York: Basic Books.
Joseph, Gloria, and Jill Lewis
    1981   *Common Differences: Conflicts in Black and White Feminist Perspectives.* New York: Avon.
Journal of Negro Education
    1982   Special issue: "The Impact of Black Women in Education" 51.
Jowitt, K.
    1979   "Scientific Socialist Regimes in Africa." Pp. 133–73 in *Socialism in Sub-Saharan Africa: A New Assessment,* ed. C.G. Rosberg and T.M. Callaghy. Berkeley: Institute of International Studies, University of California.
Jurkat, Ernest
    1944   "Prospects for Population Growth in the Near East." *Milbank Memorial Fund Quarterly* 22:383–408.
Kamin, L.J.
    1974   *The Science and Politics of I.Q.* New York: Wiley.
Kanter, Rosabeth Moss
    1977   *Men and Women of the Corporation.* New York: Basic Books.
Kaplinsky, R.
    1982   *Comparative Advantage and Development.* London: Frances Pinter.
    1985   "Electronics-Based Automation Technologies and the Onset of the Systemofacture: Implications for Third World Industrialization." *World Development* 13 (March).
    1986   "Microelectronics and Employment Revisited: A Review." Report prepared

for the International Labor Office, World Employment Program, University of Sussex, Institute of Development Studies.

Kelly, H.H. and J.W. Thilbaut
    1978   *Interpersonal Relations: A Theory of Interdependence*. New York: Wiley.

Kessler, Richard J.
    1991   "The Philippines: The Making of a 'People Power' Revolution." Pp. 194–217 in *Revolutions of the Late Twentieth Century*, ed. Jack A. Goldstone, Ted Robert Gurr, and Farrokh Moshiri. Boulder, Colo.: Westview Press.

Kessler, Suzanne, and Wendy McKenna
    1978   *Gender: An Ethnomethodological Approach*. New York: Wiley.

Kiernan, V.G.
    1969   *The Lords of Human Kind*. Boston: Little, Brown.

Kinch, A.
    1962   "A Preliminary Report from the Sweden-Ceylon Family Planning Pilot Project." In *Research in Family Planning*, ed. C.V. Kiser. Princeton: Princeton University Press.

King, Mae C.
    1973   "The Politics of Sexual Stereotypes." *Black Scholar* 4:12–22.

King Jr., Martin Luther
    1963   *Strength to Love*. New York: Harper & Row.

Kiray, Mubeccel
    1976   "The New Role of Mothers: Changing Intrafamilial Relationships in a Small Town in Turkey." Pp. 261–71 in *Mediterranean Family Structures*, ed. J.G. Peristiany. Cambridge: Cambridge University Press.

Kirk, D.
    1966   "Factors Affecting Moslem Natality." In *Family Planning and Population Programs: A Review of World Developments*, ed. B. Berelson. Chicago: Chicago University Press.

Kirkman, Cecelia
    1986   "Militarism and Violence Against Women: The War at Home." *Nonviolent Activist* 3:3–6.

Kirkpatrick, C., and F. Nixson
    n.d.   "The North-South Debate: Reflections on the Brandt Commission Report." Manchester Discussion Papers in Development Studies No. 8104. International Development Centre, University of Manchester, 12–18.

Kiser, Clyde V.
    1944   "The Demographic Position of Egypt." *Milbank Memorial Fund Quarterly* 22:383–408.

Kitschelt, Herbert
    1985   "New Social Movements in West Germany and the United States." *Political Power and Social Theory* 5:273–324.

Kitsuse, John I.
    1980   "Coming Out All Over: Deviants and the Politics of Social Problems." *Social Problems* 28:1–13.

Klandermans, P.G.
    1984   "Mobilization and Participation in a Social Movement: Social Psychological Expansions of Resource Mobilization Theory." *American Sociological Review* 49:583-600.
    1985   "Unionists, Feminists and Pacifists, Comparisons of Organization, Mobilization and Participation." Paper presented at the American Sociological Association meetings.

Klandermans, P.G., and D. Oegema
　1984　　"Mobilizing for Peace: The 1983 Peace Demonstration in the Hague." Paper prepared for the 79th annual meeting of the American Sociological Association.

Klandermans, P.G., and S. Tarrow
　1985　　Participation in "New" Social Movements in Western Europe and the United States, a research planning group. European Studies Newsletter, Center for European Studies, Columbia University.

Knodel, J.E.
　1974　　*The Decline of Fertility in Germany, 1871–1939*. Princeton: Princeton University Press.
　1982　　"Child Mortality and Reproductive Behaviour in German Villages in the Past: A Micro-Level Analysis of the Replacement Effect." *Population Studies* 36:177–200.

Kollias, Karen
　1981　　"Class Realities: Create a New Power Base." Pp. 125–38 in *Building Feminist Theory: Essays from Quest*, ed. Quest staff. New York: Longman.

Konvitz, M.R.
　1983　　*A Century of Civil Rights*. Westport, Conn.: Greenwood Press.

Kramarae, C., ed.
　1988　　*Technology and Women's Voices*. New York: Routledge & Kegan Paul.

Kriesi, Hanspeter
　1985　　*Bewegungen in der schweizer Politik, Fallstudien zu politischen Mobilisierungs prozessen in der Schweiz* (in German). Frankfurt: Campusverlag.
　1989　　"New Social Movements and the New Class in the Netherlands." *American Journal of Sociology* 94: 1078–1116.

Kuratowska, Zofia
　1991　　"Present Situation of Women in Poland." UN paper prepared for the UN regional seminar of the Impact of Economic and Political Reform on the Status of Women in Eastern Europe and the USSR.

Lado, Maria
　1991　　"Women in the Transition to a Market Economy: The Case of Hungary." UN paper.

Lapidus, Gail Wershofsky
　1978　　*Women in Soviet Society: Equality, Development and Social Change*. Berkeley: University of California Press.

LaRue, Linda
　1976　　"The Black Movement and Women's Liberation." In *Female Psychology: The Emerging Self*, ed. Sue Cox. Chicago: Science Research Assoc.

Lazonick, W.
　1979　　"Industrial Relations and Technical Change: The Case of the Self-Acting Mule." *Cambridge Journal of Economics* 3:231–62.

Lee, A. McClung
　1966　　*Multivalent Man*. New York: George Braziller.
　1968　　"Race Riots are Symptoms." Pp. vii–xxviii in *Race Riot*, ed. A. McClung and N.D. Humphrey. 2nd ed. New York: Octagon Books.

Lefort, Claude
　1986　　"Outline of the Genesis of Ideology in Modern Societies." In *The Political Forms of Modern Society: Bureaucracy, Democracy, Totalitarianism*, ed. John B. Thompson. Cambridge: Polity Press.

Leibenstein, Harvey
　1957　　*Economic Backwardness and Economic Growth*. New York: Wiley.

Lemert, Edwin
    1967   *Human Deviance, Social Problems, and Social Control*. Englewood Cliffs, N.J.: Prentice Hall.

Lerner, Daniel
    1958   *The Passing of Traditional Society: Modernizing the Middle East*. New York: Free Press, Macmillan.

Lerner, Gerda
    1973   *Black Women in White America: A Documentary History*. New York: Vintage.

Lesthaeghe, R.J.
    1977   *The Decline of Belgian Fertility, 1800–1970*. Princeton: Princeton University Press.

LeVan, H. John
    1991   "Vietnam: Revolution of Postcolonial Consolidation." Pp. 52–87 in *Revolutions of the Late Twentieth Century*, ed. Jack A. Goldstone, Ted Robert Gurr, and Farrokh Moshiri. Boulder, Colo.: Westview Press.

Lever, Janet
    1976   "Sex Differences in the Games Children Play." *Social Problems* 23–24:478–87.

Levy, Marion J.
    1966   *Modernization and the Structure of Society: A Setting for International Affairs*. Princeton: Princeton University Press.

Lewis, Arthur W.
    1955   *The Theory of Economic Growth*. London: Allen and Unwin.

Lewis, Diane K.
    1977   "A Response to Inequality: Black Women, Racism, and Sexism." *Signs* 3:339–61.

Lewis, Elizabeth Clark
    1987   "'This Work Had a End': African-American Domestic Workers in Washington, D.C., 1910–1940." In *"To Toil the Livelong Day": America's Women at Work, 1780–1980*, ed. Carol Groneman and Mary Beth Norton. Ithaca, N.Y.: Cornell University Press.

Lewis, O.
    1960   *Tepostlan: Village in Mexico*. New York: Holt, Rinehart and Winston.

Lewis, Paul
    1994   "Agency Hopes for Fall in Number of Refugees." *New York Times*, March 20, 21.

Lewis, W.A.
    1953   *Report on Industrialisation and the Gold Coast*. Accra: Government Printing Department, para. 253.

Lieberson, Stanley, and A.R. Silverman
    1965   "The Precipitants and Underlying Conditions of Race Riots." *American Sociological Review* 30:887–98.

Liff, S.
    1986   "Technical Change and Occupational Sex-typing." In *Gender and the Labor Process*, ed. D. Knights and H. Willmott. Alsershot: Gower.
    1988   "Gender, Office Work and Technological Change." Working Paper 176. Management Studies, Loughborough University of Technology.

Lim, Hyun-Chin
    1985   *Dependent Development in Korea, 1963–1979*. Seoul: Seoul University Press.

Linebarger, Charles
    1989   "All the Rage: Angry AIDS Activists Pump Up the Volume on Deaf Policy-

Makers." *San Francisco Sentinel*, February 23,3–5.
Lipman-Blumen, Jean
   1976   "Toward a Homosocial Theory of Sex Roles: An Explanation of Sex Segregation of Social Institutions." *Signs* 1:15–31.
Lipset, Seymour
   1959   *Political Man: The Social Bases of Politics*. London: Heinemann.
Loewenberg, Bert James, and Ruth Bogin, eds.
   1976   *Black Women in Nineteenth-Century American Life*. University Park: Pennsylvania State University Press.
Lofchie, M.F.
   1985   "The Roots of Economic Crisis in Tanzania." *Current History* (April): 159–63, 184.
   1986   "Kenya's Agricultural Success." *Current History* (May): 221–25, 231.
Loo, H.v.d., E. Snel, and B.v. Steenbergen
   1984   *Een Eenkend perspectief? Nieuwe sociale bewegingen en culturele veranderingen*. Amersfoort: De Horstink.
Lorde, Audre
   1982   "Scratching the Surface: Some Notes on Barriers to Women and Loving." *Black Scholar* 13:20–24.
   1984   *Sister Outsider: Essays and Speeches*. Trumansberg, N.Y.: Crossing Press.
Lorenz, Konrad
   1966   *On Aggression*. New York: Harcourt, Brace and World.
Lubeck, P.M.
   1985   "Authoritarianism, Crisis, and the Urban Industrial Sector: Nigeria's Role in the International Division of Labor." Paper delivered at the ISA Conference on the Urban and Regional Impact of the International Division of Labor. Hong Kong, August.
Lugones, Maria C., and Elizabeth V. Spelman
   1983   "Have We Got a Theory for You! Feminist Theory, Cultural Imperialism and the Demand for 'The Woman's Voice.'" *Women's Studies International Forum* 6:573–81.
Macfarlane, A.
   1978   *The Origins of English Individualism: The Family, Property and Social Transition*. Oxford: Basil Blackwell.
MacKenzie, D.
   1984   "Marx and the Machine." *Technology and Culture* 25:473–502.
MacKenzie, D., and J. Wajcman, eds.
   1985   *The Social Shaping of Technology*. Milton Keynes: Open University Press.
Malthus, Thomas Robert
   1970   *An Essay on the Principle of Population* and *A Summary View of the Principle of Population*. Edited with an introduction by Anthony Flew. Harmondsworth: Penguin.
Mandelbaum, D.G.
   1970   *Society in India: Continuity and Change*. Berkeley: University of California Press.
Mannheim, Karl
   1936   *Ideology and Utopia*. Trans. and ed. Louis Wirth and E. Shils. New York: Harcourt, Brace and World.
Marable, Manning
   1983   *How Capitalism Underdeveloped Black America*. Boston: South End Press.
   1985   *Black American Politics*. London: Verso.

Marchand, John F.
    1943   "Tribal Epidemics in the Yukon." *A.M.A. Journal* 123.
Marriott, McKim, ed.
    1955   *Village India: Studies in the Little Community*. Chicago: University of Chicago Press.
Marshall, Alfred
    1898   *Principles of Economics*. 4th ed. London: Macmillan.
Martin, David
    1978   *A General Theory of Secularization*. Oxford: Basil Blackwell.
Martin, M. Kay, and Barbara Voorhies
    1975   *Female of the Species*. New York: Columbia University Press.
Marx, K.
    1975   "Preface to a Contribution to the Critique of Political Economy." In *Karl Marx, Early Writings*. Harmondsworth: Penguin.
    1976   *Capital: A Critique of Political Economy*. Harmondsworth: Penguin. First published 1867.
Marx, Karl, and Frederick Engels
    1968   "Manifesto of the Communist Party." In *Selected Works in One Volume*. London: Lawrence & Wishart.
    1973   "Manifesto of the Communist Party." Pp. 67–98 in *Karl Marx, Political Writings*, ed. David Fernback. Harmondsworth: Penguin.
Mauldin, W.P., and B. Berelson
    1977   "Cross-Cultural Review of the Effectiveness of Family Planning Programs." Working paper, New York: Centre for Policy Studies, The Population Council.
McAdam, D.
    1982   *Political Process and the Development of Black Insurgency 1930–1970*. Chicago: University of Chicago Press.
    1983   "Tactical Innovation and the Pace of Insurgency." *American Sociological Review* 48:735–54.
    1984   "Structural versus Attitudinal Factors in Movement Recruitment." Paper presented at the American Sociological Association meetings.
McCarthy, J.D.
    1983   "Social Infrastructure Deficits and New Technologies: Mobilizing Unstructured Sentiment Pools." Working paper. Department of Sociology and Center for the Study of Youth Development, Catholic University.
McCarthy, John, and Mayer Zald
    1977   "Resource Mobilization and Social Movements: A Partial Theory." *American Journal of Sociology* 82:1212–40.
McKeown, Thomas
    1976   *The Modern Rise of Population*. London: Edward Arnold.
McKeown, T., R.G. Brown, and R.G. Record
    1972   "An Interpretation of the Modern Rise of Population in Europe. *Population Studies* 26:345–82.
McNeill, W.H.
    1963   *The Rise of the West: A History of the Human Community*. Chicago: University of Chicago Press.
    1976   *Plagues and Peoples*. New York: Doubleday Anchor.
Mead, Margaret
    1968   "Alternatives to War." Pp. 215–48 in *War: The Anthropology of Armed Conflict and Aggression,* ed. Morton Fried, Marvin Harris, and Robert Murphy.

Garden City, N.Y.: Natural History Press.

Meillassoux, C.
1972 "From Reproduction to Production: A Marxist Approach to Economic Anthropology." *Economy and Society* 1.

Melucci, A.
1980 "The New Social Movements: A Theoretical Approach." *Social Science Information* 19:199–226.
1982 *L'invenzione del presente movimenti identita, bisogni collectivi* (in Italian). Bologna: Mulino.
1984 "An End to Social Movements? Introductory Paper to the Sessions on New Movements and Change In Organizational Forms." *Social Science Information* 24:819–35.

Michel, Patrick
1991 *Politics and Religion in Eastern Europe.* Trans. Alan Braley. Cambridge: Polity Press.

Mies, Maria
1986 *Patriarchy and Accumulation on a World Scale.* London: Zed Books.

Miljan, T.,ed.
1987 *The Political Economy of North-South Relations.* Peterborough, Canada: Broadview Press.

Mill, John Stuart
1951 *Utilitarianism, Liberty and Representative Government.* New York: Dutton.

Miller, Swasti
1991 "A Comparative Analysis of Women's Industrial Participation during the Transition from Centrally Planned to Market Economies in East Central Europe." Document prepared for the UN regional seminar of the Impact of Economic and Political Reform on the Status of Women in Eastern Europe and the USSR.

Millis, Walter
1935 *Road to War.* Boston: Houghton Mifflin.

Mills, C. Wright
1959 *The Sociological Imagination.* New York: Oxford University Press.

Mitchell, B.R.
1962 *Abstract of British Historical Statistics.* Cambridge: Cambridge University Press.

Mitchell, R.C.
1979 "National Environmental Lobbies and the Apparent Illogic of Collective Action." In *Collective Decision Making Application from Public Choice Theory,* ed. C.S. Russell. Baltimore: John Hopkins University Press.
1984 "Moving Backward vs. Moving Forward: Motivation for Collective Action." Paper presented at the 79th annual meeting of the American Sociological Association.

Moghadam, Valentine M.
1995 "Gender and Revolutionary Transformation: Iran 1979 and East Central Europe 1989," *Gender and Society* 9:328–58.

Mols, Roger
1954-56 *Introduction a la demographie historique des villes d'Europe du Xllle au XVllle siecle.* 3 vols. Louvaine: Gembloux, J. Duculot.

Moore, Wilbert E.
1944 "Agricultural Population and Rural Economy in Eastern and Southern

Europe." *Milbank Memorial Fund Quarterly* 22:279–99.

Morgan, M.
1973 *Total Woman*. New Jersey: Revell.

Morgan, Thomas
1988 "AIDS Protesters Temper Their Tactics as a Way to Reach the Mainstream." *New York Times*, July 22,A12.

Morris, Aldon
1981 "Black Southern Students' Sit-In Movements: An Analysis of Internal Organization." *American Sociological Review* 46:744–67.
1984 *The Origins of the Civil Rights Movement: Black Communities Organizing for Change*. New York: Free Press.

Morsa, J.
1966 "The Tunisia Survey: A Preliminary Analysis." In *Family Planning and Population Programs: A Review of World Developments*, ed. B. Berelson. Chicago: University of Chicago Press.

Morse, A.D.
1968 *While Six Million Died: A Chronicle of American Apathy*. New York: Random House.

Mortimore, M.J.
1968 "Population Distribution, Settlement and Soils in Kano Province, Northern Nigeria 1931-62." In *The Population of Tropical Africa*, ed. John C. Caldwell and Chukuka Okonjo. London: Longman.

Moses, W.J.
1982 *Black Messiahs and Uncle Toms*. University Park: Pennsylvania State University Press.

Mosher, William D.
1980 "Demographic Responses and Demographic Transitions: A Case Study of Sweden." *Demography* 17:395–412.

Moshiri, Farrokh
1991 "Iran: Islamic Revolution Against Westernization." Pp. 116–35 in *Revolutions of the Late Twentieth Century*, ed. Jack A. Goldstone, Ted Robert Gurr, and Farrokh Moshiri. Boulder, Colo.: Westview Press.

Mosley, W. Henry
1983 "Will Primary Health Care Reduce Infant and Child Mortality? A Critique of Some Current Strategies, with Special Reference to Africa and Asia." Paper presented at the International Union for the Scientific Study of Population Seminar on Social Policy, Health Policy and Mortality Prospects, Paris, February 28 to March 4.

Mottl, Tahi L.
1980 "The Analysis of Countermovements." *Social Problems* 27:620–35.

Mulholland, Lisa A.
1992 "After the Revolution: The Changing Position of Educated Women in Prague." Research Paper, Institute of Social Studies, The Hague, Netherlands.

Muller, E.N.
1980 "The Psychology of Political Protest and Violence." Pp. 69–100 in *Handbook of Political Conflict Theory and Research*, ed. T.R. Gurr. New York: Free Press.

Murray, Pauli
1975 "The Liberation of Black Women." Pp. 351–63 in *Women: A Feminist Perspective*, ed. Jo Freeman. Palo Alto, Calif.: Mayfield.

Myrdal, Gunnar, et al.
- 1944 *An American Dilemma.* New York: Harper & Row.

Nelson, Richard R.
- 1956 "A Theory of the Low-Level Equilibrium Trap in Underdeveloped Economies." *American Economic Review* 46 (December).

Newman, Dorothy, et al.
- 1978 *Protest, Politics and Prosperity: Black Americans and White Institutions, 1940–75.* New York: Pantheon.

Newsweek
- 1988a "Acting Up to Fight AIDS." June 6,42.
- 1988b "The Drug-Approval Dilemma." November 14,63.

Ng, C.Y., R. Hirono, and N. Akrasanee
- 1987 *Industrial Restructuring in ASEAN and Japan: An Overview.* Singapore: Institute of Southeast Asian Studies.

Nielsen, Joyce
- 1978 *Sex in Society: Perspectives on Stratification.* Belmont, Calif.: Wadsworth.

Nimkoff, M.F.
- 1965 *Comparative Family Systems.* Boston: Houghton Mifflin.

Noble, D.
- 1984 *Forces of Production: A Social History of Industrial Automation.* New York: Knopf.

Notestein, Frank W.
- 1944 "Problems of Policy in Relation to Areas of Heavy Population Pressure." *Milbank Memorial Fund Quarterly* 22:424–44.
- 1945 "Population: the Long View." In *Food for the World*, ed. Theodore W. Schultz. Chicago: University of Chicago Press.
- 1953 "Economics of Population Change." In *8th International Conference of Agricultural Economists, 1952.* London: Oxford University Press.

Nyerere, J.K.
- 1981 "Address on the Occasion of Mainland Tanzania's Twentieth Anniversary of Independence." Dar es Salaam, December. Mimeograph.

O'Donnell, C.
- 1984 *The Basis of the Bargain: Gender, Schooling and Jobs.* Sydney: Allen and Unwin.

O'Kelley, Charlotte G.
- 1980 *Women and Men in Society.* New York: Van Nostrand.

Oberschall, Anthony
- 1973 *Social Conflict and Social Movements.* Englewood Cliffs, N.J.: Prentice Hall.
- 1980 "Loosely Structured Collective Conflict: A Theory and an Application." Pp. 45–68 in *Research in Social Movements, Conflict and Change*, vol. 3, ed. L. Kriesberg. Greenwich, Conn.: JAI Press.

Oettinger, Anthony G., et al.
- 1967-68 *Fourth Annual Report of the Harvard University Program on Technology and Society.* Boston: Harvard University.

Offe, Claus
- 1985 "The New Social Movements: Challenging the Boundaries of Institutional Politics." *Social Research* 52:817–68.

Ohmae, K.
- 1985 *Triad Power: The Coming Shape of Global Competition.* New York: Free Press.

Okie, Susan
    1988   "AIDS Coalition Targets FDA for Demonstration." *Washington Post*, October 11,A4.
Okruhlicova, Anna
    1991   "The Influence of Social and Economical Changes in the Czech and Slovak Federal Republic on the Position of Women." UN paper.
Oliver, P., G. Marwell, and R. Teixeira
    1985   "A Theory of the Critical Mass: Interdependence, Group Heterogeneity, and the Production of Collective Action." *American Journal of Sociology* 91:522–56.
Olson, M.
    1965   *The Logic of Collective Action. Public Goods and the Theory of Groups*. Cambridge: Harvard University Press.
Omi, Michael, and Howard Winant
    1986   *Racial Formation in the United States*. New York: Routledge and Kegan Paul.
Opp, K.D.
    1985   "Konventionelle und unkonventionelle politische Partizipation." *Zeitschrift fur Soziologie* 14:282–96.
Oppenheimer, Valerie K.
    1970   *The Female Labor Force in the United States*. Berkeley: University of California Press.
Ortner, Sherry B.
    1974   "Is Female to Male as Nature Is to Culture?" In *Woman, Culture and Society*, ed. Michelle Z. Rosaldo and Louise Lamphere. Stanford, Calif.: Stanford University Press.
Orubuloye, I.O., and J.C. Caldwell
    1975   "The Impact of Public Health Service on Mortality Differentials in a Rural Area of Nigeria." *Population Studies* 29:259–72.
Orum, A.M.
    1974   "On Participation in Political Protest Movements." *Journal of Applied Behavioral Science* 10:181–207.
Palmer, Phyllis Marynick
    1983   "White Women/Black Women: The Dualism of Female Identity and Experiences in the United States." *Feminist Studies* 91.
Parker, Seymour, and Hilda Parker
    1979   "The Myth of Male Superiority: Rise and Demise." *American Anthropologist* 81:289-309.
Penrose, E.F.
    1934   *Population Theories and Their Application*. Food Research Institute, Stanford, Calif.: Stanford University Press.
Perkins, Linda
    1983   "The Impact of the 'Cult of True Womanhood' on the Education of Black Women." *Journal of Social Issues* 39:17–28.
Perrow, C.
    1979   'The Sixties Observed." In *The Dynamics of Social Movements, Resource Mobilization, Social Control, and Tactics*, ed. M.N. Zald and J.D. McCarthy. Cambridge, Mass.: Winthrop.
Piekalkiewicz, Jaroslaw
    1991   "Poland: Nonviolent Revolution in a Socialist State." Pp. 136–61 in *Revolutions of the Late Twentieth Century*, ed. Jack A. Goldstone, Ted Robert Gurr, and Farrokh Moshiri. Boulder, Colo.: Westview Press.

Pinard, M.
  1983   "From Deprivation to Mobilization." Paper presented at the annual meetings of the American Sociological Association, Detroit.
Piven, F.F., and R.A. Cloward
  1979   *Poor People's Movements: Why They Succeed, How They Fail.* New York: Vintage Books.
Plamenatz, J.
  1970   *Ideology.* London: Pall Mall.
  1972   "Ideology." Paper presented to the Political Theory Seminar, Department of Government, University of Manchester.
Plummer, Ken
  1988   "Organizing AIDS." In *Social Aspects of AIDS*, ed. Peter Aggleton and Hilary Homans. London: Palmer Press.
Poizner, Susan
  1992   "The Sorrows of Mother Russia." *The Guardian*, June 30.
Polenberg, Richard
  1980   *One Nation Divisible; Class, Race, and Ethnicity in the United States Since 1938.* New York: Penguin.
Pollert, A.
  1988   "Dismantling Flexibility." *Capital and Class* 34:42–75.
Powell, Linda C.
  1983   "Black Macho and Black Feminism." Pp. 283–92 in *Home Girls: A Black Feminist Anthology*, ed. Barbara Smith. New York: Kitchen Table Press.
Preston, Samuel H.
  1975a   "The Changing Relation Between Mortality and Level of Economic Development." *Population Studies* 29:231–48.
  1975b   *Proceedings of the Seminar on Infant Mortality in Relation to the Level of Fertility.* Paris: Committee for International Cooperation of National Research on Demography (CICRED).
  1978a   *The Effects of Infant and Child Mortality on Fertility.* New York: Academic Press.
  1978b   "Mortality, Morbidity, and Development." *Population Bulletin of the United Nations Economic Commission for Western Asia*, No. 15 (December), 63–75.
  1978c   "Research Developments Needed for Improvements in Policy Formulation on Mortality." Mimeograph.
  1980   "Causes and Consequences of Mortality Declines in Less Developed Countries during the Twentieth Century." In *Population and Change in Developing Countries*, ed. Richard A. Easterlin. Chicago: University of Chicago Press.
Preston, Samuel, and Etienne van de Walle
  1978   "Urban French Mortality in the Nineteenth Century." *Population Studies* 32 (July).
Purcell, K.
  1988   "Women and the Telephone: the Gendering of a Communications Technology." In *Technology and Women's Voices*, ed. C. Kramarae. New York: Routledge & Kegan Paul.
Rada, J.F.
  1982   *The Impact of Microelectronics.* Geneva: International Labor Office.
  1985   "Information Technology and the Third World." In *The Information Technology Revolution*, ed. Tom Forester. Oxford: Basil Blackwell.
Ranade, Ramabai Mrs.
  1938   *Himself: The Autobiography of a Hindi Lady.* Trans. and adapted by Katherine

van Akin Gates from a book written in the Marathi language. New York: Longmans, Green.

Ransford, Edward, and Jon Miller
    1983   "Race, Sex, and Feminist Outlook." *American Sociological Review* 48:46–59.

Raper, A.F.
    1933   *The Tragedy of Lynching.* Chapel Hill: University of North Carolina Press.

Razzell, P.E.
    1974   "An Interpretation of the Modern Rise of Population in Europe: A Critique." *Population Studies* 28:5–17.

Redfield, R.
    1955   *The Little Community.* Chicago: University of Chicago Press.

Redfield, R., and M. Singer
    1954   "The Cultural Role of Cities." *Economic Development and Cultural Change* 3:53–73.

RFE/RL
    1992   Daily Report, no.41. February 28.

Riggs, F.W.
    1964   *Administration in Developing Countries: The Theory of Prismatic Society.* Boston: Houghton Mifflin.

Robinson, Jo Ann Gibson
    1987   *The Montgomery Bus Boycott and the Women Who Started It.* Knoxville: University of Tennessee Press.

Roper Public Opinion Research Center
    1972   "The 1972 Virginia Slims American Women's Opinion Poll." Williamstown, Mass.: Roper Public Opinion Research Center.
    1974   "The 1974 Virginia Slims American Women's Opinion Poll." Williamstown, Mass.: Roper Public Opinion Research Center.

Rose, Steven
    1986   "Stalking the Criminal Chromosome." *The Nation* 242: 732–38.

Rosenberg, N., and C. Frischtak, eds.
    1985   *International Technology Transfer: Concepts, Measures and Comparisons.* New York: Praeger.

Rostow, W.W.
    1960   *The Stages of Economic Growth: A Non-Communist Manifesto.* Cambridge: Cambridge University Press.

Rucht, D.
    1984   "Comparative New Social Movements, Organizations and Strategies in a Cross-Sectional and a Cross-National View." Paper presented at the Conference of European Group of Organizational Sociologists on New Social Movements.
    1985   "Soziologie als Theorie sozialer Bewegungen, ein Auseinandersetzung mit dem Ansatz von Alain Touraine." Unpublished paper, in German. Munchen.

Rudwick, E.M.
    1964   *Race Riot at East St. Louis: July 2, 1917.* Carbondale: Southern Illinois University Press.

Rupp, Leila J., and Verta Taylor
    1987   *Survival in the Doldrums: The American Women's Rights Movement, 1945 to the 1960s.* New York: Oxford University Press.

Rushing, F.W., and Carole Ganz Brown, eds.
    1986   *National Policies for Developing High Technology Industries.* Boulder, Colo.: Westview Press.

Rutstein, Shea Oscar
1974 "The Influence of Child Mortality on Fertility in Taiwan." *Studies in Family Planning* 5:182–88.
Ruzicka, L.T., and J.C. Caldwell
1977 *The End of Demographic Transition in Australia*. Australian Family Formation Monograph No.5. Department of Demography, The Australian National University, Canberra.
Ruzicka, L.T., and H. Hansluwaka
1982 "A Review of Evidence on Levels, Trends and Differentials Since the 1950s." Pp. 83–155 in *Mortality in South and East Asia: A Review of Changing Trends and Patterns 1950–1975*, ed. L. Ruzicka and A. Lopez. Geneva: World Health Organization.
Sacks, Karen
1974 "Engels Revisited: Women, the Organization of Production and Private Property." Pp. 207–22 in *Woman, Culture, and Society*, ed. Michelle Zimbalist Rosaldo and Louise Lamphere. Stanford, Calif. Stanford University Press.
Safilios-Rothschild, Constantina
1979 "Women as Change Agents: Toward a Conflict Theoretical Model of Sex Role Change." Pp. 287–301 in *Sex Roles and Social Policy*, ed. Jean Lipman-Blumen and Jessie Bernard. Beverly Hills, Calif.: Sage.
Sagafi-Hejad, T., R.W. Moxon, and Howard V. Perlmutter, eds.
1981 *Controlling International Technology Transfer: Issues, Perspectives, and Policy Implications*. New York: Pergamon Press.
Sage: A Scholarly Journal on Black Women
1984 The Premier Issue.
Sahlins, Marshall
1976 *The Use and Abuse of Biology*. Ann Arbor: University of Michigan Press.
Sanday, Peggy
1974 "Female Status in the Public Domain." Pp. 189–206 in *Women, Culture, and Society*, ed. Michelle Zimbalist Rosaldo and Louise Lamphere. Stanford, Calif.: Stanford University Press.
1981 *Female Power and Male Dominance: On the Origins of Sexual Inequality*. Cambridge: Cambridge University Press.
Sandburg, Carl
1969 *The Chicago Race Riots: July, 1919*. New York: Harcourt, Brace and World.
Sanderson, S.W.
1987 "Automated Manufacturing and Offshore Assembly in Mexico." In *The United States and Mexico: Face to Face with New Technology*, ed. C.L. Thorup. New Brunswick, N.J.: Transaction Books.
Sardar, Ziauddin
1981 "Last Chance for World Unity." *New Scientist* 91:334–41.
Sargent, Lydia, ed.
1981 *Women and Revolution: A Discussion of the Unhappy Marriage of Marxism and Feminism*. Boston: South End Press.
Sassen, S.
1993 *The Global City*. Princeton: Princeton University Press.
Sauvy, A.
1969 *General Theory of Population*. London: Weidenfeld & Nicolson.
Scarritt, James R.
1991 "Zimbabwe: Revolutionary Violence Resulting in Reform." Pp. 235–71 in *Revolutions of the Late Twentieth Century*, ed. Jack A. Goldstone, Ted Robert

Gurr, and Farrokh Moshiri. Boulder, Colo.: Westview Press.

Schein, E.H.
1966 "The Passion for Unanimity." In *Reader in Public Opinion and Communication*, ed. Bernard Berelson and Morris Janowitz. 2nd ed. New York: Free Press.

Schneider, Beth
1988 "Political Generations and the Contemporary Women's Movement." *Sociological Inquiry* 58:4–21.

Schultz, Theodore W., ed.
1974 *Economics of the Family: Marriage, Children and Human Capital. A Conference Report of the National Bureau of Economic Research*. Chicago: University of Chicago Press for the National Bureau of Economic Research.

Schur, Edwin
1984 *Labeling Women Deviant: Gender, Stigma, and Social Control*. New York: Random House.

Schwartz, M.
1976 *Radical Protest and Social Structure*. New York: Academy Press.

Scott, A.J., and D.P. Angel
1986 *The U.S. Semiconductor Industry: A Locational Analysis*. UCLA Department of Geography Research. Monograph, Los Angeles.

Scott, Patricia Bell
1982 "Selective Bibliography on Black Feminism." In *But Some of Us Are Brave: Black Women's Studies*, ed. Gloria T. Hull et al. Old Westbury, N.Y.: Feminist Press.

Sellers, W.O.
1985 "Technology and the Future of the Financial Services Industry." *Technology and Society* 7:1–9

Shah, Nasra M.
1986 "Foreign Workers in Kuwait: Implications for the Kuwaiti Labor Force," *International Migration Review* 20: 815-34.

Shaiken, H., and S. Herzenberg
1987 "Automation and Global Production: Automobile Engine Production in Mexico, the United States and Canada." University of California, Centre for U.S.–Mexican Studies, San Diego.

Shanin, T.
1972 *The Awkward Class*. Oxford: Oxford University Press.

Shils, Edward
1958 "Ideology and Civility: On the Politics of the Intellectual," *Sewanee Review* 66:450–80.
1968 "The Concept and Function of Ideology," a reprint from the *International Encyclopedia of the Social Sciences*. New York: Macmillan and Free Press, 7:69.

Shilts, Randy
1988 *And the Band Played On: Politics, People and the AIDS Epidemic*. New York: Penguin Books.

Simon, D.F.
1986 "China's Computer Strategy." *China Business Review*. November–December.

Simons, Margaret A.
1979 "Racism and Feminism: A Schism in the Sisterhood." *Feminist Studies* 5:384–401.

Singer, J.D., et al.
1979 *Explaining War*. Beverly Hills, Calif.: Sage.

Sivard, Ruth Leger
1993 World Military and Social Expenditures, 1993. Leesburg, Va: WMSE Publications.
Skocpol, Theda
1979 States and Social Revolutions: A Comparative Historical Analysis of France, Russia, and China. Cambridge: Cambridge University Press.
1985 "Bringing the State Back In: Strategies of Analysis in Current Research." Pp. 3–37 in Bringing the State Back In, ed. Peter B. Evans et al. Cambridge: Cambridge University Press.
Small, Melvin, and J.D. Singer
1980 "Patterns in International Warfare, 1816–1965." In The War System: An Interdisciplinary Approach, ed. R.A. Falk and S.S. Kim. Boulder, Colo.: Westview Press.
Smelser, Neil
1963 Theory of Collective Behavior. New York: Free Press.
Smith, Barbara
1979 "Notes for Yet Another Paper on Black Feminism, or Will the Real Enemy Please Stand Up." Conditions 5:123–27.
1983 Home Girls: A Black Feminist Anthology. New York: Kitchen Table Press.
Soete, L.
1985 "International Diffusion of Technology, Industrial Development and Technological Leapfrogging." World Development 13 (March).
Sontag, Susan
1988 "AIDS and Its Metaphors." New York Review of Books, October 27,89–99.
Sorokin, P.A.
1928 Contemporary Sociological Theories. New York: Harper & Brothers.
1937-41 Social and Cultural Dynamics. Vols. 1-4. New York: Harper & Brothers.
1947 Society, Culture, and Personality. New York: Harper & Brothers.
Sovani, N.V., and Kumudini Dandekar
1955 Fertility Survey of Nasik, Kolaba and Satara (North) Districts. Poona: Gokhale Institute of Politics and Economics.
Squire, William
1877 "On Measles in Fiji." Transactions of the Epidemiological Society of London 4:72–74.
Stack, Carol
1974 All Our Kin: Strategies for Survival in a Black Community. New York: Harper & Row.
Staples, Robert
1973 The Black Woman in America. Chicago: Nelson Hall.
1979 "The Myth of Black Macho: A Response to Angry Black Feminists." Black Scholar 10:24–32.
Stark, Rodney, and William S. Bainbridge
1985 The Future of Religion: Secularization, Revival and Cult Formation. Berkeley: University of California Press.
State Family Planning Commission of China
1983 An Analysis of a National One-per-thousand Population Sample Survey of the Birth Rate, Special Issue, Population and Economics (in Chinese with a list of contents in English). Beijing.
Steinem, Gloria
1984 "Exclusive Louis Harris Survey: How Women Live, Vote and Think." Ms. Magazine 13:51–54.

Stern, Paul C., Oran R. Young, and Daniel Druckman, eds.
    1992   *Global Environmental Change: Understanding the Human Dimensions*. Washington, D.C.: National Academy Press.
Stewart, Abigail J., M. Brinton Lykes, and Marianne LaFrance
    1982   "Educated Women's Career Patterns: Separating Social and Developmental Changes." *Journal of Social Issues* 38:97–117.
Stewart, F., and J. James, eds.
    1982   *The Economics of New Technology in Developing Countries*. Boulder, Colo.: Westview Press.
Stimpson, Catharine
    1971   "Thy Neighbor's Wife, Thy Neighbor's Servants: Women's Liberation and Black Civil Rights." Pp. 452–79 in *Woman in Sexist Society: Studies in Power and Powerlessness*, ed. Vivian Gornick and Barbara Moran. New York: Basic.
Stolnitz, George J.
    1955   "A Century of International Mortality Trends: 1." *Population Studies* 9:24–55.
Stone, L.
    1977   *The Family, Sex and Marriage in England, 1500–1800*. London: Weidenfeld & Nicolson.
Stone, Pauline Terrelonge
    1975   "Feminist Consciousness and Black Women." In *Women: A Feminist Perspective*, ed. Jo Freeman. Palo Alto, Calif.: Mayfield.
Stowsky, J.
    1987   "The Weakest Link: Semiconductor Production Equipment, Linkages, and the Limits to International Trade." BRIE Working Paper. University of California, Berkeley. August.
Strangeland, Charles Emil
    1904   *Pre-Malthusian Doctrines of Population: A Study in the History of Economic Theory*. New York: Columbia University Press.
Sumner, W.G., and A.G. Keller
    1927   *The Science of Society*. Vol. 1. New Haven: Yale University Press.
Sumner, W.G., A.G. Keller, and M.R. Davie
    1927   *The Science of Society*. Vol. 4. New Haven: Yale University Press.
Szeftel, M.
    1971   "Zambian Humanism: Ideology and Conflict—Problems of Theory and Method." Graduate Research Seminar, Department of Government, University of Manchester.
Taeuber, Irene B., and Edwin G. Beal
    1944   "The Dynamics of Population in Japan." *Milbank Memorial Fund Quarterly* 22:222–55.
Tan, A.H.H., and B. Kapur, eds.
    1986   *Pacific Growth and Financial Interdependence*. London: Allen and Unwin.
Tarrow, S.
    1983   "Resource Mobilization and Cycles of Protest: Theoretical Reflections and Comparative Illustrations." Paper presented at the annual meeting of the American Sociological Association.
Taylor, Carl E., Jeanne S. Newman, and Narindar U. Kelly
    1976   "The Child Survival Hypothesis." *Population Studies* 30:263–78.
Taylor, Telford
    1969   *Sword and Swastika*. Chicago: Quadrangle.
Teitelbaum, Joshua, and Joseph Kostiner
    1991   "The West Bank and Gaza: The PLO and the Intifada." Pp. 298–323 in *Revo-*

lutions of the Late Twentieth Century, ed. Jack A. Goldstone, Ted Robert Gurr, and Farrokh Moshiri. Boulder, Colo.: Westview Press.

Thadani, Veena N.
1978   "The Logic of Sentiment: The Family and Social Change." *Population and Development Review* 4: 457–99.

Thilbaut, J.W., and H.H. Kelly
1959   *The Social Psychology of Groups*. New York: Wiley.

Thomas, K.
1971   *Religion and the Decline of Magic: Studies in Popular Beliefs in Sixteenth and Seventeenth Century England*. London: Weidenfeld and Nicolson.

Thompson, P.
1983   *The Nature of Work: An Introduction to Debates on the Labor Process*. London: Macmillan.

Thompson, Warren S.
1953   *Population Problems*. 4th ed. New York: McGraw-Hill.

Thurow, L., and L. Tyson
1987   "The Economic Black Hole." *Foreign Policy*. (June).

Tilly, Charles
1978   *From Mobilization to Revolution*. New York: McGraw-Hill.
1981   *As Society Meets History*. New York: Academic Press.

Tilly, C., L. Tilly, and R. Tilly
1975   *The Rebellious Century: 1830–1930*. Cambridge: Harvard University Press.

Tilly, Louise, and Joan Scott
1978   *Women, Work and Family*. New York: Holt, Rinehart and Winston.

The Times
1991   "Abortion Law in Hungary." December 18.

Toffler, Alvin
1990   *Powershift*. New York: Bantam Books.

Touraine, A.
1981   *The Voice and the Eye: An Analysis of Social Movements*. Cambridge: Cambridge University Press.
1985   "An Introduction to the Study of Social Movements." *Social Research* 52:749–87.
1988   *La Parole et le Sang Politique et Societe en Amerique Latine*. Paris: Editions Odile Jacob.

Tovias, A.
1985   "The Impact of the North-South Transfer of Technology on Developing Countries' Exports." Paper delivered at the World Congress of the International Political Science Association, Paris, July 15–20.

Treichler, Paula A.
1987   "Aids, Homophobia, and Biomedical Discourse: An Epidemic of Signification." Pp. 31–70 in *AIDS: Cultural Analysis/Cultural Criticism*, ed. Douglas Crimp. Cambridge: MIT Press.

Trevelyan, G.M.
1946   *English Social History: A Survey of Six Centuries, Chaucer to Queen Victoria*. 3rd ed. London: Longmans, Green.

Trey, J.E.
1972   "Women in the War Economy World War II." *Review of Radical Political Economics* 4:1–17.

Trimberger, Ellen Kay
1978   *Revolution from Above*. New Brunswick, N.J.: Transaction Books.

Tuller, David
  1988 "AIDS Protesters Showing Signs of Movement's New Militancy." *San Francisco Chronicle*, October 27, A4.
Turner, R.H.
  1969 "The Theme of Contemporary Social Movements." *British Journal of Sociology* 10:390–405.
United Nations
  1961 *The Mysore Population Study*. New York: The United Nations Department of Economic and Social Affairs.
  1962 *Population Bulletin of the United Nations*, No. 6.
  1980 *Demographic Indicators of Countries: Estimates and Projections as Assessed in 1980*.
  1991 "Women's Role in Making Reform Work." Division for the Advancement of Women, Vienna, April 8.
  1993 *Human Development Report, 1993*. New York: Oxford University Press.
  1993 *World Economic Survey, 1993*. New York: United Nations.
UNCTAD
  1984 *New and Emerging Technologies: Some Economic, Commercial and Developmental Aspects*. Report by the UNCTAD Secretariat, Trade and Development Board. TD/B/C/6/120. Geneva, August.
  1993 *International Monetary and Financial Issues for the 1990's*. New York: United Nations.
  1993 *World Investment Report 1993. Transnational Corporations and Integrated International Production*. New York: United Nations.
UNIDO
  1984 *International Industrial Restructuring and the International Division of Labor in the Automobile Industry*. Vienna.
U.S. Congress, Office of Technology Assessment
  1985 *Technology Transfer to China*. Washington, D.C.: Government Printing Office.
U.S. News and World Report
  1989 "The Artists' Diagnosis." March 27, 62–70.
Vallin, Jacques
  1968 "La mortalite dans les pays du tiers monde: evolution et perspectives." *Population* 23:845–68.
van de Walle, E.
  1974 *The Female Population of France in the Nineteenth Century*. Princeton: Princeton University Press.
Van der Loo, H., et al.
  1984 *Een Wenkend Perspectief?: Nieuwe Sociale Bewegingen en Culturele eranderingen*. Amersoort: De Horstink.
van Noort, Wim
  1984 *De effecten van de kraakbeweging op de besluitvorming van gemeentelijke overheden*. COMT, ultg. 15 (in Dutch). Leiden: Rijksuniversiteit.
Vogel, Lise
  1983 *Marxism and the Oppression of Women: Toward a Unitary Theory*. New Brunswick, N.J.: Rutgers University Press.
Wajcman, J., and B. Probert
  1988 "New Technology Outwork." In *Technology and the Labor Process: Australian Case Studies*, ed. E. Willis. Sydney: Allen and Unwin.

Wallace, Michelle
    1979   *Black Macho and the Myth of the Superwoman.* New York: Dial.
Waller, Willard
    1940   "War in the Twentieth Century." Pp. 3–35 in *War in the Twentieth Century,* ed. Willard Waller. New York: Dryden Press.
Watney, Simon
    1987   *Policing Desire: Pornography, AIDS and the Media.* Minneapolis: University of Minnesota Press.
Waxman, Chaim I., ed.
    1968   *The End of Ideology Debate.* New York: Funk & Wagnalls.
Weber, Max
    1930   *The Protestant Ethic and the Spirit of Capitalism.* Trans. Talcott Parsons. London: Unwin.
Webster, J.
    1989   *Office Automation: The Labor Process and Women's Work in Britain.* Hemel Hempstead: Wheatsheaf.
West, Candace, and Don Zimmerman
    1987   "Doing Gender." *Gender & Society* 1:125–51.
West, Cornell
    1984   "The Paradox of the Afro-American Rebellion." In *The Sixties Without Apology,* ed. Sohnya Sayres et al. Minneapolis: University of Minnesota Press.
White, A.D.
    1896   *A History of the Warfare of Science with Theology in Christendom.* New York: D. Appleton.
White, Deborah Gray
    1985   *Are'n't I a Woman: Female Slaves in the Plantation South.* New York: Norton.
Wilkinson, B.
    1983   *The Shopfloor Politics of New Technology.* London: Heinemann.
Willcox, Walter
    1916   "The Nature and Significance of the Changes in the Birth and Death Rates in Recent Years." *American Statistical Association* (March): 1–15.
Williams, Anne D.
    1977   "Measuring the Effect of Child Mortality on Fertility: A Methodological Note." *Demography* 14:581–90.
Williams, Robin
    1967   "Individual and Group Values." *Annals of the American Academy of Political and Social Science* 37.
Willie, Charles
    1976   *A New Look at Black Families.* New York: General Hall.
Willis, Ellen
    1984   "Radical Feminism and Feminist Radicalism." In *The Sixties without Apology,* ed. Sohnya Sayres et al. Minneapolis: University of Minnesota Press.
Wilson, J.Q.
    1973   *Political Organizations.* New York: Basic Books.
Wilson, K., and M. Orum.
    1976   "Mobilizing People for Collective Political Action." *Journal of Political and Military Sociology* 4:187–202.
Winslow, C.E.A.
    1951   *The Cost of Sickness and the Price of Health.* Geneva: World Health Organization.

Wionczek, M.S.
 1981 "On the Viability of Policy for Science and Technology in Mexico." *Latin American Research Review* 16(7).
Wiser, W., and Charlotte Wiser
 1971 *Behind Mud Walls, 1930–1960; with a sequel: The Village in 1970.* Berkeley: University of California Press.
Witherspoon, W.R.
 1985 *Martin Luther King, Jr., to the Mountaintop.* New York: Doubleday.
Wolf, Margery
 1972 *Women and the Family in Rural Taiwan.* Stanford, Calif.: Stanford University Press.
Woods, F.A., and A. Baltzly
 1915 *Is War Diminishing?* Boston: Houghton Mifflin.
Woodsworth, N.
 1990 "Namibia: Trial Run for Regional Peace." *Financial Times* (London) 22,17.
 1990 "Namibia 3: A Difficult Path to Economic Independence." *Financial Times* (London) 22,19.
World Bank
 1985 *China: Long Term Development—Issues and Options.* Washington, D.C..
 1988 *World Development Report.* Washington D.C.: World Bank.
 1993 *World Development Report, 1993.* New York: Oxford University Press.
 1993 *World Development Report, 1993. Investing in Health.* Oxford: Oxford University Press.
Wray, J.D.
 1971 "Population Pressure on Families." *Reports on Population/Family Planning*, no.9 (August).
Wright, Quincy
 1965 *A Study of War.* 2nd ed. Chicago: University of Chicago Press.
Wrigley, E.A.
 1969 *Population and History.* New York: McGraw-Hill.
Wrigley, E.A., and R.S. Schofield
 1981 *The Population History of England: A Reconstruction.* London: Edward Arnold.
Xian, Shen
 1983 "Analysis of Women with One Child." In State Family Planning Commission of China, *An Analysis of a National One-per-thousand Population Sample Survey of the Birth Rate*, Special Issue, *Population and Economics* (in Chinese with a list of contents in English). Beijing.
Young, C.
 1982 *Ideology and Development in Africa.* New Haven: Yale University Press.
Young, R.A.
 1991 "States and Markets in Africa." In *States and Markets*, ed. M. Moran and M. Wright. London: Macmillan.
Youngson, A.J.
 1982 *Hong Kong Economic Growth and Policy.* Hong Kong: Oxford University Press.
Zald, Mayer, and John McCarthy
 1979 *The Dynamics of Social Movements.* Cambridge, Mass.: Winthrop.

AUTHOR INDEX

Abrams, Ray, 37
Ahady, Anwar-ul-Haq, 283
Akrasanee, N., 126
Allan, William, 151
Almaguer, Tomas, 257
Altman, Dennis, 245, 257
Amin, Samir, 307
Andolsen, Barbara, 43
Angel, D.P., 127
Anglin, D.G., 68
Anthony, Susan B., 43
Aptheker, Herbert, 31
Ardrey, Robert, 34
Aron, Raymond, 20
Aronowitz, Stanley, 50
Arriaga, Eduardo, 157
Ascherson, Neal, 307
Ashwin, Sarah, 294
Austin, Dennis, 57

Baker, Ella, 39
Balakrishnan, T.R., 163
Balser, Diane, 54, 55
Barnes, Frances, 152
Barnes, Harry Elmer, 33, 37
Barnett, Ida Wells, 39
Barron, R.D., 112
Barry, Cynthia, 294
Bates, Marston, 150
Beal, Edwin G., 156
Beale, Frances, 39–40, 54
Beard, Charles A., 33, 37
Becker, G.C., 222
Behm, H., 158
Bell, Colin, 111
Bell, Daniel, 20
Bellah, Robert N., 154
Bendix, Richard, 144
Benn, D.M., 57
Bennett, Evelyn Brooks, 40

Berch, Bettina, 54, 116
Berelson, B., 184
Berg, E.J., 58
Berger, P.L., 26,
Berry, Mary Frances, 44
Bethune, Mary McCleod, 40
Bhalla, P., 68
Bianchi, P., 139
Blake, Judith, 183
Blau, P.M., 222
Bluestone, B., 133
Blumberg, Rae Lesser, 110, 113, 115
Bogin, Ruth, 54
Balton, C.D., 232
Borrus, M.G., 127
Boserup, Ester, 151
Bourgeois-Pichat, J., 174
Braibanti, Ralph, 143
Brand, K.W., 226, 227
Brass, W., 187
Braverman, Harry, 101
Brett, E.A., 65
Brew, Jo, 9–10, 13, 314
Briet, M., 230, 231, 232, 235
Brockington, Fraser, 201
Brooks, H., 88
Brown, Carole Ganz, 138
Brown, R.G., 155
Bruland, T., 99, 107
Bruyn, Severyn, 29
Bryant, Barbara Everitt, 55
Brzezinski, Zbigniew, 57
Burawoy, Michael, 239, 257
Burnham, Linda, 42, 46
Burroughs, Nannie, 40

Cabral, Amilcar, 59
Cade, Toni, 54
Cahill, Spencer, 112, 113
Cain, Mead, 162

357

Caldwell, John C., 11–12, 143, 145, 148, 154, 155, 157, 158, 159, 162, 164, 165, 174, 176, 177, 179, 180, 181, 184, 186, 187, 188, 316–317
Caldwell, Pat, 154, 159, 162, 164, 180, 186, 187, 188
Cammack, P., 62
Carnoy, M., 132, 137
Carson, Clayborne, 39, 41
Carter, Anne P., 74
Castells, Manuel, 14, 126, 131, 136
Catt, Carrie Chapman, 43
Celac, Mariana, 292
Chabal, P., 59
Chafetz, Janet Saltzman, 6, 7, 108, 109, 112, 115, 118, 123, 124, 313–314
Chacbonneau, Hubert, 165
Chen, E.K.Y., 127, 129
Cherlin, Andrew, 52
Cho, L.J., 187
Chodorow, Nancy, 112, 113
Cimoli, M., 139
Clapham, C., 57
Clark, Colin, 154
Clark, Kenneth B., 35
Clecak, Peter, 50, 55
Cleland, W. Wendell, 156
Cloward, R.A., 226
Coale, Ansley J., 147, 157, 187
Cockburn, Cynthia, 92, 94, 104, 106
Cohen, Jean L., 240, 241, 242, 257
Cole, L.A., 31
Comte, Auguste, 71, 311
Conklin, Nancy, 55
Connell, J., 186
Connolly, Mike, 249, 257
Constantinople, Anne, 112
Cook, P., 63, 65
Coombs, Lolagene, 187
Cooper, Anna Julia, 39, 54
Coser, Rose Laub, 113
Cox, Harvey, 82–83
Cox, Sue, 54
Cramer, James C., 116
Crimmins, Eileen, 162
Crimp, Douglas, 258
Crook, Nigel R., 144
Curtis, Richard, 110
Cutler, J.E., 31

Dandekar, Kumudini, 187
Davie, M.R., 31, 37
Davies, Merryl Syn, 5, 10
Davis, Angela, 39, 40, 43, 49, 54, 55
Davis, Kingsley, 156, 157, 160–161, 163, 164, 183
Davis, Natalie Zemon, 168, 174, 186
de la Serre, Francoise, 307
Deane, Phillis, 176
Demeny, Paul, 147
Deutsch, Karl W. 143
Deyo, F.C., 128
Diamond, Norma, 179, 180
Donovan, Josephine, 54
Dosi, G., 131, 139
Douglas, Ann, 169
Dow Jr., T.E., 187
Drucker, Peter F., 307
Druckman, Daniel, 309
Dublin, Louis I., 165
DuBois, W.E.B., 49
Dugard, Samuel, 146
Dumont, Arsene, 160, 161
Dworkin, A. Gary, 118, 123, 124
Dwyer, D.H., 220, 221

Eaton, Joseph W., 164
Eberhardt, Eva, 285, 286, 287, 288, 289, 291, 292, 293
Eder, Klaus, 241
Eichelberger, Brenda, 46
Eigo, Jim, 249, 250
Eisenstadt, S.N., 144
Eisenstein, Zillah, 54, 55
Elger, T., 107
Engels, Frederick, 17, 144, 284
Epstein, Steve, 255, 257
Erlanger, Stephen, 293, 294
Ernst, Dieter, 127, 129
Evans, P.B., 132
Evans, Sara, 39, 55

Falk, R.A., 37
Fallers, L.A., 186
Fallers, Margaret C., 186
Fanon, Frantz, 36
Fanzylber, Fernando, 130
Feldman, Arthur S., 143
Fenner, Frank, 152
Ferguson, Kathy, 111

Fernandez, Dorothy, 187
Ferree, M.M., 232
Field, Mark, 75
Fireman, B., 226, 233
Fishlow, A., 130
Fishman, Pamela, 111
Flynn, Elizabeth Curley, 49
Foner, Philip S., 54
Ford, Dave, 250, 257
Fosdick, Harry Emerson, 32
Foster, George, 144
Foucault, Michel, 240, 246, 247, 248, 256
Fox, Mary Frank, 54, 116
Frank, Andre Gunder, 10
Freedman, R., 187
Freeman, Jo, 54
Fried, M., 34
Friedl, Ernestine, 114, 116
Friedlander, Dov, 161, 165
Friedland, E.A., 68
Frischtak, C., 135
Frobel, F., 126

Galbraith, J.K., 87
Gale, Richard, 119
Gamson, Josh, 4, 8–9
Gamson, W.A., 225, 226, 233, 257
Gamson, Zelda, 257
Gandhi, Mohandas K., 36
Garrow, D.J., 31
Geertz, Clifford, 56, 57, 149–150
George, Susan, 62, 66
Gerlach, L.P., 226, 232
Giddings, Paula, 39, 44, 55
Giele, Janet Zollinger, 113, 122
Gilkes, Cheryl Townsend, 54
Gille, H., 187
Gilman, Charlotte Perkins, 49
Gilman, Sander, 251
Gitlin, Todd, 258
Goffman, Erving, 112, 247
Goh, L., 131
Gold, T., 131
Goldman, Emma, 49
Goldman, Noreen, 187
Goldstone, Jack A., 13, 260, 283
Gomers, Samuel, 47
Gouldner, Alvin, 23, 24, 25
Grant, Jacqueline, 54
Gray, R.H., 148

Green, Jesse, 242, 257
Greenberg, Susan, 287, 293
Greenough, Paul R., 165
Grimshaw, A.D., 31
Groneman, Carol, 54
Grover, Jan Zita, 250, 251
Grynspan, Devora, 283
Grump, Janice, 52
Gurney, J.N., 231
Gurr, Ted Robert, 13, 283
Guttentag, Marcia, 12
Gwatkin, Davidson, 158

Habakkuk, H.J., 161
Habermas, Jürgen, 23, 241
Hagen, Everett E., 143
Hajnal, J., 187
Halisi, C.R.D., 283
Hamer, Fannie Lou, 39
Hansluwka, Harold, 158
Harding, Vincent, 55
Harff, Barbara, 283
Harley, Sharon, 39
Harper, Frances Watkins, 39, 54
Harris, Louis, 117
Harris, Marvin, 34
Harris, N., 129
Harrison, B., 133
Hartmann, Heidi, 55, 110, 111
Hegel, Georg Wilhelm Friedrich, 33
Heinen, Jaqueline, 285, 286, 289, 291, 292, 293
Heller, Joseph, 307
Hemmons, Willa Mae, 55
Henderson, J., 126, 127
Henricks, J., 126
Henry, L., 174
Hentoff, Nat, 37
Herbst, J., 65
Hershey, Marjorie, 52
Herokovitz, M.J., 31
Hertz, Rosanna, 116
Herzenberg, S., 128
Hesse-Biber, Sharlene, 54, 116
Hill, Alan, 158, 159
Hill, Robert, 31
Hine, V.C., 226, 232
Hinojosa, R.A., 126
Hinsley, F.H., 307
Hirono, R., 126

Hitler, Adolf, 33, 35
Hofsten, Erland, 154
Hollingsworth, T.H., 174
Holloway, Ralph E., 34
Homans, G.C., 222
hooks, bell, 42, 45, 54
Hoover, Edgar, 157
Horowitz, Donald L., 31
Huber, Joan, 6, 116
Hughes, Langston, 49
Hull, Gloria T., *et al.*, 54, 55
Hurn, Christopher, 143

Inglehart, R., 227–228
Inkeles, Alex, 143

Jackson, Jesse, 31
Jalalluddin, A.K.M., 186
James, C.L.R., 49
Janiewski, Dolores, 49
Jejeebhoy, Shireen, 162
Jenkins, J. Craig, 119, 225, 240
Johnson, Chalmers, 141
Johnson, Clarence, 257
Johnson, Diane, 248
Jones, Claudia, 49
Jones, Jacqueline, 55
Joseph, Gloria, 51, 53, 54
Jowitt, K., 68
Jurkat, Ernest, 156

Kamin, L.J., 35
Kanter, Rosabeth Moss, 112
Kaplinsky, R., 126, 131, 138
Kapur, B., 128
Keller, A.G., 34, 37
Kelly, H.H., 222
Kelly, Narindar, 162
Kessler, Richard J., 283
Kessler, Suzanne, 113
Kiernan, V.G., 34
Kim, S.S., 37
Kinch, A., 187
King, Deborah K., 7–8
King, Mae C., 54
King, Martin Luther Jr., 30, 31, 32, 35, 39, 317
Kiray, Mubeccel, 170, 179, 180, 181, 186
Kirk, D., 187

Kirkman, Cecelia, 36
Kirkpatrick, C., 63, 67
Kirp, David, 257
Kiser, Clyde V., 156
Kitschelt, Herbert, 241
Kitsuse, John I., 247
Klages, H., 228
Klandermans, P.G., 8, 9, 10, 13, 225, 230, 231, 232, 233, 235, 237
Knodel, John, 162, 164, 175, 186, 187
Kollias, Karen, 44
Kollontai, Alexandra, 285
Konvitz, M.R., 31
Kostiner, Joseph, 283
Kreye, O., 126
Kriesi, Hanspeter, 241
Kuratowska, Zofia, 286, 288, 289, 290
Kwok, R.Y.W., 131

Lado, Maria, 287
LaFrance, Marianne, 116
Lapidus, Fail Wershofsky, 285
Larose, Andre, 165
LaRue, Linda, 54
Lawrence, Paul R., 89
Lazonick, William, 100, 107
Lee, A. McClung, 4, 7, 31, 37, 317
Lefort, Claude, 25
Leibenstein, Harvey, 152, 159
Lemert, Edwin, 247
Lenin, Vladimir, 269, 284, 285, 289
Lerner, Daniel, 143
Lerner, Gerda, 54
Lesthaeghe, R.J., 175, 186, 187
LeVan, H. John, 283
Lever, Janet, 112, 113
Levy, Marion J., 143
Lewis, Arthur, 68, 144
Lewis, Diane K., 39, 44, 49, 52, 53
Lewis, Jill, 51, 53, 54
Lewis, O., 168, 172, 179, 180, 181, 186
Lieberson, Stanley, 31
Liff, S., 93
Lim, Hyun-Chin, 131
Linebarger, Charles, 257
Lipman-Blumen, Jean, 110
Lipset, Seymour, 20
Lipton, M., 186
Loewenberg, Bert James, 54

Lofchie, M.F., 68
Lorde, Audre, 40, 42, 54
Lorenz, Konrad, 34
Lotka, Alfred J., 165
Luckman, Thomas, 26
Lugones, Maria C., 42
Lundstrom, Hans, 154
Lykes, M. Brinton, 116

Macfarlane, A., 169, 173–174, 186, 187
MacKenzie, D., 100, 107
Malthus, Thomas, 145–146, 147–148, 149, 150, 151, 152, 155, 156, 157, 158, 159, 163, 164, 317
Mandelbaum, D.G., 168, 171, 186
Mannheim, Karl, 19, 26–28
Marable, Manning, 31, 51, 54
Marchand, John F., 193
Marriott, McKim, 172
Marris, Robin, 89
Marshall, Alfred, 144, 154
Martin, M. Kay, 115
Marwell, G., 233
Marx, Karl, 1, 3, 16, 17–18, 19, 71, 99, 119, 144, 164, 285
Mauldin, W.P., 184
Mayer, Albert J., 164
McAdam, D., 225, 226, 230, 231, 232, 233, 234, 240, 241
McCarthy, John, 119, 232, 240
McDonald, Peter, 155, 158
McKenna, Wendy, 113
McKeown, T., 153, 154, 155
McNeill, William H., 12, 196, 201
Meillassoux, C., 169
Melucci, A., 13, 226, 229, 230, 235, 237
Mesthene, Emmanuel G., 6
Mies, Maria, 1
Miljan, T., 139
Mill, John Stuart, 30
Miller, F.D., 232
Miller, Jon, 55
Miller, Swasti, 289
Mills, C. Wright, 310
Minogue, M., 63, 65
Mitchell, B.R., 176
Mitchell, R.C., 232, 233
Moghadam, Valentine M., 10, 298
Mols, Roger, 201
Moore, Wilbert E., 156

Morales, R., 126
Morgan, M., 216
Morgan, Thomas, 257
Morris, Aldon, 41, 225
Morsa, J., 187
Mortimore, M.J., 151
Mosher, William, 161
Moshiri, Farrokh, 283
Mosley, Henry, 158
Moses, W.J., 31
Mulholland, Lisa A., 285, 286, 287, 296
Muller, E.N., 233, 234
Murphy, R., 34
Murray, John F., 248
Murray, Pauli, 39, 40, 54
Myrdal, Gunnar, *et al.*, 31

Nelson, Richard, 153, 159
Newby, Howard, 111
Newman, Dorothy K., 54
Newman, Jeanne, 162
Ng, C.Y., 126
Nielsen, Joyce, 115
Nimkoff, M.F., 187
Nixson, F., 67
Noble, David, 101–103, 104
Norris, G.M., 112
Norton, Mary Beth, 54
Notestein, Frank, 145, 146–147, 156, 161, 165, 183
Nyerere, J.K., 61

Oberschall, Anthony, 225, 233, 240
O'Donnell, C., 107
Oegema, D., 232, 235
Oettinger, Anthony G., 73, 89, 90
Offe, Claus, 241
Ohmae, K., 129
O'Kelly, Charlotte G., 115
Okie, Susan, 249, 257
Okruhlicova, Anna, 287
Oliver, P., 233
Olson, M., 225, 233
O'Meara, Patrick, 283
Omi, Michael, 248
Opp, K.D., 233, 234, 235
Oppenheimer, Valerie K.,
Orubuloye, I., 157
Ortner, Sherry B., 113
Orum, M., 232

Paine, Thomas, 144
Palmer, Phyllis M., 45
Pardoko, P.H., 187
Parker, Hilda, 110
Parker, Seymour, 110
Parks, Rosa, 39
Parsons, Lucy, 49
Penrose, E.F., 157
Perrow, C., 235
Piekalkiewicz, Jaroslaw, 283
Pinard, M., 233
Piven, F.F., 226
Plamenatz, John, 3, 57
Plummer, Ken, 249
Poizner, Susan, 290, 291
Polenberg, Richard, 54
Powell, Linda C., 54
Preston, Samuel, 154, 155, 156, 158, 159, 165
Probert, B., 106

Rada, Juan, 127, 139
Raine, George, 249, 257
Ranade, Ramabai, 186
Randall, Sara, 158, 159
Randolh, A. Phillip, 48
Ransford, Edward, 55
Raper, A.F., 31
Rayman, Paula, 29
Razzel, David, 154, 155
Record, R.G., 155
Reddy, P.H., 154, 159, 162, 164, 186
Redfield, R., 172, 187
Riggs, F.W., 58
Robeson, Paul, 49
Rodgers-Rose, LaFrances, 55
Rosenberg, N. 135
Rosenberg, Nathan, 80
Rosenbloom, Richard S., 76, 89
Rostow, W.W., 143
Rucht, D., 229, 235
Rudwick, E.M., 31
Ruffin, Josephine St. Pierre, 39, 54
Rupp, Leila J., 122
Rushing, F.W., 138
Rutstein, Shea Oscar, 163
Ruzicka, Lado, 158, 174, 176, 177, 186, 187

Sacks, Karen, 110
Sagafi-Hejad, T., *et al.*, 135

Sahlins, Marshall, 35
Saint-Simon, Comte de, 71
Sanday, Peggy, 113, 115
Sandburg, Carl, 31
Sanderson, S.W., 126
Sanger, Margaret, 49
Sardar, Ziauddin, 5, 10, 307
Sargent, Lydia, 54, 55
Sauvy, Alfred, 152, 175
Scarritt, James R., 283
Schein, E.H., 30
Schofield, R.S., 144, 147, 148–149, 153, 154, 155, 160, 161, 164
Schultz, Theodore W., 145, 148, 162
Schumpeter, Joseph, 86
Schur, Edwin, 111, 112, 113
Schwartz, M., 231
Scott, A.J., 127
Scott, Joan, 1
Scott, Patricia Bell, 55
Secord, Paul, 12
Shah, Nasra M., 308
Shaiken, H., 128
Shanin, T., 168
Shils, Edward, 20, 57, 84
Shilts, Randy, 249, 250, 256, 258
Silverman, A.R., 31
Singer, J.D., 37, 172
Sivard, Ruth Leger, 308
Skinner, R., 136
Skocpol, Theda, 12, 13, 260
Small, Melvin, 37
Smelser, Neil, 226, 240
Smith, Barbara, 54
Smith, David H., 143
Soete, L., 131, 139
Sontag, Susan, 238
Sorokin, Pitirim A., 32, 37
Sovani, N.V., 187
Spelman, Elizabeth V., 42
Spengler, Joseph, 143
Spiegelman, Mortimer, 165
Spitze, Glenna, 116
Squire, William, 193
Srinivasan, K., 162
Stalin, Joseph, 269
Stanley, Manfred, 73
Stanton, Elizabeth Cady, 43
Staples, Robert, 54
Steinem, Gloria, 55

Author Index

Stern, Paul C., 309
Steuart, James, 164
Stewart, Abigail J., 116
Stewart, Maria, 39, 54
Stolnitz, George, 156–157
Stone, L., 169
Stone, Pauline Terrelonge, 40, 54
Stowsky, J., 126
Sullivan, Oriel, 158
Sumner, W.G., 34, 37
Szeftel, M., 57

Taeuber, Irene B., 156
Tan, A.H.H., 128
Tarrow, S., 226, 237
Taylor, Carl, 162
Taylor, Verta, 122
Teitelbaum, Joshua, 283
Teixeira, R., 233
Terborg-Penn, Rosalyn, 39
Thadani, Veena N., 184
Thilbaut, J.W., 222
Thomas, K., 155
Thompson, John B., 3, 6
Thompson, P., 107
Thompson, Warren, 155
Tierney, K.J., 231
Tilly, Charles, 13, 14, 231, 240
Tilly, Louise, 1, 231
Tilly, R., 231
Toffler, Alvin, 307
Tordoff, William, 3–4
Touraine, A., 126, 229, 235, 241, 242, 257
Tovias, A., 135
Townsend, Joseph, 164
Treichler, Paula, 256
Trevelyan, G.M., 154
Trey, J.E., 117
Trimberger, Ellen Kay, 269
Truth, Sojourner, 39, 54
Tubman, Harriet, 39
Tuller, David, 257
Turner, R.H., 231, 235

Vallin, Jacques, 158
van de Walle, Etienne, 154, 155, 175, 187
van den Eerenbeemt, Marie-Louise, 159
Van der Loo, H., 226, 227
van Noort, Wim, 235
Vogel, Lise, 110, 111

Voorhies, Barbara, 115
Voss, Kim, 257

Wajcman, Judy, 7, 106, 107
Wallace, Maggie, 40
Wallace, Michelle, 39
Wallace, Robert, 164
Waller, Willard, 33
Wasson, Merrylin, 187
Waters, Pamela, 52
Watney, Simon, 250, 254
Waxman, Chaim I., 25
Weber, Max, 1, 3, 16, 17, 18–19, 109, 236
West, Candace, 112
West, Cornell, 41
Westin, Alan F., 87
Wilkinson, B., 101
Willcox, Walter, 146, 160
Williams, Anne, 162
Williams, Robin, 79
Willis, Ellen, 45
Wilson, J. Q., 225, 233
Wilson, K., 232
Winant, Howard, 248
Winchester, N. Brian, 283
Winslow, C.E.A., 155
Wiser, Charlotte, 186
Wiser, W., 186
Witherspoon, W.R., 31
Wolf, Margery, 180
Woodsworth, N., 64, 65
Wray, J.D., 187
Wright, Quincy, 37
Wrigley, E.A., 144, 147, 148–149, 153, 154, 155, 160, 161, 164

Xian, Shen, 164

Young, Andrew, 31
Young, Crawford, 4, 58, 59, 66
Young, Oran R., 309
Young, Ralph, 63
Youngson, A.J., 131

Zald, Mayer, 119, 240
Zimmerman, Don, 112

SUBJECT INDEX

Abortion, black feminism and, 44
    Bolsheviks and, 285
    Central and Eastern Europe, 10, 290, 291–292, 297, 298
    fertility levels and, 316
    sex ratios and, 202
    social movements and, 9, 229
    women's movements and, 121
Absolute monarchy, 28
ACT UP, *see* AIDS Coalition To Unleash Power.
Affirmative action, 49
Afghanistan, *see* Revolutions, Afghanistan.
Africa, AIDS and, 309
    development and, 4, 59–60, 62, 65, 66, 68, 69
    familial production in, 168
    fertility and, 184
    ideology and, 57
    migration and, 12, 190, 198, 200, 308
    mortality decline, 155
    population and, 147, 148, 150, 151
    slaves, 31, 197
    U.S. imperialism and, 51
    wealth flow, 181
    Westernization, 173
African Blood Brotherhood, 48
Aid, development, 4, 62, 63, 66, 135, 139, 140, 143, 158, 263, 281, 287, 301
Aid, international, *see* Aid, development.
AIDS, 8–9, 238–257, 308, 309
AIDS Coalition To Unleash Power (ACT UP), 8, 238–257
Albania, EU and, 301
Algeria, development and, 59, 69
America, *see* United States.
American Federation of Labor (AFL), 47
Amerindians, disease from European contact, 193
    nationalism and, 31
Angola, development, 59, 63, 64, 65

Argentina, world market, 130
Armies. *See also* military.
    population sumps as, 12, 192–193, 194, 197
    raiding and, 195
Asceticism, 18
Asia, development and, 60, 65, 68, 69, 130, 131, 132, 133, 140
    familial production and, 168
    internationalization of manufacturing, 126, 127, 128, 315
    Malthusian ceiling, 150
    migration, 12, 200, 309
    U.S. imperialism and, 51
    Westernization, 173
Asians, South African revolution and 271, 272, 275
    unions and, 47
Association of South-East Asian Nations (ASEAN), 67, 68
Australia, female labor, war and, 91
    fertility and 174, 175, 176
    gender, industrial conflict and, 92
    Malthusian equilibrium and, 146
    migration, 199
    mortality decline, 156
    policies, ideology and, 67
    telecommuters, 97, 106
Austria, internationalization of automobile manufacturing, 315
    post materialist values, and social movements, 228
Autocracies, 32

Balkanization, 303, 304
Bangladesh, conversation, and mode of production, 186
    fertility and, 162
    natural disasters, and development, 66
Belgium, development, 65
    fertility, 175, 186, 187

Subject Index 365

internationalization of automobile
manufacturing, 315
Birth control, *see* Contraception.
Birth rates, 146, 147, 148, 149, 160, 164,
197, 290, 297, 308, 312
East Germany, 297
Poland, 290
United States, 308
Bisexuals, 250.*See also* Gays;
Homosexuals; Lesbians.
Blacks. *See also* Movements.
AIDS and, 245, 249, 255, 257–258
cities in, 75, 84, 89
feminism, 38–55
migration, urban, 200
Muslim, 31
new social movements and, 241
South African revolution and, 264,
267, 270, 273, 275, 277, 282
revolts, 31
urban riots, 120
working class divisions and, 100
Body, the, 2, 9–10, 11, 256
Bolivia, revolution and, 259
Boycotts, ACT UP, 249
women's movements, 120
Brain drain, 135, 140
Brandt Report, 67
Brazil, development, 62, 65, 66, 129, 130,
131, 132, 134
position in global economic order, 299
Britain. *See also* England; United Kingdom.
female labor, and war, 91
migration and, 199
religion, 25
Rhodesia and, 268, 177
sexual politics, production and, 92, 99
Third World and, 66, 67
women's movements, 120
Zimbabwe and, 281
Brotherhood of Sleeping Car Porters, 48
Bulgaria, EU and, 301
nationalism and, 303
women in, 289, 293
Bureaucratization, social movements and,
228
West of, 19
Burma, revolutionary conflict, 259, 177

Cambodia, *see* Revolutions, Cambodia.
Canada, income inequality and, 318

international division of labor in, 128,
133, 316
Capital, 7, 69, 95, 100, 101, 103, 106, 296,
316. *See also* Monopoly capital.
Capitalism, 1. *See also* Production.
black feminism and, 40, 47, 49, 50, 51
development and, 4, 58, 59, 60, 63,
64, 65, 66, 67, 68, 69
Eastern Europe and, 299, 301, 305,
306
family and, 168, 169–170, 172
fertility and, 166, 173
ideology and, 16–19, 29
men and, 298
morality and, 170
pros and cons of, 318
sexual politics, and production, 98, 99
social movements and, 229
West and, 178
women and, 10, 169–170, 171–172,
284, 285, 289, 290, 295,
296–297
Capitalists, *see* Capital.
Caribbean, colonialism and, 60
Center, 300. *See also* Core; Periphery.
Central Europe. *See also* Eastern Europe;
Europe; States, Central and Eastern
Europe; Western Europe.
democracy and, 13, 282
revolutionary movements and, 259,
276, 277, 278
women and, 2, 9–10, 13, 285
Charisma, 29, 56
Chicago Household Economists, 144, 162
Child mortality, 155, 158, 159, 162, 163,
164, 176, 182, 184, 185, 187, 192,
291
Child strikes, Central and Eastern Europe,
1, 10, 287, 297
Child care, 10, 97, 110, 112, 172, 202
Central and Eastern Europe, 284, 285,
286, 288, 289, 290, 291, 295
Children. *See also* child care; child
mortality; child strikes; fertility.
education and, 35, 73
development and, 59
disease and, 192
female labor and, 116, 117
gender, and care of, 202, 203, 216,
220
labor, 100

militarization and, 36
population checks and, 146, 149, 150
returns on, pretransitional society, 162
wealth flows theory and, 11–12, 168, 169, 170, 172, 173, 174, 176, 177, 181, 182, 185
Chile, development, 63, 129
Cities. *See also* Development corporations; Urbanization.
   emergence, 191
   German, unemployment and, 286
   migration and, 19, 194, 195, 197, 200
   mortality and, 12, 152, 155, 191, 192, 198, 199, 201
   technology and, 75, 77, 85
   Third World, 133, 302
   West German, and racism, 303
China, child mortality, 164
   "classic" revolution, 260
   democracy movement, 259, 277
   development and, 134, 137, 138
   migration and, 191, 194, 196
   Westernization, 187
Civil rights, *see* Rights, civil.
Civil Rights Act, Title VII, 122
Class, 311. *See also* Elites; Marxism.
   black feminism and 38, 40, 41, 42, 43, 44–46, 47, 48, 50, 51, 52, 53, 55
   development and, 65
   Eastern Europe in, 5
   fertility and, 149
   gays and, 253
   heterosexual pairing and, 211
   ideology and, 28, 29
   ideology, and political power, 56
   lower, AIDS and, 258
   Marxism and, 4, 6, 18, 19
   migration and, 194–197
   mortality and, 155
   multivalence and, 7
   revolution and, 261, 262, 263, 266, 267, 269, 270, 271, 273, 274, 275, 280, 281
   social movements and, 8, 13, 118, 227, 228, 229, 240, 241, 242, 245
   technology and, 7, 91, 94, 95, 98–99, 100, 101, 103
   violence and, 34
Classism, 38, 45, 51, 52, 53

Clerical workers, *see* Workers, clerical.
Cognitive dissonance theory, 117
Collective action, state and, 13
   women's movements, 314
Collective behavior, theory of, 226, 240
Colonialism, 5, 59, 301, 302, 305. *See also* Decolonization.
Combahee River Collective, 51, 52
Communism. *See also* Class; Marxism; Socialism.
   Afghanistan revolution and, 263
   blacks and, 55
   black women and, 39, 47, 49
   Cambodian revolution and, 262
   Eastern Europe, 299, 300, 302, 305–306
   end of ideology theory and, 21, 24
   Philippine revolution and, 263
   secularization and, 20
   social movement as, 224
   Vietnam revolution and, 262, 276
   women, Central and Eastern Europe, 284, 285, 287, 293, 297
Communist bloc, former, 289, 295–296, 299
Communist Party, blacks and, 50
   Czechoslovakia, 273
   East Germany, 273
   feminism and, 50
   Hungary, 273
   Poland, 269, 273, 276
   South Africa, 271
Communities, AIDS activism and, 243, 246, 257–258
Comparable worth policies, 49, 123
Computers, 308. *See also* Telecommuters.
   development and, 131–132, 137, 138, 139
   education and, 73
   labor and, 74
   location of work and, 96
   management control and, 102–103
   participatory democracy and, 80
   productivity and, 72
   sexual division of labor and, 92, 97–98, 103, 104–105
Conflict, 2, 4, 22, 32. *See also* Struggles.
   armed, 35
   class, ideology and, 28
   ethnic/racial, 5, 30–32, 54

ideology and, 30, 36, 56
industrial, 100
industrialized countries, 228
migration and, 12
nationalist, 304
revolution and, 259, 264, 265, 266, 267, 268, 272, 274, 275–276, 277, 278, 282
sexual groups, 54
social movements and, 241, 242
technology and, 79, 91
women's position and, in familial production, 171. *See also* Women.
values of, and social planning, 79
Congress of Industrial Organizations, 49
Consciousness, 2, 8
AIDS, 244
black feminism and, 51, 52, 53
gender, 39, 40, 119, 120, 241. *See also* Feminism; Consciousness-raising.
media and, 23
worker, 119, 133
Consciousness-raising, 42, 45, 122, 217, 221
Conservatism, 20
Consumption, conspicuous, capitalism and, 306
mortality rates and, 152
social movements and, 227
societies based on market production in, 11, 169, 176, 178
Third World in, 134
women's, familial production in, 11, 185
Contraception. *See also* Abortion.
Central and Eastern Europe in, 291, 292, 293
fertility levels and, 316, 317
Third World in, 184
West in, 173, 176, 177
women's movements and, 121
Core, 126, 139, 141. *See also* Center; Periphery.
Costs and benefits, external, 77–78, 80, 81, 289
male-female relationships in, 207–209, 212, 213, 214, 218, 220. *See also* Exchange theory.

social movement participation of, 225, 230, 233, 234
Countries, developing, *see* Third World.
Coups, 263, 265, 270
Cuba, development and 63, 69
Czechoslovakia, EU and, 301, 304
men, 289
nationalism and, 302, 303
revolution in, 273
women, 287, 288, 290, 292, 293

Darwinism, 29
Death. *See also* Death rates; Mortality.
abortion, Polish law and, 298
AIDS activism and, 249, 251–252, 253, 256, 257
familial production and, 167
fatalism and, 144
population growth and, 145, 146, 198
social movements and, 9, 229
Death rates, 145, 146, 147, 148, 149, 152–153, 155, 157, 160, 316
Debts, Eastern and Central European states, 296, 301
Iranian revolution and, 261. *See also* Fiscal crisis.
Third World, 62, 65
Decolonization, 5, 36, 267, 305. *See also* Colonialism.
Democracy, development aid and, 66
economic, 306
ethnic conflict and, 30–31
Eastern Europe and, 5, 306
ideology and, 28
Newly Industrializing Countries and, 129
participatory, 80, 88, 306
revolution and, 13, 262, 268, 272, 273, 274, 276, 279, 281–283
socialist, 51
technology and, 6, 71, 80, 88
war and, 32, 35
Demography, 1, 2, 10–12, 14, 144, 145, 183, 310, 313, 314, 316, 317. *See also* Population Studies.
armies and, 192
cities and, 199
French fertility and, 175
gender division of labor and, 115, 117
male-female relations and, 203, 206, 210

revolutions and, 266
schooling and, 179
superstructure and, 172
Demographic change, 7, 11, 143, 166, 178, 311. *See also* Demographic transition; Fertility; Mortality.
Demographic transition, 1, 11, 143, 145–146, 156, 159, 162, 169, 171, 173, 186
Demographic transition theory, 143, 146, 164, 183
Demystification, 17–18, 19. *See also* Marxism.
Denmark, 316
Dependency, African States of, 69
   Eastern Europe, 5, 300, 301, 303, 304, 306
   Newly Industrializing Countries, 129
   periphery of, 126
   revolutions and, 262, 263, 265
   Third World, 60, 67, 139, 300, 306
   Turkey, 304
Development, 1, 4, 57, 58–69, 125
   Asia, 133
   Eastern Europe, 300, 301, 304, 305, 306
   ideology and, 4, 58–60
   Iranian revolution and, 261
   morality and, 168
   mortality and, 144, 153, 155, 157, 158
   multinational corporations and, 138
   Newly Industrializing Countries, 129, 131–132
   social movements and, 230
   South American countries, 130, 131–132
   technology transfer and, 135, 138, 139, 140, 141
   Third World, 300, 301, 306
   Vietnam, 280
Development corporations, 89
Diffusion, 12, 19, 20, 98, 100, 101, 132, 195, 196
Discrimination, AIDS and, 248
   black women against, 38, 41, 42
   class, 42
   gender, 10, 41, 120, 121
   race, 42, 44
   race-gender, 48
   union, 47
   wage and job, 48, 287
   women against, in Eastern Europe, 10, 287
Deskilling, 7, 99, 101, 102, 107
Disease. *See also* Health care; Public health.
   endemic, 12, 194, 198
   epidemic, 12, 33, 148, 149, 151, 152, 192, 193, 198, 239, 249, 252, 253, 256, 309
   death rates and, 153
   migration and, 191–194, 198–200
   population size and 145, 148, 149, 150, 152, 157, 159, 201
   public health measures and, 199
   world connectedness and, 309
Division of labor, 314, 315
   gender, 7, 91, 93, 96, 98, 109, 110, 111, 112, 113, 114, 115, 116, 117, 123, 293, 313
   international, 14, 96, 126, 127, 128, 129, 131, 133, 141
Dodge Revolutionary Union Movement, 48
Dominance, *see* Domination.
Domination, 4, 34–35. *See also* Power.
   AIDS activism and, 240, 246–248, 251, 253, 254–255, 256
   body of, by society, 9
   capitalist, 95, 104
   colonies of, 60, 260
   Communist Party, Soviet Union in, 293
   elite, 306
   ethnic group and, 272
   ideology and, 3, 25
   male, 39, 51, 91, 92, 94, 95, 104, 175, 313
   racial, 260
   racial solidarity, black women and, 41
   regional, 68
   regional, Vietnam, 280
   revolutions and, 260, 267
   states and, 5
   superpower, 260
   Western nations by, 5, 60, 67, 68, 300
   whites by, 31, 51
Domostroika, 290
Dual-earner couples, 116

East, the, 66, 228, 299
East Germany. *See also* Germany; West Germany.

Subject Index 369

racism, 303
revolutionary coalition and, 273
West German take over and, 305
women, 286, 287, 289, 297
East Java, women, views on fertility and
  family size, 187
Eastern Europe. *See also* Central Europe;
  Europe; States, Central and Eastern
  Europe; Western Europe.
  ideology, end of, 21
  revolution and, 268, 308
  Third World and, 5, 66, 299–307
  Western capital and, 69
  women in, 2, 9–10, 285, 297, 314
Economic growth, core economies, 132
  mortality decline and, 154
  New Social Movements Theory and,
    9, 13, 226, 227, 228, 230
  Newly Industrializing Countries
    (NICS), 129, 131
  revolution and, 261, 262, 266, 272
  technology and, 74
  Third World and, 14, 56, 58, 59
  Third World fertility change and,
    183
Economy. *See also* Capitalism;
  Communism; Socialism.
  informal sector, 96
  mixed, 21, 64, 65
Education. *See also* Schools.
  AIDS and, 243, 245
  compulsory, and privacy, 84
  development and, 64, 136, 138, 139,
    140
  ERA and 44
  fatalism and, 144
  fertility and, 147, 317
  ideology and, 28, 30, 36
  inequality and, 35
  mortality decline and, 11, 145, 155,
    157, 158, 163
  Newly Industrializing Countries in,
    132
  production and, 127, 128, 129, 131,
    138
  revolutions and, 267, 269
  rural migrants and, 200
  social movements and, 228, 229
  technology and, 71, 72, 73, 76, 77, 86,
    89

Third World, and family change, 179,
  185
war and, 32
women and, 52, 117, 118, 119, 121,
  219, 314
Egalitarianism. *See also* Equality;
  Inequality.
  development and, 4, 59, 144
  fertility and, 178
  ideology and, 28
  labor market and, 184
  revolutions and, 268, 280
  schooling and, 169
  socialism and, 296
Egypt, ancient, 194, 196
  global economic position, 299
  mortality decline and, 156
  revolution, 259
Elderly, 230. *See also* Old.
Electronic cottages, 96, 98
El Salvador, revolt, and aid from
  Nicaragua, 261
Elites. *See also* Class.
  development and, 66.
  Eastern Europe, 5, 301
  migration and, 191, 194, 196
  religion and, in familial production,
    172
  revolutions and, 13, 260, 261, 262,
    263, 264, 265, 266, 267, 268,
    269–270, 271, 272, 273, 274,
    275, 276, 277, 279, 280, 282
  urban, and early civilization, 195
  women and, 7, 110–111, 113, 114,
    115, 116, 120, 121, 122–123,
    124
England. *See also* Britain; United Kingdom.
  factory system, 72
  family patterns in, 169, 187
  fertility and, 148, 160, 161, 163, 173,
    174
  mortality and, 144, 153, 154, 155,
    156, 160, 161, 163, 164
  population equilibrium and, 147
  wars and, 32
Enlightenment, 19
Entrepreneurism, 28
Environment, natural, 77. *See also* Nature.
Epidemics, *see* Disease, epidemic.
Equal Pay Act, 122

Equal Rights Amendment (ERA) 44, 49,
   120, 122
Equality. *See also* Egalitarianism;
   Inequality; Stratification.
   development and, 58, 59
   Eastern Europe in, 306
   gender, 108, 114, 118, 119, 124,
      221–222
   multiple jeopardy and, 51
   Newly Industrializing Countries and,
      129
   political means and, 317
   scientific decision making and, 88
   violence and, 34
   women's, 42, 285, 295, 296, 297
Equity, *see* equality.
Essentialism, 95
Estonia, women in, 291
Ethiopia, natural disasters, and
   development, 66
Ethnicity. *See also* Race; Racism.
   Eastern Europe and 5, 302–303, 305,
      306
   gender systems and, 109
   ideology and, 29, 30–32
   masculinities and, 95
   revolutions and, 260, 263, 264, 265,
      266, 267, 268, 271, 272, 282
   technological expertise and, 7
   violence and, 34
   working class divisions and, 100
EU, *see* European Union.
Eurasia, migration and, 191, 195, 196, 197,
   198
Europe. *See also* Central Europe; Eastern
   Europe; Western Europe; States,
   Central and Eastern Europe.
   Balkanization and, 303
   decentralization of manufacturing and,
      126, 128, 315, 316
   Eastern Europe States and, 304
   grain cultivation, migration and, 190
   fertility decline and, 161, 187
   migration and, 191, 192, 194, 199
   mortality decline and, 11, 146
   mortality, urban areas, 201
   population, checks on growth, 147
   preindustrial, and ideology, 24, 27
   price control, and colonies, 60
   research on teleworkers, 97

revolution and, 268, 281
secularization and, 16, 19
social movements and, 224, 227, 230,
   235–237, 240–241
wealth flows and, 176
wars and, 32, 33
European Community, 287
European Union (EU), 5, 301, 303–305
Exchange theory, 110, 205, 206–222. *See
   also* Costs and benefits, male-female
   relationships in.
External costs and benefits, *see* Costs and
   benefits, external.

Factionalism, revolutions in, 262, 263, 273,
   274, 275
Factory workers, *see* Workers, factory.
Family Violence, *see* Violence, family.
Famine. *See also* Hunger.
   alleviation of, 156
   development and, 66
   population check as, 145, 149, 150,
      152, 201
Fascism, 21, 224
Fatalism, 11, 144
Fathers, Muslim in Morocco, 220
   Russia in, 290
   Third World, and family change, 179,
      180
Females, *see* Women.
Femininity, 109, 111, 117
Feminism, 1, 7, 105, 108, 113, 114,
   216–217, 222. *See also* Movements,
   women's; Movements, women's
   suffrage.
   black, 7, 38–55
   Central and East Europe, 10, 286,
      290, 292, 293–295, 297
   lesbian separatism and, 42
   liberal, 45
   Marxist, 45, 110
   Neo-Freudian, 112
   radical, 45
   social movements theory and, 241
   socialist, 45, 48
Feminization of poverty, 46
Feminization of work, 92
Fertility, agricultural societies in, 316
   capitalism and, 166, 169, 170, 177
   decline, 12, 143, 144, 145, 146, 148,

152, 160–164, 166, 173, 174, 176, 177, 182, 183, 184, 185, 187, 316, 317
familial production and 11, 166, 169, 183, 185, 186
family change and, 178, 183
female labor and, 116, 317
hunting and gathering bands, 167
income and, 153
market economies in, 316
modernization and, 146, 162–162, 163, 186
mortality, relation to, 146–148, 153, 160–164, 184
superstructure and 166, 173, 175–176, 177, 183, 185, 186
Third World, 12, 173, 183, 185
West in, 174, 185, 187
wives' attitudes toward, 175
women's, government control of in Eastern and Central Europe, 291
Films, acceptance of homosexuals and, 3
First World, Eastern Europe and, 5
ideology and, 67
Fiscal crisis, revolutions and, 260, 279. *See also* Debts
France, alliances, for research and development, 309.
empires, 305
fertility and, 175, 176, 188
income inequality and, 318
internationalization of automobile manufacturing, 315
migration and, 194
mortality and, 144, 155, 156
population equilibrium and, 160
premodern, 186
revolution, 259, 260
revolution, and "age of ideologies", 20
wars and, 32
wealth flows and, 174, 187
Freudianism, 29

Gays. *See also* Bisexuals; Homosexuals; Lesbians.
AIDS activism and, 240, 241, 242, 243, 245, 247, 248, 249, 251, 253, 254, 255, 256, 257
mass media and, 3

Gender, 1–2, 6–7. *See also* Men; Women; Roles, women; Sex roles.
black women's poverty and, 46
class politics and, 38
cultural superstructure and, 167
discrimination, and black women, 41
equality, 108–118, 119
familial production and, 168
ideology and, 29
inequality, 313
mortality trends and, 155
politics, black women and, 51
relations between the, 203
sex ratios and, 207, 212, 215
social movements and, 9, 227
technology and, 104, 106
work and, 97, 98, 99, 101, 103, 106
Germany. *See also* East Germany; West Germany.
fertility and, 162, 175, 186
foreign investment, and world connectedness, 309
income inequality and, 318
internationalization of automobile manufacturing, 315
marriage, and wealth flow, 187
migration and, 194
prostitution, 287
racism and, 303
Ghana, birthrate, early twentieth century, 164
family change and, 180
ideology and, 57
industrialization and, 68
old people, and benefits from high fertility, 162
women, views on fertility and family size, 187
Global warming, 309
Globalization, 1, 11, 14, 178, 183, 185. *See also* Internationalization.
Grand narrative of cultural transformation, 3, 16–25
Great Britain, *see* Britain.
Greece, ancient, 32
textile industry, investment in by NICS, 133
Grievances, social movements and, 8, 13, 225, 226, 236
revolution and, 270, 279, 280

Gross national product (GNP), 130, 308
Guinea, socialism and, 58
Guinea Bissau, ideology and, 59

Harvard University Program on Technology and Society, 72, 73, 79, 84, 90
Health care. See also Disease; Public health.
 AIDS activism and, 244, 245
 black women and, 46
 Central and Eastern Europe, 286, 289
 mortality decline and 163, 185
 technology and, 75
Hispanics, AIDS and, 245, 255, 258
 nationalism and, 31
Holland, peace and, 32
Home work, computer-based, see Telecommuting.
Homophobia, 251
Homosexuals. See also Bisexuals; Gays; Lesbians.
 acceptance of, and media, 3
 ACT UP and, 8, 251
 AIDS and, 249–250
 identity politics and, 255
 middle America and, 253
Hong Kong, international division of labor and, 127
 Newly Industrializing Country as, 129, 130, 131, 132, 133, 134
Housing, black women and, 46
 recurrent patterns and, 312
 Third World urban centers and, 65
 vested interests and lack of, 77
Humanism, revolutionary movements and, 268
 war and, 32
 Zambian, 57
Hungary, EU and, 301, 304
 material success and, 281
 nationalism and, 303
 revolutionary coalitions and, 273
 women, 285–286, 287, 288, 291, 292, 293
Hunger. See also Famine.
 black women and, 46
 ideology, states and, 30
Husbands, Eastern Europe, views on women holding jobs, 286
 exchange theory and, 110, 205, 220, 221
 familial production in, 172
 family change and Third World countries, 180
 fertility decline and, 177, 178
 French, eighteenth and nineteenth century, 175
 power and, 114, 168, 202
 Russian, 290
 school, effects on during industrialization, 169

Identity, 2
 black women and, 39, 53
 communism under, 287
 "deviant", 247
 East European, 305
 gay, 240, 243, 247, 253–254
 gender, 39, 112, 202, 204, 215, 216, 219
 masculine, 7, 94, 95
 revolutions and, 280, 281
 social movements and, 8, 228, 241, 242, 247–248, 257
 Third World and, 56
 women and, 39, 53, 217, 219
Identity politics, 247, 255
Ideological multiplicity, 26–27
Ideology, 2–4, 14, 311, 314
 activists and, 108
 African states and, 68–69
 black feminist, 38, 40, 43, 53
 conflict and, 28, 30, 32, 36, 56
 demographic transition theory and, 164
 development and, 4, 58–60, 63, 64, 66, 67
 domination and, 3
 Eastern Europe, 300, 306
 economic growth and, 56
 education and, 30, 36
 egalitarian, and European cultural heritage, 184
 end of, 17, 20–22, 23, 24, 25, 30, 36, 69, 78, 306
 ethnicity and, 30–32
 gender, 111, 113, 119, 121–122, 123, 313
 gender definitions of skill and, 93, 94

Grand narrative of cultural transformation and, 16–17, 19, 20–25
Hong Kong, and economic growth, 131
industrialization and, 24
ingredients of, 28
legitimation of power and, 24, 25, 28–29, 30, 56
management control and, 103
mass media and, 3, 6, 23, 28
modernization and, 3
national integration and, 56
resource mobilization theory and, 3
revolutions and, 261, 262, 263, 265, 267, 268, 282
SADCC and, 67
social movements and, 232, 233
superstructure and, 3
Third World leaders and, 56, 57, 58
Third World, and productivity, 65
typology of, 29
war and, 32–35, 36
women, Central and Eastern Europe and, 296
Zimbabwe in, 65
Illiteracy, 144. *See also* Literacy.
IMF, *see* International Monetary Fund.
Immigrant Workers, *see* Workers, immigrant.
Imperialism, activism against, 1960s, 39, 50, 51
Vietnam revolution and, 262
Impoverishment, *see* poverty.
Incentives, collective, social movements and, 233
selective, social movements and, 233. *See also* Costs and benefits, social movements.
Independence, Eastern Europe and, 299, 300, 302, 303
Namibia, and dependence on South Africa, 64
state, and development, 60, 64, 65
state, and ideologies, 56, 58–59
India, birth and death rates, early twentieth century, 148
demographic and family change, 162, 164
export-oriented industrialization and, 130

global economic order, position in, 299
high technology manufacturing and, 127
independence, and nonviolence, 36
migration and, 191, 194, 196
mode of production, and conversation, 186
mortality trends, 155, 156, 164
old people, and dignity, 168
Pakistan, and territory, 302
privatization, 62
religion, 172
rural, attitudes toward sickness, 154, 159
wives, 171
women, views on fertility and family size, 187
Industrial revolution, technological change since, 5, 72
revolution, economic growth and, 154
Industrial Workers of the World, 49
Industrialization, 311
agricultural base and, 68
Brazil, 131
demographic transition and, 160, 161, 163
Eastern Europe, 302
England, 154
export-oriented, 129, 132
fertility decline and, 12, 185
ideology and, 24
mortality decline and, 11
periphery of, 127, 129, 132, 133, 135
productive structure and, 128
social movements and, 9, 228, 229
unions and, 47
women
 Central and Eastern Europe, 285
 USSR, 285
 West in, 314
women's movements and, 118, 121
Inequality. *See also* Egalitarianism; Equality; Stratification.
black women and, 40, 42, 45, 49
class, 95, 318
gender, 95, 109, 112, 114, 115, 124, 217, 221–222, 217–218, 296, 297, 313
gender, technical skills and, 95

ideology and, 4, 34–35
men, technical skills and, 95
states, ideology and, 59
Intellectuals, end of ideology thesis and, 21
  feminist, Central and Eastern Europe, 295, 297
  ideology and, 23, 29, 36
  revolutions and, 272
  socialism and, 49
Intelligentsia, black male leadership in, 40
  Polish revolution and, 265, 273
International Ladies' Garment Workers' Union, 47–48
International Monetary Fund (IMF), 5, 60, 62, 63, 67, 68, 69, 300, 301, 302
Internationalization, 315–316. See also Globalization.
Invention, adoption of, and views on technology, 72
  agriculture of, 190
  automatically controlled machine tools of, 101
  cannon of, 198
  computers of, 74
  gender and, 98
  self-acting male of, 100
  war and, 32
  wheel of, 74
Iran, Kurds and, 302. See also Revolutions, Iran.
Iraq, Kurds and, 302
  war with Iran, 261, 281
  See also Revolution, Iraq.
Ireland, fertility and delay of marriage, 187
  textile industry, investments in by NICS, 133
Israeli-Palestinian conflict, 260, 266, 268, 269, 270, 271, 275
Italy, income inequality and, 318
  internationalization of automobile manufacturing and, 315
Ivory Coast, inequality and, 59

Jamaica, IMF/World Bank and, 69
Japan, ASEAN and, 68
  competition with Western Europe, 304
  computer needs, ability to supply own, 131
  decentralization of companies, 126, 128, 133

demographic transition and, 160
development and, 136
foreign investment and, 309
income inequality and, 318
internationalization of automobile manufacturing and, 315
technology transfer and, 137, 140
Java, equilibrium population and, 149
mortality decline, 156

Kenya, development and, 58, 59
  women, views on fertility and family size, 187
Knights of Labor, 49
Ku Klux Klan, 31
Kuwait, foreign workers, 308

Labeling Theory, 110, 247. See also Labels, AIDS activism.
Labels, AIDS activism and, 240; 246–248, 252, 253–256. See also Labeling Theory.
Labor, children, familial production and, 171
  children, industrial conflict and, 105
  decentralization of manufacturing and, 126–129
  Eastern Europe, 5, 301–302
  gender, and industrial conflict, 7, 98, 99–100, 103, 105, 106
  ideology and, 36
  migrant, see Workers, immigrant.
  militancy, postwar period, 102
  organized, 14, 47, 49, 51, 92, 122, 126
  organized, male, 92, 122
  revolution and, 263, 269
  Third World, 124, 126, 128
  women, 116, 117, 118, 123, 314
  women, Central and Eastern European, 288, 289, 290, 295
  women, familial production and, 171
Labor power, 10, 19
Laos, domination of by Vietnam, 280
Latin America, computer industry and, 131
  debt and, 62
  decentralization of manufacturing of, 126
  development and 131, 132

Subject Index

export-oriented industrialization, 129–130
manufacturing trade balances, 129
Marxism and, 268
migration and, 12, 200
mortality decline, 157
mortality/fertility link, 163
protectionism and, 133
Latvia, women in, 291
Law, canon, 174
colonial, mortality decline and, 156
premodern era, 147
secularized states and, 19
Western, matrilineal societies and, 173
women and, 122, 220, 284, 285, 288, 290, 291–292
Lawsuits, gender discrimination and, 120
Leadership, black women and, 39
black men and, 40
European working class, blacks and, 50
generational, 180
male, the New Left and, 51
military, views on technology, 71
minority, AIDS and, 258
Namibia, Marxist-Leninism and, 64
revolutions and, 263, 268, 269, 271, 272, 273, 275, 277–278, 279–280, 282
social movements in, 226
South and Southeast Asia, capitalism and, 69
state, development goals and, 60
state, ideologies and, 56, 57, 58
women, public attitudes toward in the U.S., 117
League of Revolutionary Black Workers, 41
Legitimation, gender systems and, 109, 110, 111, 112, 113, 121
ideologies and, 20, 28, 29, 34
religion and, 82
Lebanon, development and, 64
Left (U.S.), 47, 49, 51, 55. *See also* Old Left; New Left.
Lesbians, *See also* Bisexuals; Gays; Homosexuals.
directionality of change and, 312
ideology and, 20, 36
war and, 32
ACT UP in 242, 243, 244, 245, 253

media, and acceptance of, 3
stigmatization and, 255
Lesbian feminist separatism, 42
Liberalism, 20, 32
Liberation Theology, 271
Literacy. *See also* Illiteracy.
directionality of change and, 312
ideology and, 20, 36
war and, 32
Lithuania, women in 291
nationalism and, 303
Lynching, 31, 39, 48

Malaysia, export-orientation and, 129, 130
men, views on fertility and family size, 187
peripheral industrialization and, 127
Males, *see* Men.
Mali, development and, 59
demographic equilibrium and, 159
Malthusian population theory, 145–146, 147–148, 149, 150, 151, 152, 155, 156, 157, 158, 159, 163, 164, 317
Management, decentralization of manufacturing and, 126, 128
development and, 138
industrial conflict and, 92, 94, 99, 100, 101, 102, 105
information technology and, 132
peripheral industrialization in, 135
technology transfer and, 140
telecommuters as, 97
Marxism. *See also* Class; Communism; Demystification; Socialism; Revolution.
class struggle, 4, 6
definition of ideology, 56–57
development and, 59, 60, 63
Eastern Europe, 305
end of ideology theorists and, 24
gender and, 45, 115
ideology as, 21–22, 28, 29, 57, 58
revolutions in, 266, 269–270, 272, 273, 274, 275, 280
social movements and, 228, 229, 236
superstructure and, 2–3
women and, 284, 295–296
Masculinity, engineering culture and, 103
social definitions, change in, 117, 118
technological expertise and, 7, 94, 95

Mass communication.. *See also* Mass
  media; Mediazation.
  benefits of, 76
  ideology and, 23, 28
  social unrest and, 76
  urban crisis and, 75
  women's movement and, 122, 124
Mass media. *See also* Mass communication;
  Mediazation.
  AIDS and, 9, 250–251
  domination and, 3
  homosexuals and, 3, 9, 250
  ideology and, 6
  social movements and, 258
Mass mobilization, revolutions in, 260, 261,
  262, 263, 264, 265, 269–272
Media, *see* Mass Media.
Mediazation, 3, 22–24. *See also* Mass communication; Mass media.
Medical care, *see* Health care.
Medical establishment, AIDS and 9, 252
Medical science, AIDS and, 246, 250
  mortality and, 154
Medicalization, moral positions and, 250
Men, 1, 2. *See also* Gender; Sex roles.
  black, 40, 46, 47, 48, 49, 51
  Central and Eastern Europe, 284, 285,
    286, 287, 289, 290, 293, 295,
    297
  elite, and women's movements, 123
  familial production and, 11, 171, 185
  female service occupations and, 124
  feminist analysis and, 45
  fertility levels, and gender separation,
    316
  gender stratification and, 109–119,
    313–314
  household and family work, 123
  Mexican, and purity of wives, 172
  protective legislation and, 48
  sex ratios and, 12, 202–222
  technological change, and the sexual
    division of labor, 91–106
  telecommuting and, 96–98
  traditional family in, 169
  women's movements, support of, 121
Mesopotamia, 190, 192, 194
Messianism, 28
Mexico, debt and, 62
  decentralization of manufacturing,
    126, 128
  elite, and self-interest, 66
  export-oriented industrialization, 129
  export performance, compared, 130
  family change in, 179, 180, 181
  fertility, 187
  IMF/World Bank and, 69
  marriage, and familial production,
    168–172
  parastatals, and development, 65
Middle East, migration and, 191, 194, 195,
  196
Middle East, oil production and balance of
  payments, 61
Migration, conflicts and, 12, 200–201
  demography and, 11
  diffusion and, 12, 195, 196
  elite, 194–196, 197
  fertility link and, 12
  gender system changes, 7, 117
  historical, 189–200
  international, 312
  life cycle and, 189
  mass, 191–194, 196–197
  policy and, 201
  population growth, changes caused by,
    198–200
  urban, and delay of fertility decline,
    161
  urban, Third World in, 65
Militarization, authoritarianism and, 33
  barbarian world, 195
  U.S. Society and, 36
  women and, 36
Mississippi Freedom Democratic Party, 39
Modernism, 32
Modernity, 11, 19, 24, 25
Modernization, demographic transition and,
  143, 146, 162, 163
  fertility and, 161
  ideology and, 3, 22
  mortality decline and, 11
  social movements and, 8, 226, 227,
    229, 230
  technology transfer and, 138, 139
  Third World, and regional integration,
    139–140
Monism, and social movements, 7, 38, 39,
  42, 45, 47, 51, 55
Monopoly capital, 300. *See also* Capital.

Mortality, *see also* Child mortality.
  cities and, 191, 192, 193, 198, 199, 201
  decline, 143, 144–146, 152–164, 171, 176, 316
  development and, 144
  demographic transition and, 143
  demography and, 11
  familial production and, 170
  Malthusian equilibrium and, 147–153
  migration and, 12
  modernization and, 146
  population growth and, 145–146
  society, nature of, 145
Mortality rates, *see* Death rates.
Moscow trials, 21
Mothers. *See also* Mothers-in-law.
  Eastern Europe in, 169, 290–291, 292, 296, 297
  economic sacrifice, familial production in,
  education of, and child mortality decline, 155
  exchange theory and, 222
  family change and, 177, 179, 180, 181
  generational change and, 205
  labor force participation and, 116, 117
  mortality transition, before, 145
  sex ratios and, 216, 219
  traditional role, 210
Mothers-in-law. *See also* Mothers.
  familial production and, 172
  family change and, 180, 181
Movements, 1, 2, 13, 14, 224–237, 238–258, 313, 314. *See also* New Social Movements Theory; Resource Mobilization Theory; Revolution.
  abolition, 39
  AIDS activist, 8, 238–258
  antinuclear, 235
  antiwar, 50
  black feminist, 38–53
  black Garvey, 31
  black liberation, 7, 8, 51
  black nationalist, 40, 50
  civil rights, 39, 40, 224, 230, 236
  class, 7
  Communist, Philippines, in, 263
  democracy, 259, 277
  environmental, 224, 226, 229, 232, 241

  ethnic rights, 30
  free speech, 50
  ideologies and, 20
  independence, 303
  labor, 54, 132
  liberal humanitarian, 235
  liberation, 38
  local-autonomy, 241
  nationalist, 118
  opposition, 64
  peace, 224, 226, 235, 236, 241
  political, 24
  race, 39
  religious, 232
  revolutionary, 17, 259, 268, 270, 271, 272
  socialist, 118, 235
  student, 224, 229
  temperance, 118
  violence and, 35
  women's, 7, 8, 39, 40, 42, 43, 51, 52, 118–124, 184, 226, 235, 236, 241
  women's suffrage, 39, 43, 49, 120, 176, 224
  workers', 224, 226, 229, 236
Mozambique, development and, 64, 65, 69
Multinational corporations, 308
  decentralization of production and, 125, 126, 128, 129
  Eastern Europe, 300, 302
  Newly Industrializing Countries in, 131
  power of, 14
  technology transfer, 131–132, 137
  Singapore, and upgrading of technology, 134
  Third World dependence on, 63–64, 67
  Third World workers and, 133
  U.S., offshoring and, 133
Multiple jeopardy, 7, 38, 42, 44, 51, 52, 53
Multivalent ideology, 53
Multivalent personalities, 30
Multivalent societies, 7, 27, 28

Nambia, development and, 64, 65
Nation of Islam, 41
National Association for the Advancement of Colored People, 41

National Association of Wage Earners, 40
National Black Feminist Organization, 52
National Negro Labor Council, 48
National Organization for Women (NOW), 44
National Union for the Total Independence of Angola (UNITA), 64
National Welfare Rights Organization, 41
Nationalism, black women, 40, 41
    blacks, 31
    Central and Eastern Europe, women and, 296, 297
    Eastern Europe, 297, 302–303, 304, 305
    elite self-enrichment and sacrifice of, 66
    Germany, 303
    revolution and, 261, 262, 263, 264, 265, 266, 267, 268, 270, 271, 272, 275, 276, 278, 282
    SADCC and, 67
    U.S. historians of, 33
    women and, 38
Nationalization, Namibia, 65
    Third World in, 64
Native Americans, *see* Amerindians.
Nature. *See also* Environment.
    conquest of, and Protestantism, 154
    fatalism, mortality and, 144
    gender ideologies and, 111, 284, 296
    new social movements and, 227
    technology and, 72
Nazism, 21, 33
Near East, trade expeditions and, 194
Negro American Labor Council, 48
Netherlands, the, fertility transition, 175, 186, 187
    internationalization of automobile manufacturing, 316
    mortality decline, 156
    social movements and, 228, 235
New international division of labor, *see* Division of labor, international
New Left, 39, 46, 50, 51, 55
New Social Movements Theory, 8, 13, 224, 226–230, 234, 239, 241–242, 243, 256–257
New Zealand, European settlement, 199
    ideology and, 67
    mortality decline, 156

Newly Industrialized Countries (NICS), 14, 68, 125, 129–132, 133, 138
Nicaragua. *See also* Revolutions.
    administrative/technical workers, and development, 65
    IMF/World Bank and, 69
    U.S. support of *contras*, and development, 64
Nigeria, child mortality, 164
    family change and, 180
    fertility, 187
    ideology and autonomy, 59
    mortality levels, medical facilities and, 157
    state farms, 66
Nonviolence, 35–36
Normalization, 9, 240, 246, 247–248, 251, 254, 255, 256. *See also* Stigma.
Norms, gender, 111, 112, 119, 296
North, conflicts with other regions, 228
    manufacturing facilities, relocation back to 127, 128
    technological gap as compared to South, 135
    Third World firms in, 133
North Atlantic Treaty Organization (NATO), 137
North Korea, 69

OAU, *see* Organization of African Unity.
OECD, *see* Organization for Economic Cooperation and Development.
Offshore production, 96, 126, 133
Old. *See also* Elderly.
    capitalism and, 170
    familial production and, 185
    Ghana, lifetime gains from fertility, 162
    Hungary, full-employment policy and, 285
    India, and familial production, 168
    industrialization and, 169
    welfare states and, 10
    women's care of, and social change, 2, 289
Old Left, 47, 49, 55
Organization for Economic Cooperation and Development (OECD), 67–68, 127, 128, 130, 132, 133, 134, 140
Organization of African Unity (OAU), 68

Organization of Petroleum Exporting
    Countries (OPEC), 61, 62

Pakistan, division into "West" and "East,"
    and colonialism, 302
    privatization and, 62
Palestine, see Revolutions.
Parastatals, 65, 66, 68
Patriarchy, Combahee River Collective
    Statement and, 51
    family production and, 168, 173
    the Soviet Union and, 285
    Western, black women in, 39
Perestrokia, 290
Periphery, 126, 127, 300
Personalities, androgynous, 114
    gendered, 109, 111, 112, 113
Peru, Marxism and, 268
Philippines, the. See also Revolutions.
    industrialization and, 127, 130
    mortality decline, 156
    parastatals, and debt, 65
    World Bank and, 66
Plagues, see Disease.
Pluralism, 22, 66
Poland. See also Revolutions.
    EU and, 301, 304
    nationalism and, 303
    theocracy, 10
    women in, 287–288, 289, 290, 291,
        293, 297
Poor, see Poverty.
Population growth, fertility and, 152, 316
    mortality and, 145, 149, 152, 153, 316
    preindustrial societies, 151
    migration and, 198–200
    revolution and, 261, 262, 263, 264,
        265, 266, 271
    "social mobilization" and, 143
Population studies, 182, 186. See also
    demography.
Pornography, Central and Eastern Europe,
    10, 287
Portugal, ideology and, 67
    textile industry, investment in by
        NICS, 133
Postindustrial theory, 96
Poverty, black women and, 45
    blacks, 41
    class politics and, 47, 49, 50

Eastern Europe, 5, 297, 300, 301, 305
    migration and, 12
    population size and, 149, 150
    Rights of Man in, 144
    Third World in, 59
    urban, 75, 77
    women, Central and Eastern Europe,
        290–291, 296
    women, and feminism, 38, 43, 44, 45,
        46
    working-class exploitation and, 46
Pragmatism, end of ideology thesis and, 21
    states and, 67
Praxis, 53
Privatization, Central and Eastern Europe,
    effects on women, 286, 291
    Third World, 62, 63, 65
Production. *See also* Capitalism.
    automobile, internationalization of,
        314–316
    communal, 59
    Communist bloc, former, 296
    customized, 126
    familial, 11, 166, 167, 168, 169, 171,
        174, 176, 179, 183, 185, 186
    gender and, 98, 103–106, 115–116
    industrial conflict and, 96, 99, 100,
        101, 102, 103
    market, 11
    men, Central and Eastern Europe, 289
    methods of, corporations and, 86
    mortality decline and, 155
    social movements and, 228
    techniques of, and U.S. economy, 74
    Third World, 65, 126, 128, 129, 131,
        133, 134, 136, 138, 139, 140
    women, Central and Eastern Europe,
        296
Professionals, female, 95, 219, 290
    male, 97–98
Progressive era, 49
Proletariat, 49. *See also* Class.
Propaganda, definition of, 28
    ideological multiplicity and, 27
    inequality and, 34
    social conflict and, 36
    war in, 32
    women, Poland, 290
    women's status, Soviet Union in, 293
Prostitution, AIDS and, 250, 255

Central and Eastern Europe, 10, 287
France, eighteenth and nineteenth
    century, 175
Protectionism, 14, 125, 128, 132–134, 138
Protestant ethic, 28
Public health. *See also* Disease; Health
    care.
    measures, mortality decline and, 11,
        152, 155, 157, 199, 200, 316
    officials, AIDS and, 248

Race. *See also* Ethnicity; Racism.
    black feminism and, 38, 39, 40, 41,
        42, 46, 47, 48, 50, 51, 53, 55
    gays and, 253
    revolution and, 269
    sociological study of, 6–7
    violence and, 34
Racism. *See also* Ethnicity; Race.
    AIDS and, 258
    black feminism and, 38, 39, 43, 44,
        50, 51, 52, 53
    Central and Eastern Europe, 297
    EU and, 304
    Germany, 303
    states and, 30, 248
Rape, abortions and, Poland, 291
    attitudes toward, Central and Eastern
        Europe, 293, 294
    public opinion, and elite response to,
        124
    war, and former Yugoslavia, 295
Rationalization, 3, 6, 17, 18–19, 22–23, 88
Reconstruction, Southern, 31
Reference-group theory, 119
Refugees, 309
Relative Deprivation, 13, 119, 224, 225,
    231
Relativism, 32
Religion, attitudes toward sickness, India,
        154, 159
    capitalism, development of, 18
    decline of, 16–17, 19, 20, 176, 317
    familial production and 168, 172
    family change and, 178
    female fertility decision making and,
        175
    fertility and, 147, 183
    ideological multiplicity and, 27
    individual choice and, 84

inequality, and black women, 42
imigration and, 194
mode of production and, 167
persistence of, 23, 25
revolution and, 260, 267, 268, 269,
    271–272
secular, 31–32
technological change and, 82–83
women and, 124, 296
Republic of Korea, development and, 14,
    63, 68, 127, 129, 130, 131, 132, 133,
    134, 136
    revolution and, 259
Reserve labor force, women as, 288
Resource Mobilization Theory, 3, 8, 13,
    119, 224, 225–226, 230, 234, 240, 241
Revolutions, 1, 2, 13, 14, 17, 20, 50, 241,
    259–283, 296, 314, 317. *See also*
    Capitalism; Factionalism; Movements;
    Socialism; Violence; War.
    Afghanistan, 260, 263, 266, 267, 268,
        269, 271, 272, 273, 274, 277,
        278, 279, 280, 281, 282
    anti-racist, 51
    Bolivia, 259
    Cambodia, 262, 266, 267, 268, 269,
        270, 271, 273, 274, 276, 277,
        278, 279, 280, 281, 282
    capitalist, 5, 10, 267
    Chinese, 260
    Egypt, 259
    European, 260
    feminist, 51
    French, 259, 260, 276
    Iran, 260, 261, 266, 267, 268, 269,
        270, 271, 273, 276, 278, 279,
        280, 281, 282
    Iraq, 259
    Latin American, 260
    Nicaragua, 260, 261, 266, 268, 269,
        270, 271, 273, 274, 277, 278,
        279, 280, 281, 282
    Palestine, 265, 266, 267, 268, 270,
        271, 272, 275, 282–283
    Philippines, 259, 260, 263, 266, 268,
        269, 270, 271, 273, 275, 276,
        277, 280, 281, 282
    Poland, 260, 265, 266, 267, 268, 269,
        271, 273, 276, 279, 280, 281,
        282

Romanian, 292
Russian, 260, 274, 284, 285, 293
scientific, 11, 163
sexual, 296, 297
South African, 264, 266, 267, 268, 269, 270, 271, 272, 275, 277, 278, 280, 281, 282
South Korea, 259
Vietnam, 262, 266, 268, 269, 270, 271, 274, 276, 277, 278, 279, 280, 281, 282
Zimbabwe, 260, 264, 266, 268, 270, 272, 277, 278, 279, 280, 281
Rhodesia, revolutionary conflict in, 267, 268, 269, 271, 272, 276, 277, 281
Rights, civil, 4, 13, 39, 40, 50, 58, 248, 273, 281
democratic, Palestine, 283
political, revolutions and, 13, 273, 281, 282
proactive social movements and, 231
regal divine, 28
universal, and secularized states, 19–20
white, Zimbabwe, 264
women's, 111, 117, 121, 219, 314
women's Central and Eastern Europe, 284, 291–292, 297
Riots, food, 1
race, 31, 33, 35, 47, 120
Roles, women, 112, 118–120, 121, 145, 169, 216–218, 219, 220, 221, 222, 248. *See also* Sex roles; Women.
Romania, EU and, 301
revolutionary conflict, 276
women, 288, 289, 292, 293
Russia. *See also* Soviet Union.
"classic" revolution and, 260
war and, 32
women, 290, 292, 293–294, 297

SAARC, *see* South Asian Association for Regional Cooperation.
Sanitation, mortality decline and, 154, 155, 156, 199
Third World in, 65
Sapphire Sapphos, 52
Schools. *See also* Education.
black women, and founding of, 39
desegregation of, 48
fertility decline and, 176, 177
industrialization and, 169
Polish, and women, 292
Russian feminists and, 294
technology and, 73, 76
Third World, and Westernization, 178
Science. *See also* Medical Science; Revolutions, scientific; Scientists; Social Sciences.
decision making and, 88
ideology and, 28
inequality and, 35
mortality decline and, 11, 154–155, 199
Newly Industrializing Countries and, 132
normalization and, 248
peripheral development and, 127, 135, 138, 140
positive age and, 311
power and, 20
war and, 32
women and, 296
Scientists. *See also* Science.
development and, 132, 135, 136, 137.
technology and, 71, 77, 78
Scientific Management, 71, 87
Secularization, female fertility decision making and, 175
industrial capitalism and, 3, 17, 19–20, 22–23, 24
Iranian revolution and, 267
Segregation, occupational, 48
racial, 31, 38
sex, 106, 116, 171
Seneca Falls Declaration, 43
Serfs, 19
Sex, *see* Gender.
Sex ratios, 12, 117, 203, 205, 210, 211–212, 213–216, 217, 218, 219
Sex roles, 12, 112, 175, 202–203, 204, 205–206, 209, 218, 219, 220, 221, 229. *See also* Gender; Men; Roles, women; Women.
Sexism, 30, 38, 39, 40, 44, 45, 50, 51, 52, 53, 296, 297. *See also* Inequality, gender.
Sexual Division of Labor, *see* Division of Labor, Gender.
Sexual harassment, Russia in, 293–294

Sexual politics, black women and, 40, 51, 52
    New Left in, 51, 55
    technological work, 92, 94
Silicon Valley, 133
Singapore, development and, 14, 68, 127,
    129, 130, 131, 134
Slavery, 31, 38, 39, 197
Slovak Republic, nationalism, 303
    women, 287
Slovenia, women, 292
SNCC, *see* Student Nonviolent
    Coordinating Committee.
Social exchange theory, *see* Exchange
    theory.
Social movements, *see* Movements.
Social problems, revolutions and, 279
    social movements and, 235, 236
    technology and, 6, 71, 74, 76, 77, 78,
        85, 86, 89
    violence and, 35, 317
Social sciences, 236, 313
Socialism. *See also* Class; Communism;
    Marxism.
    Afghanistan revolution and, 267
    black women and, 49, 51
    development and, 4, 58, 59, 60, 63,
        64, 65, 66, 67, 68, 69
    ideology as, 20, 57
    left and, 47
    social movements and, 224
    women, Central and Eastern Europe,
        10, 284, 285–286, 293, 296
Socialist democracy, *see* Democracy,
    socialist.
Socialization, blacks', 38, 52
    gender and, 52, 112, 113, 171, 205,
        220
    ideology and, 30
    social movements and, 241
South, 135, 228
South Africa. *See also* Revolutions, South
    Africa.
    dependence of Namibia on, 64
    left and, 51
South Asian Association for Regional
    Cooperation, 68
South Korea, *see* Republic of Korea.
South Vietnam, *see* Vietnam.
South West African People's Organization
    (SWAPO), 64

Southern African Development Coordina-
    tion Conference (SADCC), 67, 68
Soviet Union. *See also* Russia.
    revolution and, 263, 265, 268, 269,
        274
    sex ratio after World War II, 117
    Westernization, relations of
        production, 187
    women and, 285, 289, 293
Spain, internationalization of automobile
    manufacturing and, 315
    world market and, 130
Sri Lanka, development and, 64
    women, views on fertility and family
        size, 187
Stalinism, 21, 299
Starvation, *see* Famine; Hunger.
States, AIDS and, 246, 248–249, 254, 256,
    257
    autonomous actors as, 12
    Central and Eastern Europe, 5, 268,
        285, 286, 287, 288, 290, 291,
        293, 296, 297, 299, 300, 301,
        302, 303, 304, 305, 306, 307
    churches and, 25
    communist, 285, 287, 297
    development and, 4, 14, 58, 60, 61,
        62, 63, 64, 65, 66, 67, 131
    developmental, 131, 141
    ideologies and, 4, 27, 30, 32, 56, 57
    international position, postrevolution,
        280–281
    migration and, 200–201
    morality and, 168, 170, 172, 185
    protective legislation and, 48
    public decision making and, 85
    rationalization and, 18
    reconstruction of, postrevolution, 260,
        269, 274, 278–279
    revolution and, 13, 260, 261, 262,
        263, 264, 265, 266, 267, 269,
        270, 272, 278, 279, 281
    secularized, 19
    social movements and, 13, 229, 241,
        246, 254, 256
    technology and, 71
    Third World, 306
    violence and, 30, 32, 35, 276
    wealth flows, familial production in,
        174

welfare, *see* Welfare states.
women, Central and Eastern Europe, 9–10, 13, 293
world interconnectedness and, 308, 309
Status of Women, the, Presidential Commission on, 122
Stereotypes, gender, 111
Sterilization, black women, 44
  East German women, 287
Stigma. *See also* Normalization.
  AIDS and, 8, 9, 246–248, 249, 250, 251, 253, 254, 255, 257, 258
  gender and, 111
Stratification. *See also* Equality; Inequality.
  class, 45, 47
  gender, 2, 6–7, 108, 109, 110, 111, 112, 115
Strikes. *See also* Unions.
  black women and, 49
  technical innovation, and sexual politics, 92, 99, 100
  women and, 48, 120
Struggles, 2, 4. *See also* Conflict.
  AIDS activism and, 254–255, 256
  anti-colonialist, 59
  armed, 276
  black women, 53
  class, 4
  ideology and, 4
  independence for, 65
  political, and the women's movement, 122–123
  production, and women, 91, 92
  revolutionary, 259, 260, 261, 262, 263, 264, 265, 268, 271, 277
  states, between, 5
Student Nonviolent Coordinating Committee (SNCC), 39, 40
Students for a Democratic Society (SDS), 50
Sudan, development, constraints on, 66
  instability and, 302
Suffrage, *see* Movements, women's suffrage.
Superstructure, demographic change and, 166, 167, 170, 171, 172, 173, 174, 175, 176, 177, 183, 185, 186
  Marxism and, 3
  social movements and, 9, 227

Sweden, fertility and, 187
  internationalization of automobile manufacturing and, 315
  mortality decline and, 153–154, 155, 161
Switzerland, internationalization of automobile manufacturing and, 315
Symbols, AIDS activism and, 8, 243, 244, 247, 251–254, 257
  ideology and, 28, 36
  religious, and technology, 82, 83
  social movements and, 258
Symbolic interaction theory, 111

Taiwan, decentralization of manufacturing and, 127
  demographic transition and, 163
  development and, 14, 68, 129, 130, 131, 133, 134
  family change and, 179, 180
  marital fertility and, 187
Tanzania, development and, 58, 59, 60, 61, 63, 69
Technological determinism, 96, 101
Technological transfer, *see* Transfer, technological.
Technology, 2, 5–6, 14, 313, 314, 317
  cities and, 75, 77, 85
  decision making and, 6, 80, 85–86, 87–88
  definition of, 73
  democracy and, 6, 71, 80, 88
  development and, 125–141
  diffusion of, 98, 195
  Eastern Europe, 299, 302
  education and, 73, 89
  fertility decline and, 162
  gender and, 7, 91–107, 115–116
  individuals, and, 83–84
  industrial conflict, and gender, 7, 91–107
  internationalization of automobile manufacturing, 316
  medical, 11, 75, 156, 157, 158, 163
  migration and, 189
  mortality decline and, 11, 156, 157, 158, 163
  rationalization and, 6, 80, 88
  religion and, 71, 82–83
  simple, 139

social control and, 248
social movements and, 228
telecommuting and, 96–98
values and, 6, 73, 78–83, 90
war and, 33, 74
world connectedness and, 309
Telecommuters, 96–97, 106, 314
Television, ideology and, 3, 23
   men, Eastern Europe in, 293
   participatory democracy and, 80
   social unrest and, 76
Thailand, industrialization and, 127, 130
   privatization and, 62
Third World, development and, 14, 56–69, 138, 139, 140
   Eastern Europe, comparison, 5, 299–307
   family change and, 170
   female labor from, 104
   female labor in industrial societies and, 124
   fertility and, 148, 166, 173, 174, 177, 178, 179, 183, 184, 185
   industrialization, 127
   international division of labor and, 126, 128
   international sexual division of labor and, 96
   mortality and, 156, 158, 159, 163
   Nestlé, the women's movement and, 120
   violence and, 35
   workers, 133
Third World Women's Alliance, 40
Tokenism, 38
Trade Unions, *see* Unions.
Transfer, technology, Third World and, 14, 125, 131, 132, 135–140
Transportation, black women and, 46
   cities and, 75, 85
   decentralization of manufacturing and, 125, 127, 316
   development and, 134
   distance, and effects, 86
   individualism and, 81
Tunisia, women, views on fertility and family size, 187
Turkey, EU and, 301, 304
   family change and, 179, 180, 181
   Kurds and, 302
   patriarch, familial production in, 171, 186
   revolution and, 269
   women, views on fertility and family size, 187

Ukraine, abortion and, 292
Underground railroad, 39
Unions. *See also* Strikes.
   black women and, 39, 44, 46–49, 51
   participation in, 230, 235
   sexual division of labor and, 92, 94, 99, 101, 103, 105
   Third World, and privatization, 63
   women and, 55, 120
United Kingdom. *See also* Britain; England.
   foreign investment and, 309
   income inequality and, 318
   India's independence from, 36
   internationalization of automobile manufacturing, 315
   post materialist values, and social movements, 228
   textile industry, investment in by NICS, 133
United Negro Improvement Association, 41
United States, black women in, 38
   computer manufacturing and, 131
   democracy and, 80
   demographic transitions, 144, 146
   dependency of colonies on, 60
   ideologies, black action groups, 29
   female labor, and wars, 91, 117
   foreign investment, 309
   gender inequality, 313
   Hutterites, and fertility, 164
   imperialism, 51
   income inequality, 318
   internationalization of automobile manufacturing, 315
   internationalization of manufacturing, 126, 127, 128
   Nicaragua, support of *contras* and effect on development, 64
   privacy, 84
   social movements and, 224, 228, 230, 235–237, 240, 241
   race riots, 120
   radicalism, 49
   religion and, 25

revolutions and, 20, 262, 263, 265,
    268, 273, 274, 276, 277, 280, 282
technology, sexual politics and, 92
technology transfer and, 137
telecommuters, gender and, 97
textile industry, investment in by
    NICS, 133
Third World and, 67
wars and, 32, 33
women, and feminism, 222
U.S. Agency for International Development
    (USAID), 60, 62
Urban development corporations, *see*
    Development corporations.
Urban League, 41
Urban League's Negro Workers Councils,
    48
Urbanization, 47, 118, 121
USSR, *see* Russia; Soviet Union.

Values, black feminism and, 42, 45
    exchange theory and, 209
    family, 219
    fertility decline and, 12, 183
    gender and, 111, 112, 202, 203, 204,
        209, 215, 219, 220
    ideology and, 28
    normalization and, 246
    political power and, 56
    religious, decline of, 17
    revolutions and, 282
    social movements and, 226, 227–228,
        234, 235
    technology and, 6, 71, 73, 78–83, 85,
        89, 90, 101
    universal, and state, 19
Vested interests, Marxist analysis in, 57
    technology and, 76, 77
Vietnam, *see* Revolutions, Vietnam.
Violence, 1. *See also* Revolution; War.
    alternatives to, 35–36
    black sexual politics and, 40
    domestic, Serbia in, 295
    family, 124
    gays and, 257
    independence movements and, 303
    Ku Klux Klan and, 31
    Marxism and, 21
    organized, diffusion of, 195
    peace and, 317

population check as, 150, 152, 201
population growth and, 198
revolutions and, 13, 264, 270, 274,
    275–277, 282
social control as, 9, 246
social learning and, 34
social movements and, 13
states and, 30
women's movements and, 120

War. *See also* Revolution; Violence.
War, civil, 259, 268, 276, 281, 295
    former Yugoslavia, 295
    fertility and, 316
    gender and, 7, 117, 313
    guerrilla, revolution and, 263, 277
    ideology and, 32–36
    just society and, 144
    population check as, 149, 151
    revolutionary, 259
Wealth flows, 11, 164, 166–167, 168, 170,
    171, 172, 173, 175, 176, 177, 181,
    182, 187
Weather Underground, 50
Welfare states, end of ideology and, 21
    privacy and, 84
    social movements and, 8, 9, 13, 228
    women, Central and Eastern Europe,
        10, 284
West, cultural diffusion and, 196
    demographic transitions, 163, 164,
        166, 167
    Eastern Europe and, 300, 301
    equality, lack of, 306
    exchange theory, heterosexual
        relationships and, 213
    family change and, 169
    fertility decline and, 173–179,
        184–185
    ideology and, 21, 25
    Iran and, 281
    mass media and, 3
    migrant clothing workers in, 104
    mortality decline and, 153, 155
    social movements and, 226, 228, 230,
        248
    technology and, 86
    Third World and, 63, 66, 300
    women, compared to communist
        Europe, 285, 289

West Germany. *See also* East Germany; Germany.
  Brandt Report and, 67
  effects on East Germany of take over, 305
  racism and, 303
  social movements and, 228, 235
Western Europe. *See also* Central Europe; Eastern Europe; Europe; States, Central and Eastern Europe.
  decentralization of manufacturing and, 128
  democracy, encouragement of in revolutionary regimes, 282
  Eastern Europe and, 5, 301
  fertility decline and, 173, 175
  Polish revolution and, 265
  wealth flows and, 176, 187
Whites, AIDS activism and, 245, 253
  ethnic conflict and, 31
  feminist, and black women, 52
  South African revolution and, 264, 267, 271, 272, 277
  Zimbabwe revolution and, 264, 280
Women, 1–2. *See also* Gender; Movements, women's; Movements, women's suffrage; Roles, women; Sex roles.
  AIDS activism and, 257
  black feminism and, 7, 38–55
  capitalism and, 10, 169–170, 171–172, 284, 285, 289, 290, 295, 296–297
  Central and Eastern Europe, 2, 10, 284–298
  familial production in, 11, 171–172, 185
  family change and, 180
  fertility and, 11, 175, 185, 316
  French, and nineteenth-century equality, 175
  gender inequality and, 7, 108–124, 313–314
  mortality transition, before, 145
  Muslim, in Morocco, 220–221
  revolutions and, 1
  sex ratios and, 12, 202–222
  social movements and, 1, 230
  technological change, and the sexual division of labor, 7, 91–101, 103–106

telecommuting and, 96–98
violence and, 36
welfare states and, 10
white, 39, 41, 42, 44, 45, 46, 47, 48, 49, 51
Wives, Central and Eastern Europe in, 286, 290, 292, 297
  exchange theory and, 205, 206, 210, 219, 220
  familial production in, 168, 171, 172
  family change and, 169, 177, 178, 180
  fertility, interest in limiting, 175
  mortality transition, before, 145
  power, lack of, 111, 113, 114
Women's Trade Union League, 47
Workers, clerical, 55, 97–98
  craft, 91, 92, 93, 94, 99
  domestic (domestics), 40, 48, 49
  factory, 40, 84, 94, 95
  female, 91–101, 103–106, 109, 110, 115, 116, 117
  garment, 49, 104
  immigrant, 48, 104
  male, 91–95, 96, 97–98, 99–101, 103–106, 115, 117
Working Women's Association, 47
World Bank, 5, 60, 62, 63, 65, 66, 67, 69, 300, 301, 302, 309

Yugoslavia, EU and, 301
  nationalism and, 302
  women in, 289, 295
  world market and, 130

Zaire, development and, 59, 65
Zambia, development and, 63, 65, 66
  ideology and, 57
Zero population growth, 148
Zimbabwe, development and, 65, 68. *See also* Revolutions, Zimbabwe.